Introduction to Magazine Writing

Conrad C. Fink
Donald E. Fink

Macmillan Publishing Company
New York

Maxwell Macmillan Canada
Toronto

Maxwell Macmillan International
New York   Oxford   Singapore   Sydney

We
dedicate this book to all students
of magazine writing.
May you carry the craft to new heights.

Editor: Kevin M. Davis
Production Editor: Christine M. Harrington
Art Coordinator: Ruth A. Kimpel
Text Designer: Willis Proudfoot
Cover Designer: Cathleen Norz
Production Buyer: Pamela D. Bennett

This book was set in Garamond Light by American–Stratford Graphic Services, Inc., and was printed and bound by Semline, Inc., a Quebecor America Book Group Company. The cover was printed by Phoenix Color Corp.

Macmillan Publishing Company
866 Third Avenue
New York, New York 10022

Macmilllan Publishing Company is part of the
Maxwell Communication Group of Companies.

Maxwell Macmillan Canada, Inc.
1200 Eglinton Avenue East, Suite 200
Don Mills, Ontario M3C 3N1

Library of Congress Cataloging-in-Publication Data

Fink, Conrad C.
    An introduction to magazine writing / Conrad C. Fink, Donald E. Fink.
        p.   cm.
    Includes bibliographical references and index.
    ISBN 0-02-337561-2
    1. Authorship.   I. Fink, Donald E.   II. Title.
PN147.F445   1993
808′.02—dc20   92-43182
                                                                CIP

Printing: 1 2 3 4 5 6 7 8 9   Year: 4 5 6 7 8

Preface

We have written this book to introduce you to the challenges and creative joys—and the difficulties—of successful magazine writing. In the pages ahead, you will learn how to select story ideas for magazines, research stories, then write clearly and directly in a style that will make you and your writing attractive to editors of a wide variety of magazines. You'll also learn how to start positioning yourself now, as a student, for an eventual career in magazines.

Although our separate media careers took us to different parts of the world as reporters and writers, we now join forces as co-authors of this book to share with you lessons we learned the hard way, searching out news and feature stories under difficult conditions and writing under deadlines. We learned how to handle those pressures and still write effectively, and we'll share our techniques with you.

One important lesson, however, we must share with you immediately: We can only *introduce* you to magazine writing and this book can serve only as your *starting point*. Developing the solid writing skills that will get your work published, either as a staff writer or free-lancer, is mostly up to you. The place to develop those skills is on your keyboard, writing, rewriting and experimenting with the language until your own distinctive, effective writing style emerges. The time to start developing those skills is *now,* under the guidance of your instructor, with lessons you will learn in this book.

Therefore, you'll note we structured this text as a "beginner's platform." Throughout it, we suggest ways you can begin writing immediately for magazines, on campus and off. As a beginner, you'll encounter more challenges and difficulties than successes. But stick with it. Perseverance and hard work—lots of it—are behind every successful magazine writing career.

In studying magazine writing you've chosen a rapidly evolving sector of the American media. Magazines are dramatically revising their publishing strategies and editorial content to meet changing reader lifestyles and meet stiffening competition from newspapers and broadcast media. More change is ahead, and it will directly impact on you as a writer.

Four things to remember:

First, to write successfully for magazines you must understand the broader magazine industry and its economic and competitive dynamics. You must learn how magazines target "markets" of readers, then create editorial strategies to win the selected readers who can be "sold" to advertisers. (Just a few magazines try to get along with circulation revenue only.) Everything you do as a writer—from generating a story idea to polishing your final manuscript—will revolve around deep understanding of a specific magazine's strategy, whether that is to reach a narrow audience with special interests, as do trade magazines (*Advertising Age, Editor & Publisher,* and so forth) or to reach a wider audience, as do consumer magazines (*Ladies' Home Journal, Reader's Digest*).

Second, as a writer, you must understand your readers as well as why and how they read particular magazines. Do they search for news and information? Entertainment? Escapism? Something else? Knowing a magazine readership's *demographics* (ages, incomes, educations, etc.) and *psychographics* (lifestyles, attitudes, reading habits) helps you properly select a subject, then correctly structure your writing to catch and hold those readers. For example, if you are writing a story on, say, extramarital sex, you must take one writing approach for a largely youthful audience of campus readers and quite another approach for older readers of a retirees' magazine!

Third, you greatly improve your chances of being published if you develop an aura of professionalism. Editors are quick to recognize and appreciate writers who understand a magazine's editorial mission and who can submit story ideas and copy that are expertly tuned to aid in that mission. Throughout this book we present a wider professional context that will enable you to operate more effectively as a professional writer.

Fourth, if there are "natural" writers born with polished ability to craft superb, publishable copy, we haven't met them in the combined total of more than 60 years that we've been in journalism. We *have,* however, met hundreds of successful writers who began as you perhaps are beginning—tentatively, uncertainly, maybe even a little frightened at the challenge of fulfilling a dream of writing for a living. You can learn this craft, as they did, proceeding one step at a time, first by mastering the basics of strong, clean writing and then by building an array of skills on that foundation that will constitute your own personal writing style. We've organized this book to take you through those steps one at a time.

ORGANIZATION OF THIS BOOK

We open Part One with "Setting the Scene: The American Magazine Today." Chapter One, "Understanding the Magazine Industry," describes the burgeoning numbers of magazines that target narrow niches or sectors of readers with special interests. Somewhere, right now, somebody publishes magazines for virtually every special interest, vocation or hobby a reader could have. You will look at this diversity in the first chapter.

In Chapter Two, "You and the Magazine Reader," we discuss what you must know about magazine readers and the income, age and lifestyle characteristics that make them readers. This chapter defines reader targets.

Part Two, "The Writer's Craft," opens with Chapter Three, "Developing Strong Language Fundamentals." This covers techniques we've developed in our own careers for using language with telling impact. We discuss writing that is colorful, lean, "people-oriented"—and how to avoid the Four Deadly Sins: bloated language, abstractions, redundancies and cliches.

Chapter Four covers "Writing with Authority and Credibility." Quoting authoritative sources and official documents is one way to build credibility into your writing. Weaving in graphic, you-are-there detail is another.

Chapter Five, "Selecting and Reporting Your Story," covers the crucial technique of selecting stories appropriate for the magazine you target, researching them properly and writing with an angle, an approach likely to meet the special interests of your magazine's readers. You'll learn in this chapter what every beginning writer must understand: Strong reporting can cover weaknesses in your writing, but not even the fanciest writing will cover poor reporting, inaccuracies or factual holes in your story.

Your next step in the writing process is selecting a story structure—a framework—that communicates best with your target audience. We turn to this in Chapter Six, "Story Form and Structure (I)," with discussions of information/news articles, personality profiles, how-to approaches and narrative structures.

There are many ways to write magazine stories, so we carry our discussion of structures into Chapter Seven, "Story Form and Structure (II)," which covers the service article, question-and-answer and other formats.

Once you settle on a story structure, you must carefully fashion an introduction or lead that catches readers. Then you must build a narrative style that pulls them through to the end. That's the subject of Chapter Eight, "How to Attract and Hold Readers."

All your efforts as a reporter and writer are useless if you cannot convince an editor to publish your story. So, in Chapter Nine, we turn to the art of "Selling Your Story—and Yourself." Here, we provide hints on formulating story ideas and writing an offering—or "query"—letter that's likely to attract editors.

Thousands of specialty magazines with a narrow editorial focus are published these days and they offer an appealing market for writers. In Part Three, "Writing for Specialized Magazines," we discuss how to penetrate this market. Chapter Ten, "Writing for Your Readers' Pocketbooks," covers one of the most rapidly expanding specialty sectors—business, economics and finance.

Chapter Eleven, "Writing Sports," provides hints on how to break into one of the most popular fields for writers: sports. You'll learn that saying who won often is just a minor part of sports writing today.

"Writing for Technical Magazines" is the subject of Chapter Twelve. If you are mechanically inclined, or can apply sound reporting techniques to technical subjects, these magazines offer you many chances to get published.

Another "hot" category for writers is covered in Chapter Thirteen, "Writing for Entertainment Magazines." Movies, music, theater, dance, the club scene—all are subjects for entertainment stories.

In Part Four, "The Legal and Ethical Context of Magazine Writing," we discuss two areas you must understand *before* writing for publication. Chapter Fourteen covers "You and the Law." Chapter Fifteen focuses on "You, Ethics and Honest Writing."

In the book's final section, Part Five, we turn to "You, Editors and the Production Process," an important aspect of magazines many writers ignore, to their disadvantage.

In Chapter Sixteen, we discuss how you must craft your stories ever mindful that your words often will be packaged with illustrations, charts and photos. You can strengthen your pitch to editors if you provide such illustrations, or at least suggest how they can be obtained for design layout. This single chapter in Part V also features a quick but substantive discussion on how manufacturing and distribution of a magazine affect your performance as a writer. We discuss, for example, how timely and topical stories you write won't reach readers for days or weeks because of delays inherent in the still-cumbersome magazine production process.

Each part and chapter opens with a brief explanation of points we'll cover. A summary concludes each chapter. These opening and closing features should help you isolate important points for studying and reviewing for tests. Recommended Reading lists are positioned throughout the book to signal where you can find additional background material. We urge you to range widely in your reading. Good writers are voracious readers.

We've woven into our text many examples of professional magazine writing. We do not mean to suggest you mimic other writers in developing your own style but, rather, simply to illustrate techniques used by successful writers. Study how the pros write, but proceed through this book determined to develop your own personal writing style. Build your career on *your* distinctive use of the language, not somebody else's.

In magazine writing there isn't a commonly accepted, industrywide standard for style, punctuation and usage. For uniformity in this book, we follow *The Associated Press Stylebook and Libel Manual,* revised edition, 1989. However in reproducing examples of writing we use the style in which magazines originally published them, even if that style contradicts AP style. Before writing for any magazine, be sure to learn its particular style.

ACKNOWLEDGMENTS

This book is not the product of its authors alone.

The many magnificent editors and writers we've been privileged to work with had a hand in the book, for it is their collective wisdom we've tried to capture.

Those writers and editors who, many deadlines ago, encouraged us in our own careers deserve special thanks. Memories of their advice and counsel inspired us to try to help beginning writers.

Students at the University of Georgia also helped us. For more than a decade, they have taught the teacher, and any pedagogical validity in this book flows from their lessons.

Special thanks to Dean Tom Russell of Georgia's Henry W. Grady College of Journalism and Mass Communication. His continued support of this and other writing projects by one of your co-authors is most appreciated. Kent Middleton of the Grady faculty, and an expert on media law, critiqued our chapter on law and provided valuable insights. Ernie Hynds of the Grady College, a long-time teacher with special background in magazines, provided helpful views on the book's overall structure. Thanks to both colleagues.

Our thanks, too, to Allison Dollar, managing editor of *In Motion,* for her contribution of hints for free-lancers (Chapter Nine). The American Society of Journalists and Authors, Inc., was helpful in permitting reproduction, also in Chapter Nine, of its letter of agreement for writers and its Code of Ethics and Fair Practices. In that same chapter, we reproduce a Crain Communications, Inc., letter agreement, through the assistance of Fred Danzig, editor of *Advertising Age.* Our thanks to him.

Throughout our research and writing, we received valuable help from Magazine Publishers of America, the industry's leading trade association. We are most grateful for this.

We thank Kevin Davis, administrative editor at Macmillan Publishing Company, who saw merit in our proposal for this book. We owe Christine Harrington, production editor at Macmillan, a very low bow for putting up with grumpy authors and guiding the manuscript through the production process.

Finally, extremely valuable guidance came from colleagues in academia who reviewed the manuscript. Our profound thanks to Carole Eberly, Michigan State University; Katherine C. McAdams, University of Maryland, College Park; Chuck Marsh, University of Kansas; Judy Polumbaum, University of Iowa; and David E. Sumner, Ball State University.

ABOUT THE AUTHORS

Conrad C. Fink and Donald E. Fink are brothers who have both served as reporters, editors and foreign correspondents in media careers that took them on assignments throughout the world. Conrad Fink worked for the Associated Press in many countries in Asia and Europe before becoming a vice president of that news-gathering organization at its New York City headquarters. He served in a number of management positions with the AP, a diversified media company, and has taught at the University of Georgia since 1982. Conrad is the author of five books and has won many awards for his teaching.

Donald Fink worked first as a newspaper reporter, then joined McGraw-Hill's *Aviation and Space Technology* magazine. He traveled much of the world on reporting assignments and was the magazine's bureau chief in Geneva and Los Angeles before becoming editor in chief. Donald is now based at McGraw-Hill's New York City headquarters, in charge of the company's aviation and space publications.

Contents

Part One

Setting the scene: The American magazine today

American magazines today are incredibly diverse and editorially imaginative. They are bigger, bolder and more colorful than ever. As a group, they represent a multibillion dollar industry. Their numbers are expanding rapidly, despite stiff competition from other print and electronic media, and magazines will no doubt continue as major contenders for reader time and advertiser dollars in decades ahead, as they already have for more than 250 years since Colonial times.

For you, the student writer, there is both challenge and opportunity in all that.

Your challenge lies in mastering the precision writing skills demanded by editors who increasingly have finely tuned ideas of what marketplace niches their magazines must occupy, who their readers are and what they want to read—and how writers like you fit (or don't fit) into their editorial scheme of things. That means you, more so than the generations of student writers who preceded you, must come up to speed quickly on the magazine industry and its marketing and economic dynamics. Understanding these basics is a sign of professionalism, and if you desire success in magazine writing, that's what you must be—professional.

Your opportunity lies in that same industry diversity. Among the many thousands of magazines published today are some just right for you—magazines that cover topics of interest to you and that write them in a style you can handle. Find those magazines, develop the fundamental writing skills they demand, and you can become a published writer.

To set the scene for helping you develop your writing skills, we open Part I with Chapter One, "Understanding the Industry." This sketches the structure of the magazine industry today and its economics and strategies. Understanding the medium is essential to learning how to write for it.

Understanding readers, what they want from magazines and how they go about getting it is essential for you as a writer, too. We turn to this in Chapter Two, "You and the Magazine Reader." You'll learn in this chapter that successful magazine writers don't shout in broad generalities at large, faceless crowds. Rather, they speak directly and in precise language to individuals whose lifestyles, backgrounds and reading needs and interests they understand thoroughly.

Now, let's start your introduction to magazine writing.

Chapter 1

Understanding the magazine industry

Readers in America have many reasons to *never* pick up a magazine. They can read newspapers, more colorful and journalistically stronger than ever—and now selling a record 62 million copies daily.[1] Punching a button opens an electronic treasure chest of 30, 60 or more cable TV channels of news, information and entertainment. Books on countless subjects are everywhere, as are many other lifestyle diversions that beckon readers away from magazines.

Advertisers have many reasons to *never* put a dollar into magazines. Newspapers, radio, TV, direct mail, the Yellow Pages—all deliver attractive audiences who will purchase goods and services.

In sum, the American magazine industry has every reason to collapse. Yet. . . .

Yet . . . consumer magazine circulation is growing tremendously—up 74 percent from 1964 to 1989, compared with 52 percent growth in U.S. adult population over the same period. U.S. adults in 1991 bought an average of 36 magazines, compared with 30 in 1981.[2]

Yet . . . magazine advertising revenue more than doubled from 1979 to 1989, hitting a record $6.6 billion, then forging ahead to $6.8 billion in 1990. Then, a nationwide economic recession struck all media, and magazine revenue dropped to $6.5 billion in 1991.[3]

Yet . . . the number of magazines is increasing rapidly—from 9,434 in 1969 to 11,143 in 1992, with hundreds more being launched every year.[4]

How can this be? How can magazines flourish against such strong media competition? How, in this satellite age of stunning electronic and visual communications technology, can we still meet reader and advertiser needs by putting ink on paper, much as Johann Gutenberg did when he popularized movable type in Germany in the 1400s?

More to the point for you as an aspiring magazine writer: What will the future of magazines likely be? What career options will they offer?

We'll examine these and other questions in Chapter One. You will get a glance at turning points in magazine history and learn key characteristics of the magazine industry today: what its competitive strategies are, where the industry gets its economic support, how it maintains circulation growth, which magazines are strongest and who owns them.

THE WRITER AND MAGAZINE STRATEGY

Through all the twists and turns in American magazine history, two things remain constant.

First, magazines can change their publishing strategies quickly and dramatically in response to changes in American habits and lifestyles. Magazines thus are still able, after more than 250 years in business, to meet reader needs for news, information and entertainment in ways other media cannot.

Second, this continuing success in our extremely competitive communications marketplace is driven not by modern marketing or managerial techniques or new technology, although all are present today in magazine publishing. Rather, the success of magazines is driven by writers and editors. It is creative minds, not sales gimmicks or futuristic equipment, that give magazines their basic competitive strength—editorial content finely focused on readers' needs and desires, as no other medium can focus it, and all appealingly packaged to be informative, entertaining or just plain diverting.

Because of that basic editorial strength and flexibility in changing as reader desires change, magazines from their beginning have been a unique and unifying thread in our evolving American society. Regardless of how we change as a nation—in how we govern ourselves, in the subjects we discuss, or how we style our hair— magazines are on the cutting edge of spreading word of that change or, indeed, *leading* change.

That more magazines than ever are doing this today, with more success than ever, is major tribute not only to magazines as a medium but, also, to the men and women who create their editorial strategies and who write and edit their content.

Folio, the industry's leading trade publication, reflected on all this in an editorial marking the 250th anniversary of the first efforts by Benjamin Franklin and Andrew Bradford to launch magazines in Colonial America in 1741 (see Box 1–1). The magazine said in an editorial:

We have to believe . . . that the men and women who choose this profession don't do so just because it's a good business proposition: Anyone who has spent any time in magazine publishing knows that there are easier ways to earn a living! No, most of us do it for reasons not easily contained in an editorial prospectus or a publishing spread-sheet. We make magazines because we believe they are fundamentally important to us and to our fellow citizens. The framers of the Constitution recognized this importance over 200 years ago. Responding to the impulse of Franklin and his peers, they made publishing the only business protected by the Constitution. It's called the First Amendment.

BOX 1–1 Highlights in U.S. Magazine History

1741 America's first magazines are launched—and quickly fail. Benjamin Franklin's *General Magazine and Historical Chronicle* survives for six issues, Andrew Bradford's *American Magazine* survives for three.

1820 By this year, several "cause" magazines are established, primarily to fight slavery. Among them is Elijah Embree's *Emancipator*.

1821 *Saturday Evening Post* is founded. The magazine eventually builds a content mix of educational journalism and entertaining copy that makes the magazine a national institution.

1850 By this year, "trade" publishing is well established. Magazines with narrowly defined target audiences include *General Shipping & Commercial List* (founded in 1815, now known as *Journal of Commerce*), *American Rail-Road Journal* (1831, now *Railway Age*) and *Scientific American* (1845).

1855 *Frank Leslie's Illustrated Newspaper* is launched with broad coverage of news, music, drama, fine arts and fiction, all abundantly illustrated; eventually becomes *Leslie's Weekly*, a crusading magazine that finances Leslie's successful creation of America's first publication "group"—*Frank Leslie's New Family Magazine* (1857), *Frank Leslie's Budget of Fun* (1858) and, after the Civil War, *Frank Leslie's Boys and Girls Weekly* and *The American Magazine*.

1857 *Harper's Weekly* is published, featuring new engraving techniques that transform illustration in American magazines; Civil War coverage boosts circulation over a then-phenomenal 100,000.

1860 Competition is driving subscription prices steadily downward, and by this year, advertising revenue has major importance for magazines; however, total content still is about 75 percent editorial, 25 percent ads.

1865 *The Nation*, a journal of news considered a direct ancestor of today's news magazines, is launched by E. L. Godkin.

1869 First transcontinental railroad is completed, strengthening a rail network that permits widespread circulation of magazines.

1879 Development of mass circulation is boosted by Postal Act, which provides relatively cheap postal rates for magazines.

1883 *Ladies' Home Journal* is published, becomes core of Cyrus Curtis' hugely successful Curtis Publishing Company and first magazine to hit one million subscribers (in 1903). By 1920, the *Journal* is described as world's most valuable magazine.

1888 Schoolteacher James H. McGraw acquires *American Journal of Railway Appliances*, launching what becomes McGraw-Hill Inc., today a diversified publishing giant.

1893 *McClure's* is launched with 15-cent cover price; *Munsey's Magazine*, launched in 1889, drops to 10 cents from 25 cents; mass-circulation sales strategies drive publishing.

1896 National Geographic Society, founded in 1888, converts its *National Geographic Magazine* from irregular to monthly publication; magazine becomes one of America's all-time reader favorites.

1907 *Saturday Evening Post*, published by Curtis since 1897, becomes first magazine to achieve $1 million annual advertising revenue.

1919 Burnarr Macfadden launches *True Story*, and confession and detective magazines are off and running.

1922 *Reader's Digest* is launched by DeWitt Wallace; initially contains only reprints from other publications, and quickly evolves into one of world's most carefully packaged and successful magazines.

1923 Henry Luce and Briton Hadden publish *Time*, foundation of today's international media conglomerate, Time Warner.

1925 Harold Ross publishes *The New Yorker*, still regarded by many media critics as a leader in magazine sophistication.

1933 *Esquire* is launched as a quarterly, setting a standard still emulated by upscale men's magazines.

1936 Photojournalism is redefined as a major communications technique as *Life*, the weekly picture magazine, is launched.

1939 *Business Week* is launched, then goes on to become a leader in niche publications aimed at business executives, along with *Forbes* and *Fortune*.

1942 John Johnson launches Johnson Publishing Co. in Chicago on a borrowed $500; by 1989, the company, publisher of *Jet* and *Ebony*, has revenues of $216.5 million and is the nation's second-largest black-owned company.

1950 Large numbers of highly specialized magazines emerge, such as *Playboy*, *Sports Illustrated*, *Mad*.

1953 Walter H. Annenberg creates *TV Guide* from a New York City magazine published since 1948; high-quality commentary on TV and regionalized listings build largest circulation for its time in magazine history.

1955 *Reader's Digest* accepts ads for first time, heading for industry leadership in revenue as well as circulation.

1956 Soaring costs plus advertiser and reader defections to TV force *Collier's*, a general-interest magazine founded in 1888, to fold. Other mass-circulation magazines also shut down. *Life* folds in 1972 (but is reborn as a monthly in 1978).

| BOX
1–1 | *continued* |

1967 With $7,500 in borrowed funds, Jann Wenner launches *Rolling Stone* to cover the rock music world.

1972 *Ms.* magazine is published as women's movement develops momentum; it struggles for advertising pages and profitability, and in 1991 management decides to rely solely on circulation revenue.

1977 Average cost to reader for an American magazine passes $1 for first time, and industry as a whole moves strongly toward obtaining more revenue from readers than from advertisers.

1985 For first time, number of American magazines surpasses 11,000.

1988 Per-issue circulation of magazines rises to 190.9 copies sold per 100 American adults, up from 150.9 per 100 adults in 1954.

1990 Magazine industry ad revenue hits record $6.8 billion.

1991 Severe nationwide economic recession forces magazines, like all media, to search for new revenue sources in video productions, electronic publishing, trade shows and other areas. Many magazines trim staffs, reduce page numbers and sizes and cut other costs.

Magazines are entirely different from newspapers, which tend to serve a local populace with generalized content. In many ways, magazines are peculiarly American. Because magazines have unique voices and specialized viewpoints, they reach individuals that other periodicals can't. They serve institutions, ideologies and interest groups in ways no other medium can. Magazines—there are over 10,000 published in this country today—help integrate our society; they are vital stitches that hold together the crazy quilt that is the cosmopolitan American culture. (*"Magazines: A Fundamental Importance,"* Folio *March 1991, 67*)

Folio editors make two points that an aspiring magazine writer should note.

First, your principal media competitors are newspapers which today publish much magazine-like writing. You need to develop story ideas and reporting approaches not covered in the daily press, then fashion writing techniques that carry your readers beyond what is in newspapers, particularly those fat, feature-laden Sunday newspapers. In numbers, edition size and revenue, Sunday papers are the fastest-growing sector of the American newspaper industry.

Second, magazine marketing strategy must provide, as *Folio* says, "unique voices and specialized viewpoints" that are packaged distinctively and inserted in the marketplace for readers and advertisers with a precision other media cannot match.

Sound simple? It isn't.

Three Crucial Elements of Strategy

Successful magazine strategy is complex. But it can be broken down into three broad elements crucial to writers.

First, magazine strategy involves identifying a market or group of readers with common interests who can be enticed into reading regularly about those interests.

Generally, these reader-targets are sought anywhere in the United States. An important distinction for you as a magazine writer: Only three daily newspapers (*The New York Times, The Wall Street Journal, USA Today*) are truly significant national papers that seek readers coast-to-coast. Most newspapers serve smaller geographic markets—a city and, say, five or six adjacent counties. By contrast, many magazines are national or even international in their reach, and writers must think in those broader terms.

Some magazines, such as city or regional publications, define their markets as groups of readers in more restricted geographic areas. But, generally, in magazines you write for readers identified by their common interests, not whether they live in a small slice of geography. Even that classic city magazine, *New York,* serves a far-flung audience. Fully 26.5 percent of its subscribers live outside metropolitan New York City. They read the magazine, obviously, because of their shared interest in *New York*'s coverage of the theatre, movies, music, and not just the city itself.

A second principal element in magazine strategy is to target readers with characteristics attractive to advertisers. Successful magazines depend in large measure on ad revenue, and that requires editors and writers to deliver readers the advertisers want—those with attractive *demographics* (income, age, educational level and so forth) and *psychographics* (interests, thinking, lifestyle and spending attitudes).

It's important to note that pulling in large numbers of readers who are not attractive to advertisers can ruin a magazine. Costs of serving readers—in paper, manufacturing and distribution—are enormous, and "unattractive" readers generate only costs, not ad revenue, if advertisers won't pay to reach them. Indiscriminately adding demographically and psychographically unattractive readers will drain a magazine's profits. Some magazines offer advertisers precise targeting by selling subscriptions only to people whose demographic profiles match those desired by advertisers. For example, McGraw-Hill's *Aviation Week & Space Technology*, launched in 1916, seeks only subscribers involved in aviation and space industries—pilots, engineers, sales executives, and so forth. Maintaining such subscriber purity enables magazines to charge higher ad rates. For advertisers, it offers the efficiency of paying to reach only people who are potential customers.

In the third broad element of magazine strategy, editorial content must be fashioned expertly to pull in the target audience. Readers must be enticed into the magazine regularly and deeply, into pages where advertisements are located. Content must be appealing, predictable in its uniformity and subject matter, and written with precision to match the interests and understanding of readers. And, content must build—week after week, month after month—an environment in which both readers and advertisers know their needs will be met.

Besides thus fulfilling their role in the commercial marketplace, magazines also have a wider historic responsibility. Their editorial content must be socially responsible and journalistically valid. We'll discuss this later in detail, but as a writer you must approach your task—as have generations of writers before you—with a sense of great responsibility for the impact you have on society. As purveyors of ideas, architects of social trends and as builders of public opinion, writers have an obligation to be accurate, truthful, balanced and fair.

For magazine strategists, the three broad elements of planning—market, audience, content—are easy to put on paper. But many strategies fail in execution because they lack a key to successful follow-through: precision. Unfortunately, the margin for error is narrowing for magazine strategists, editors and writers.

For example, identifying the market often requires sorting through a multitude of subtleties, and making the wrong judgment call on any can lead to disaster. An illustration: You wouldn't assume that the market for a fishing magazine includes elk hunters. That's obvious. But not so obvious, perhaps, is that a magazine for people who fish cannot identify its reader-market broadly as including those who wade upstate New York streams in search of trout *and* those who troll off the Florida coast for saltwater fish. The two groups use—and want to read about—different equipment and angling techniques. A dairy farmers' magazine cannot lump together those who farm in Wisconsin with those in Georgia. They operate under different climatic, soil and market conditions, and they require separate magazine content that reflects those differences.

In assessing a magazine and a story you want to write for it, be certain to research the target audience so you understand the subtleties of its interests and information needs.

Precision is equally important for magazines in delivering readers who are attractive to advertisers. Top-of-the-line car companies, stockbrokerage houses and exotic travel companies won't buy ads in a magazine delivering readers with down-scale demographics—say, $10,000 annual household income—who cannot afford high-cost goods and services. Cosmetic manufacturers and high-style fashion houses want their ads seen by readers whose lifestyles and interests make them potential buyers, not merely window-shoppers. Readers whose psychographics tend toward cut-off jeans and back-to-mother-earth lifestyles are, for these advertisers, "wrong" readers. Any magazine that fails to deliver the right readers can fail financially.

Many subtleties are involved in delivering right readers. For example, magazines must deliver *exclusive readers*, who as a group cannot be reached easily or economically by advertisers using other media. *Life* had millions of readers but failed as a weekly in 1972 because its type of readers—and millions more—could be reached by advertisers using TV. TV also offered advertisers a lower cost for reaching each 1,000 persons—lower cost-per-thousand or "lower CPM," in industry parlance—than did *Life*.

In writing, remember that your story must dovetail with a magazine's overall effort to attract the type of readers wanted by its advertisers. Don't submit to *Forbes*, a business executives' magazine that claims one in three subscribers is a millionaire, a story on, say, how impoverished retirees can grow vegetables cheaply in their own gardens.

And, do remember—every time you touch a keyboard—your competitors, especially those Sunday newspapers. They're presenting analytical, in-depth writing, colorfully packaged in appealing formats once exclusive to magazines. They are attracting to newspapers many readers who formerly saw magazines as the best once-weekly stopping point for catching up on all the news they were too busy to read during the week. Evidence of this is Sunday newspaper growth, up from 586 Sunday papers with 49.2 million circulation in 1970 to 865 with 62.4 million circulation in 1990. Your writing style must compete against these papers as well as against other media and lifestyle diversions that pull "time-starved" Americans away from reading.

Begin thinking now—as all magazine strategists must—about how you and your writing techniques can fit into the intensely competitive media marketplace.

Magazine Advantages over Competitors

Magazines have some enormous advantages over other media competitors because so many advertisers these days are emphasizing target marketing—creating special products, then launching tightly focused ad campaigns at only those potential customers most likely to purchase them. Magazines have unique strengths as advertising vehicles in target marketing. To explain:

Most newspapers serve general audiences of readers. Some readers are old, some young; some are wealthy, some aren't. Much more so than magazines, newspapers attract readers across wide demographic and psychographic ranges. Yet, many advertisers employing target marketing techniques want to "shoot" at potential customers with the accuracy of a rifle, not the scattered pattern of a newspaper shotgun. Simply, target marketing often requires reaching young consumers and the old—but not at the same time. Or, it often requires reaching only those consumers who are young *and* wealthy.

Newspapers attempt to deliver such niche audiences by creating within their pages a series of special subject news sections likely to attract readers with commonality of interests (and demographics). Examples are business and sports sections. Newspapers also publish geographically zoned editions, stressing local news, to serve limited areas of their broader market. But only specialized newspapers, such as *The*

Wall Street Journal and business news weeklies, are having much success in narrowly focused target marketing.

Broadcast television cannot provide target marketing. Its generalized content and wide-ranging signal indiscriminately scoop up large masses of viewers of all kinds, in all places. TV, therefore, attracts advertising for products likely used by millions—the young and old, the wealthy and not-so-wealthy. Watch TV tonight and note the commercials for beer (aimed, probably, at those who drink more than one), razor blades, shampoo and other everyday products. For ads on diamond rings, Rolex watches and expensive vacations or cars check your favorite upscale magazine.

Broadcast TV also is disadvantaged in the fight for ad dollars because people who spend many hours watching the tube generally are downscale in income and education, compared with readers of magazines and newspapers. It's a fact: Among all media "consumers," people who read the most generally are better educated, have higher incomes and thus are more attractive to upscale advertisers.

Cable TV has some target marketing capabilities because it devotes channels to specialized information and entertainment formats consistently likely to attract viewers similar in interests and background. Radio has targeting capabilities, too, because it attracts audiences of similar listeners through specialized music programming—"golden oldies" for older Americans, country and western for yet another audience and so forth.

However, direct mail most seriously competes with magazines for ad revenue, because it can deliver messages to extremely narrowly defined markets—all dentists (but not physicians) in a county, wine drinkers (not beer drinkers), credit card users (not cash buyers). But direct mail to many means junk mail, and it doesn't carry the credibility of ads in publications.

Table 1–1 shows where magazines fit into the fierce struggle under way for advertising dollars in the American free enterprise media marketplace.

Although currently seventh in the race for ad dollars, magazines are well positioned to prosper in what is certain to be increased target marketing by advertisers in the future. Evidence of this is in the current rapid growth in the number of magazines, most of them highly specialized, at a time when the number of daily newspapers is diminishing (see Table 1–2).

TABLE 1–1 How the Media Share Advertising Revenue

Medium	Ad Revenue (in Millions)	Percentage of Total
Newspapers	$ 32,281	25.1%
Television	28,405	22.1
Direct mail	21,945	18.2
Miscellaneous	15,955	12.4
Yellow pages	8,926	6.9
Radio	8,726	6.8
Magazines		
Weeklies	2,864	
Women's	1,713	
Monthlies	2,226	
Total	6,803	5.3
Business newspapers	2,875	2.2
Outdoor	1,084	0.8
Farm publications	215	0.2
TOTAL	128,640	100.0

Source: Robert J. Coen, McCann Erikson. Figures for 1990.

	TABLE 1–2 Magazine Numbers Growing Rapidly	Year	Number of Magazines	Number of Daily Newspapers
		1950	6,960	1,772
		1960	8,422	1,763
		1970	9,573	1,748
		1980	10,236	1,745
		1990	11,092	1,611
		1992	11,143	1,586

Sources: Magazine Publishers Association and American Newspaper Publishers Association.

The Rise of Specialized Publishing

For writers, the single most important continuing change in American magazine publishing is the explosive growth of specialized publications targeted on niche audiences.

Concurrent with that is the weakening—or near death—of mass-circulation magazines that seek general audiences with wide-ranging editorial content.

Of hundreds of new magazines launched annually (584 in 1989, by one count, 541 in 1991), almost all are highly specialized.[5] These are the 10 most popular interest categories for new magazines launched in 1991.[6]

Rank	*Category*	*Number of new magazines*
1	Sex	66
2	Sports	42
3	Lifestyle/service	38
4	Media personalities	34
5	Crafts/games/hobbies	32
6	Military/naval	26
7	Metropolitan/regional/state	24
8	Gay/lesbian	22
9	Automotive, puzzles	19
10	Fishing & hunting, home/home service, music	18

Not all new publications (*Erotic Lingerie* and *Sexual Secrets* were among them in 1989) survive, of course. The University of Mississippi's Dr. Sami Husni, a leading scholar in new publications, reports only 18.6 percent of new magazines launched in the early 1980s were still publishing four years later.[7] Nevertheless, large publishing firms and individual entrepreneurs, all hoping to strike a rich vein of reader interest and advertiser support, continue to launch new magazines in niche markets. Mass-circulation weekly magazines, once virtual publishing icons in the United States, have all but vanished. *Look* and *Collier's* were among them. Those that hang on—*Life* and *Saturday Evening Post*, for example—now are published much less frequently and in dramatically changed form.

For you as a writer the meaning is clear.

First, the day is ending in magazines for generalist writers who know a little about many things but not much about anything. Readers of specialized magazines—such as *Adhesives Age* ("all the news about glue") or *American Agriculturist*—likely are experts in the subject you're writing about. That means you can create journalistically valid copy for specialized magazines *only* if you possess in-depth understanding of the subject. Alert writers/reporters can develop specialist knowledge on the job and through interviews, of course. But strong academic training can be extremely helpful. Why not consider majoring in journalism/writing and minoring in, say, business, science or agriculture, if you think you would like to write about one of those subjects?

Second, you must build a network of highly qualified news sources and develop interviewing techniques if you want to write with authority and credibility for specialized magazines. You must understand how to find those in your chosen specialty field who know what is new, what is happening—and you must know how to get information from them. The experts among specialty magazine readers know much of what is happening in their field, and your writing will be dismissed quickly if you continually serve up "old news." That is, your success as a writer will depend in large measure on your reporting skills.

Third, your ability to handle the language must be polished. Experts in a specialty magazine's audience—bankers, scientists, business executives—don't communicate in sloppy, imprecise language. You can't, either. You must develop a style that clearly and directly expresses your meaning. Vague, verbose writing will kill your career in magazines. You also must strike a balance between writing in the language of experts and picking up so much of their communications shorthand—their lingo—that your writing becomes unintelligible to all but a highly expert few. We'll address this later in the book. For now, concentrate on creating a basic writing style that communicates effectively to a broad-based audience. Raising the level of sophistication in your writing to address experts, as well as non-experts, can come later.

Clearly, in deciding directions for your magazine career you'll need to reflect deeply on your personal interests, your reporting/writing skills and what types of magazine writing are suitable for you. But you obviously must determine, also, which skills the industry *needs*. There are several ways to get a sense of this.

Finding "Hot" Specialties for Writers

The clearest signal on which writing specialties are in greatest demand comes from the circulation successes of magazines and the content and writing that build those successes.

Tables 1–3 and 1–4 list magazines with the largest combined subscription and single-copy circulation in America. Examine their content, isolate the specialty coverage that makes them so popular, and then reflect on what you can offer them as a writer.

The magazines listed in Table 1–3 (p. 12) derive much of their circulation from home-delivered subscriptions. Editors of those magazines fashion long-term contracts with readers: In return for your subscription fee, we'll provide a certain quantity, quality and type of coverage over time.

Quite another editor-reader relationship exists for magazines with strong single-copy sales. Editors and writers for these magazines must fashion covers and content that shout from crowded newsstands and supermarket shelves and create a new "buy" decision in readers' minds every week or month. The magazines most successful at that are listed in Table 1–4 (p. 13).

Of course, the most important sign of how a magazine's writing and marketing formula is working is whether the magazine can turn its editorial and circulation efforts into financial success. You'll rarely get enough inside information on magazines, particularly their costs, to calculate precisely whether they are profitable. But

TABLE 1–3 Top-circulation U.S. Magazines

Rank	Magazine	Combined Circulation
1	*Modern Maturity*	22,450,000*
2	*Reader's Digest*	16,306,007
3	*TV Guide*	15,353,982
4	*National Geographic*	9,921,479
5	*Better Homes & Gardens*	8,003,263
6	*Family Circle*	5,151,534
7	*Good Housekeeping*	5,028,151
8	*McCall's*	5,009,358
9	*Ladies' Home Journal*	5,002,900
10	*Woman's Day*	4,751,977
11	*Time*	4,248,565
12	*Redbook*	3,841,866
13	*National Enquirer*	3,706,030
14	*Playboy*	3,498,802
15	*Sports Illustrated*	3,444,188
16	*Newsweek*	3,420,167
17	*People*	3,235,120
18	*Star*	3,207,951
19	*Prevention*	3,109,562
20	*American Legion Magazine*	2,984,389
21	*Cosmopolitan*	2,679,356
22	*AAA World*	2,630,944
23	*Scholastic Teen Network*	2,591,130
24	*First for Women*	2,393,722
25	*Southern Living*	2,385,058
26	*U.S. News & World Report*	2,351,922
27	*Smithsonian*	2,204,298
28	*Glamour*	2,012,305
29	*Field and Stream*	2,003,041
30	*NEA Today*	1,980,823

*Members of the American Association of Retired Persons automatically receive this magazine.
Source: Audit Bureau of Circulations. Figures are for first six months of 1991.

you can determine which magazines are leaders in total circulation and advertising revenue. Table 1–5 (p. 14) lists the top U.S. magazines according to ad revenue.

Yet another measurement exists for which types of editorial content are popular and, therefore, where your writing skills are in demand. This is a study by R. Russell Hall Co. of 74 magazines that in 1991 published 1.9 *billion* editorial pages (or 2,122 pages for every U.S. household). Table 1–6 (p. 15) reports this breakdown in types of content.

Note in Table 1–6 that fiction accounts for only 1.3 percent of all pages. Only one notable weekly magazine, *The New Yorker*, publishes fiction regularly. A few monthlies do—*The Atlantic, Harper's, Esquire, Playboy,* and *Seventeen,* are among them. Not many years ago, weekly and monthly magazines were primary outlets for American fiction writers.

Why the change? About 500 or so literary journals and quarterly reviews have

TABLE 1–4 Most Successful U.S. Single-Copy Circulation Magazines

Rank	Magazine	Average Single-Copy Circulation
1	*TV Guide*	6,975,652
2	*Woman's Day*	4,058,500
3	*National Enquirer*	3,621,137
4	*Family Circle*	3,246,839
5	*Star*	3,137,419
6	*First for Women*	2,764,667
7	*Cosmopolitan*	2,170,997
8	*People Weekly*	1,690,542
9	*Woman's World*	1,542,582
10	*Good Housekeeping*	1,385,090
11	*Penthouse*	1,361,298
12	*Glamour*	1,299,262
13	*Globe*	1,260,247
14	*Soap Opera Digest*	1,031,546
15	*Ladies' Home Journal*	909,378
16	*Reader's Digest*	908,000
17	*National Examiner*	873,867
18	*Playboy*	832,576
19	*Weekly World News*	754,850
20	*Vogue*	749,931
21	*Redbook*	734,966
22	*Mademoiselle*	641,050
23	*New Woman*	624,019
24	*Self*	585,574
25	*Country Living*	568,166
26	*Shape Magazine*	533,288
27	*Better Homes & Gardens*	525,334
28	*Life*	513,799
29	*Muscle & Fitness*	497,664
30	*Seventeen*	434,606

Source: Audit Bureau of Circulations. Figures are averages for first six months of 1990.

sprung up as showcases for short stories and other creative writing. More importantly, magazine strategists generally say fiction doesn't attract advertisers as well as service articles. These are articles, for example, about cars. They pull in auto advertisers that want their ads positioned adjacent to editorial copy that potential car buyers will read. Cosmetic manufacturers want their ads positioned next to service articles about beauty care, travel companies want ads next to travel stories, and so forth. Advertisers know that potential consumers read service articles and that they are in an information-seeking buying mode when they do. Who knows whether potential consumers are "pulled" by fiction? And, if they are, does fiction create a buying mode? Or does it merely relax, entertain and provide escapism?[8]

How such factors influence editorial decision making is yet another reason why you, as a writer, must understand publishing economics.

TABLE 1–5 U.S. Magazines with the Highest Advertising Revenue

Rank	Magazine	Headquarters	Total Revenues (in Millions)	Owner
1	*TV Guide*	Radnor, PA	$884.1	News Corp.
2	*People*	New York	663.4	Time Warner
3	*Time*	New York	578.4	Time Warner
4	*Sports Illustrated*	New York	563.3	Time Warner
5	*Reader's Digest*	New York	440.1	Reader's Digest Association
6	*Parade*	New York	388.6	Advance Publications
7	*Newsweek*	New York	377.8	Washington Post Co.
8	*Better Homes & Gardens*	New York	291.9	Meredith Corp.
9	*PC Magazine*	New York	271.5	Ziff Communications
10	*U.S. News & World Report*	Washington	267.4	U.S. News & World Report
11	*Business Week*	New York	263.5	McGraw-Hill
12	*Good Housekeeping*	New York	262.5	Hearst Corp.
13	*National Geographic*	Washington	246.4	National Geographic Society
14	*Family Circle*	New York	225.7	New York Times Co.
15	*National Enquirer*	Lantana, FL	216.8	G.P. Group
16	*Ladies' Home Journal*	New York	216.5	Meredith Corp.
17	*Cosmopolitan*	New York	206.5	Hearst Corp.
18	*Forbes*	New York	196.9	Forbes Inc.
19	*Fortune*	New York	189.5	Time Warner
20	*McCall's*	New York	186.5	New York Times Co.
21	*Playboy*	Chicago	180.1	Playboy Enterprises
22	*Star Magazine*	Tarrytown, NY	171.3	G.P. Group
23	*Woman's Day*	New York	168.8	Hachette Publications
24	*Money*	New York	158.2	Time Warner
25	*Vogue*	New York	143.9	Advance Publications
26	*Glamour*	New York	139.4	Advance Publications
27	*USA Weekend*	New York	137.4	Gannett Co.
28	*Redbook*	New York	126.1	Hearst Corp.
29	*Southern Living*	Birmingham, AL	122.3	Time Warner
30	*Cable Guide*	Horsham, PA	116.6	TVSM

Source: Advertising Age. Figures are for 1991.

THE WRITER AND INDUSTRY ECONOMICS

The magazine industry's *business* strategy revolves, in major part, around building readership that can be "sold" to advertisers. Industrywide, 48 percent of total consumer magazine revenue comes from advertisers.

Looking ahead, you can estimate fairly well which types of magazines will flourish with advertiser support (and which types of specialty writing will thus be in demand) by examining where the ad dollars come from. Table 1–7 lists the leading sources of magazine ad revenue, while Table 1–8 (p. 16) shows the top individual advertisers.

TABLE 1–6 Top Editorial Content Categories for 75 Magazines

Rank	Type of Editorial	Percentage of Total Pages
1	Culture/humanities	15.9
2	Food/nutrition	8.8
3	Sports/hobbies	8.6
4	National affairs	7.7
5	General interest, health/medical science	7.2(tie)
6	Home furnishings/management	5.7
7	Amusements	5.6
8	Wearing apparel	5.3
9	Travel/transportation	4.4
10	Miscellaneous	4.3
11	Beauty/grooming	4.0
12	Foreign affairs	3.8
13	Business/industry	3.3
14	Children	2.6
15	Building	2.5
16	Gardening/farming	1.8
17	Fiction/stories	1.3

Source: Magazine Publishers of America reproduced elements of this study in *The Magazine Handbook, 1992–1993,* p. 35, quoting R. Russell Hall Co.; Audit Bureau of Circulations and SRDS on circulation; Sales & Marketing Management Survey of Buying Power, 1991, on households.

Industry Profit Levels

Although there are many failures among magazines, particularly among the hundreds of new titles launched annually, the industry generally is profitable.

A leading investment bank, Veronis, Suhler & Associates, estimated that consumer magazines as a group achieved 13.3 percent operating (or pretax) profit margins in 1989. For trade and professional magazines, the figure was 12.1 percent.[9] In 1991, the profit figure was 10.6 percent, according to the Magazine Publishers of America.

TABLE 1–7 Leading Sources of Magazine Advertising Revenue

Rank	Type of Ad	Ad Revenue (Millions)
1	Automotive, automotive accessories/equipment	$940.5
2	Toiletries/cosmetics	629.4
3	Direct response companies	560.5
4	Business/consumer services	460.2
5	Foods/food products	433.6
6	Apparel, footwear, accessories	415.4
7	Travel, hotels/resorts	358.8
8	Computers, office equipment/stationery	285.9
9	Cigarettes, tobacco, accessories	264.4
10	Liquor	228.3

Source: Publishers Information Bureau. Figures for 1991.

TABLE 1–8 Top Corporate Advertisers, 1991

Rank	Company	Magazine Ad Spending (Millions)
1	General Motors Corp.	$250.4
2	Philip Morris	215.6
3	Ford Motor Co.	149.9
4	Procter & Gamble Co.	142.8
5	Chrysler Corp.	106.8
6	Toyota Motor Corp.	105.5
7	Grand Metropolitan PLC	83.1
8	Unilever NV	81.0
9	Nestle SA	77.0
10	Time Warner	67.0
11	American Brands	64.3
12	RJR Nabisco	61.8
13	Honda Motor Co.	58.1
14	Johnson & Johnson	56.3
15	Sony Corp.	55.6
16	AT&T Co.	48.8
17	Mazda Motor Corp.	46.4
18	Bradford Exchange	45.3
19	Estee Lauder Inc.	42.1
20	Allied-Lyons PLC	38.8

Source: Magazine Publishers of America.

Operating profit essentially is what's left *after* publishing cost—salaries, rent, printing and so forth—are deducted from total and circulation revenue, and *before* taxes, interest payments and other non-operating costs are taken out. Magazine margins generally are below those for television stations, which often enjoy 35 percent or more operating profit, and newspapers, many of which have 20–30 percent margins. However, magazines as a group are more profitable than many non-media businesses.

Broadly, two factors (aside from general economic conditions) most influence magazine margins.

First, many competitors—including proliferating magazines of all types—are scrambling for the same reader's attention and advertiser's dollar. New circulation and

FIGURE 1–1 Where the Money Comes From (*Source: Magazine Publishers of America, quoting Price Waterhouse Annual Financial Survey, 1992*)

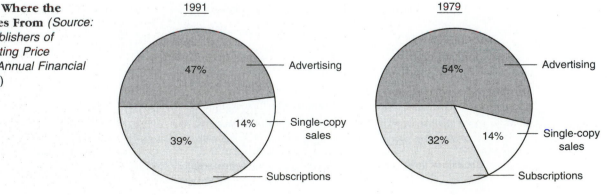

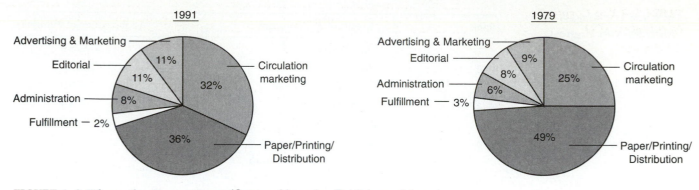

FIGURE 1–2 Where the Money Goes *(Source: Magazine Publishers of America, quoting Price Waterhouse Annual Financial Survey, 1992)*

ad revenue is, simply, harder to find. Moreover, advertisers have so many alternatives for reaching potential customers—through TV, newspapers, direct mail, and so forth—that magazines have difficulty raising ad rates.

Second, magazine publishing is a high-cost enterprise. Color printing on slick or "calendared" paper used by most magazines is much more expensive than newspaper production. The cost of selling ads and getting and keeping readers is soaring. Another problem is a magazine's major expense in maintaining home-delivered subscriptions. It easily can cost $10 to $20 to sell one subscription because of the need for mailing expensive sales promotion and, often, granting deeply discounted subscription rates. Because mailing costs are so high, single-copy selling—by simply stacking magazines on racks—is the most profitable form of distribution.

Figure 1–1 shows a breakdown of changes, 1979–91, in revenue sources for consumer magazines.

Of consumer magazines' total costs, 70 percent are for circulation and marketing, paper, printing and distribution. As Figure 1–2 indicates, editorial costs are relatively small. Many magazines have small staffs, use free-lance writers and contract out many production and distribution functions. "Fulfillment" covers payment to outside contractors that handle mailing and shipping.

What It All Means for Writers

For you as a writer, the cost/revenue squeeze on magazines has two particularly significant meanings.

First, producing high-quality editorial content doesn't guarantee financial success. If advertisers stay away, as many did in the 1990–92 recession, even the best writers and editors cannot create profitable magazines. In 1991, two nominees in that year's National Magazine Award contest, *7 Days* and *Wigwag*, were among many magazines forced to close down when revenue slumped. To survive economically harsh times, some high-quality magazines sharply cut their editorial expenditures. One technique is downsizing, reducing a magazine's size to save on paper, production and mailing.

Second, as in other media, the economics of publishing tend to favor group ownership. Only large companies can afford massive investment in research and development of successful new magazines. And groups achieve certain economies of scale that small individual owners cannot. For example, many large publishers have core magazines around whose infrastructure they build a cluster of similar spin-off magazines. Some use essentially the same editorial matter in different types of products. In 1990, Reader's Digest Association worldwide sold 43 million books, 5 million

TABLE 1–9 U.S. Magazine Publishers with Highest Ad Revenue

Rank	Publishing Company	Ad Revenue (in Millions)
1	Time Warner	$1,928.0
2	Hearst Corp.	1,002.0
3	Advance Publications	859.0
4	Thomson Corp.	774.4
5	Reed International	760.0
6	Reader's Digest Association	729.2
7	International Data Group	627.0
8	News Corp.	575.0
9	McGraw-Hill	448.0
10	Meredith Corp.	441.7

Source: Advertising Age. Figures for 1991.

musical compact discs and cassettes and 800,000 videos—all worth $1.2 billion. *Reader's Digest* itself (with a circulation of 28 million in 16 languages) had revenues of $623.9 million.

In magazine publishing, the big get very big, indeed. Most are diversified conglomerates involved in other media and, often, publish many magazines. As you can see in Table 1–9, the biggies count advertising and circulation revenue in many millions of dollars.

Despite setbacks during the 1990–92 recession, huge companies with assets worth millions are betting the future of magazines is strong. See Box 1–2 for one magazine mogul's opinion.

As you can see, as a writer, either on staff or free-lance, you are part of a magazine team organized to meet reader needs and desires. You should understand how you fit into that team.

HOW MAGAZINES ARE ORGANIZED

The number of writers employed by a magazine varies widely with the type of magazine and its chosen editorial mission.

Some magazines, such as newsweeklies, employ large staffs of writers stationed throughout the world. *Time* deployed 25 staff writers and photographers in the Middle East alone during the Persian Gulf War in 1991; *Newsweek* and *U.S. News & World Report*, 15 each. These magazines use few free-lance writers.

BOX 1–2

Is Print Dead?

"Today we live in an age of stratified, separated, targeted markets that are information-hungry. The future of all advertising-supported media is narrowcasting, not broadcasting . . .

"The idea that print is dead is preposterous. Electronic media are tiny and will occupy niches that print never occupied—basically search and retrieval, and database areas." (William Ziff of Ziff Communications, a magazine publisher with more than $500 million in annual sales)[10]

FIGURE 1–3 Table of Organization for a "Typical" Magazine

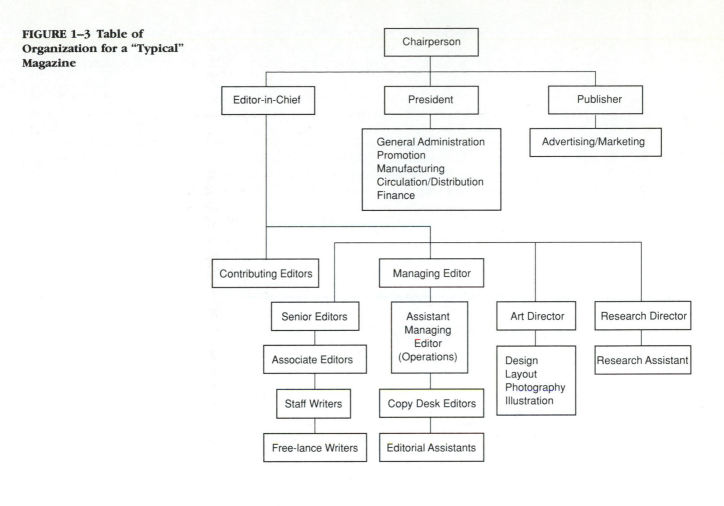

What Those Titles Mean

Titles and job descriptions vary from magazine to magazine. Generally, however, this is what they signify:

Chair—In overall charge of magazine policy, finance, operations, planning. Sometimes is the owner.

President—Oversees administration and general business operations. Answers directly to chairperson.

Publisher—Normally responsible primarily for advertising sales and marketing, but sometimes carries title and responsibilities of president, as well. Reports to chairperson.

Editor in chief—Top editorial policy strategist; supervises all editorial content, including text and art. In many companies is responsible for more than one magazine. Reports to chair or publisher.

Managing editor—In charge of day-to-day editing and proofreading; coordinates editorial, art, production departments; ensures deadlines are met.

Art director—Powerful position on many magazines; responsible for design and layout—general appearance of magazine.

Senior editors—Key players who plan and write articles, oversee staff writers and free-lancers; need highly creative ideas for developing stories and new editorial programs.

Contributing editors—Non-staff writers and consultants; often paid retainer for their expertise in particular areas—foreign affairs, medicine, science and so forth. Frequent writers for the magazine.

Research director—Provides backup for editors, writers; checks accuracy of copy, particularly from free-lancers.

Associate or assistant editors—Create and execute story ideas, edit, assign articles, write on specialty subjects.

Generally, magazine staffers with "editor" attached to their names are experienced reporters and writers, as well as editors. They need strong skills in use of the language—and excellent "people skills" that enable them to supervise other writers and editors.

Other magazines, including some with enormous circulations, have small staffs and rely primarily on free-lance writers. *Cosmopolitan*, with 2.7 million circulation in 1990, normally has only 40 or so employees in its New York City editorial headquarters.

Organization of a magazine's editorial department varies in accord with its editorial mission. See Figure 1–3 for an illustration of a typical organizational structure.

Titles and their meanings vary, too. See Box 1–3 for a general explanation.

In examining magazine industry economics it occurred to you, of course, that big, money-making magazines are best able to afford salaries that will help you achieve a lifestyle to which you would love to become accustomed! Start now aiming for magazines that can provide an outlet for your creative talents *and* a decent salary. You can get both (see Box 1–4). Incidentally, if you want to work on the staff of a "big

---

BOX 1–4

Where the Money Is

Entry-level magazine editorial jobs are extremely competitive, and that can mean low salaries for beginners just out of college. Starting annual salaries of around $15,000–$18,000 are common at low-circulation magazines in small cities.

In large cities, writers and editors with a few years' experience can demand more. In New York City, for example, McGraw-Hill in 1991 offered starting salaries of $29,000–$36,000 for editorial staffers with three years' experience.

Substantially higher salaries are paid writers and editors talented enough to rise in managerial ranks. Robert M. Steed, managing director of Performance Plus ... Inc., a New York consulting firm, finds these commonalities in a national survey for *Folio*: of magazine professionals:[11]

1. Business magazines pay higher salaries than do consumer magazines.
2. Women earn 82–95 percent of what men earn for comparable jobs, but the "gender gap" in total compensation is closing.
3. Highest salaries are paid in the Northeast by large-circulation magazines published weekly or biweekly. Lowest salaries are paid in the South Atlantic region.

Steed's 1992 survey of 542 professionals shows editorial managers who supervise a staff or more than 10 persons earn an average of almost 2.4 times as much in salary as do non-supervisors, four times as much in total compensation. The Steed survey finds these *average* annual salaries in the Northeast:

Top editorial management	Average salary
All respondents	$74,847
Business magazines	78,397
Consumer magazines	63,411

Editors	Average salary
All respondents	$54,613
Business magazines	55,092
Consumer magazines	53,692

Managing editors	Average salary
All respondents	$46,620
Business magazines	44,792
Consumer magazines	48,440

Senior or associate editors	Average salary
All respondents	$48,724
Business magazines	49,750
Consumer magazines	48,529

Art directors	Average salary
All respondents	$47,458
Business magazines	47,632
Consumer magazines	47,183

For all but a relatively few highly talented writers, free-lancing is *not* where the money is. Free-lance writing can be creatively fulfilling, but it's a difficult way to earn a good living.

Thousands of writers compete for space in those magazines that pay top rates—*Harper's*, $1,500 or so; *Playboy*, $3,000–$5,000 and up; *TV Guide*, about $1,000. Some leading magazines receive *tens* of thousands of manuscripts annually.

Nevertheless, free-lance writing now, as a student, can be your way of breaking into magazine staff jobs after graduation. Just don't count on free-lancing to pay your tuition and rent.

league" magazine, odds are you'll end up in New York. Many magazines, particularly smaller, start-up publications, locate elsewhere, but New York City still is the nation's media capital.

You also should consider launching your own magazine someday. For those willing to take risks, ownership opportunities are many (see Box 1–5).

The biggest risk for all publishers—big and small, corporate and private—is whether they can attract and hold readers. We now turn, in Chapter Two, to the writer's perspective of that.

BOX 1–5

The Golden Idea plus Courage

Magazine history has many examples of men and women who had a "golden idea" for a new publication *and* the courage to stake all on pursuing it to success.

In 1967, a dropout from University of California at Berkeley, 21-year-old Jann Wenner, borrowed $7,500 to launch a new magazine about rock music. He called it *Rolling Stone*.

Today, the magazine has well over 1.1 million circulation, is worth $150 million or more and is the core publication in Wenner's expanding media conglomerate.

Particularly with development of relatively inexpensive desktop publishing on small personal computers, magazines offer low-cost entry into ownership. But it takes more than a "golden idea." Strong journalistic and business skills are needed to succeed.

Christopher Whittle displayed both business and journalistic skills in developing his "golden idea"—that traditional media, their pages and airwaves cluttered with thousands of messages, no longer can grab audience attention and deliver ads or commercials with stand-out impact.

After graduation in 1969 from the University of Tennessee, he published a survival guide for UT students, *Knoxville in a Nutshell*. From that grew Whittle Communications, publisher of many specialized magazines and advertiser services. Time Inc. (now Time Warner) paid $185 million for half the company in 1988. Whittle retained 11 percent, estimated then to be worth $44 million.

One highly successful Whittle idea: single-advertiser publications. For a (large) fee, advertisers such as medical equipment or pharmaceutical companies can have special magazines published that contain their ads only.

In 1974, Jan and Paul Roman put their entire savings, $12,880, into a publication titled *Fine Woodworking*—and did they find a magazine niche! Today, the magazine has more than 290,000 circulation, and the Romans have added "cluster" magazines—*Fine Homebuilding*, with 245,000 circulation, *Threads* (125,000), *Fine Gardening* (125,000)—and a new one, *Boats & Gear*.

Forbes' magazine estimated in 1990 the Romans had $25 million in annual revenue from magazines, how-to-do-it books and video cassettes. To get started the Romans gambled everything they had—and won.[12]

Robin Wolaner took a different approach with her golden idea. She told Time Inc., in 1986 a new magazine was needed for parents and soon-to-be parents. Time liked her idea so much it scrapped plans for a similar publication and became her partner in *Parenting*, now enjoying circulation more than 500,000. In 1990, Time's successor corporation, Time Warner, bought out Wolaner for, *The New York Times* estimates, $5 million to $10 million. Wolaner now works for Time Warner locating and evaluating new magazine ventures.[13]

Caution: It's easy to fail and lose your entire investment in magazine publishing. Learn the business on somebody else's payroll before taking the plunge. Robin Wolaner worked in magazines for 15 years before letting loose her entrepreneurial spirit.

SUMMARY

American magazines are incredibly diverse, editorially imaginative and, as a group, prosperous, despite strong competition from other media for reader attention and advertiser dollars.

Consumer magazine circulation is growing more rapidly than the U.S. adult population, and magazine advertising revenue in 1990 hit a record $6.8 billion (although it slumped to $6.5 billion in 1991, due to a nationwide recession). The number of U.S. magazines is increasing, too—to 11,143 in 1992, from 9,434 in 1969.

Magazines, one of the oldest communications media in America, have lasted more than 250 years since Colonial times because they adapt to changing American habits and lifestyles. Their continuing success is driven by the creative minds of editors and writers who fashion editorial content finely focused for readers' needs and desires.

Three crucial elements in magazine strategy are identifying a market of readers with commonality of interest, delivering readers who are attractive to advertisers and creating an editorial environment where readers and advertisers know their needs will be met.

Magazines have advantages over media competitors, particularly the ability to deliver niche audiences of readers desired by advertisers in target marketing. This involves creating special products and launching tightly focused ad campaigns only at those potential customers most likely to buy them. Newspapers, principal print competitors of magazines, have difficulty delivering such narrowly defined audiences.

For writers, the most important continuing change in publishing is explosive growth of specialized publications. Of 541 new magazines launched in 1991 and 584 in 1989, almost all are highly specialized and targeted to niche audiences. The failure rate of these magazines is high. One study shows only 18.6 percent of magazines launched in the early 1980s were still publishing four years later.

Specialized publishing means writers who are generalists have difficulty. Writers need in-depth understanding of the subjects they cover plus highly developed networks of expert sources—and interview techniques to extract information from them. Precision language skills are mandatory in writing for expert readers of specialized magazines.

To determine which writing specialties are in demand, study content of large-circulation, financially successful magazines.

Entry-level editorial jobs are extremely competitive, and that keeps beginner salaries low. Business magazines pay the highest salaries. Regionally, large-circulation magazines published weekly or biweekly in the Northeast pay the best. Average salaries are lowest in the South Atlantic.

Magazine profits are higher than those of many non-media businesses, but generally lower than those of newspapers and television stations. For this and other reasons, industry economics tend to favor ownership of magazines by large media conglomerates, although individual private entrepreneurs with a golden idea have succeeded throughout magazine history.

RECOMMENDED READING

For current developments in magazine publishing, see research reports issued periodically by Magazine Publishers of America, 575 Lexington Ave., New York, N.Y. 10022. Excellent coverage of magazine topics and new titles being launched is published by *Folio, Advertising Age, Adweek, Magazine Week, Marketing & Media Decisions, Media Week, Publishing News.* Media news sections of *The New York Times, The Wall Street Journal* and *The Los Angeles Times* cover the magazine industry regularly and well.

For names and addresses of magazines, see *Gale Directory of Publications and Media, National Directory of Magazines* and *Standard Periodical Directory.*

To read further about the industry, see Leonard Mogel, *The Magazine: Everything You Need To Make It in the Magazine Business* (Chester, Ct.: Folio: Book Pequot Press, 1988), William Rankin, *Business Management of General Consumer Magazines* (New York: Praeger, 1980), and William Taft, *American Magazines for the 1980s* (New York: Hastings House, 1982).

For magazine history: Theodore Peterson, *Magazines in the Twentieth Century*, 2d ed. (Urbana: University of Illinois Press, 1964), and Michael Emery and Edwin Emery, *The Press and America: An Interpretive History of the Mass Media* (Englewood Cliffs, N.J.: Prentice-Hall, 1992, 7th ed.)

NOTES

1. *Facts About Newspapers '92*, published by the American Newspaper Publishers Association, estimates daily newspaper circulation in 1991 at 60,687,125 and 62,067,820 on Sundays.
2. *The Magazine Handbook, 1992–1993, No. 64*, Magazine Publishers of America, New York, 2–3.
3. *Facts About Newspapers '92.*
4. *The Magazine Handbook*, 2–3.
5. Deirdre Carmody, "A Guide to New Magazines Shows Widespread Vitality," *The New York Times*, 25 Feb. 1991, C-1. See also Patrick M. Reilly, "Magazines Fail to Shake Off Ad Slump," *The Wall Street Journal*, 17 July 1990, B-7.
6. Magazine Publishers of America, quoting Sami Husni's *Guide to New Magazines*, 1992.
7. Deirdre Carmody, "A Guide to New Magazines Shows Widespread Vitality," *The New York Times*, 25 Feb. 1991, C-1. See also Patrick M. Reilly, "Magazines Fail to Shake Off Ad Slump," *The Wall Street Journal,* 17 July, 1990, B-7.
8. For superb treatment of this subject see Deirdre Carmody, "The Short Story: Out of the Mainstream But Flourishing," *The New York Times*, National Edition, 23 April 1991, B-1.
9. Liz Horton, "Profit Gap Between Magazine Groups Shrinks," *Folio* March 1991, 39, quoting John Suhler, president and co-chief executive officer of Veronis, Suhler & Associates in that firm's 1990 Communications Industry Report. The 1991 figure is from Deirdre Carmody, "Power to the Readers: *Ms.* Thrives Without Ads," *The New York Times*, 22 July 1991, D6.
10. Christopher Palmeri, "The Idea That Print is Dead is Preposterous," *Forbes*, 10 June 1991, 42.
11. Robert M. Steed, "1992 Editorial Salary Survey," *Folio*, August 1992, p. 39.
12. Rita Koselka, "Editor Makes Good," *Forbes*, 19 March 1990, 100.
13. Deirdre Carmody, "Beating Time Warner At Its Own Game," *The New York Times*, 8 April 1990, F-1.

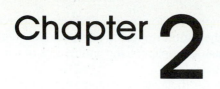

Chapter 2

You and the magazine reader

So, who *are* these magazine readers, these mysteriously elusive targets chased so vigorously by more than 11,000 magazines and competing media of all kinds?

Why do they read magazines, and what do they seek from them? Where and when do they read? What is their frame of mind when they do?

For a magazine, successfully answering those questions is crucial. If it doesn't, all the marketing theory and strategic planning we discussed in Chapter One will fail.

For you as a writer, understanding your reader must guide your every step on the creative path, from selecting a story idea to writing, with precision, in style, structure and language that will communicate best. If you don't keep your reader firmly fixed in mind, you will fail.

In Chapter Two, we will discuss what a writer must know about readers. You will learn four things about magazine readers.

First, magazine readers generally are better educated than the average American and have higher incomes. But most functionally literate Americans, of all demographic and psychographic types, read magazines at least occasionally.

Second, readers approach magazines with varying intensity and loyalty. Some select magazines randomly and flip hurriedly through the pages, grazing here and there or sometimes simply looking at ads. Others read thoroughly and regularly in specific magazines for which they have impressive loyalty. For example, 85 percent of *National Geographic* subscribers renew their subscriptions, a phenomenally high rate for all print media. (For some metropolitan newspapers, the annual loss of subscribers—called "churn"—exceeds 50 percent).

Third, readers seek various rewards for their efforts. Some want to travel vicariously to far-off places with *National Geographic* writers; some seek titillation from peeking into private lives of the rich and famous with personality magazine writers; others seek simple diversion, a relaxing turn-off from the hurly-burly of their daily lives. Increasingly, however, research shows magazine readers are information seekers.

Fourth, regardless of what they seek, readers are pressed for time. The demands of modern living leave them time starved, and they will challenge you to entice them with stories truly important to them personally and written colorfully and compellingly.

Let's turn now to the chase after the American magazine reader, your target as a writer!

THE WRITER'S PROCESS OF DISCOVERY WITH READERS

Picture yourself discussing music with friends. Early in the conversation, perhaps without even thinking about it, you engage in a process of discovery to determine their interest and expertise.

Even a quick glance gives you a starting point: You carefully note your friends' body language and tone of voice. Do they appear bored? Or are their eyes beginning to light up? Are they speaking excitedly about new songs and new groups? Are your friends pushing forward with their opinions?

Thus, in a chat, do you seek signals on what musical interests and expertise of your conversational partners possess? Thereby armed, you can determine precisely how best to communicate your views and information. You can decide how to structure your side of the conversation—whether, for example, to tell an anecdote or two, or stick to a technical discussion. You can even determine which language usage will best communicate your thoughts—down, even, to individual words and technical terms you use.

Now switch scenarios: You've got a new job as a New York-based writer for *Tennis* magazine (yes, dreams *do* sometimes come true) and you are doing a piece on a young Swedish woman player blossoming into international stardom.

You stare at the VDT screen (you'll do lots of that in a writing career), trying to decide which writing approach will best communicate with your magazine's 420,000 subscribers. Which story structure will work? Which level of tennis terminology will be understood? Indeed, which language usage is appropriate?

Well, you obviously can't look for clues in your readers' body language or tone of voice. Your readers are distant and mostly anonymous. Yet, you *do* have clues about them and how to approach them in your writing.

For example, your subscribers have a deep interest in tennis, and probably expertise as well. They pay to receive a tennis magazine, after all. That's the first clue on how to pitch your writing. Others are available in the standard marketing information (or media kit) that *Tennis*, like most magazines, publishes. The kit provides this reader information:

- The average *Tennis* subscriber's annual household income is $86,000.
- Of those employed, 70 percent have professional/managerial jobs.
- 87 percent are homeowners.
- 89 percent are college educated.

■ 74 percent are men; 26 percent, women.
■ Their average age is 39.[1]

Now, think of the enormously valuable reader information you already have that will determine which direction your writing should take.

First, you know your readers are tennis buffs and thus more interested in a story about a tennis star than about a young woman. Let *People* magazine write about her love life; you do a piece on her playing technique (particularly that vicious backhand everybody in the tennis world is talking about). Still, a personality profile (a story built around her as an individual) might be the perfect story structure—as long as you profile her tennis abilities.

Second, you know most of your readers are college educated and, thus (we hope) have above-average reading abilities. You can pitch the sophistication level of your writing accordingly.

Third, you know your readers' average age is 39, so you shouldn't orient your story toward information important primarily to, say, teenagers or retirees.

Well, you get the point: A discerning writer can draw extraordinarily helpful hints from even limited information about a reader audience. Let's check clues on magazine readers in general to help you fashion your personal writing style that will reach them.

Educated, Upscale Adults Read More

Magazine readers generally are better educated and more affluent than most Americans. This challenges you to position your writing at a level likely to attract and hold relatively knowledgeable, well-to-do people.

A study by Mediamark Research Inc. (MRI), showed that during one four-week period (an average month), 89 percent of all American adults read one or more magazines. The average number of issues read in the month was 10.3. A demographic breakdown of readership is shown in Table 2–1.

Note from Table 2–1 the relationship among education, higher income and increased readership. Although 89 percent of all American adults read magazines in an "average" month, 95.3 percent of those with at least some college education do so. Of adult Americans with $50,000 or more in annual household income, 94.3 percent read magazines.

The relationship between employment and magazine readership is tight, as well. Among employed adults, the MRI survey shows that 94.9 percent of those with professional/managerial jobs read magazines—12.2 issues each month, on average. The

TABLE 2–1 Magazine Reader Demographics

Reader Group	Percentage Who Read One or More Magazines	Average Number of Issues Read
18–44 years old	91.4%	11.5
25–54 years old	90.6	10.9
Attended or graduated from college	95.3	12.4
$40,000-plus household income	93.8	12.0
$50,000-plus household income	94.3	12.2
Professional/managerial	94.9	12.2

Source: Reach & Frequency Analysis of 1992 Spring MRI, magazines published in a four-week period, quoted in Magazine Publishers of America's *The Magazine Handbook 1992–1993*, research document No 64, p. 38.

Magazine Publishers Association says its research shows that employed women depend more heavily on magazines for information of all types than do non-employed women.

MRI research also profiles the average reader of an average magazine:

- Median age: 40.3 years (U.S. median: 41).
- 40 percent are at least high school graduates.
- 60 percent are married.
- 57 percent are heads of households.
- 56 percent live in a household of three or more persons.
- 56 percent are employed full-time.
- Median household income is $35,800.
- 67 percent own their home (median value $87,686).
- 78 percent live in a metropolitan area.[2]

It's dangerous, of course, to draw sweeping conclusions from general data in the two tables above. For a writer, however, valuable clues emerge.

First, the high percentage of readers—94.9 percent—among professionals or managers is very significant. Advertisers love to reach these people because they have high incomes and can influence their *companies'* purchasing, in addition to changing their *personal* buying habits, in response to ads. So, whether you're a staff writer or free-lancer, many magazines you write for will try to create editorial content to attract this group of readers. Professionals and managers, like many people, read for sheer pleasure and relaxation. But as a group, they seek information from their reading, and your writing for them should be fact-filled, precise and, of course, accurate.

Second, note the high percentage of average readers who are married, heads of households and live in households of three or more persons. These people have responsibilities—paying bills, making marriage work, raising children—that in large measure dictate their reading habits. Regard them as people who are trying to cope with their responsibilities, and write stories that will help them save money, do a better job of child rearing and, in general, live more fulfilling lives.

Third, magazine readers have identifiable lifestyle characteristics that you should consider when selecting and writing stories. For example, the information presented earlier shows that magazine readers own things. Fully 67 percent own homes (that certainly helps explain why, as we learned in Chapter One, *Better Homes & Gardens* is a circulation leader, and why other large magazines emphasize stories on home buying and maintenance). You also can deduce from Tables 2–1 and 2–2 that magazine readers' median household income (above the national average) gives them purchasing power for hobbies, vacations, sports and other participatory activities. As a group, your reader-targets are movers, doers, shakers. Note also, that most do it and shake it in metropolitan areas, where 78 percent of magazine readers live. This bears directly on you as a writer. It can mean, for example, that a story on, say, how to live in a mountaintop log cabin should be written not from the viewpoint of someone lucky enough to already live in one, but rather from the wistful viewpoint of a harried commuter and city dweller who dreams of living in one.

Among competing media, newspapers come closest to magazines in types of target audiences. Newspaper readers, like magazine readers, generally are upscale in education and income. Therefore, skills you develop in reporting and writing for magazines can also apply to much newspaper work—particularly specialized writing on business, science, the arts and so forth.

Entirely different creative impulses and skills are used, however, to reach television audiences. Many people who watch TV also read magazines, of course, but readers and viewers are very different, a point illustrated in Table 2–2. The table summarizes results of an MRI study that compared magazine reading and TV viewing in various demographic groups.

TABLE 2–2 Magazine Reading Versus TV Viewing by Demographic Group (U.S. Average: 100)

Category	Magazines	TV
Attended/graduated from college	140	61
Graduated high school	90	104
Did not graduate high school	48	160
Household income $40,000 plus	135	63
Household income $50,000 plus	141	58
Household income $60,000 plus	148	55
Professional/managerial	157	50
Technical/clerical/sales*	128	67
Precision/craft*	99	103
Unemployed	60	142

*Based on employed adults
Source: The Magazine Handbook 1992–1993, 41.

Table 2–2 clearly shows magazine readers are upscale demographically compared to TV viewers in education, income and types of jobs. The gap widens between magazine and TV audiences further upscale on the demographic charts. This is revealed in research that divides the marketplace into media imperatives—a study of which medium is imperative, or essential, to reach a specific audience.

For example, among those who own residences valued at $100,000 or more, magazines reach 43 percent; TV, 22 percent. Among those with household income of $50,000 or more annually, magazines reach 48 percent and TV, 17 percent.[3]

With statistics such as these, magazine and newspaper editors increasingly are opting out of downscale mass media strategies, leaving them to TV's wide net. Instead, magazine editors are going for the upscale audiences so desired by advertisers—and that forces you, as a writer, to be more sophisticated in selection of stories and writing level. Clearly, you must strive for information-packed reporting and a writing style that is stimulating and, in every sense, suited for fast-track readers.

Your Readers Are Activists and Achievers

A portrait of relatively successful, career-oriented readers emerges from research that divides media consumers into Values and Lifestyles (VALS) typologies.

Table 2–3 summarizes one study comparing exposure to various media among different VALS typologies.

TABLE 2–3 Media Usage by Various VALS Types

Typology	Mean Level of Exposure (U.S. Average: 100)			
	Magazine	TV	Radio	Newspapers
Actualizer	143	86	98	140
Fulfilled	124	96	98	125
Experiencer	112	101	104	90
Achiever	116	87	106	120
Maker	103	90	116	120
Striver	92	95	104	92
Believer	82	112	93	99
Struggler	55	123	81	71

Source: The Magazine Handbook 1990–1991, quoting 1988 SMRB/VALS 2.

A writer always must avoid the temptation to draw sweeping conclusions from limited data. But there certainly are points to ponder in Table 2–3.

First, magazine reading is heaviest among individuals characterized as successful, motivated and well-educated—Actualizers, Fulfilleds, Experiencers and Achievers. TV viewing is heaviest among less-educated individuals with limited social, economic and emotional resources—Strivers, Believers, Strugglers. Perhaps your story selection and writing tone should be upbeat, affirmative and motivational, if you want to meet the needs of magazine readers. TV writers, conversely, might be better rewarded for comfortable, non-challenging sitcoms.

Second, the similarity between magazine and newspaper readers is clear. Newspapers, as well as magazines, are a medium of choice for those who have made it, who are fulfilled. If you're writing about ways to finance a new home in today's credit market, for example, what will you give your readers that they cannot find in their newspaper's daily business section? What reporting strengths and writing techniques will you use for a story on, say, health problems associated with jogging beyond what superb personal health writers provide in *The New York Times*, *Los Angeles Times* and scores of other newspapers?

Table 2–4 shows that magazine readers are more active in public affairs than the average American or TV viewer. Note the guidance a magazine writer can draw (cautiously, generally) from this study.

When trying to get a grip on what magazine readers in general are like, note their involvement and activity carries into other areas: They are more likely than average Americans to travel domestically or internationally, to attend conferences and conventions, to rent cars.

Now that we've identified many demographic characteristics of our target readers, how can we move closer, as writers, to catching those readers? Let's track their reading habits.

How, When and Where Readers Read

American readers transmit clear signals on how, when and where they read magazines. These reading habits reveal attitudes and other lifestyle, or psychographic, characteristics that you, as a writer, must understand.

TABLE 2–4 Community Activities of Magazine Readers Versus TV Viewers

Activity Past Year	Media Imperatives (U.S. Average: 100)	
	Magazine Readers	TV Viewers
Voted in election	109	92
Wrote something that was published	154	55
Addressed public meeting	155	64
Active in local civic issue	134	66
Did fund-raising	124	74
Volunteer non-political work	122	80
Member		
church board	132	63
business club	185	44
civic club	124	76
country club	122	87
health club	164	48

Source: The Magazine Handbook 1990–1991, 41.

TABLE 2–5 Single-Copy Sales Versus Subscriptions for Magazines

Year	Single-Copy Sales (Millions)	Percentage of Total	Subscriptions (Millions)	Percentage of Total
1955	66.4	40	99.8	60
1965	63.9	30	147.7	70
1975	82.2	33	166.8	67
1980	93.9	34	181.1	66
1985	80.5	25	240.8	75
1989	79.6	22	283.5	78
1991	71.6	20	296.3	80

Source: Audit Bureau of Circulation figures in general and farm magazines (excluding comics and newspaper supplements) for first six months of each year.

In sum, most American readers read their magazines at home during leisure hours. *However,* some magazines—particularly the trades—are read elsewhere, particularly in offices, at times when readers clearly are in an information-gathering mode.

These habits are revealed, first, in how and where readers purchase magazines. Table 2–5 indicates this changing pattern.

Note in Table 2–5 the decided swing toward subscription delivery of American magazines, primarily to homes. Of all copies sold in 1991, 80 percent went to subscribers.

Of course, single-copy sales—totalling 71.6 million in 1991—are extremely significant. Their importance forces editors to strive for layout design, distinctive content and editorial tone—particularly in cover design—that shout, "Buy me!" from crowded sales racks. This is where single-copy sales are made:

Supermarkets/grocery stores	53.9%
Convenience stores	10.3
Drugstores	8.8
Bookstores	7.4
Others (bus and train stations, airport, newsstands, etc.)	19.6[4]

When the magazine is sold, what happens to it? A Magazine Publishers of America study tracked what follows the sale:

- Adult readers spend 52 minutes on the average magazine copy.
- On average, 4.7 adult readers are exposed to the copy.
- Each reader accesses the copy over 2.1 days.
- Each copy is kept accessible, on average, 28.8 weeks.[5]

For a writer, the single most important fact from this is reading time—52 minutes—devoted to the average copy of a magazine. That's substantially longer than time normally devoted to newspapers. Most research indicates readers give 26 minutes or so to their daily newspaper, a bit more on Sundays. TV viewers have very short attention spans—flipping channels during commercials, changing programs and less frequently settling down for lengthy, concentrated viewing on any in-depth subject.

That is, reading time devoted to magazines underlines the serious, information-seeking attitude readers take to what you produce through your keyboard. Further clues to reader frame of mind:

Where readers read

In own home	59.2%
Workplace	12.2
Another's home	10.1
Doctor's/dentist's office	7.5
All other	11[6]

Day of week (100 = daily average)

Sunday	82
Monday	103
Tuesday	111
Wednesday	88
Thursday	97
Friday	106
Saturday	113[7]

Time of day

Before and during breakfast	10%
After breakfast through lunch	19
After lunch through dinner	35
After dinner to retiring	42
In bed before sleeping	5[8]

Note in all three preceding lists that magazine writers gain access to most of their readers under the best possible circumstances—leisurely reading at home (59.2 percent), mostly on Saturdays and during those hours of relaxation between dinner and retiring. (The time of day percentages add up to more than 100 because the same magazine sometimes is read at different times of the day.) These other clues emerge for a writer:

First, although you'll catch most of your readers at home, a significant number—40.8 percent—must be reached elsewhere, sometimes at work (12.2 percent), or "on the fly," in a doctor's office and so forth. Many of those reading in their workplace undoubtedly are after primarily current information about their jobs, from trade publications and other career or work-oriented magazines.

Second, day-of-the-week reading is strong on Mondays and Tuesdays (again, mostly of trades) as the workweek begins and then again on Fridays and Saturdays (during leisure time). If you're writing for a magazine that is delivered early in the week, consider your audience generally to be information seekers. Weekend readers often read for relaxation and entertainment.

Third, time-of-day statistics show one thing that magazines do *not* do: compete with newspapers and TV in early-morning hours. People getting their day started and hurrying to work turn to newspapers and TV for their morning news fix. As a magazine writer, you're not competing to be first to deliver overnight news. Your time comes when things slow down a bit—after lunch and through dinner (35 percent of magazine reading is done then), and after dinner to sleep (42 percent). It's an article of faith among afternoon newspaper editors that readers must be caught between, say, 4 p.m. and 7 p.m., when they turn to the evening's meal and TV watching. Magazines, however, seem to be doing well in the evening. (Incidentally, there is little seasonal variation in magazine reading. American readers spread their magazine habit almost evenly throughout all 12 months.)

Successful writers and magazines react alertly and with sensitivity to clues on who their readers are and what shape their reading habits take. *Time*, for example, demonstrates it understands that reader "time starvation" means magazines can get pushed aside due to lifestyle pressures and demands of daily living. In 1989, when the Berlin Wall came down, *Time* bought full-page newspaper ads that counseled readers: "To understand the fall of the wall . . . make time for *Time*."

What Readers Seek in Magazines

Readers' needs and desires are as varied and complex as readers themselves, of course, and editors constantly seek clues on what readers seek in their pages.

A magazine's circulation success or lack of success is one good gauge of whether it provides what readers want. But many magazines go well beyond that, conducting expensive research into reader desires. Strong evidence emerges that, as a group, magazine readers primarily seek knowledge about subjects important to them personally and ideas they can use in daily life.

Sensing this, editors increasingly are stressing editorial content on how to cope with the pressures of family, job and school. *U.S. News & World Report* sums up its function in a slogan to attract readers: "News you can use."

In one study for the Magazine Publishers Association, American consumers give magazines particularly high marks over newspapers, TV and radio in providing the "most knowledge and usable ideas" in these areas:

1. Furnishings and management
2. Farming, gardening, landscaping
3. Hobbies
4. Beauty and grooming
5. Home buying, building, remodeling
6. Self-improvement, clothing/fashions (tie)
7. Health
8. Food
9. Raising, caring for pets
10. Automobiles, raising children (tie)[9]

Let's search the list above for general guidelines for writers. A few jump out.

First, high marks are given magazines for coverage of *personal, lifestyle-oriented issues.* Broad, international issues—what happened yesterday in Afghanistan, what the Yugoslavs are up to today—aren't on that list. Newsmagazines (*Time, Newsweek, U.S. News*) and thought leaders (*Atlantic, Harper's* and so forth) do well with such issues. But in the list above, what's noted is information about buying a new sofa, raising roses and building birdhouses in your basement. The list portrays readers as asking, "How can *I* get by—looking better, feeling better, doing better in *my* personal responsibilities?"

Second, the list suggests readers seek in magazines types of stories other media have difficulty providing as well as magazines can. With their panoramic news and information responsibilities, newspapers *do* cover Afghanistan and the Yugoslavs, along with business, economics, finance, crime, comics, horoscopes—you name it, newspapers cover it. That means furnishings, landscaping or hobbies, mentioned so prominently on the list, cannot be covered regularly in great depth. TV doesn't regularly cover such subjects in depth, either, although cable TV promises some similar editorial focus through specialized channel programming. As a magazine writer you must know what other media can and cannot provide your readers.

Third, the list suggests readers turn to magazines for information *when making important decisions*—on, for example, which furnishings or automobiles to buy, how to remodel a home, how to raise children (and pets), how to eat better and live healthier lives. For the writer, the lesson is obvious: Your reporting and writing must be informative, accurate and helpful to decision makers.

Fourth, the list suggests only tightly focused writing can meet reader demands today. If you were writing about beauty and grooming, for example, you would take one focused writing approach on this subject for, say, *Seventeen*, popular with teenage women, and quite another for *Lear's*, whose covers often carry faces of women in their 40s and 50s and whose slogan is, "The magazine for the woman who wasn't born yesterday." If writing about autos (No. 10 on the list), you would not concentrate on bulky, family-size sedans in an article for *Rolling Stone* and its youthful readers. And, mobile homes and vacation trailers might be a better subject for *Modern Maturity* than low, racy convertibles!

Obviously, the full story of what readers seek from magazines is not told by the list of subjects in which magazines get high marks for providing knowledge and usable ideas. Recall from Chapter One the study showing that, in pages devoted to editorial, magazines pay much attention to culture/humanities, sports, national affairs and so forth. And, flip through magazine pages and you'll often encounter gentle, sweet, off-beat human interest stories that have nothing to do with achieving life goals, striving for success or trying to look more beautiful. Much magazine content clearly is designed to divert, amuse or entertain.

So, let's examine other factors you must consider when structuring your writing.

Reader Perceptions

By far the most crucial indicator of what you should report and how you should write is what readers themselves perceive to be important. In a competitive media market-place, where readers can turn to many sources for news and information, you must respond to what readers say they want.

That is, you indeed must make elaborate efforts to understand your audience's demographics and psychographics before you touch your keyboard.

However, as a trained reporter and writer you have the enormous responsibility of sifting through available information and placing before your readers what they *need*, as well as *want* to know. Afghanistan and the Yugoslavs *are* important, even to Americans whose universe seems restricted to automobiles, building birdhouses or looking beautiful. Your challenge as a writer is to determine why and how such apparently unpalatable subjects are important, then highlight that importance in terms your readers will understand. Avoid "castor oil" writing: here, read this—it's good for you. You are dealing, as you have learned, with readers who are above the American average in education, awareness and involvement. They will understand the importance of distant, seemingly esoteric subjects if you do your writing job well.

Impact

In searching for keys to reader interest, look for the impact a subject will have on people in general and your readers in particular, right now.

Readers seek mostly news and information that has impact on people, not things. Acid rain and what it will do to trees in a decade is a pallid subject, compared to what environmental damage does to your readers' health, their children, the world in which they live—today, right now, right here. See the difference?

Stop at the magazine rack next time you're in a supermarket and note how magazines respond to readers' desire for information on people and things that have impact on their lives. Note the stories on money (how *you* can get it, save it, spend it wisely), politics (how *you* are governed and what *you* can do about it), crime (what it's doing to *you* and your loved ones), education (how *your* children are or aren't being taught). The subject list is endless—but, always, it leads to direct impact on readers.

Proximity

Listen—*truly listen*, as all good writers must—next time you're with friends or family. Note how extremely self-centered the conversation often becomes. People relate even distant events to themselves, where they live, study and work every day. Readers tend to consider almost any subject in terms of their own tight little worlds.

For newspaper and TV news writers, local news offers a perfect vehicle for responding to the proximity factor. Note the huge blocks of space and time newspapers and TV news programs devote to news about local people, things and events.

For you as a magazine writer, proximity has different meaning. Your readers often are geographically widespread, and "local news," as interpreted by a local newspaper, often isn't what they seek from magazines. (You'll recall from Chapter One that even *New York*, ostensibly a magazine about a city, has readers in Missouri and elsewhere.) So, proximity for you requires explaining to magazine readers how, for example, Afghanistan or Yugoslavia actually is near—if the United States gets sucked into their civil wars and if that means American troops (men and women from *your* neighborhood) and tax dollars (*your* tax dollars) will be involved.

For magazine writers, proximity doesn't have a particularly geographic meaning. Rather, it often means *subjects* near to your readers and their daily lives.

Prominence

Unquestionably, readers seek from magazines news and information about prominent people. Believe it: Your readers are more interested in Donald Trump's financial and marital fortunes than in those of Mr. and Mrs. Average, who live on a quiet side street in Smalltown, USA. (See Box 2–1.)

BOX 2–1 Personalities Readers Love to Read About

Free-lance writer Jill L. Sherer checked into how editors select personalities for cover stories they hope will appeal to their target audiences. In an article on cover champions for *Advertising Age*, Sherer determined the five leading personality favorites for leading magazines:

Life, 1960–89: John F. Kennedy (15 covers), Jacqueline Kennedy Onassis (14), Lyndon B. Johnson (10), Elizabeth Taylor (8), Marilyn Monroe (7).

Rolling Stone, 1967–89: John Lennon (16), Mick Jagger (13), Bob Dylan (12), Bruce Springsteen (7), Lyndon B. Johnson (7), Ted Kennedy (6).

Ladies' Home Journal, 1960–89: Princess Diana (18), Jacqueline Kennedy Onassis (14), Elizabeth Taylor (11), Barbara Walters (10), Marlo Thomas (9).

Esquire, 1960–89: John F. Kennedy (10), Elizabeth Taylor (7), Richard Nixon (7), Lyndon B. Johnson (7), Ted Kennedy (6).

Time, 1960–89: Richard Nixon (36), Jimmy Carter (24), Ronald Reagan (19), Gerald Ford (19), Lyndon B. Johnson (15).

McCall's, 1960–89: Jacqueline Kennedy Onassis (9), Mary Tyler Moore (8), Princess Diana (8), Elizabeth Taylor (7), Marie Osmond (6).

People, 1976–89: Princess Diana (35), Elizabeth Taylor (29), John Travolta (16), Jacqueline Kennedy Onassis (15), Farrah Fawcett (15).

TV Guide, 1953–89: Lucille Ball (26), Michael Landon (19), Mary Tyler Moore (17), Johnny Carson (16), Arthur Godfrey (16).

There is a science in picking the right cover personality to attract the right audience. Free-lancer Sherer explored this in interviews with leading editors.

Myrna Blyth, editor of *Ladies' Home Journal*: "Princess Diana is never bad. And even when she's bad, she's not bad. She is a superstar personality of the world."

Elizabeth Sloan, editor of *McCall's*: "(British) royals do well. If you run Shirley MacLaine, you will attract older audiences; if you run Rob Lowe you will attract younger audiences. Very few people, with the exception of Jackie Kennedy, Fergie (another "royal") and Princess Di, can attract the entire spectrum."

Jann Wenner, editor-in-chief of *Rolling Stone*: "A cover subject must be current or journalistically valid at that moment. If Madonna has a new album coming out, she's the best choice for the cover."

Henry J. Muller, managing editor of *Time*: "There is an incredible competitiveness about cover subjects in that there are more and more magazines on the newsstands. Everybody is trying harder to find a way to shout in order to get attention." (Source: Jill L. Sherer, "Celebrities Sell Magazines—Sometimes," *Advertising Age*, 24 May 1989, 82)

However, unless you are careful the intense reader interest in personalities can lead you badly astray, into pursuit of trivial details about the meaningless lifestyles of irrelevant people. Again, check the supermarket magazine racks: So many soon-to-be-forgotten writers waste precious time reporting gossip for little-known magazines that seek to titillate readers by peeking into the private lives of inconsequential personalities.

Readers have legitimate interest in people who have political and economic power and social meaning. Write to meet those interests, but don't waste your time on peek-and-tell journalism.

Timeliness

Americans turn to the media for timely information on topics and personalities of importance. But critical time delays are inherent in the cumbersome process of creating, manufacturing and distributing magazines, so being first with news isn't likely to be your mission in magazine writing. Radio, TV and newspapers have the jump on you in that regard.

As a magazine writer, therefore, you must offset your time disadvantage with reporting and writing techniques other than speed. We'll discuss them later in the book, but your writing job includes interpreting, analyzing and presenting information in a context of background detail and understanding. To see how professionals do this, read the hard news sections at the front of *Time*, *Newsweek* and *U.S. News & World Report*.

However, a sense of timeliness must guide your writing. For example, a story on that Swedish tennis star we discussed earlier in the chapter will be much more meaningful to your readers if written shortly before or after she appears in a major international tournament televised throughout the United States. Reader interest in issues fades quickly, and if you want to write on the meaning Afghanistan has for Main Street, USA, do so quickly after a major battle outside Kabul, the capital. "Peg"—or hang—your story on Yugoslavia on a recent presidential statement issued in a White House news conference that is front-page news in all newspapers and on each TV network's evening news show.

Conflict

Sad to say, conflict—between people, issues, ideologies—is news to all media. Readers, viewers and listeners alike are drawn to conflict.

Again, however, your magazine-writer definition of what's important differs from how writers for other media define it. For example, newspaper writers will "front" tomorrow morning a timely, "spot news" account of a husband-wife quarrel that led to a shooting death. TV writers will air tonight a hard-news, "bang-bang" story, complete with video of flashing red lights on police cars and body bags being carried from the house. *Your* story—next week or next month—might be what psychologists and counselors say is the root of conflict in the American family, and how your readers can handle tension and conflict in *their* families. The actual shooting might be simply your peg for an in-depth, thoughtful analysis that the newspapers and TV news shows didn't have time for as they rushed to be first with the news.

A danger for writers in all media is automatically regarding *all* conflict as news, *all* noise and hubbub as important. Next time you see two politicians hotly debating on TV, raising their voices and pointing their fingers, look closely at their faces. Why do they seem to be enjoying themselves? Because the pretense of conflict so often suckers the media into providing what all politicians love: exposure. Listen carefully to the clamor of voices. Think deeply about the conflict so apparent. Then, decide whether it's truly of compelling interest to your readers.

The Novel and Unusual

Do you ever tire of listening to lectures or reading textbooks (not this one, of course)? Ever think you can't absorb one more important fact or consider another crucial issue?

Well, readers are the same. They, too, want to swing away from serious matters on occasion and seek simple relief in a relaxing read about something that is merely novel or unusual. Writers who can provide the novel and unusual in a light, engaging style are at a premium in magazine work. Even the most serious magazines make room for their writing.

Note, for example, the "formula" approach many editors take to fashioning content: One story at least on an important political, economic or social issue (written, of course, in basic, understandable language); a little sex (cloaked in suitably clinical instructional terms); inspiration ("How I overcame a tortured relationship with my father"); consumerism ("Why your telephone bills are so high"); and a cute story (about, say, sweet little ladies in West Virginia who make violins out of matchboxes).

After our steady drumfire of stories that are timely, important and filled with conflict, your readers seek—and deserve—something mildly diverting. Give it to them.

Incidentally, we can't knock the American editor's success in fashioning desirable content. It withstands nicely the severest test, how valuable readers regard it. (See Box 2–2.)

Well, that's a look at readers past and present who have made the magazine industry so successful. But, what's ahead?

YOU AND READERS OF THE FUTURE

By the year 2000, profound changes will take place in the American reader audience you and your magazine will be striving to capture.

BOX 2–2

Testing Reader Perception of Value

Reader willingness to pay substantial single-copy and subscription prices is a sure test of the perceived value of magazines. Note below that in the period 1960–1989 magazine prices increased at a rate faster than the consumer price index:

Year	Average Single-Copy Price	Index 1960 = 100	Average Yearly Subscription Price	Index 1960 = 100	Consumer Price Index
1960	$ .39	100	$ 4.58	100	100
1965	.46	118	5.32	116	106
1970	.63	162	7.16	156	131
1975	.87	223	10.14	221	182
1980	1.48	379	16.75	366	278
1985	2.10	538	23.15	504	364
1986	2.20	564	23.24	507	370
1987	2.20	564	24.45	534	384
1988	2.29	587	25.29	552	400
1989	2.44	626	25.96	563	419

Base: The single-copy and one-year subscription prices reported to the Audit Bureau of Circulations, in effect December 31 of each year, for 50 leading magazines in advertising revenue for that year.
Source: Magazine Publishers of America.

The U.S. Census Bureau projects an American population that is larger (268 million, or so) and older (36.3 median age, up from 28 in 1970) and considerably different in demographic and psychographic characteristics.[10] Your definition of what makes a magazine story—and how you write it—will need to take into account the changed audience.

Some Things to Expect

You'll be writing, by the year 2000, for an increasingly diverse America.

The Census Bureau projects blacks will number 36 million or 13.3 percent of total population in 2000, up from 29 million and 12.2 percent in 1985. Hispanics will number, conservatively, 25 million and 9.4 percent, up from 17 million and 7.2 percent in 1988. Our Asian population will increase, too.

Among women readers, lifestyle changes indicate dramatically different attitudes toward magazine content. By 2000, an estimated 61 percent of American women will be working outside the home, up from about one-third in 1972. Among well-educated, affluent women, so often the target of magazine writers, an even higher percentage will have out-of-home careers. The traditional family of employed father, stay-home mother and 3.1 children (average for the nuclear family) will be the exception.

If educated, affluent women are your target as a writer in the future, better think of stories about juggling careers and homemaker responsibilities, how to handle job stress and not recipes—what to wear on a business trip, not what you laze around in while drinking mid-morning coffee in the kitchen.

William Dunn, demographics reporter for *USA Today*, finds in Census Bureau projections these additional signals for writers:[11]

- Median family income will rise, boosted by wives who join their husbands in the workplace. (They will have more money for more things—and, thus, more interest in stories about participant sports, hobbies, exotic travel and so forth).
- The divorce rate will stabilize, but 6 in 10 children will spend at least a year in a single-parent home, due to divorce, separation, death or out-of-wedlock birth. (And think of the many how-to-cope story ideas that arise from that stunning statistic!)
- Baby Boomers born between 1946 and 1964, the upwardly mobile generation so sought after by the media, will force America's median age upward (because they work out to stay in good health), will delay retirement beyond the usual age (because they'll need the money) and will join their parents in the suburbs. (Note how all that fits into our earlier characterization of the most fervent readers of magazines being employed professionals/managers who read for career information and who live in a metropolitan area.)
- The workweek in 2000 will average 35.7 hours, down from 38.4 in 1970. (Requiring more articles on leisure-time activities and hobbies?)
- Americans will continue moving, particularly toward the South and West, and clustering along the Atlantic and Pacific coasts. (By now, we hope, you are thinking of a feature on a family moving to Virginia from Minnesota, or one on how to fit your children into a new neighborhood and school, for instance.)

Kris McGrath of MORI Research, a leading analyst of reader habits, looks ahead and sees several trends emerging:[12]

First, McGrath says, America is becoming a nation of specialists who "consume only information they feel is directly relevant to them, which often does not include general news provided by mass media." She finds working women often choose magazines for their relevant information.

Second, the daily newspaper habit is declining, McGrath says, with people speaking of "catching" the news, rather than keeping up with it. This means you will be writing for people who increasingly "don't have the frame of reference they need to understand the news," she says. As a magazine writer you'll need to provide background and context for hurried readers on the move.

Third, readers, particularly of newspapers, are becoming "cherry-pickers" who browse through written material, stopping here and there. This, says McGrath, underlines the importance of graphics—charts, lists of high points, photos—that catch readers' eyes and quickly deliver important information.

What It All Means for Writers

It's often difficult to understand readers and, of course, it's impossible to accurately predict their future needs and desires. It's easy, however, to predict the future role of writers in the magazine industry: They'll be more important than ever.

Looking ahead to the changing complexion of America and rising media competition, magazine strategists constantly stress the need in the future for improved editorial content. The core of that is improved writing.

Joe Hanson, chairperson of the editorial board, *Folio* magazine, says: ". . . the role of the editorial department will be substantially strengthened. It's the rare publisher who doesn't recognize that his primary customer is the reader, and that if he fails to serve the reader, he won't have anything to sell his advertisers."[13]

Jack Rehm, president and chief executive officer of Meredith Corp. (*Better Homes & Gardens*, *Ladies' Home Journal* and others), says: "Editorial vitality is our livelihood. It's what we have to sell."[14]

Such advice that magazine executives keep their eyes on basics is underlined by the industry's commitment to giving readers strong servings of editorial content in each issue. In 1991, a survey showed 190 magazines devoting 54.3 percent of total space to editorial, 45.7 to advertising, compared to a 51.9/48.1 ratio in 1976. Remember, that space is costly. Every inch of space provided for editorial is an inch that cannot be sold to advertisers. By contrast, newspapers are devoting more space to advertising—67 percent on Sundays and 60 percent throughout the week.[15]

The magazine industry is coming up with many techniques to catch readers. They include personalizing each issue (putting each subscriber's name on the cover, for example) with processes called ink-jet printing and selective binding.

Another technique is hard-sell circulation promotion. More people are being contacted more often and asked to subscribe. Not all current promotion is quite as catchy as one that *National Lampoon* did. That humor magazine once carried a cover photo of a cute little puppy with a gun being held to its head. The headline: "If you don't buy this magazine, we'll shoot this dog."[16]

All the sales glitz and promotional push is secondary, however, to the editorial integrity of the magazine—to the accuracy, credibility and skill of your writing.

In Chapter Three we'll begin our detailed discussion of how you can develop writing skills to meet the challenge.

SUMMARY

As a writer, you'll find valuable clues about your readers and their interests in your magazine's standard marketing information kit. In general, magazine readers are better educated and more affluent than average. Your challenge is to write articles at a level likely to attract relatively knowledgeable, well-to-do people.

The relationships between education, higher income or meaningful employment and magazine readership are tight: Of all American adults, 89 percent read magazines in an average month; 95.3 percent of those with college education do so.

Of adults with $50,000 or more annual household income, 94.3 percent read magazines. Of adults with professional/managerial jobs, 94.9 percent read magazines—12.2 issues monthly, on average.

Research indicates that upscale readers seek information and how-to-cope hints in magazine stories.

Of all competing media, newspapers attract audiences most similar to magazine audiences. That means your magazine writing skills can be used in many types of newspaper writing, too. That's not the case in TV, whose audiences tend to be less educated and to seek entertainment, not information.

Research that divides media consumers into Values and Lifestyles (VALS) typologies shows magazine readers tend to be "Actualizers," "Fulfilleds," "Experiencers" and "Achievers." TV and radio are strong among "Strivers," "Believers" and "Strugglers."

Readers generally read magazines at home during leisure hours. However, some magazines, particularly trades, are read in offices by persons seeking job-oriented information.

Adults on average spend 52 minutes reading a magazine, compared with about 26 minutes on newspapers. This underlines the serious, information-seeking attitude of many readers when they pick up magazines.

Most magazine readers seek knowledge about subjects important to them personally, plus ideas they can use in daily life. What they perceive as important is your first clue about what and how to write for them. Readers also want timely information with *impact* on people and events that affect their daily lives. They also like information about prominent people and conflict—between people, issues, ideologies. And, well-written articles of novel or humorous people or events always draw readers.

The U.S. Census Bureau says that by the year 2000 you can expect to write for a larger, older, more diverse population that works fewer hours weekly but, in two-family homes, has higher household income. You'll have to select and write stories accordingly in the future.

Many techniques are being used to increase magazine circulation—selective binding to personalize each issue, more aggressive sales promotion and so forth. Clearly, however, the future success of magazines will depend on improved editorial content—and you and your writing will be central to that.

RECOMMENDED READING

The best way to track editors and writers in the great chase for readers is to read widely in magazines. Pick a representative sample of magazines—particularly in subject areas you might want to cover—and read them each week or month. Note carefully how editors pick a menu of articles and package them in a style likely to attract readers. Watch carefully how professional writers structure their stories to provide what readers want.

The best research on magazine reader attitudes comes from Magazine Publishers of America. But enormously helpful research also comes from the Newspaper Association of America's publication, *presstime*, the American Society of Newspaper Editors' *ASNE Bulletin* and various studies published by The Associated Press Managing Editors Association. This work is done principally from a newspaper viewpoint, of course, but much is directly applicable to magazine writing.

For current coverage of magazines see *Folio* and the media sections of *The New York Times* and *The Wall Street Journal*.

If you're seeking demographic information on audiences in specific markets, *Circulation* is a valuable reference. U.S. Census Bureau material is available in most libraries. And, of course, the media information kits that magazines provide generally profile their reader audiences.

NOTES

1. List Services Corp. advertisement, *Folio,* March 1991, 4.
2. Reach & Frequency Analysis of 1989 Spring MRI, magazines published in a four-week period, quoted in Magazine Publishers of America's *The Magazine Handbook 1992–1993,* 39.
3. *The Magazine Handbook 1990–1991,* quoting SMRB 1989, 40.
4. Magazine Publishers of America, quoting Curtis Circulation Company.
5. *The Magazine Handbook 1992–1993,* 39.
6. Magazine Publishers of America, quoting MRI, Spring 1992.
7. Magazine Publishers of America, quoting "The Level of Magazine Reading," Mediamark Research Inc., March 1980.
8. *Ibid.*
9. "A Study of Media Involvement," conducted in 1986 by Audits & Surveys Inc., for the Magazine Publishers Association.
10. An excellent study of Census Bureau projections within a media context, from which we have drawn, is by William Dunn, demographics reporter, *USA Today,* titled "A Demographic Primer," and published in *Future of Newspapers Report* by the American Society of Newspaper Editors, April 1988, 33.
11. *Ibid.*
12. Kris McGrath, *Future of Newspapers Report,* 93.
13. Joe Hanson, "Looking Back, Looking Ahead," *Folio,* March 1991, 147.
14. Diane Cyr, "Rehm: Editorial Must Come First," *Folio,* March 1991, 30.
15. Magazine content figures from *The Magazine Handbook 1992–1993,* p. 17, quoting Price Waterhouse Annual Financial Survey, conducted for Magazine Publishers of America, 1992. Newspaper figures from *Facts About Newspapers '92,* published by Newspaper Association of America, 11.
16. If you fail to see the humor in this, you may not be alone. *National Lampoon* circulation has fallen dramatically since that cover was published in 1973. As *The New York Times* says, its "sense of humor wore thin." See Michael Lev, "Lampoon Seeks to Repeat Its Best Bottom Lines," *The New York Times,* national edition, Feb. 26, 1990, C-8.

Part Two

The writer's craft

We now focus on the difficult, sometimes painful and always wondrous process of learning to write effectively for magazines.

Our discussions of the complex magazine industry, in Chapter One, and the elusive reader, in Chapter Two, were designed to give you essential background for the primary thrust of our book: extended examination of the writer's craft.

Just as the magazine industry is complex, so, too, is learning to write effectively for it. Indeed, this is where a little pain can enter your writer's life. If you're really serious about writing well you must try so hard sometimes it hurts. And you (like all writers before you) inevitably will suffer the occasional anguish of trying so very hard to get it right, but knowing deep in your heart that you're failing. Worse, even when *you* think you've succeeded, you'll encounter the hurt of watching *editors* slash and whack at what you've created.

That's our warning to you.

Our promise is that learning to write well is a truly wondrous experience. There is magic in reporting and researching a story, then lacing together colorful, vibrant words in a strong language net that captures readers and controls them in a manner of your choosing. That is what effective writing does: It beckons and entices readers, then pulls them into your story and informs, amuses or entertains them according to your plan.

With hard work in this course and constant writing practice outside the classroom you can learn at least the fundamentals of such writing. If you've got talent and are willing to work very hard, you may be able to launch a great writing career. Right here. Now.

We begin in Chapter Three, with "Developing Strong Language Fundamentals." Your writer's plan for capturing readers is only as effective as your ability to weave colorful, precise language into a strong story-telling fabric. We'll discuss how to do that.

Much of your writer's challenge is to come across as credible, and we turn to that in Chapter Four, "Writing with Authority and Credibility." You're dead as a writer if you come across as a shallow, uninformed keyboard artist who can do little other than manipulate words. You must build authority into your writing.

In Chapter Five, "Selecting and Reporting Your Story," you will learn how you can apply your new understanding of the magazine industry to choosing story topics and researching them for individual magazines. It's important to remember throughout that strong reporting skills are the foundation of effective writing.

Once you've researched a story, you must decide which writing structure to use. We discuss this in Chapter Six, "Story Form and Structure I," and in Chapter Seven, "Story Form and Structure II." You have many types of story organization at your disposal, and it's crucial to select and master those that best fit your writing abilities.

In Chapter Eight, "How to Attract and Hold Readers," we discuss writing techniques that will help you capture readers despite competition from lifestyle diversions and the many demands in modern society on readers' time, attention and energy. You must construct for each story a lead or introduction that grabs and holds readers.

In Chapter Nine, "Selling Your Story—and Yourself," we discuss how to carry the process through the essential next step and convince editors you are an accomplished, credible writer. Editors have two things you need—paper and ink—and we'll discuss how you can get some of both.

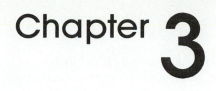

Chapter 3

Developing strong language fundamentals

I t's likely that much of what you already know about writing you learned in a basic newswriting course (remember Who, What, Where, Why, When and How?) and in reading newspapers.

If so, relax. We want you to understand that in magazine writing you've got a little more latitude in how you use language than when hammering out a straight-news lead of the Five W's and How. Your writing pace can be quite different than when shaping an inverted-pyramid news story.

Don't misunderstand us: The information content of the Five W's and How must be in any magazine story. The reporter's *approach* to conveying facts is very much part of magazine writing. Certainly, the need for accuracy, fairness, professional integrity and social responsibility in ethical newswriting can and must be applied to magazine writing.

But, as you learned in Chapter Two, many magazine readers differ from newspaper readers or TV viewers. Those who pick up trade magazines are, like newspaper readers, after information. And, magazine readers, like those who watch TV, often seek diversion and entertainment. Generally, however, readers of consumer magazines seek whatever they're after with a more leisurely or "off-duty" mindset. This permits you—indeed, requires of you—a writing approach often more leisurely and expansive than you would use in straight newswriting.

Let's begin with language fundamentals crucial to such a writing approach.

BUILD ON STRONG SENTENCES

Ever watch master carpenters at work? They painstakingly build their most majestic designs for even towering structures from the ground up on strong underpinnings—foundation blocks and beams carefully placed, one by one, for maximum support.

So, too, must you build strong structures—story organization—for your writing. Your foundation blocks, of course, are sentences.

The strongest sentence structure, as well as the one most easily understood by readers, keeps sentence parts in simple order: *subject* + *verb* + *direct object*. Examples:

> The *painter sketched* the *landscape*.
>   (subject) (verb)   (direct object)
>
> The *writer typed* the *manuscript*.
>   (subject) (verb) (direct object)

Note that it's impossible not to understand the meaning of the two preceding sentences. It's also impossible not to see that a steady drumfire of subject + verb + direct object would drive readers crazy with the monotony. Remember, in magazine writing you generally are addressing audiences with better-than-average educations. So, your challenge is to construct sentences with the strength of subject + verb + direct object but also to write with variety, flow and rhythm that readers find enticing.

For example, you can inject variety into your writing by varying the order of sentence parts:

> The landscape was sketched by the painter.
> The manuscript was typed by the writer.

Still, you've got a very basic (and dull) sentence structure. So, flesh out those sentences with *phrases* (you remember them: two or more related words conveying a thought but lacking subject or verb, or both). They can introduce color into your writing:

> The painter, mumbling under his breath, sketched the landscape.
> The writer, ignoring her ringing telephone, typed the manuscript.

Clauses also give you "elbow room" in your writing. (To refresh your memory, clauses are related words with a subject and verb.) Independent clauses form complete thoughts: The painter wants the commission. Dependent clauses are not complete thoughts: The painter sketches the landscape *because he needs to finish it*.

Remember that whatever order or form you come up with, your sentences must express complete thoughts. Except in special circumstances, which we'll discuss later, don't write in sentence fragments. And you should forget what you might have heard about "writing like you talk." When talking with friends, you talk in bits and pieces. In bursts. Or haltingly. Like this. It doesn't work. On paper.

Conversely, avoid run-on sentences that ramble without apparent direction, pulling together associated and disassociated facts in sprawling masses of verbiage that have no central thrust and, certainly, are terribly confusing to your readers who, of course, have many more things to do each day than sit still, staring at your writing, trying to figure out what in the world you are trying to say. Get our point?

Here's a trick professional writers use: When you've crafted a few paragraphs, sit back and read them aloud. Your ear will signal sentence fragments or run-on sentences. If you hear yourself gasping for breath, start breaking up those run-on sentences. Listen to the rhythm of your writing. Your eye—used to sorting out complex language structures—sometimes will mislead you (particularly when your writer's ego is whispering, "Just fine. Everything's just fine.").

Use Strong Verbs and Active Voice

In sorting through your writer's tool chest, look for parts of speech that enable you to communicate clearly and effectively. You'll find, of course, these:

1. *Nouns* name or denote things, persons, places, ideas, qualities (Rembrandt, Holland, gallery).
2. *Pronouns* take the function and place of nouns (it, they, us).
3. *Verbs* express action and tell what nouns or pronouns are doing (Rembrandt *paints*).
4. *Adjectives* describe nouns and pronouns by limiting, qualifying or modifying them (*moody* Rembrandt, *weak* Holland).
5. *Adverbs* modify verbs, adjectives or other adverbs by manner, time, degree and so forth (paints *quickly*, types *slowly*).
6. *Interjections* are exclamations (darn!), *prepositions* link nouns and pronouns to another element in the sentence (*after* sketching, *in* the typing), and *conjunctions* connect sentences, phrases, clauses and words (the painter *and* typist, paint *or* type).

Picking the right verbs and using them effectively is crucial to elevating your writing from pedestrian to professional level. Let's pause for a refresher on them.

In most magazine writing, *present tense* (the painter sketches the landscape, the writer types) is much more effective than *past tense* (the painter sketched), *future tense* (the painter will sketch), or certainly, *present perfect tense* (the painter has sketched), *past perfect tense* (the painter had sketched) or *future perfect tense* (the painter will have sketched).

Much magazine writing is timeless, compared to, say newswriting for newspapers or TV. Magazines are issued mostly weekly or monthly, of course, and thus cannot deliver the yesterday, today or tomorrow impact of spot news. Although your story consequently will lack immediacy, you can create a you-are-there atmosphere for your reader by shifting verbs into present tense. That is, don't write you *were* in the studio as the painter *sketched*. Rather, write you *are* there, watching the painter *sketch*—and transport your readers right along with you.

Here's how Betty Goodwin, writing for *Entertainment Weekly*, transports us to an interview with singer Tony Bennett:

> Little-known fact: Tony Bennett likes to dine alone.
> He's the man over in the corner, back to the wall, eating in an Italian restaurant at the Hilton hotel in Anaheim, California . . . (here, writer Goodwin describes what Bennett is wearing).
> The maitre d' sends over the best the house has to offer (a detailed description of Bennett's meal follows).
> This is how I first meet Tony Bennett, crooner of enduring love songs, eternal smoothy, and champion romantic vocalist. . . . (*Betty Goodwin, "The Zen of Tony Bennett,"* Entertainment Weekly, *26 July 1991, 22*)

Using verbs in the active voice generally is most effective. This makes the subject of the sentence the doer of action (the painter sketches the landscape). In *passive voice*, the subject is receiver of action (the landscape is sketched by the painter).

Link active voice to strong, colorful verbs and you effectively communicate a *word picture*. We have added emphasis to the following examples:

> Mayor Gavrill K. Popov, a short, round-edged, sadly smiling figure, *is shambling* around on the edge of his city as the grayness overtakes the night. . . .
> The Mayor *hefts* his briefcase and heads out into a light, mercifully clean snow. . . . (*Francis X. Clines, "Moscow 1991,"* The New York Times Magazine, *19 May 1991, 37*)
> Two high-heeled, young women engulfed by the building's massive lobby, *hoof it* toward the string of revolving doors at the main entrance. A courier makes a solitary

sprint to the administrative offices. . . . (*Marie Powers, "No Room at the Inn,"* Business Atlanta, *Nov. 1990, 40*)

As the first seaborne assault wave approaches, the first wave of airborne Marines is *clattering* overhead. . . . (*Tom Post with John Barry and Douglas Waller, "To the Shores of Kuwait,"* Newsweek, *11 Feb. 1991, 28*)

You'll recognize immediately in these examples something that's alive and, well, more active about a sentence with an active-voice verb in present tense. You'll recognize just as quickly, of course, that you shouldn't make a rule of using only active-voice verbs. Note passive voice sometimes can be more effective:

Active	*Passive*
The painter destroyed the $1 million landscape.	The $1 million landscape was destroyed by the painter.

Using passive voice here emphasizes the $1 million value of the landscape, a fact likely to catch reader imagination. This illustrates that, with few exceptions, your basic rule in writing should be simple: *Avoid restrictive "rules" and use language forms that communicate effectively and avoid those that don't.*

Many editors today (unlike some your predecessors wrestled with) generally establish one guideline: Write clearly and with impact to best accomplish your goal, whether that be to inform, entertain, divert or amuse.

However, every editor has *some* rules for what constitutes effective writing. Whether you're a staff writer or free-lancer, learn those rules. Sometimes they're formalized in style books or desk manuals. At many magazines, however, they're unwritten, and your best way to learn them is to read carefully which language forms are published and which aren't.

We can tell you right now, though, when your friendly editor likely will turn mean: It's when you misuse *adjectives, adverbs* and *interjections* and, often, *prepositions.*

Language Traps to Avoid

Editors are called gatekeepers because they decide what goes and doesn't go into publications. You must get by the gatekeepers before you even start to chase readers. Following are some language misuses that can get the gate slammed in your face.

Misuse of Adjectives

Of all parts of speech, adjectives are most misused by beginning writers. Adjectives limit, qualify or modify nouns and pronouns, of course, and thus describe them (*beefy* painter, for example, or *thin* typist). Misuse generally takes two broad forms.

First, writers indiscriminately throw too many adjectives into a sentence: The beefy, white-haired, red-nosed, scowling, bandy-legged painter sketched the landscape. (Don't laugh; we've seen lots of sentences just as ridiculous.)

Second, lazy writers substitute adjectives, which *tell* readers something, for imaginative, colorful language that *shows* them and lets them imagine. Note the difference:

No: The beefy painter sketches the landscape.
Yes: The painter, wheezing as he shifts his 290-pound body, sketches the landscape.

Consider the impact of these sentences, which use adjectives sparingly.

Light from a street lamp penetrates the gloomy studio, striking his *white hair.* He coughs three times, *scowls* and then shakes his head.

"Too many cigarettes," he says. "Too much booze, too," he adds, touching a forefinger to his *red, heavily veined nose.*

Good writing is a mosaic of nuances, hints, clues, bits and pieces trailed alluringly before readers. It beckons, cajoles, entices and before they know it, readers are tumbling helter-skelter after you, joyously discovering your hidden delights and drawing their own imaginative pictures. Don't stick your thumb in their eyes with that beefy, white-haired, red-nosed, scowling, bandy-legged painter. He's beyond belief. Let your readers discover for themselves.

Another example: If you ever interview Sylvester Stallone, don't write, "The nervous, high-strung Stallone exudes energy." Do as a professional does:

> Now he's pacing around the desk while he talks on a speakerphone. He doesn't sit down if he can avoid it. Confined to a chair, he doodles, worries a paper clip in his fingers, taps his palms on tabletops. (*Elizabeth Kaye, "Sly's Progress,"* Esquire, *Feb. 1989, 95*)

Here's an example from a leading magazine of how you can go wrong with adjectives (we'll omit the writer's name to protect the guilty):

> His pear-shaped body, round, cherubic face, and deep drawl call Arthur Godfrey to mind.

Note here how ineffective it is to stack so many adjectives in a sentence and to use such awful cliches (pear-shaped, cherubic). Incidentally, note the references to Arthur Godfrey. You remember him, don't you? No? Well, neither will many of your readers. He was a radio entertainer well known in the 1940s and 1950s. Reach that far back to draw comparisons for your readers and you'll mystify many of them.

Lesson on adjectives: If you must use them, choose the damned things carefully. (There, you see? We've both been editors, and just *writing* about misuse of adjectives makes us angry.)

Misuse of Adverbs

This, too, can get you in trouble with editors and, most important, can shortchange readers. Adverbs, of course, modify verbs, adjectives or other adverbs by time, degree, manner and so forth. (The painter sketches *slowly.* The writer types *furiously.*).

Again, lazy (and, thus, ineffective) writers are most likely to misuse this part of speech. Note the difference:

No: The runner sped quickly around the track.
Yes: The runner lapped every competitor, twice passing three "tail-end Charlies."

Or, see the difference here:

No: The senator screamed angrily.
Yes: The senator's screaming could be heard in a corridor off the Senate floor, and reporters lounging there scurried into the press gallery to see what was happening.

Selected properly and placed carefully, adverbs strengthen your writing. Don't take a shortcut by misusing them. Only amateurs do that.

Another misuse is with *subordinating conjunctions*, those dependent clauses that link a sentence or previous clause. For example:

No: The painter was sketching the landscape *when* he feared it might be worthless.
Yes: The painter was sketching the landscape *though* he feared it might be worthless.

Make sure adverbs in your writing say precisely what you want to say.

Misuse of Interjections

These are exclamations (darn! whew!), and if you really want to sound like amateur night, sprinkle them throughout your writing. Note:

No: The car skidded into the ditch and narrowly missed the tree. Whew! Close call!
Yes: The car skidded into the ditch. Measurement showed it missed a 40-foot oak by 16 inches.

It's much more effective, obviously, to give readers specific details in the illustration above and let them discover precisely how narrowly the car missed the tree. Let them say it to themselves: "Whew! Close call!"

Sometimes, of course, interjections belong in your writing, particularly in quotes that catch for your readers the personality of individuals and how they express themselves. An example is a personality profile quoting Raghib (Rocket) Ismail, a football player who opened his pro career with a 73-yard run on the 110-yard field used in Canadian football:

"That's a long field, man. I was out there thinking like, 'Whew.' But even then. . . ." (*William F. Reed. "3, 2, 1 . . . Blast Off!"* Sports Illustrated, *21 July 1991, 22*)

Cleansed of the interjection, this quote would not communicate as well to the readers how The Rocket talks and thinks. Interjections even work sometimes (though less frequently) outside quotes. An example from a *Life* article on food riots in Russia:

One lady got so desperate for a bottle of milk that she bit the arm of the woman selling it. Well, she got her bottle of milk, all right. It came—wham!—right on top of her head. . . . (*Jeanne Marie Laskas, "Yeltsin's Backyard," Life, June 1991, 36*)

Misuse of Prepositions

Grammarians once considered this a felony offense; today, it's a misdemeanor. Either way, misuse of prepositions can cost you heavily with some editors.

Prepositions relate a noun or pronoun to another word to show the relationship between two words: The landscape *in* the art show was the best work *of* the painter. In, at, to, up are *simple prepositions*; *compound prepositions* are more than one word: because of, in front of, along with.

Some editors won't let you end sentences with prepositions (It was a heavy burden to put up with. He turned the screw in.). Most of the time you can sidestep the argument by rewriting to avoid ending sentences with prepositions. But sometimes that can read just awful (It was a heavy burden up with which to put.). So, the "rule" against ending sentences with prepositions is another that many editors don't argue over.

By now, it should be apparent to you that we—like many editors—feel a basic rule of good magazine writing is simply that you must *give readers reason to read*. Let's look at a few ways to do that.

INDUCE READERS TO READ

Why does some writing soar above the clamor of daily life, demanding and getting reader attention? Why does some, however, only murmur ineffectually, then vanish virtually unnoticed? Those are highly complex questions that defy simplistic answers. But we can draw a few basic guidelines for beginning writers who want to soar, not vanish.

Keep It Simple

One of the worst temptations for beginning writers is to try to write beyond their capabilities. Try it and, like beginning acrobats who try too hard, you can fall flat on your face.

With experience, writers can use complex writing forms like handy tools. But even highly experienced writers often opt for simple, straightforward structures. They have to because many readers today simply won't devote time to figuring out writing puzzles.

Here's how one of the finest writers of our time takes you easily, directly and simply forward in his story:

> They came in the night, of course, full of God and certainty, moving through a heavy Gulf fog. Two men and two women. It was Christmas Eve. The streets of Pensacola were empty. They slipped through the covering fog into the parking lot of a two-story house on North Ninth Avenue. Then, in the name of life, they planted a bomb. And hurried on to other targets. At 3:23 a.m., the first bomb exploded, damaging an abortion clinic called the Ladies Center. The second bomb went off at 3:38, the third at 3:45, wrecking the offices of doctors who also performed abortions.
> That was 1984.
> More than four years later, on a hot, hazy Saturday evening, I sat parked in an air-conditioned car on North Ninth Avenue, staring at the two-story building that houses the Ladies Center, trying to imagine the night thoughts of people who would use violence in the name of life. . . . (*Pete Hamill, "America's Holy War,"* Esquire, Nov. 1989, 61)

Now, read (only once) the following, then quickly jot down what it's all about.

> On a rainy Thursday night in late February, at the Cathedral of St. John the Divine in northern Manhattan, a choir of celebrities staged the political analogue of an Academy Awards ceremony in honor of the president of Czechoslovakia, Vaclav Haval, and on the way uptown in the subway I wondered if I could expect to see Ivana Trump and the Solid Gold dancers. The invitation listed the names of some of the illuminati scheduled to appear on the program (among them Warren Beatty, Henry Kissinger, Meryl Streep and Sting), and the sum of their collective Q ratings foretold an evening decorated in pious tinsel. . . .

Note in both examples above the writers use the same approach: They draw a mood picture (fog, rain) and invite you along with them. But which is more understandable? Were you able to understand the second example in one reading? The short, punchy sentences of the first example are much more easily comprehended than are the long, convoluted sentences of the second.

Note how the example below almost defies understanding in one reading because the writer packs so many thoughts into two sentences:

> Viacom Enterprises, which has scored big with off-network sitcoms, and which has had some recent success with first-run weekly shows, is testing three new shows this summer that the company hopes will put it on the map in the first-run entertainment strip business. The last time the company had a big hit in that category was with the Richard Dawson-hosted version of Family Feud.

However, note below how a writer focuses on a single characteristic to lead you simply, yet effectively, into a personality profile:

> Beware of what you say to Coca-Cola's Robert Goizueta, one of Atlanta's Most Respected CEOs. The man does not forget. A crisp memory and attention to detail enable him to look at the fine points that often become blurred or lost in the rush of corporate life. "I handed him a proxy statement once and his first comment was it was printed on lighter paper than in the previous year," recalls Ugo Ippolito, a former Coca-Cola executive who now is an attorney with Glass, McCullough, Sherrill & Harrold. "I called the printer to verify and he was right."

Of course, noticing what a piece of paper weighs does not a great CEO make, but Goizueta is as meticulous about small matters as he is the big picture.... (*Faye McDonald Smith, "Vision," Business Atlanta, Nov. 1990, 31*)

With experience, you'll be able to fashion long, meandering sentences and yet always maintain control, gently leading readers through a succession of thoughts all woven nicely into a single and easily understood, if complex, fabric. Until then, keep it simple.

Handle the Time Element Carefully

Reread the example of Pete Hamill's writing on abortion clinic bombings. Note how less effective he would be if he opened this way: "It was 1984, and they came in the night...."

When Hamill's story was published, the 1984 time element was *five years old*. Who wants to read a story pegged to a five-year-old incident? Hamill figures not many, so he tucks his time element deep in his story, where readers will encounter it only after being hooked by the imagery of that smooth and simple first paragraph.

Of course, *precisely* when the bombings occurred is irrelevant in Hamill's story, as is the time peg in much magazine writing. And, that's a good thing because of the often lengthy delay between the time a story leaves your keyboard and when it arrives, weeks or months later, in a reader's hands.

Newspaper writers in the spot news business must include the "when" time element of the Five W's early in their stories. Indeed, writers for afternoon newspapers labor to find "this morning" or "today" time elements for news stories that give readers fresh details they didn't get from morning newspapers or TV. Tony Silber, writing for *Folio*, simply ignores the time element in this story:

Lang Communications' chairman, Dale Lang, says that after more than a year of trying, he is close to a deal to buy back Time Inc. Magazine Co.'s share of the soured *Working Woman* and *Working Mother* partnership venture. There are indications, however, that he may not be as close as he claims.

"I think 30 to 45 days at the latest it will be accomplished," Lang says. "We'd struck a price with Time, at the time we sold *McCall's*, what the buyout price would be. I've been in the process of pulling those funds together." (*McCall's* was sold in 1988 to The New York Times Magazine Company.) Lang says Time Inc. ... (*Tony Silber, "Is the 'Time' Near for Lang's Buyout?" Folio, July 1991, 15*)

We have two thoughts on time elements.

First you can ignore the time element and cast your story in present tense. Note how Silber does that with "says" and "claims." Readers don't need to know precisely when he interviewed Lang. However, magazines, particularly weekly trades, need to stay close to timely events. Often they include time elements, but subordinate rather than ignore them. Note the handling by *Electronics Media*, published on Mondays:

LOS ANGELES—Bill Cosby and The Carsey-Werner Co. plan to bring the comedian out in a new syndicated version of the TV classic "You Bet Your Life" in the fall of 1992.

The announcement Thursday of the move.... (*William Mahoney and Thomas Tyrer, "Cosby to Host First-Run Strip of TV Classic," Electronic Media, 24 June 1991, 1*)

Because it's published on Mondays, *Electronic Media* cannot reach many readers before Tuesdays at the earliest. Note how ineffective it would be to lead a story, for reading on Tuesday, this way:

LOS ANGELES—It was announced last Thursday that Bill Cosby ...

Of course, whether you omit the time element or subordinate it deep in your story, there's always the danger your story will be outdated before it reaches readers.

Writing for *Folio*, Tony Silber must have wondered whether Lang's deal with Time Inc., would go through while *Folio* was still on the presses or being mailed to subscribers. In handling the time element you must fashion a writing approach that will "stand"—be journalistically valid—weeks or months ahead. It's tricky, and every writer occasionally gets caught by developments that outdate a story before it reaches readers. But don't get caught that way too often, or the gatekeepers will slam the gate on you.

And this brings us to our second thought on handling time elements: Try to give your story a "look-ahead" dimension. Note in the *Folio* example above that Tony Silber's interview with Lang obviously took place days or weeks before publication. But Silber doesn't linger on that "old" development. He pitches his story ahead, to expected developments, in his lead: "There are indications, however, that he may not be as close as he claims."

Here are two examples of how *U.S. News & World Report*, a weekly newsmagazine, pitches stories ahead:

For days, newspapers and TV report the Bush administration had planned (past perfect tense) punitive air strikes against Iraq. *U.S. News*, therefore, doesn't look back. Rather, it looks ahead:

> Another Desert Storm? The United States *is actively preparing* to mount air attacks against Iraqi nuclear installations *as early as this week* if Saddam Hussein does not immediately comply with the United Nations mandate to dismantle the facilities.... (emphasis added) (*Charles Fenyvesi, editor, "Washington Whispers," U.S. News & World Report, 29 July 1991, 16*)

After weeks of speculation about the political future of John Sununu, a top aide to President Bush, *U.S. News* weighs in with a look-ahead dimension:

> The fate of John Sununu *remains* a question. Senior Republicans *now favor* leaving Sununu at the White House as chief of staff because they *think* he has learned from past mistakes and *is no longer* as domineering. But they *continue to insist....* (emphasis added) (*Kenneth T. Walsh and David Gergen, "Tomorrow," U.S. News & World Report, 29 July 1991, 27*)

Be Concrete, Not Abstract

One of the complex issues you must consider thoughtfully is the important question of whether abstractions can create a state of mind among your readers that perhaps is one you would not wish to create.

Now, read again that preceding paragraph. It's nothing but fluff—gaseous words that say nothing. What "issues"? What "question"? What "state of mind"? Those are abstract nouns that name attributes, qualities or ideas. They are vague and if misused, they will destroy your writing.

Note how even a leading trade magazine gets trapped:

> Although the Persian Gulf war has been over for four months, journalists continue to grapple with problems caused by military restrictions during the 40-day conflict. (*"Journalists Call for Meeting with Cheney," Broadcasting, 1 July 1991, 26*)

The "problems" and "restrictions" mentioned earlier should have been described in concrete terms:

> Although the Persian Gulf war has been over for four months, journalists are attacking military limits on movements by reporters that they say were a form of censorship.

Incidentally, note in the *Broadcasting* example the phrase "*continue* to grapple...." *Nothing* kills a story quicker than telling readers, "Folks, we've got more of the same news here for you: Things are *continuing....*"

Here's another example of language that says nothing:

Preston Padden, senior vice president, affiliates, Fox Broadcasting Co., pulled no punches during his keynote speech to the Broadcast Promotion & Marketing Executives Association last week in Baltimore. (*"Fox's Padden Broadsides Competition at BPME,"* Broadcasting, *24 June 1991, 59*)

As the *Broadcasting* story itself subsequently revealed, there were plenty of concrete news pegs in Padden's speech: He criticized network TV's programming as "copycat" and said CBS, NBC and ABC are "saddled with bloated infrastructures from a bygone era. . . ." Now, there is something concrete, not abstract, to catch readers' attention.

Remember from Chapter Two the research showing how many readers turn to magazines for *information*? Your job as a writer is to give it to them. Stuart Newman opted for concrete details, not abstraction, to pass on operative information in a *New York* article about day trips New Yorkers can make into the nearby countryside:

Niles Davies likes to say that his orchard, Dr. Davies Farm (914-268-7020), in Congers, is "45 minutes from Broadway." Considering the likelihood of a traffic snarl or two, that estimate is perhaps a bit optimistic. To get there, take Palisades Parkway north to Route 303 (Exit 5N), then Route 9W to Route 304.

You're flagged into a parking spot near the farm stand, which sells Dr. Davies's homegrown squash, tomatoes, and corn and homemade cider. From there, you're guided to the picking area.

There are some 4,000 pick-your-own trees on Dr. Davies's 40 acres. The atmosphere is idyllic. To your right as you enter, you'll see a reservoir lined with weeping willows: Canada geese float gingerly across the still water. Turn around and take in the Tilcon Quarry, whose vertical ridges make the rock face look like a staircase turned on end. . . . (*Stuart Newman, "The Hunt for Red September,"* New York, *17 Sept. 1990, 60*)

When writing to inform, rather than amuse or entertain, don't try too hard for a cutesy, subtle writing style. Just list the facts, as this writer did in presenting lifestyle hints for heart attack survivors:

- Vegetarian diet . . .
- Moderate exercise . . .
- No smoking . . .
- Stress-management techniques . . . (*John Poppy, "Inner Peace for Regular Guys,"* Esquire, *June 1990, 79*)

Lists can pack maximum information in minimum space.

Attribute to Authoritative Sources

What's your first question after you read this sentence: The authors say magazine readers are demographically upscale, well-educated information seekers.

Isn't your question, "How do the authors know?"

Well, we made statements like that in Chapter Two—and gave you elaborate attribution, including many endnotes, to indicate our sources. Similarly, it's your job in magazine writing to attribute tightly and to *authoritative sources*. You have an ethical responsibility to seek accurate, reliable information from sources in a position to know and to tell your readers where you got it.

Note our stress on *authoritative*. A White House guard isn't an authoritative source to quote on how the president regards the chairperson of the Federal Reserve Board. The president is the most authoritative source for that. And if he won't talk—as George Bush wouldn't during a controversy over Federal policies in 1991—you should seek, as *U.S. News* did, other sources: "senior White House officials," "Robert Brusca, chief economist at Nikko Securities," "Chris Varvares, an economist with Laurence H. Meyer & Associates in St. Louis," and so forth.[1]

The best attribution is "he said," "she said"—complete, as above, with name, title, organization. Readers then can judge for themselves the authoritativeness of your writing. Anonymous "senior White House officials" is a fallback to use only when sources won't go on record. Beware anonymous sources. They're often floating trial balloons—using you to launch unattributed statements, then sitting back to see what public reaction develops. Many important stories won't get into print, however, unless you (with agreement from your editor) grant anonymity. But when you do, try to signal your readers on how believable your sources are. "Officials" isn't as believable as "White House officials" and neither is as strong as "*senior* White House officials."

Incidentally, not even the best reporters know what people think, feel, sense or expect. We know only what they *say*. Note these examples of how you can go wrong by trying to get inside a source's head:

> As a 23-year-old reporter for *The Washington (D.C.) Post,* Leonard Downie Jr. *never expected* to be in management, let alone as executive editor (emphasis added).

> When the phone rang at 6 a.m., the day after Christmas, 21 years ago, Frank Nanney Jr. *sensed trouble* (emphasis added).[2]

Now, note how easy it is to fix these two preceding examples by inserting attribution so subtly that readers won't stumble over it:

> Leonard Downie Jr. *says* that as a 23-year-old reporter for *The Washington (D.C.) Post* he never expected to be in management, let alone as executive editor.

> The phone rang at 6 a.m., the day after Christmas, 21 years ago, and Frank Nanney Jr. *recalls* sensing trouble.

Following is an example of how not to insert attribution. This is from a *New York Times Magazine* story on photographer Sebastiao Salgado:

> Salgado, says Arthur C. Danto, a professor of philosophy at Columbia University and the art critic for *The Nation*, has an advantage over Hine, in that Hine's photographs, now more than 50 years old, are valued more for their historical interest.[3]

There is no doubt about who is the source quoted above or his credentials. But the cumbersome insertion of attribution disrupts narrative flow and forces you to read the paragraph a couple of times to extract its meaning. Busy readers won't labor through such dense writing. Isn't the following better?

> Salgado has an advantage over Hine because Hine's photographs are more than 50 years old and valued more for their historical interest, according to Arthur C. Danto, Columbia University professor of philosophy and art critic for *The Nation*.

Use Plenty of Colorful Quotes

When it comes to inducing readers to read, you can't go wrong by weaving strong, colorful quotes into your writing. People like to read what other people say—in their own words, at their own tempo, with their unique conversational rhythms and patterns.

Beware: Beginning writers are tempted (as we were tempted, many deadlines ago) to rewrite everything in their own words. There is a feeling (which we felt) that a story isn't really yours unless you filter everything in it through your vocabulary and restructure it in your thought patterns. But note below how highly successful professional writers recognize strong quotes and give way to them, "backing out" of the story and letting the words of others tell the tale.

U.S. News writers were describing former President Bush flying by helicopter over Maryland and telling his passenger, former Soviet Union President Mikhail Gorbachev, how real estate agents help Americans find and buy houses:

Gorbachev jerked his head upward and waved his arms in amazement. "In my country," he declared, "such an agent would be shot." (*Kenneth T. Walsh, Carla Anne Robbins, Robin Knight and Louise Lief, "The True Believer,"* U.S. News & World Report, *1 July 1991, 24*)

Business Week personality profile writers knew when to get out of the way and let quotes describe Lawrence A. Bossidy, who moved from General Electric Co. to become chief executive of Allied-Signal Inc.:

Still, Bossidy's intense style can be tough. "There's nothing subtle about the guy," says a former Kidder (Peabody & Co.) investment director. "You either deliver the goods or you're out." Under him, the pressure at GE is like "having to kill a lion every day," adds Nelson Gurman, general manager of GE's lighting operations in South America. (*Joseph Weber and Lisa Driscoll, "'Jack Welch's Jackhammer' Nails a Corner Office,"* Business Week, *15 July 1991, 28*)

It would be criminal to omit or rewrite such colorful, telling quotes as in the two preceding examples.

Full quotes are particularly useful in backing up your characterization of an individual's attitudes. Note this tight tie between a writer's characterization and the backup quote in an *Organic Gardening* story about a physician-researcher:

Levin is plainly contemptuous of lab-bound researchers. "I used to be an academic," he says. "Now I'm a hands-on doctor. I no longer pay the rent by publishing papers. What academics do has nothing to do with reality. People who publish papers in medical journals don't see patients, and people who see patients don't publish papers in medical journals." (*William Legro, "Under Siege,"* Organic Gardening, *April 1988, 66*)

Often, quotes ramble on, and using them in full will bore your readers stiff. If so, select the few words that capture precise meaning and use a *partial* quote:

Robert Pepper, FCC Office of Plans and Policy chief, said the only problem with his staff "is they're so good, they keep getting job offers." That staff, Florence Setzer and Jonathan Levy in particular, was responsible for.... (*"The People Behind the Pepper Paper,"* Broadcasting, *8 July 1991, 24*)

Sometimes, quotes create a word picture that readers can "see." If so, *use 'em!* Note how a *New York* writer lets Jane Pauley's own words open a personality profile on herself:

"I call myself Tom's sub-anchor," says Jane Pauley. "Nobody's asked me to stop saying that yet, although I realize it's not very elegant." Pauley, dressed in anchorwoman red, is scribbling some last-minute notes on her news copy. Right behind her in NBC's Washington bureau sits Steve Friedman, her old boss at Today and the new executive producer of the Nightly News. It's his first night on the job. But it's not Jane's. She sat in for Tom Brokaw just the week before, when he took off for the Memorial Day weekend.

"How do you pronounce forte?" she asks a newsroom editor. "'Fort' or 'fortay'?" "[NBC News president] Michael Gartner would say 'fort,'" says Peggy Hubble, director of publicity for NBC News. "'Fort' is the first choice," says a producer, consulting a dictionary. Pauley adjusts her copy, making several other changes. Then she leans forward and stares into the lights, the camera, and three monitors. She watches carefully as Brokaw, in San Francisco, finishes the lead story, about Gorbachev's U.S. visit. "And Jane Pauley will have more news from Washington in a moment".... (*Phoebe Hoban, "The Loved One,"* New York, *23 July, 1990, 23*)

Now, a warning about quote leads: Only seldom does exactly the right quote present itself in precisely the right way as you are writing a lead. People normally don't talk in well-rounded sentences that sum up a situation and thus qualify to lead your story. But, there's a temptation, particularly when you stare at your keyboard, completely out of ideas, to grab a quote and lead with it—regardless of whether it's suitable. Don't take the lazy writer's way out. If the quote works, use it. But don't use inappropriate quotes as a crutch.

We have two additional points on using quotes.

First, never pass up a quote that graphically sets up the reader's understanding of the thrust of your story. You're not in the business of shocking people simply for the sake of shocking them, but note how this *Mademoiselle* writer lets quotes tell a terrible story that emerged after a jogger was raped and beaten in New York's Central Park:

> . . . a shaken city learned that the boys who attacked her laughed and joked after they were arrested, and when the police asked why they whipped the jogger with a metal pipe, one of them answered, "because it was fun." Only one of the teens expressed any misgivings; he admitted that "it got to me when her blood started to spurt" . . . (*Jill Neimark, "The Legacy of the Central Park Rape,"* Mademoiselle, *Sept. 1989, 226*)

Second, using direct quotes sometimes can embarrass people unnecessarily. So, if the President of the United States and Leader of the Free Western World suffers a slip of the tongue and utters a clanger—"Him and me are going to Moscow"—take the quotes off and paraphrase: The president said he and the Secretary of State are going to Moscow. (Of course, if the president repeatedly butchers the language, *that* may be a stand-alone story.)

Never change a quote, for any reason, and leave the quote marks on it. If it's in quotes you signal your readers that's *precisely* what was said.

Often, particularly in writing profiles or color stories, you achieve great impact if you reproduce full quotes, clangers and all. Note in the next example how a *Modern Maturity* writer creates a special word-picture by using a quote filled with clangers:

> "This deer don't look too healthy," comments Ken Jafek as he examines the remains of a mule deer. "But it means Bill's right close." Bill is a mountain lion who stalks the snowy slopes of the Albion Mountains in southeastern Idaho. And Jafek and his two Walker hounds, Bones and Tex, are hot on the elusive cat's tail. (*Charles Creekmore, "Highlights,"* Modern Maturity, *Aug.–Sept. 1991, 12*)

How about cleaning up the preceding quote: "I say," Ken Jafek comments, "but this deer doesn't look too terribly healthy."

Nah. That's awful. Let your readers "hear" a mountain man talk like a mountain man!

Translate for Your Readers

As a magazine writer you go places, see things and talk to people—and report on all that for your readers who aren't lucky enough to go, see and talk for themselves. You, in fact, translate for them what you encounter.

Broadly, your translator duties take two forms: First, you translate the meaning of an event, an idea or a personality with a story structure your readers can understand. Second, you ensure that every technical word, term or principle you use is restated for your lay readers.

First, let's look at how some real pros translate the meaning of a complex development that many American readers have trouble comprehending: unemployment in Europe. The following story *could* open with mind-boggling statistics. Rather, the writers translate it into human terms any reader can understand:

> These days, Bill Goodliffe, a British truck driver, lives anything but the good life. Seven months ago, the 29-year-old was laid off. Unmarried, he manages to make ends meet by combining his weekly $75 unemployment benefits with a little help from his folks. Every day, Goodliffe checks the bulletin boards at a local employment center for new jobs. But so far, no luck. "Quite frankly, being unemployed stinks," he says.
> European companies are suddenly cutting workers at a furious pace. Goodliffe counts among the 900,000 Europeans who have lost their jobs in the past year, most of them in the past five months. . . . (*Blanca Riemer, Richard A. Melcher, Patrick Oster and*

> *bureau reports, "'Quite Frankly, Being Unemployed Stinks,'"* Business Week, *15 July 1991, 44*)

Two *Advertising Age* writers sort through the complicated inner workings of a leading ad agency and translate the bottom-line meaning for their readers in just a few words:

> Saatchi & Saatchi Co. Chief Executive Robert Louis-Dreyfus is taking a stronger hand in the management of troubled Backer Spielvogel Bates Worldwide.
>
> In exclusive interviews with *Advertising Age,* Mr. Louis-Dreyfus said part of his job is to ensure that "the right people are in the right place," and that it was clear he had to step in when Backer began hemorrhaging during the past year.
>
> Mr. Louis-Dreyfus' increased role in the day-to-day affairs of Backer is significant because, until now, those duties had been the closely guarded and exclusive province of agency CEO Carl Spielvogel. . . . (*Jon Lafayette and Laurel Wentz, "Louis-Dreyfus Making His Moves at Backer,"* Advertising Age, *24 June 1991, 1*)

Three points about the example above:

1. Note the short lead, just 21 words, keeps it simple and thus effectively translates for readers the single most-important development.

2. In the second paragraph, the writers use a partial quote to expand on the central thought of the first paragraph. That continues the translating process. (Note, also, how the writers take credit for an exclusive interview. A little such chest-puffing is okay in our business.)

3. The writers expand their translation considerably by explaining, in the third paragraph, the significance of the lead's "stronger hand" angle. Don't be reluctant to stop the action in your writing and explain, flat out, in straightforward language, the central point of your story.

Translating for readers always must include restating, in terms they understand, unusual or technical language. Often, you can slip your translation into your story with barely a ripple. Note:

> He has the reputation of a "rainmaker," *a lawyer who attracts new clients* (emphasis added). (*Bill Shipp, "No-Name Guru,"* Atlanta Magazine, *April 1991, 27*)

Writing in *Elle* (February 1991, 80), Pamela Bloom refers to "Thor, *god of thunder* . . ." In the same magazine (p. 88), in a feature on fountain pens, Heidi Ellison refers to "Ebonite, *a hard rubber.* . . ." Just a few words can fill in the blanks for readers without disrupting narrative flow.

Quick! Do you know what "encomium" means? Well, even if you do, many of your readers don't. So, a *Lear's* writer could do a better job of translating if he used, "the ultimate high praise . . ." instead of, as he did, "the ultimate encomium . . ."[4] Don't play word games with your readers. If they want puzzles, they'll move on to the crossword page.

Comparisons are enormously helpful in translating. Note how this writer helps her women readers understand a piece of apparel:

> The apron Ada Patton puts on in the morning is different from the aprons worn by chefs and homemakers; hers is made of leather, and it's meant to protect her from the hooves of the 1,000-pound horses she shoes every day at Santa Anita Race Track and at Hollywood Park in California. Patton has been doing this job for a little over 12 years and is still the only female blacksmith ever to shoe thoroughbreds at a major American track. (*Jane Schwartz, "Thoroughbreds: Women in Horse Racing,"* Lear's *Feb. 1991, 32*)

Below, a writer compares Cable News Network's ratings after the Persian Gulf war with those it achieved *during* the conflict and thereby translates clearly CNN's success in attracting viewers:

Twenty-four-hour ratings before the war were averaging about a .7 rating/2.2 share in CNN's universe of 57 million homes, for a reach of 404,000 households. During the 42-day war, CNN's 24-hour rating averaged a 4.3/12.3, and reached 2,458,000 cable homes. By April, ratings were back down to a .7/2.2, and in May ratings were a .6/1.9, reaching 332,000 households, the same ratings level as in May 1990.

Ratings may be back down to pre-war levels because there's "a burnout" from all the news, according to Turner. "When the news tempo resumes its normal pace, people will come back," he said. "When we have the next major news event in the world, we'll see a resurgence".... (*"CNN: Where Have All The Viewers Gone?"* Broadcasting, *1 July 1991, 45*)

A couple of points about this example.

- At times, sweeping generalities ("CNN's ratings are up ... CNN's ratings are down") won't do the job. Translate for readers with *precise* numbers and details.
- Translating must be conducted with extreme care to ensure it's at a level appropriate for your reader audience. For example, referring above to "rating" and "share" without translation is fine for *Broadcasting*'s audience of TV executives. For the readers of a general-circulation magazine, such as *Reader's Digest* or *Life,* your usage must be, "Rating, *the ratio of a station's viewers to all people in its market....*"

Sometimes, a comparison can be light, sweeping and, indeed, imprecise—if it creates an image readers understand. For example, how would you translate for readers the lifestyle of tennis star Ilie Nastase? An *Esquire* writer tries (successfully, we think):

There is something very cosmopolitan about all this, very man-of-the-world. Except that even at forty-four, Ilie Nastase does not act anything like a man of the world. As always, *he acts like a teenager playing hooky from school* (emphasis added). (*Mike Lupica, "Tennis Without Balls,"* Esquire, *July 1990, 39*)

You can characterize an event or statement and thus translate, too. Here, a writer characterizes a *smile* by cigar-smoking David Frost, a British TV star:

"I suppose you could say my philosophy of interviewing is—whatever works," says Frost, between puffs. "But I believe you can be testy without being abrasive. You can put somebody on the spot without overt confrontation." Then he pauses, smiles. *There's a wink in this man's smile.* "Sometimes confrontation is essential. You have to ask certain questions." (emphasis added) (*Linda Ellerbee, "Talk to Me,"* Elle, *Feb. 1991, 96*)

Below, a writer characterizes, twice in the same sentence, the size of a movie's budget. Note how ineffective it would be to simply peg the budget at "$90 million" and leave it at that.

"Terminator 2: Judgment Day" is reported to have cost Carolco Pictures over $90 million to produce—*almost 15 times more than the original*—giving it what is apparently the *largest budget in Hollywood history.* (emphasis added) (*Benjamin Svetkey, "Cash Flow,"* Entertainment Weekly, *12 July 1991, 14*)

GETTING PERSONAL (AND OTHER TRICKS OF THE TRADE)

Have you noticed that throughout this book we refer to you, our reader?

That's our effort to get personal with you, to achieve a special intimacy even though we've never met you. It's a writer's trick we learned long ago: The best-told tale is one spun not for distant masses of faceless, anonymous readers but, rather, one-on-one—by us for you (singular), as if you're sitting on a sofa beside us. Let's discuss this and other tricks of the trade.

Take Your Readers by the Hand

Magazines, more than any other medium, offer you, as a writer, special opportunities to get personal with individuals in your audience. Newspapers avoid first-person writing and force writers into the background ("a source told *The Times* today . . ." is the much-favored impersonal—and cold, distant—form.) In TV, too much first-person ("I'm here on the White House lawn . . .") is regarded as show-biz stunting. In magazines, however, first-person writing is a favored form of communication.

Note how a travel writer takes you by the hand and leads you around Thailand:

> You can travel the 427 miles north from Bangkok to Chiang Mai by air—and most visitors do. But you can also get there by train or by bus as I did. . . .
>
> Everywhere, I saw Thai spirit houses. . . . Taxes and tribute had passed over the mountains I traveled through . . . Teak for temples and palaces had been carted over the roads I followed. . . . (*John Rember, "Thailand's Highland Treasure,"* Travel and Leisure, *Feb. 1990, 141*)

Sometimes, you can send your reader off on a solitary journey, using the intimate "you" to transport the reader along on an imaginary trip. Note how beautifully that is done by *The New York Times Magazine*'s wine writer who reports from Paris on buying wine in France:

> Take the Burgundy run, for example. In this country, when your cache of Gevrey-Chambertin and Volnay Les Caillerets begins to dwindle, you mortgage your home, head for your favorite wine shop and stock up.
>
> In Paris, you call several friends who, it turns out, are also low on Burgundy. "It's time," you announce, "for a Burgundy run."
>
> In no time, you have orders for more than your car can carry. Like most Parisians, you have your favorite suppliers—Jacqueline Jayer in Vosne-Romanée, perhaps, or Jacques d'Angerville in Volnay. You call them to say you will arrive on Saturday. You book a quiet room at the Hotel de la Poste in Beaune for Friday and Saturday, and take a table for dinner there on Friday night. (*Frank J. Prial, "Winerunning,"* The New York Times Magazine, *26 May 1991, 48*)

Have a pleasant trip? *We* did!

A very special intimacy can be created with your reader through a first-person account of something you've experienced. There are two ways to get into this type of story. Both are tricky.

The first is to recount a personal experience worthy of recounting. The trick is to not select first-person approaches on stories that, simply, aren't worth telling ("How I Learned to Study" or "How I Stopped Chewing My Fingernails"). Can you doubt the following story, titled, "My Name Is Jessica . . . I Do Not Drink," is worthy of a first-person approach?

> Although I don't go to AA meetings anymore, I am a believer. Not in everything that is said or done in AA. Not in all the ways one is taught to behave. Not in most of the culture that surrounds AA. But I believed then and I believe now and I think I will always believe that when one is ready to be a recovering addict, the way is through the AA system. But when one is done with AA, one is done with it. . . . (*"My Name Is Jessica . . . I Do Not Drink,"* Lear's, *July/Aug. 1989, 56*)

Another way into the "I-do-it" story is as a reporter, seeking out an experience for the express purpose of writing about it. The trick here is to inject your first-person self into the story but not so strongly that it becomes a meaningless gee-whiz tale of adventure, rather than an informative story that communicates important facts to your reader. A *Business Week* reporter achieves nice balance in describing the business aspects of Bell Atlantic Corp.'s Training & Education Center in Valley Forge, Pa., then taking readers along as he learns the safe way to climb an electrical pole:

> For obvious reasons, I'm interested to know if there have been any injuries in recent years. (The instructor) says no—with the exception of injured pride. But working around high-voltage wires and clinging to the top of a swaying pole strike me as a bit risky.... (*Mark Lewyn, "The Last Cowboys of The Information Age,"* Business Week, *15 July 1991, 20F*)

Take readers along as you learn to fly, swim, sail, skate or climb poles.

Always, in writing on the personal level, your goal is to insert your reader into the equation. Here, for example, is an extract from an *Esquire* story on U.S. Marine Corps uniforms:

> A Marine can't just mix and match based on his own sense of the occasion, of course. What to wear, when, and how exactly to wear it is spelled out in a 228-page document entitled "Marine Corps Uniform Regulations" [MCO PI020.34]. The instructions are nothing if not precise: two pages alone on the proper wearing of the sword, for example. *Keep that in mind the next time you begin to feel a little hemmed in by your own job's dress code....* (emphasis added) (*"Semper Finery,"* Esquire, *Feb. 1989, 135*)

Set the Scene Carefully

Ever watch truly great comedians set up their audiences? With painstaking care they hint and suggest, luring listeners toward just that right moment when—bang!—they deliver the punch line and bring down the house.

So, too, must you set up your readers, not only to get them into your story, but to create a reading *environment* that pulls them deeply into your story. Here, for example, is a word picture drawn to set up readers of a story about a cool, laid-back jazz musician:

> A summer evening in Manhattan. Stan Getz is stretched out on his bed in a plush suite at the Parker Meridien Hotel, exhausted, chain-smoking Gauloise cigarettes. He is a barrel-chested, raspy-voiced man with a fondness for sharp clothes, intimidating when he wants to be, but tonight his face is as round and devoid of malice as a baby's. Getz is happy about last night's show at Carnegie Hall. It was the first public airing of some tricky new material from his new album, "Apasionado," and the crowd responded warmly. (*Joseph Hooper, "Stan Gets Through The Years,"* The New York Times Magazine, *7 July 1991, 30*)

Above, the scene is set by "stretched out on his bed in a plush suite...." By contrast, below is another scene designed to set up readers—to catch their interest—for a story about a Broadway producer imprisoned for grand larceny:

> Controlled electronically by an invisible hand, the wall of bars slides open as if of its own accord, but as soon as one enters the enclosure, the metal grid closes abruptly with an ominous clank. The only furniture is a few molded-plastic chairs and child-size tables; each is made from one seamless piece of material, with no parts or hardware that could be removed and sharpened into a shank that could be used to stab someone. This is where Adela Holzer is permitted to see her visitor.... (*Leslie Bennetts, "Springtime For Holzer?"* Vanity Fair, *Feb. 1991, p. 40*)

Both of the preceding examples were leads, designed to introduce readers to the subject matter. You can use word pictures just as effectively in the body of your story to maintain reading momentum. An *Esquire* writer traveled with David Duke, former grand wizard of the Ku Klux Klan, campaigning as a Louisiana state representative. Deep in his story, the writer carefully sets the scene by detailing how Duke works a crowd:

Blow-dried and coiffed, Duke is standing just outside the arena, near the gate end of the pens that are at this moment full of Brahma bulls . . . a gray one with a hideously black, flopping, fat neck . . . a brown one, snorting and pawing the earth, great gobs of drool dangling from his nostrils, black eyes like death pools. . . . Around Duke, the riders are strapping on huge, corsetlike structures and taping their midriffs, wrapping straps around boot tops, wrists, and hatbands, and at the same time gripping Duke's hand and pounding his back. "Go get 'em, David," one young dude, sixteen, 150 pounds, a peewee Marlboro Man, drawls.

"I've got to shake that man's hand," says a bronc rider in his twenties. "I'm from over to Texas, and man, if we had more people like David Duke back home, we wouldn't have no more problems with the niggers 'n' wetbacks . . . hell, we wouldn't have no more problems!" Duke shakes his hand happily.

A few hundred words further into the story, the *Esquire* writer gives readers another scene-setting jolt to maintain the story's momentum:

Duke (turns) with some relief to shake the hand of a stout woman who is approaching at good speed.

"Got me out of the kitchen to meet this man, my husband did," says the woman. She reaches up to kiss Duke on the cheek. Duke leans down. The woman grins widely, exposing both teeth. Duke recoils slightly, but manages a glancing peck.

Her husband steps up to shake Duke's hand, too, after struggling to free his fingers from the handle on his cattle prod, a wandlike electric shocker that will later coax bulls and broncs from pen to pen.

"I need one of those up to the legislature," says Duke. "Maybe then we'll get something done."

"I hear that!" barks the stout woman's husband. "Take this one here!"

Duke laughs and turns toward a pickup truck laden with T-shirts, baseball caps, and plastic Mardi Gras doubloons bearing his name. . . . (*Lucian K. Truscott IV, "Hate Gets a Haircut,"* Esquire, *Nov. 1989, 174*)

A lesson in the *Esquire* example: Don't *tell* us who David Duke's political supporters are. Let us discover.

Following is scene-setting detail from *Gray's Sporting Journal* that transports you onto a lake with fishermen:

But when we glanced over our right shoulders as we rhythmically worked the jigs, we saw something coming. A squall line hove in from the north, its leading edge like cotton balls swabbed through the barrel of a dirty gun. The clouds were dark and roiling and ominous, and advancing at a menacing pace. . . .

Finally, the center of the lake went dead calm. The sky assumed a peculiar greenish cast. The air thickened. We could see the waves at the north end of the lake break back against themselves. Then, as if it were subject to the laws of plate tectonics, the whole surface seemed to shift and rearrange into two converging halves, with us at the seam. I opened the throttle as wide as it would go, and pointed the dinghy for home. . . . (*Tom Davis, "The Toothsome Pike-Perch,"* Gray's Sporting Journal, *Spring 1990, 62*)

We don't know whether you've ever fished. But we do know this: If you have, you won't be able to resist reading the full article after you've sampled the scene-setting detail above.

You've seen above four examples of writing that we think succeeds because its scene-setting detail stirs reader imagination, creating word pictures of unmistakable clarity. What follows is an example of outdoor writing that fails on two counts: (a) It tries to *tell* you something, rather than letting you discover, and (b) its imagery stretches so far that it's ridiculous. Imagine (if you can) the following:

Try to imagine yourself as a wild carnivore. Should you be tossed into the woods on some frigid winter night with only your scanty body hair to protect you from the cold, with only your teeth and fingernails as weapons of defense, with no well-developed sense of smell or hearing and limited endurance, you certainly would not last long.

With this in mind, I enjoy following the winding trail of a red fox, marveling at the attributes this superb hunter demonstrates as it travels through its world. . . .[5]

Lesson: Don't stretch so far in grasping for scene-setting detail that you ask your reader to imagine the unimaginable. Your writing will fall flat if you do.

Note how the writer below fails to set the scene properly for a story about antique toys because his language invites in only those readers who remember a poem—and invites out those who don't remember:

Remember poet Eugene Field's little toy dog "covered with dust" and the little toy soldier "red with rust"?[6]

Next, a writer fails because his scene-setter casts a net for "everyone," when, in fact, roses make some people sneeze:

Everyone likes the fragrance and beauty of roses, but no one wants the bother of season-long spraying to keep them healthy and in bloom. Luckily, this dilemma is no longer a problem. You can avoid the extra work and effort by growing low-care roses. . . .[7]

Lesson: In structuring scene-setting detail be careful not to narrow your focus so much that, as in recalling a poem, you eliminate vast numbers of potential readers who can't understand your point. Conversely, don't address everyone in the world. Really, not everyone goes crazy over roses.

Capture Your Story's Rhythm

Every story you report has its own tempo, pace, rhythm. Match that rhythm in the tempo of your writing—catch that pace in words—and you improve enormously your chances of communicating effectively.

In this example, a writer depicts a woman who, unlike her career-oriented neighbors, wants to be a housewife. The writer captures the tempo of life—hers and her neighbors'—with carefully crafted detail:

The street is a cul-de-sac. The houses are new. The first interior light, a bedroom lamp, is switched on before 6:00 a.m., followed by lights in the bathroom, the hallway, the kitchen. Before long, up and down the street, more lights come on as people hurry to shower, dress, assemble children, feed babies, pack diaper bags, load cars, get on their way. By sunrise, the migration has begun. Lights go off, doors are locked, garage doors rise, cars pull away. The rush is toward the highway and downtown Cincinnati, and as the last car turns out of sight, Red Clover Court seems suddenly abandoned.

At one house, however, a woman still stands by the front door. Her name is JoAnn Stewart, and she is waiting for her husband, Scott, who is coming down the hallway in a charcoal suit, his shirt wrinkle-free, his red tie knotted tightly, his briefcase in hand.

"Bye, honey," she says, rubbing him on the back.

Next comes her son, Ben, blond and fresh, who will take the school bus to first grade.

"Use your manners," she says, kissing him on the cheek.

Then comes her other son, Brian, a big, happy boy, who will spend the morning in preschool.

"You have a good morning, okay?"

The door closes, and JoAnn is alone, and with no hesitation, she sets out to do what she does every day, what her mother used to do, and her grandmother before that. She sets out to be a housewife.

She clears the breakfast dishes. She reaches for the vacuum. She reaches for the dustcloth. She reaches for the laundry. There is a smile on her face, and soon she begins to whistle. . . . (*David Finkel, "The Last Housewife in America,"* Esquire, *June 1990, 102*)

Note the staccato, bang-bang way the writer illustrates how commuters start their day—"assemble children, feed babies, pack diaper bags, load cars. . . ." The tempo is unmistakable.

Then, the writer shifts to his housewife subject, depicting her standing by the front door as, one by one, her family streams by. Again, the rhythm is portrayed effectively.

Here, a writer catches a different "rhythm" of life. See if you can discover the writing device she uses:

> From the back they look like any other family lunching in a restaurant. The mother attends her children with graceful gestures, calmly answering the animated questions of the six-year-old boy, picking up the spoon the toddler repeatedly drops from her high chair, feeding the dark-haired child sitting quietly on the side.
>
> But from the front, this is no ordinary family. The mother is Norma Claypool, an unmarried former college professor who is totally blind. With her are three of her adopted children—all severely handicapped. The talkative little boy, Richard, is blind and so disfigured from a birth defect that strangers sometimes gasp when they see him. The noisy toddler, Dawna, has slanting, wide-set eyes and a short, stocky body—unmistakably a Down's syndrome baby. The quiet one is Tommy, four and a half, severely abused by his natural parents and so badly brain-damaged that he cannot walk, talk or feed himself.... (*Dinitia Smith, "Hard to Place—But Not to Love,"* Woman's Day, *3 April 1984, 78*)

The writing device used so effectively, of course, is the language used to open both paragraphs: "From the back . . ." and, "but from the front. . . ."

Sometimes, just a few words catch tempo. A *Life* writer described a fast-track, brilliant, 17-year-old finalist in the Westinghouse Science Talent Search. At five, she was intrigued by neurosurgery. At seven, botany . . . on and on, year after year, the tempo of her life picked up. So, several hundred words into her story, the writer sums up the rhythm:

> First. Youngest. Only. Best. Those words had defined Tessa's life.... (*Allison Adato, "To Be The Best,"* Life, *June 1991, 47*)

A Few Other Language Tricks of the Trade

Now, a few isolated language tricks you can use to put punch in your writing. Remember: In effective writing the *little* things count.

Play with Words

Special effect is achieved if you get playful on occasion in your writing. Be certain, however, that you do it on a playground you understand. The following examples wouldn't work for the serious readers of, say, *Harper's, Atlantic* or another "thought-leader" magazine. We think, however, they're perfect for the magazines that used them. (Emphasis is added to italicized words in each example.)

The irreverent *Spy* on rapacious Wall Street and a New York City brokerage house with an outpost in Brooklyn:

> At the corner of Kings Highway and Coney Island Avenue stands Dean Witter Reynold's sole Brooklyn outpost, *only 7.8 miles* (*as the vulture flies*) from their headquarters in the World Trade Center. (*Andy Aaron, "When Dean Witter Talks, People Listen to E. F. Hutton,"* Spy, *May 1989, 46*)

A *People* writer on reggae rap singer Daddy Freddy:

> We already know the Jamaican-born Freddy has a *turbotongue*.... (*David Hiltbrand, "Stress,"* People, *22 July 1991, 18*)

A *Rolling Stone* writer on singer Chris Robinson's complaints that he was misquoted by reporters:

What Robinson, the Black Crowes' singer and *resident superyap,* actually said. . . . (*David Fricke, "The Black Crowes,"* Rolling Stone, *30 May 1991, 30*)

New York reports that Peter S. Kalikow, owner of the zesty *New York Post,* reveals details of the paper's financial troubles:

Kalikow's grim news has a *certain tabloidy twist.* . . . (*Edwin Diamond, "Tab Terror!,"* New York, *17 Sept. 1990, 19*)

Slang Works Sometimes, Too

Don't overdo it, but judicious use can add zest to your writing:

It was not your typical Palm Beach event. . . . (*Linda Marx, "Feud in B Minor,"* Connoisseur, *July 1991, 19*)

". . . gardening grabbed him young . . ." (*Barbara Walder, "The Avant-Gardener,"* Organic Gardening, *Nov. 1990, 19*)

A *Smithsonian* writer follows an oil wildcatter in a rough-and-tumble Kansas oil patch and discovers that he neither negotiates leases with landowners nor converses with them. Rather:

He *dickers* with landowners, and chats with contractors. . . . (*James R. Chiles, "There Are New Signs of Energy out in The Kansas Oil Patch,"* Smithsonian, *March 1991, 37*)

Structure for Emphasis

You can highlight points—important points—in your writing by using several devices. The dash is used effectively in this story about arm wrestlers:

Brzenk has also defeated the well-known Rick Zumwalt, one of the sport's most flamboyant—and largest—personalities. (*J. David Miller, "Tough Guys Don't Flinch,"* American Way, *15 July 1991, 16*)

Note the double emphasis here:

Chambers, just FYI, is one of the wealthiest women—wealthiest people, period—in the world. (*Melissa Harris, "Anne The Obscure,"* Atlanta Magazine, *April 1991, 47*)

Using a colon singles out points, too:

What's needed is a way of calling the bluff of each side: a course on tolerance that both sides might find difficult to disavow. (*Arthur M. Melzer, "Tolerance 101,"* The New Republic, *1 July, 1991, 10*)

Sometimes, interrupting the smooth flow of a sentence lends special emphasis. This from a story about organized crime:

No one, it should be pointed out, has accused (him) of any organized-crime involvement. (*"Crime,"* Vanity Fair, *Nov. 1989, 162*)

Repeating a point, particularly with a backup quote—a *telling* quote—emphasizes a point:

Jackson believes it was her own role as the eldest of four sisters that gave her the authority that has been the hallmark of her drama career: "I blame my bossiness on the fact that I was the oldest child and told to take control of my sisters. . . ." (*Christopher Silvester, "Labour Pains,"* Connoisseur, *July 1991, 17*)

You'll recognize, of course, that repeating for emphasis should be done only sparingly. Constant repetition, making readers read everything twice, can be a turn-off. It can drive readers away. See what we mean? Understand?

Sometimes, a single word can achieve emphasis:

He learned to outmaneuver opposing linemen by mastering a variety of moves, countermoves and tricks, changing his mode of attack from play to play.

Still, Millard's most effective asset may be his intensity.... (emphasis added) (*Jill Lieber, "Deep Scares,"* Sports Illustrated, *29 July 1991, 36*)

One of the most effective devices for achieving emphasis is to present diametrically opposed emotions side by side, which provides jolting contrast. Note how this writer places talk of murder next to "tea and thin sandwiches" in a story about an Ethiopian princess who spent nine years stuffed in a prison cell with her mother and others:

"There were times I could quite cheerfully have strangled my mother," Princess Rebecca Asrate Kassa said over tea and thin sandwiches in the lounge of my London hotel several days before I was to leave on a journey to Ethiopia. And who could blame her, or anyone forced to spend nine years in an Ethiopian prison cell with her mother, sister and six aunts—charged with no crime, permitted no visitors, offered no hope of release, itching with fleas, plagued by rats, sleeping on mattresses on concrete, chronically ill, and blinded by a light that was never once, in all that time, extinguished? (*Thurston Clark, "The Princess and The People,"* Vanity Fair, *Nov. 1989, 108*)

Finally, *lighten up!* Readers desperately need a smile. Provide one and you'll win their hearts. Leave 'em laughing and they'll read everything you write. Note:

My maternal uncle, James Francis "Harp" O'Connor (may he rest in schnapps) was a disbarred lawyer, an undischarged bankrupt, a fair-to-middling bird hunter and a keen, almost mystical fly-fisherman, but first and foremost—in keeping with his hallowed Hibernian heritage—he was a world-class bullshitter. He taught me all I knew.... (*Robert F. Jones, "Voracity,"* Gray's Sporting Journal, *Spring 1990, 21*)

SUMMARY

Your ability to win readers is only as strong as your skill in handling basic language structures, particularly the *sentence*.

Subject + verb + direct object is the strongest sentence structure, but gets monotonous if used too frequently. Vary your order of sentence parts and use phrases and clauses. And avoid writing in fragments and run-on sentences; both drive off readers.

Strong *verbs* are extremely important for writers. Using them in present tense and active voice puts punch in your writing. Avoid misuse of adjectives, which *tell* readers something. Use, instead, strong, colorful language that lets readers *discover.* Adverbs are misused by many beginning writers, as are interjections and prepositions.

Inducing readers to read is a complex challenge. One key is to write in simple structures, being careful not to stretch beyond your writing abilities. As your writing experience increases you can reach for more complex structures.

Handling time elements carefully is important. Because of delays inherent in manufacturing and shipping magazines, much of what you write must be timeless. But casting your story in present tense can give it "you-are-there" impact.

Avoid abstract nouns and strive for stories filled with concrete details. Remember, readers seek information, not abstractions, in magazines.

Weave strong attribution into your writing. Use authoritative sources to give readers faith in what you write. Avoid writing what people think, feel, sense, expect. You know only what they *say.*

Often, your story will tell itself if you get out of the way and let strong, colorful quotes carry readers forward. Readers like to read what other people say in their own words, at their own tempo, with their unique conversational rhythms and patterns.

As a writer, your job is to go to places, see things and talk to people, then translate for your readers what you encounter. That often involves using warm, personalized writing structures that tell readers, in terms they can understand, the meaning of complex developments. It also means describing in lay terms every technical term, idea and principle you use in your story.

Other tricks of the writing trade include using first-person, "I-am-there" detail to personalize your writing. Take your readers by the hand and lead them forward. You also should set the scene carefully, using colorful, specially selected language to create word pictures that entice readers into your story. Be certain to *catch the rhythm* or tempo of your story. Find language that matches it and you'll win readers. And don't forget to *lighten up*! Leave 'em laughing when you can.

RECOMMENDED READING

The best way to learn about outstanding magazine writing is, of course, in *discerning* reading of leading magazines. Professional writers are voracious readers. You should develop a hearty reading appetite, too. Now. Read to learn how to write.

For language basics, see Brian S. Brooks and James L. Pinson, *Working With Words: A Concise Handbook for Media Writers and Editors* (New York: St. Martin's Press, 1989), William Strunk Jr., and E. B. White, *The Elements of Style,* 3rd ed. (New York: Macmillan Publishing Co. Inc., 1979) and Rene J. Cappon, *The Word* (New York: The Associated Press, 1982). Also helpful are James J. Kilpatrick, *The Writer's Art* (Kansas City: Andrews, McMeel & Parker, 1984) and Terri Brooks, *Words' Worth* (New York: St. Martin's Press, 1989).

NOTES

1. Eva Pomice with Robert F. Black, Don L. Boroughs and Sara Collins, "Bush's Leap of Faith," *U.S. News & World Report,* 1 July 1991, 48.
2. These examples appeared as, respectively, Debra Gersh, "A Hard Act to Follow," *Editor & Publisher,* 6 July 1991, 12, and Tom Riordan, "Weekly Editor," *Editor & Publisher,* 29 June 1991, 15.
3. Mathew L. Wald, "The Eye of the Photojournalist," *New York Times Magazine,* 9 June 1991, 28.
4. Richard Atchenson, "What We Did For Love," *Lear's,* Nov. 1989, 176.
5. Ronald Andrews, "The Carnivores: A Success Story," *The Conservationist,* March–April 1991, 8.
6. Skip Korson, "Old Dolls and Toys Evoke Memories," *Macon Magazine,* Nov./Dec. 1990, 18.
7. Eric Rosenthal, "Low-Care Roses," *Organic Gardening,* June 1991, 38.

Chapter 4

Writing
with authority
and credibility

I t is so important that you inject *authority* into your writing and build *credibility* in
your byline that we devote this entire chapter to special hints on how you can
accomplish those goals.

This topic requires special focus for two reasons:

First, whatever else you offer as a writer, your fundamental appeal to *editors*
must be your credibility as an honest writer who can report accurately and fairly, then
fashion a story with balance, integrity and professionalism. Develop a reputation for
that, or the gatekeepers won't open your way into their pages, no matter how facile
your writing.

Second, magazine *readers,* ever more educated and more discerning, will skip
over your story if they sense in your reporting or writing the slightest amateurism,
structural weakness or lack of authority. Recall from Chapter Two research showing
readers seek, above all, *information* from magazines. They'll quickly recognize any
lack of substance, even if it is masked by writing glitter.

Clearly, editors and readers alike are setting high standards for writers these
days.

Public opinions polls show strong undercurrents of disaffection in general with
American media. Magazines, newspapers and TV are regarded by many as biased,
unreliable and inaccurate. Readers show their desire for credible, authoritative writ-

ing by increasingly turning to specialized magazines that feature writers who are experts in their fields and who can *write with believability*. With the financial fortunes of their magazines at stake, editors must respond by ensuring their writers possess— and display—expertise in the subjects they cover.

In Chapter Four, we'll discuss how you can achieve authority and credibility: Build into your writer's soul a passion for accuracy, detail, precision and integrity, *then* fashion writing techniques that demonstrate to editors and readers that you're a professional doing a reliable, authoritative job.

You will learn in this chapter how to anticipate questions that arise in readers' minds—questions that, if left unanswered, erode faith in your reporting and writing. You will learn how to ensure that your efforts to write with color and impact don't obscure the strong factual base of your reporting. You will learn, also, that fact-checking is a responsibility that writers cannot leave to editors or magazine re-searchers.

THE GOAL: FACTUAL WRITING WITH STRUCTURAL INTEGRITY

Learning to build authority and credibility into your writing is an enormously com-plicated challenge. It involves every aspect of reporting and writing, and can take years to truly master. But if you want to get started in magazine writing, you must learn to handle immediately two broad dimensions of the challenge.

First, you must learn to report accurately and precisely the factual elements of your story—its basic building blocks—accurately reporting all names, ages, titles, occupations and so on.

Second, you must learn to write with absolute integrity, ensuring that your story, broadly and as a structural whole, is balanced and fair. It's possible, of course, to build a completely erroneous story structure on factually correct building blocks.

Let's start with the foundation.

Making the Five W's and How Work Harder for You

The foundation for any story—a hard-news piece or soft feature—must be built on answers all readers seek: *who* is involved, *where, why, when, what* is this all about, and *how* is it happening? The only difference in how you handle those basic elements is the immediacy and emphasis you assign them in your story structure.

As you have learned in basic newswriting courses or from reading newspapers, the Five W's and How are jammed tightly into the first few paragraphs of a hard-news story. Readers seeking from newspapers a quick news fix may be attracted by writing grace and wit, but above all they want the basic elements laid out quickly and in unmistakably clear order.

In magazine writing, you can make those Five W's and How work harder for you by threading them more gracefully and subtly throughout your story fabric. You can tease, hint at, suggest and beckon readers alluringly as you reveal those elements one by one. But don't get so carried away with your writing artistry that you omit any of the Five W's and How from your story. Leave them out of even a soft feature and your readers will depart dissatisfied—and unlikely to seek out your byline in the future.

Let's examine how magazine professionals build strength into their writing through sophisticated use of the Five W's and How.

Who

Is *Forbes*, which calls itself "Capitalist Tool," a magazine about business? No. It's a magazine about people in business and about how business affects people. *Sports*

Illustrated isn't about sports. It's about athletes, fans, spectators, coaches, trainers and other people involved in, and affected, by sports. *Esquire*, *Family Circle*, *Parents*, *Vanity Fair*, *New York*—all focus on people and things, events, happenings, occurrences that have impact on people. That's the who element.

Of course, successful writers in all media find the human element in their stories and treat it deftly to make their writing come alive. So, what's the difference in magazine writing? It lies in the space, detail and prominence you give the human element in your story. You've got to develop keen judgment about how strongly to stress the "who" factor, how much detail to use and where to insert it.

Below are examples of how two *Forbes* writers take entirely different approaches to the "who" element:

In a story of more than 1,000 words about bankruptcy laws in Florida, Rosalind Resnick only briefly interrupts the flow of her story to insert—with precise detail—her "who":

> Last year a record 36,552 people filed for bankruptcy in Florida, a 30% jump from 1989. (*Rosalind Resnick, "The Deadbeat State,"* Forbes, *8 July 1991, 62*)

Note several factors: Resnick doesn't write "a great many people" filed for bankruptcy, or "about 36,000"; she is precise with "36,552." Resnick also *characterizes* the number as a record (not "new record," incidentally; all record-setting developments are "new") and adds further perspective for her readers by pointing out bankruptcies were up 30%. In this example, the writer slides her readers into and out of the "who" element very quickly, with a minimum of words or interruption of her narrative flow.

Another *Forbes* writer, Carolyn T. Geer, opens with stress on the people factor and makes it the central thrust of her narrative flow. Although her story is about an insurance company, here is how she opens it:

> *Joseph Macchia's* Gainsco, Inc., is something of an ugly duckling in the insurance business.... (emphasis added)

That personalized intro emphasizes the writer's main thrust—that the company and its success revolve around the personality, drive and business smarts of its chief executive, Joseph Macchia. With that point made up front, the writer then weaves her story about a *company* around a real, live, warm *human being*:

> Bronx-born Macchia, 56, a milkman's son.... (third paragraph)
> Macchia, who peppers his conversation with corny aphorisms like "A promise made is a debt unpaid" ... After working his way through Fairfield University in Connecticut, graduating in 1957, Macchia did a stint in the Marine Corps.... (fourth)
> ... Macchia ... borrowed $500,000 from a bank, rented an office, set up a card table and three folding chairs, and was soon in business.... (sixth)

Then, a closing quote that further illuminates the personality of a human being rather than a company:

> "You don't have to be a rocket scientist to do what we do," Macchia says. "All you have to do is exercise discipline, not get greedy and be patient as hell." (*Carolyn T. Geer, "Be Patient and Don't Get Greedy,"* Forbes, *8 July 1991, 80*)

The writer in this example builds credibility by letting you discover that Joseph Macchia makes the company go. She doesn't open with the ordinary, blatant "Joseph Macchia is the driving force behind...."

The writer also scatters throughout her story clues to what motivates the insurance man—the "who" element—to succeed: "milkman's son" (he's scrambling up the socioeconomic ladder), "corny aphorisms" (he has the common touch), "working his way" through college and "stint in the Marine Corps" (knows hard work, discipline), "borrowed $500,000" (takes risks).

In just that manner can you make an otherwise dull business story come alive with in-depth exploration of the person who runs the company.

Much magazine writing, of course, focuses on the "who," not companies or things. Personalities are favorite reading subjects for millions of magazine subscribers. For those readers, you'll take on an entirely extra dimension of authority if you go beyond the usual, "The 5-foot-10-inch, 180-pound man...." Note below how a *New York* writer handles in few words such "housekeeping" detail in a story on Robert Redford:

> Unavoidably, you begin with what Redford disparagingly calls the "handsome thing"—the burnished blond hair, windblown and yet somehow still perfectly coiffed; the blue eyes; the square jaw; the lithe build; the delicate tension between beauty and manliness ...

The *New York* writer doesn't quite dismiss such physical descriptions, you understand. They, after all, *are* essential to any well-drawn portrait of a personality. But the language signals that the story (which we don't have room to reproduce here) goes on for many thousands of words, *exploring in depth* what's behind the "handsome thing." For example:

> Born and raised in Southern California, Redford remembers his childhood as a "velvet haze." He was only a fair student ...
>
> He may have looked like an insider, but Redford grew up poor, rebellious, liberal, and felt very much outside ...
>
> He never relinquished that feeling of separateness. Instead, he invested it in his roles.... (*Neal Gabler, "Redford Talks,"* New York, *10 Dec. 1990, 34*)

Incidentally, we emphasized earlier your need not only to report a story strongly but also to establish credibility with readers by demonstrating that you have done the job for them. Well, here's how Neal Gabler makes you believe he got the goods on Redford in the preceding example:

> Initially, Redford was wary about granting *an interview....* Even when he did relent, he kept *voicing misgivings.* As he was about to begin *a second* session after *two hours the previous day*, he sucked in his breath and grimaced. (emphasis added)

You'll note that the writer provides fascinating insights into Redford's character while simultaneously (yet with endearing indirection) giving you a backstage look at how time-consuming and careful his in-person reporting was. Build your credibility by taking your readers behind the scenes to watch you at work.

What

Here's a little game you can play to illustrate perfectly how you can build into your writing an element of expertise and authority many writers don't display in other media.

Watch one of tonight's network TV newscasts. List the stories focused on—but limited to—the *what* element of events around the world. You'll find interest rates rise (but the cause isn't mentioned), games are won or lost (period), governments totter and fall (end of story), the stock market is up or down (and that's all folks).

Now read the first three or four paragraphs of every story on today's front page of your newspaper. How many are limited to simply telling you *what* happened?

Daily journalism is obsessed with *what*. Space and time limitations in newspaper and TV journalism restrict chances for elaboration. Deadline pressures force writers to go now, without taking time to seek deeper meaning. In all that lies enormous opportunity for you to create a magazine-writing style that adds whole new dimensions to reader understanding of what is going on in this crazy world.

It's easy to define, complex to deliver: You must get beyond *what* to explain the *real* what, beyond what is happening and explain what caused it to happen and what it all means. For example, a TV newscast might report banks are raising their interest rates. So? So, an *Atlantic Monthly* writer, not diverted by a need to report the latest ax murder or plane crash, takes time to elaborate on the real what:

> If a company wants to modernize a factory, it almost always has to borrow money, usually by approaching a bank or by issuing bonds. In either case it must pay interest— sometimes quite a bit of interest. The higher the cost, the more difficult it is to justify the investment. Right now it is more expensive to invest in the United States than it is to invest in Europe or Japan. . . .
>
> Crudely speaking, money costs more in this country because there isn't enough of it available to private investors. Americans save much less of their incomes than other peoples do; as a result, banks have less to lend. Last summer, Commerce Department figures show, the American personal-savings rate was 5.1 percent, meaning that the nation saved a nickel of every dollar of disposable income; in Japan the savings rate for 1988, the most recent figure available from the Organization for Economic Cooperation and Development, was 15.2 percent. With Americans not putting much in the bank, American banks have less money to lend. . . . (*Charles C. Mann, "The Man With All the Answers,"* The Atlantic, *Jan. 1990, 45*)

That basic explanation must give many readers their first understanding of the real what behind the what of rising interest rates. That is how to impress readers with your expertise and authority.

Following is another example of how you can insert the real what into a story. A *Forbes* writer takes several hundred words to describe the what: A big city landlord (Smith) conducts an elaborate scam by buying cheap rental properties and then using them as collateral in persuading banks to lend him more on the properties than they are worth. Can't you just hear a TV news anchor trying to explain the "real what" of that in six seconds? The *Forbes* writer uses a simple but effective device:

> (Smith's) strategy was taken from the pages of those how-to-get-rich-in-real-estate books. He would buy rundown buildings cheaply, fix them up with money from the banks, slap new mortgages on them and use the proceeds to buy more properties. With every uptick in values, he could borrow more. To maximize his control over his properties, he kept his leases as short as three years.
>
> Case in point: 451 D Street, a huge converted warehouse bought in 1983 for $4.7 million, or $10.60 per square foot. Fixed up, it could rent for up to $12 a foot. (Smith) played musical mortgages, refinancing ever increasing amounts—from (banks) which lent him $28 million in April 1989—two years after the market peak. Today, the building, not yet fully renovated, is at most worth $20 million. . . . (*Laura Jereski, "Tell Them Anything to Get the Loan,"* Forbes, *5 Aug. 1991, 58*)

Sometimes (but not too often, we hope), you'll be unable to explain the real what. Will your credibility suffer? Not if you level with readers and explain why there are holes in your story. For example, Loren Feldman, writing for the *New York Times Magazine,* easily finds the what in a story about the New York Mets hiring a psychiatrist, Dr. Allan Lans, to analyze its baseball players:

> Since 1988, it has been Lans's job to wander baseball fields, watch workouts, treat drug and other personal problems and ponder such questions as: Why can't Mickey Sasser throw the ball back to the pitcher? Why can't Sid Fernandez stop eating? Why couldn't Davey Johnson communicate with his players? Does anybody miss Darryl Strawberry? And how have the Mets managed, simultaneously, to win more games and disappoint more people than any other team in baseball?

But where is the real what in all that? Author Feldman doesn't know—but actually bolsters your faith in him as a writer by telling you flat out he doesn't know and explaining why he doesn't know:

Sadly, if Lans has found the answers to those questions, doctor-patient confidentiality precludes his sharing them. Because there aren't many questions he can answer publicly and because it's almost impossible to evaluate the performance of a psychiatrist, little has been written about his role, and he remains a figure of some mystery—both outside the clubhouse and in. . . . (*Loren Feldman, "Baseball Psych-Outs,"* New York Times Magazine, *7 July 1991, 11*)

Where

It's an essential element of any story, of course. And it's easy to insert—"in Connect-icut". . . "in his office in Los Angeles" and so on.

But can't you insert the *where* with a ring of authority and make it do something special for your story? Yes, and here is how:

He walks slowly across the soccer field on ruined knees, past the red-brick dorms of the small Connecticut college and toward the white spire of the library. And as Joe Namath walks, somehow the years disappear in the morning mist, and it is 1969 all over again. It is First Avenue in Manhattan. It is night. And he is Broadway Joe, who liked his women blond and his Johnnie Walker red. Broadway Joe, who said he couldn't wait until tomorrow, 'cause he got better looking every day. (*Mike Lupica, "The Neon Nights of Broadway Joe,"* Esquire, *Oct. 1989, 67*)

Looking out of his 12th-floor windows of the World Savings building in West Los Angeles, Eli Broad points to the Executive Life building about a mile south on Olympic Boulevard.

Broad thinks a great deal about Executive Life these days, because he, too, is in insurance and in Los Angeles. . . . (*Matthew Schifrin, "Cherry-Picking,"* Forbes, *8 July 1991, 44*)

Note how the following writers (a) insert where, (b) take you behind the scenes on their reporting jaunts and (c) thus inject unmistakable authenticity into their writing.

A *Smithsonian* writer reports on her investigation into the so-called "greenhouse effect":

To find out more, I talked to John Mitchell of the British Meteorological Office. Mitchell illustrated his explanation by pointing out his window. "Those high clouds," he said. . . .

"On the other hand," he continued, pointing to some lower, puffy cumulus clouds in another part of the sky. . . . (*Margaret Scott, "Modeling Earth's Future Climate Requires Both Science and Guesswork,"* Smithsonian, *Dec. 1990, 29*)

For *The Atlantic,* a writer reports that U.S. armed services face declining budgets, reduced forces and changing missions, then asks, "How will the armed forces adapt?" He continues:

To find out, I paid a visit to the Army War College, in Carlisle, Pennsylvania. The college serves as a sort of graduate school in war-making. . . . For several days I became a student at the war college. I attended lectures, pored over assigned readings, and participated in seminar discussions. I chatted with students in the hallways, joined them on the softball field, took breakfast with them in the morning, and downed beers with them at night. I stayed on campus, in a century-old guesthouse named after George Washington. The college officials asked only that I not quote any student by name. . . . (*Michael Massing, "Conventional Warfare,"* The Atlantic, *Jan. 1990, 28*)

Note the final sentence in Michael Massing's War College example above. What do you think he adds by telling you, "The college officials asked only that I not quote any student by name . . ."? He adds strength to his story by explaining why he doesn't name officers. But he also helps explain *where* he is: not at just a military installation but at a top-secret installation where the army grooms men and women for senior leadership. That is how to insert "where" in your story and make it work harder for you.

When

In magazine writing you cannot match the immediacy of newspaper or TV news-writing, of course, and thus cannot strive for a "today" time element. But you *can* establish authenticity in your writing with deft insertion of the *when* element.

First, this element must be in even a seemingly timeless or old story because without some sense of time, without some context for understanding when, your readers will have difficulty tracing your footsteps.

Second, you must establish a meaningful time context without unnecessarily diverting your readers from the narrative path or dating your story, thus rendering it nonessential.

Philip Caputo shows you how to insert a sense of time into a story that's months old before it hits print, yet give it an active, present-tense "today" feeling:

> He wakes up late on what he knows will be the last day of his life.... (first paragraph)
> Let us try to imagine how he looks as he gets out of bed and stands in the curtained light of room 104.... (second)
> As the eyes of our imagination grow accustomed to the dimness, we see other things in the room, things that baffle and alarm us.... (third)
> He wraps the rifle and magazines in a blanket and steps out into the cool brightness of the day. The midmorning sun enriches the pale yellow of the El Rancho's stucco walls.... (sixth)
> It is close to 11:00 when he gets behind the wheel and drives off.... (11th)

Thus does Caputo reveal to you that his tale opens early one morning (but *which* morning?) and moves toward mid-day. Which day? More importantly, however, Caputo lets you infer that you're at the dawning of something horrible ... and that it's late in someone's life. In fact, Caputo is reconstructing the day on which Patrick Edward Purdy takes an AK-47 assault rifle to his old school, Cleveland Elementary, in Stockton, Calif., and shoots into 400 children in the playground, hitting 35 and killing 5. Only as if in passing, 1,000 or more words into his story, does Caputo specify what a newspaper or TV newswriter would emphasize in the lead: The precise date. Caputo does that indirectly by reconstructing the killer's drive under an overpass en route to the school, and adding:

> In the cars and trucks rumbling above him the radios are abuzz with music, the idiot chatter of disc jockeys, weather reports, news. One of the big stories of this day, January 17, 1989, is of the impending execution in that other sun-kissed state across the country. A serial killer and rapist named Theodore Bundy will be executed in Florida.... (*Philip Caputo, "Death Goes to School,"* Esquire, *Dec. 1989, 136*)

Obviously, for magazine readers the precise date is almost irrelevant in the chilling tale above. But, like any good newspaper reporter, Caputo ensures readers get it.

Incidentally, readers know neither Caputo nor any other writer truly can get inside the killer's head or be there, to collect graphic details, the morning he arises to do his deadly work. To suggest otherwise would destroy a writer's credibility. Note how Caputo levels with readers and, without weakening the fabric of his story, invites them to imagine with him what happened: "Let us try to imagine"... (second paragraph) and "As the eyes of our imagination grow accustomed...." (third)

Following is an example of how the precise date is totally irrelevant. But the writer in the next example neatly inserts a sense of time: a "fresh spring morning" contrasted vividly with bloody horror that follows. This is from a story about a woman with a disorder that causes her to harm herself while sleeping:

On a fresh spring morning last year, K., a young New York woman, woke up on the floor of her bedroom. Catching a glimpse of herself in the mirror as she struggled to her feet, she saw that there was blood all over her face. Her two front teeth were loose, a bottom tooth had pierced her upper lip, her nose was broken, and she had what she would later discover was a concussion. She remembered having had a terrifying dream, then a feeling that she was running, then something hard against her knees and face. Otherwise, she couldn't recall a thing.

Six months later, as she prepares to spend her second of two nights under observation in Neil Kavey's sleep lab at the Columbia-Presbyterian Sleep Disorders Center in New York City, she still isn't sure exactly what happened. . . . (*Rachel Urquhart, "Night Shift,"* Vogue, *Jan. 1991, 192*)

Sometimes, the "when" of a story is not a day, week, month or even a year but rather a bygone era. How to catch that? Hans Koning, writing in *Harper's Magazine*:

When I was a boy in high school in Amsterdam, there were images in my mind from the First World War of English soldiers, little fellows under their saucer helmets, marching down a village street with French children running after them crying, "Tommy, Tommy!" Then the soldiers are standing in a trench waiting for dawn, rain is falling, it isn't possible to sit down in the heavy mud. When the subaltern blows his whistle, they climb out and start charging forward, holding their rifles with bayonets pointing upward at forty-five degrees. After that, very few of them will stay alive for more than a few minutes longer.

I could not conceive of myself as being one of those men, of their gentle docility in obeying the whistle. Such a fate (like being burned as a heretic or broken on the wheel by the Spaniards who waged war on Holland 300 years earlier) belonged to a past of before me. . . .

I am talking of Amsterdam in the Thirties. It was a town in which our milkman came to the door mornings with a cart holding a large metal urn with fresh farm milk. This cart had a dog walking under it in harness, to help pull. . . . (*Hans Koning, "A Life Colored by War,"* Harper's Magazine, *May 1990, 67*)

In this example, the writer's sense of time really is one of mood. The when is not a calendar date but, rather, an *era,* a distant past of disciplined, perhaps unthinking willingness to meet death, a time of dogs pulling milk carts. . . .

Why and How

Of all basic building blocks in a story's foundation, *why* and *how* are both a magazine writer's greatest challenge and a great opportunity to construct an authoritative, credible style.

The challenge is the need to give your readers a dimension of understanding they cannot get from spot-news media, which gain access to your readers each day, before you do. Newspapers are making great efforts to build explanatory background into their pages, so often dominated by hurried topical writing. The *New York Times* front-page "News Analysis," for example, is an effort to tell readers why and how. Columnists and op-ed writers featured on the page opposite the editorial page offer in-depth background. TV has "60 Minutes," "20/20" and other in-depth, analytical programs.

Your opportunity in handling why and how is that if you consistently advance reader understanding beyond what the spot-news media do, you can join those professional magazine writers whose bylines are eagerly awaited each week or month by regular audiences seeking their authoritative expertise. Note *consistently* and *regular.* The only way to get a regular following is to deliver the goods each time your byline goes atop a story.

The reporting and writing approach you take to "why and how" depends, of course, on the complexity of your material and the sophistication of your audience.

In industry trade journal writing you often can—indeed, must—assume your readers have considerable technical expertise. Write to that expertise. For example, *Aviation Week & Space Technology* is read by, of course, engineers and others deeply familiar with aviation and space matters. So, in reporting that NASA is contemplating a space shuttle mission to the Hubble space telescope, the magazine explains briefly and simply the why and how:

> Two of the observatory's six main gyros have already failed and a third has begun to degrade.... NASA could replace the gyros and repair the optics in a single shuttle mission.... (*Washington Staff, "Hubble Dilemma,"* Aviation Week & Space Technology, *5 Aug. 1991, p. 17*)

You wouldn't hold for long a reader audience of aviation and space experts if you made them wade through what to them is elementary:

> ... gyros have already failed and a third had begun to degrade. Gyro is a colloquial term for gyroscopic stabilization system, consisting of a continuously driven gyroscope whose spinning axis is confined to a horizontal or vertical plane that senses any deviation from a desired altitude and ...

The next example shows how you should treat why and how just a bit more fully if your audience isn't as narrow as *Aviation Week*'s. This story is from *Advertising Age,* a weekly whose audience is drawn from a broad range of media-related industries: advertising agency employees, marketing executives, newspaper and TV people and others. The what is in the lead:

> Coca-Cola Co. is striking back against Pepsi-Cola on all fronts.

The how and a bit of the why follow in the second paragraph:

> The No. 1 soft-drink marketer is preparing its first coordinated worldwide ad campaign, moving to solidify its lead over Pepsi in the U.S. and planning to boost ad spending, particularly for Diet Coke.

More expansive treatment follows in the sixth paragraph on *why* Coca-Cola and its ad agency, McCann-Erickson Worldwide, are moving so vigorously:

> Executives at the cola giant and McCann are under pressure from Pepsi, credited by industry observers with outdating Coca-Cola on the marketing front in recent years. (*Alison Fahey and Gary Levin, "Coke Plans 'Real Thing' Global Attack,"* Advertising Age, *5 Aug. 1991, 1*)

Such in-depth treatment of why and how in the story above won't be found in most daily newspapers, which serve wide-ranging general audiences of readers, many unlikely to be interested in soft-drink marketing esoterica. And, of course, even if TV news could shake its habit of flitting from one spot-news story to another it still wouldn't cover Coca-Cola in depth that matches *Advertising Age.* Why? Because depth on such a specialized story would be a turn-off for TV viewers, even more general in demographic makeup than newspaper readers and far more diverse in their information interests. Thus, TV and, to some extent, newspaper writers must seek consensus stories aimed at the widest-possible audiences. That leaves *Ad Age*'s Fahey and Levin with the specialized audiences their magazine attracts. If those two writers can provide such why and how explanation week after week they'll have readers searching out their bylines in each issue.

Forbes goes into detail on the why and how of a story that, for its audience of profit-oriented business executives, must be astonishing: A successful executive, Charles Battey, drops out of the high-paying corporate circuit to do volunteer work in the Third World. Why? Because:

> Vacationing in Indonesia in 1985, he felt guilty about being a tourist living in luxury amidst poverty. Back home he volunteered to help a Cambodian family resettle in the Minneapolis area. "I noticed how resourceful these people were if just given a little help."

Then, *Forbes* addresses how: For $100 weekly he went to work for a Christian organization specializing in business development overseas. *Forbes* adds:

> Do you or someone you know want to emulate Charles Battey's experience? Here are some of the main players in overseas small-business development.... A few of them accept volunteers (there follows a list of seven organizations, complete with addresses and telephone numbers). (*Dyan Machan, "Chucking It All,"* Forbes, *8 July 1991, 106*)

Note that *Forbes* extends the "how" to how you, the reader, can get into volunteer work. Such "how-you-can-do-it" detail strengthens your writing enormously. It places in your readers' own laps a development otherwise remote and affecting only strangers.

So far, in our discussion of why and how, we've dealt with three examples drawn from specialized magazines. You undoubtedly noticed the gradually expanding amount of explanatory detail in each: *Aviation Week*'s simple, brief explanation that's sufficient for its expert readers (the gyros are going bad); *Advertising Age*'s more in-depth detail on cola marketing for a wider audience; *Forbes,* with the most diverse audience of the three magazines, treating why and how even more expansively. Now let's look at a fourth example, this time showing how a general interest newsmagazine, *U.S. News & World Report,* assumes no expertise among its readers in discussing the why and how of Alzheimer's disease:

> It has been called the disease of the '80s, because that's when Americans became aware of it, but Alzheimer's will really hit home in the 21st century. (First paragraph—and note the "look-ahead" angle there!)
>
> The devastation the disease wreaks is far worse than most imagine.... (second paragraph)
>
> Over a period of time lasting from as few as five years to as many as 20, the disorder destroys brain cells, and harmless forgetfulness gives way to a cruel and capricious insanity: One sufferer refuses to bathe or change clothes, another eats fried eggs without utensils, a third walks naked down the street, a fourth has the family's beloved cats put to sleep while yet another mistakes paint for juice and drinks it. The outlandish acts committed by Alzheimer's patients take as many forms as there are people who suffer the disease.... (third paragraph) (*Shannon Brownlee, "Alzheimer's: Is There Hope?"* U.S. News & World Report, *12 Aug. 1991, 40*)

Note the graphic examples in the third paragraph illustrating for a general audience the behavior of victims. Describing the why and how in that manner would be inappropriate for, say, the expert readers of *The New England Journal of Medicine.*

Skillfully handling the Five W's and How builds authority and credibility into your writing. But judge carefully your audience's expertise. Giving expert readers too much elementary background will bore them; giving general audiences too little will confuse them. Either way, you'll drive off readers.

INSERTING THE RING OF TRUTH

As a student, you develop—probably almost unthinkingly—the ability to sense quickly whether lecturers have prepared properly for your classes. Only a few minutes into lectures, you know whether what follows likely will be rewarding or a waste of time.

Readers also can sense quickly, often after just a few paragraphs, whether your story is properly researched and reported—whether it has the ring of truth—and is written in an engaging, easy-to-understand style.

Professional writers (like good lecturers) use many devices to get a grip on readers early in their stories, and then scatter incentives throughout the narrative to maintain the momentum. Let's look at some.

Using Believable Detail

The scenario: Betty Fussell is writing for *Lear's* about her son, an Oxford graduate who, under California's influence, turned to bodybuilding. How can you *not* believe her when she opens her story this way:

> As I deplaned in the LAX terminal, I thought only in California would I see a monster like the one approaching from the distance—low-thighed, arms flared by a massive chest, neck engulfing his jaw—an incredible hulk who parted the crowd like the Red Sea and kept on coming, kept on grinning. What was that supposed to mean? "Hi, Mom." I recognized the voice, if not the man. It was Sam—my son the bodybuilder.
>
> All 6 feet 4 inches and 250 pounds of him bent over and gave me a kiss. In Valleyspeak, it was awesome. I hadn't seen Sam for a year, and I couldn't stop staring, which was just what he wanted. He played it cool, picking up my suitcases as if they were paper bags. He could have slung me over his shoulder like a towel, this Samson, who a mere 30 years ago was born a perfectly normal Sam—weighing 8 pounds 10 ounces, measuring 16¼ inches long. I felt like a character in "Invasion of the Body Snatchers," struggling to recognize in this mutant alien my own flesh and blood. . . .

If you doubt that's a real mom writing about her own real son, Fussell pushes you further toward believability by recounting, deeper in her story, the days when Sam was growing (and pumping) up:

> The larger my offspring grew, the smaller I felt as proud mother. While other mothers spoke of their son the brain surgeon or the nuclear physicist, I pulled out photos of my son the bodybuilder and watched eyes roll and mouths drop. One friend to whom I showed a photo at lunch said, "Oh, God, not while I'm eating." Others asked discreetly, "Why is he doing this?" meaning "Why is he doing this to you?" (*Betty Fussell, "My Son the Bodybuilder,"* Lear's, *Nov. 1989, 79*)

Of the many devices you have for achieving credibility with readers, inserting believable first-person detail, as in this example, is one of the strongest.

However, most of your magazine writing will be based on reporting, not first-person experience. As successful as she was with Sam the Bodybuilder, Betty Fussell can't construct a writing career around him. She—and you—can use the how-it-happened-to-me approach a couple of times. Then, you must move on. When you do, strive to collect the same type of believable detail for your writing.

Jennifer Conlin, writing for *Newsinc*, describes the late Robert Maxwell, British media mogul and owner of *The New York Daily News*, as "anything but a hands-off owner." She adds believable detail on "Maxwell's obsession with the phone—he calls from the barber, from his yacht, from wherever, and keeps a 90-button console in his office. . . ."[1]

Dominick Dunne, writing in *Vanity Fair*, hides believable nuggets throughout a lengthy story on a once-rich financier now imprisoned on criminal charges: ". . . his yacht gone, his planes gone, his dozen houses gone, or going, and his reputation in smithereens—he has recently spent three months pacing restlessly in a six-by-eight-foot prison cell. . . . True, he dined there on gourmet food from the Schweizerhof Hotel, but he also had to clean his own cell and toilet. . . ." And, deeper in the story: ". . . accompanied by Swiss law-enforcement agents, he arrived in New York from Geneva first-class on a Swissair flight, handcuffed like a common criminal but dressed in an olive-drab safari suit with gold buttons and epaulets. . . ."[2]

Robert Scheer, writing for *Esquire* about Paul Newman on a movie set: "It's midnight in the woods near Winnfield, Louisiana, and Newman walks out of the kitchen in the rented ranch-style house where he is living for the duration. He is wearing white BVD briefs. An apple is stuck in his mouth, and his hands are clutching a cold Bud and a salad doused with some of Newman's Own."[3]

Lessons from the preceding examples: If you want readers to believe, you must collect and reveal to them details that prove you were there: the color of buttons (gold), the number of buttons on a console (90) and the kind of beer Paul Newman drinks (Bud).

Weaving in Facts and Figures

They're central to the American idiom: "Is that a fact?" "It's a fact." "Let's look at the facts." We are a fact-oriented society. (That's a fact; you can count on it.)

So, get facts into your writing! Doing so pulls your reader along the simplest, most direct route toward believing.

Inexperienced writers encounter two primary difficulties in handling facts.

First, a feeling that facts can get in the way of a narrative, can destroy mood and scene-setting flow.

Second, once the need for facts and figures is accepted, learning how to weave them into the fabric of a story, how to build writing strength on them, yet not leave them jutting out where they snag the eye and rip patterns and interrupt smooth movement.

Well, as shown in the examples we've studied, facts *don't* interrupt narrative flow, if handled correctly, and are essential to creating mood and descriptive atmosphere in your writing. Recall: Paul Newman dressed in white BVD briefs—not shorts, not plain old underwear. He's got an apple (not just food) stuck in his mouth and is clutching a Bud (not any old beer). Creates a mental image that sticks, doesn't it?

So, just as coaches tell beginning swimmers to first lose their fear of water, we'll tell you to lose your fear of facts. You'll learn to love 'em. But, how to get facts and figures neatly woven into your story? How to build your story on them, rather than smother your story in them?

To begin, don't worry too much about being subtle with facts. Wherever you think your story needs strength, simply insert—bang!—a sentence or paragraph of unadorned facts or figures. Readers don't find that nearly as interruptive as you might imagine. Recall again the research in Chapter Two showing that magazine readers *seek* information. They're after facts and figures! Reflect on your own reading habits. Don't you mentally underscore facts and figures as you move through a story, building your own mosaic of understanding from bits and pieces?

A writer in the next example enormously strengthens a paragraph with a short, quick transfusion of figures. This is from a lengthy story for *Entertainment* on Arnold Schwarzenegger and director James Cameron:

> "I always felt we should continue the story of 'The Terminator,'" Schwarzenegger says. "I told Jim that right after we finished the first film." Shot in 48 days on a stripped-down $6.4 million budget, the sleeper Cameron calls "a lean street thriller" went on to earn a healthy $100 million in worldwide ticket sales and attract an enormous audience on video. To a post-apocalyptic theme "The Terminator" added the expected genre mayhem plus unexpected dollops of emotion (between Linda Hamilton and Michael Biehn, who played the father of her child) and loopy, sociopathic humor (from Schwarzenegger). It's now seen as a sci-fi classic, but at the time it was simply the product of a team of creative people who had nothing to lose. . . . (*Donald Chase, "He's Big, He's Back, and He's Really A Pretty Nice Guy, Once You Get To Know Him,"* Entertainment, *12 July 1991, 12*)

This story is a critique of film-making, the type of writing that spurs some writers to plunge poetically into artsy, impressionistic froth. Note, however, how weak that paragraph would be if writer Chase simply used "stripped-down budget" (without the $6.4 million figure) and "healthy ticket sales" (without $100 million). Used wisely, precise figures add believability to the most poetic of musing.

Also, note how Chase carefully characterizes the figures. To readers who don't understand Hollywood, a $6.4 million budget may sound high. It isn't, so Chase characterizes it as "stripped-down." And in this era of megabucks and millions being spent for this, billions for that, some readers might not know whether $100 million in ticket sales is a rewarding take. Chase unobtrusively lets you know: it's "healthy."

Lesson: When writing for an audience of non-accountants, be careful in lacing your writing with facts. Space them out. Throwing in bunches of them frightens off readers. And, do signal what the figures mean. It aids reader comprehension.

Here, a writer slides a single figure into the interior of a sentence and immediately widens reader comprehension. This is from a story about Israel's quarrel with Syria over an area known as Golan Heights:

> The Shamir government makes no historic claim to the area—a 450-square-mile ridge of rocks and farmland commanding the Galilee—appealing instead to geography, physics and survival. (*Carla Anne Robbins, "The Long Walk to Peace,"* U.S. News & World Report, *12 Aug. 1991, 17*)

It's a good bet many Americans have heard of Golan Heights; it's also a good bet that in the preceding example Carla Anne Robbins, with that 450-square-mile figure, tells those same Americans something they don't know.

Just 200 words into his narrative, a *People* writer devotes an entire paragraph to figures designed to bolster his story about an Alabama civil rights lawyer, Morris Dees, under attack for suing white supremacist groups:

> Now he rides with his 9 mm automatic stuck into his blue jeans. His third wife, Elizabeth Breen Dees, 35, keeps a riot gun on her side of the bed. In 1983 Dees' office in downtown Montgomery was firebombed; since then, both it and Dees' 250-acre ranch have been turned into fortresses. (*Bill Shaw, "Morris Dees,"* People, *22 July 1991, 50*)

Note that the figures, far from diverting reader interest, add to it by citing specifics that reveal how severely threatened the lawyer feels.

Demonstrating Balanced Skepticism

Reflect briefly on your relationship with your readers.

You use all your writing skills to attract those readers and pull them deeply into your story. You demonstrate in every way possible your credibility and professionalism.

Your readers, in turn, invest their money for your magazine and their time—and perhaps even emotional commitment—in what you have to say. They in effect appoint you their surrogate, their witness of events they cannot attend, their reporter of developments beyond their reach. They're vulnerable in that dependence on you.

You have a huge responsibility, therefore, to serve as reader surrogate with integrity and to demonstrate that by achieving and displaying healthy, balanced skepticism in your reporting and writing. We're not recommending attack-dog adversarial journalism, popular with some newspaper and TV reporters, as a way of building authority and credibility into your writing. We *are* suggesting that readers expect you to look behind the obvious for what's hidden, to uncover the bad as well as the good, to point out what works in our society, as well as what doesn't.

With experience, you can move into investigative journalism, doing stories on evangelists who bilk the gullible, bankers who skip with the dough, government programs that fail. Now, however, your challenge is to ensure that on even the most routine story you protect your readers' interests. One way to do that is to carefully qualify information you pass to your readers. You can accomplish that with minimal interruption of your narrative flow, using just a few words to tell readers you are attempting to give them a balanced view. For example, Robert Karen, writing for *The Atlantic*, discusses psychological research into infant-mother bonding and how emotional tendencies are passed down through the generations. In his second paragraph, Karen puts his readers on guard:

Theories to explain this unwanted inheritance are plentiful. But scientifically ver-
ifiable explanations *have been elusive.* Indeed, until the past two decades *nothing could
be said with scientific authority* about most any dimension of the mother-child bond. . . .
(emphasis added)

In the fourth paragraph, Karen balances his story further by elaborating on controversy within research circles:

One group of researchers and clinicians, known as attachment theorists, claims
that they've discovered some answers and are on the road to finding the rest. But
although they've dazzled many of their peers, altering some of our most basic attitudes
toward early child care, their contributions have frequently met with skepticism, op-
position, or rebuke. (*Robert Karen, "Becoming Attached,"* The Atlantic Monthly*, Feb.
1990, 35*)

This example raises several points:

First, we find some beginning writers feel obliged to discover and report truth
to their readers. But who knows what truth is? Who knows which infant-mother
bonding theory is correct? You discharge your obligation to readers if you instead
report facts—counterbalanced by other facts, theories weighed against other theories.

Second, don't try to be subtle about demonstrating that you write balanced,
credible copy. State your disclaimers and qualifiers—"theories," "claim," "skepticism"—early and emphatically. What we're talking about here is being fair with your
readers.

Being fair extends, of course, to giving all parties in a dispute chance to comment. That's elementary stuff you learned in basic newswriting. In advanced magazine
writing, however, you must go beyond that and characterize for your readers the
balancing information you present.

For example, a *Forbes* writer asks film company owners for comment, reports
faithfully what they say but then signals readers the officials are providing just fluff and
actually "aren't saying much."[4] Another *Forbes* writer asks a computer company official for comment and is told the company's position is "a nice position to be in." The
Forbes writer adds, "Or is it?" and produces evidence that the company's position
perhaps isn't so nice.[5]

An even more blatant challenge of official comment is made by yet another
Forbes writer in a story on the embryonic World League of American Football. It seems
ratings for the league's televised games on ABC are dismal:

ABC *admits* it's disappointed with the ratings, but a spokeswoman *says bravely* that
the league "just needs some fine-tuning."
A league spokesman says boosting TV ratings by 50% to 75% is doable with
improvements in the action and promotion. *Can anybody name a single player in the
league?"* (emphasis added) (*"Last WLAF?"* Forbes, *22 July 1991, 17*)

One point about the last example: We don't like "admits." That has a legal or
confessional connotation to us. "Acknowledges" (or just plain "says") is preferable.
But we sure do like other qualifiers in both those paragraphs. As surrogate for your
readers you are responsible for passing along "balancing comment." You also are
responsible for signaling when it's nonsense.

Sometimes, you'll encounter a quote that makes a point crucial to your story but
is wildly exaggerated. What to do? A top automobile writer, Jerry Flint, had this
problem in a story on the struggle between American and Japanese auto manufacturers. His lead:

Walter Hayes, retired vice chairman of Ford of Europe, ponders the future of his
company and his industry. "We are engaging in the Third World War," he says. . . .

You can see how that quote characterizes the embattled thinking from Detroit
automakers, and thus deserves the prominence Flint gives it. But it is so exaggerated
that Flint cannot merely let it stand:

> Hayes is being a bit dramatic, but it's a question of survival for a good number of companies and literally hundreds of thousands of jobs.... (*Jerry Flint, "Will the (New) Maginot Line Hold?" Forbes, 8 July 1991, 58*)

Skillful writers insert balance in their writing in ways that round out the story they're trying to tell. For example, in the Paul Newman profile we mentioned earlier, *Esquire* writer Robert Scheer faces a problem confronting all writers doing stories on film personalities: how to get beneath the Hollywood glitter and close to the real person. Scheer avoids the gushy adulation that spoils so much writing about film stars and lets Newman describe himself:

> "I'm a kid from Shaker Heights who benefited from the luck of the draw."

Scheer asks Newman who or what he is once he's finished acting out other people's lives. Newman's answers are vague. Scheer presses the question, and:

> Once again, quite sadly: "I have no idea."

Still, Scheer bores in, again letting Newman himself insert the balance of reality vs. Hollywood glitter:

> One other thing: Modesty comes off Newman's skin like musk. He mixes it up with the locals at the 7-11, tries to like the deep-fried catfish at Tom's in Shreveport. On the set, he dashes the image of the prima donna. "You don't know how sh—— they can get in this business," says *Blaze* director Rob Shelton. "Actors refuse to come out of their trailer for a scene because they haven't been stroked fifteen times that morning. But this guy Newman—you don't have to f—— around." Teamsters and gaffers and grips want to protect him.
>
> Mention his lack of arrogance and he says, "Maybe it's false modesty." Ask him if he's a hero and he answers, "By what standard? That I put my makeup on better than anyone else, that I get my eyebrows blacker, or I've got baby blues blinking endearingly at the audience? What is that? That's horse——."
>
> "Don't paint me like some goody-two-shoes," he warns later. "I've screwed up just like everyone else does. I've behaved badly and hung from chandeliers, but I figure that's part of growing up and figuring out what the hell is happening. I've had some very tough times, but I seem to have weathered them somehow." (*Robert Scheer, "The Further Adventures of Paul Newman,"* Esquire, Oct. 1989, 164)

That's a balanced, multidimensional portrait drawn of Paul Newman. And note how writer Scheer steps aside and lets Newman provide extra dimensions by wrestling with himself. Those quotes let readers watch the struggle, which dramatically adds credibility to Scheer's let-me-take-you-there style of writing.

Incidentally, note above our coy attempts to protect you from the shock of all those obscenities. Quoting people faithfully, gutter language and all, can lend enormous credibility to your writing. Writer Scheer filled in all the blanks in his account, so his readers (unlike you) didn't have to figure out the words. But Scheer wasn't writing for retiree subscribers to *Modern Maturity,* and obviously figured his *Esquire* readers (a) could stand the shock, and (b) couldn't get a proper look at Newman without the naughty words.

Good rules on writing dirty: Do so only if it's essential to the thrust of your story and not likely to offend readers of your magazine. We decided that filling in the blanks above wasn't essential to getting our point across and that doing so might offend you.

OTHER THREATS TO YOUR CREDIBILITY

A cartoon strip character, Pogo, once got himself clipped out of newspapers and pasted on the walls of writers' offices all over America. His creator had captured him with a bewildered look on his face, muttering, "We have met the enemy, and he is us."

In striving to build credibility into your writing, look closely for the enemy: It may be you. As many professional writers will tell you, wounds to your credibility can be self-inflicted.

Let's look at some danger signals.

Beware Overwriting

Here is how it feels: Your adrenalin is pumping. Your mind is racing. Your fingers are dancing across the keyboard. Words. Color. Images. All are pouring out. You're on a roll. This story is the greatest you've ever written.

Whoa.

Get a cup of coffee (decaf). Cool down a bit. Look at that copy again. Is it smothered in adjectives? Riddled with generalizations? Stretched by exaggeration?

It can happen, especially when you let your writer's ego dominate your reporter's instinct. We all have writer's ego. Writing, after all, is creative. It's *fun*. Not all of us have reporter's instincts, however. Reporting is laborious, time-consuming. Dredging for facts isn't always fun—and, what the hell, let's write around holes in our story. Let's dazzle readers with our keyboard mastery so they'll overlook our lack of substance.

Think about this chapter's examples of good writing. None can be termed "color" writing. All are effective because they are simple, straightforward and packed with facts. Don't forget your primary mission as a writer is to communicate information—whether that be embodied in figures, word pictures, mood or whatever. Writing is ineffective when it gets so colorful that accuracy suffers and communication fails.

In the next example, the writer *really writes*. He's into a story about NBC News and comes upon Michael Gartner, president of the network's news division:

> With his trademark bow tie slightly askew, his hands folded across his belly, gazing out from behind a deceptively meek face featuring eyebrows that rise like popovers when he makes a point, Michael Gartner looks and sounds like a genial college professor. But in action he's the feared dean of students. (*Tad Friend, "Would You Buy A Used TV-News Show From This Man?"* Esquire, *Dec. 1990, 155*)

You make the call: Is that effective writing? Before you decide, let us make a couple points: We can hang in there with "trademark bow tie" and "meek face." We start to weaken with eyebrows likened to "popovers" and really fade with "genial college professor," a storied figure, to be sure, but one in short supply these days. And "feared dean of students"? C'mon! When was the last time *you* feared a dean of students, even if you knew who she or he was?

Beware of Generalizations

Have you noticed in this book that we don't write, "*Most* writers . . .", but rather "*Many* writers . . ."? We also try to avoid "all, always, biggest, smallest, fastest, slowest. . . ." We learned long ago that such generalizations always—or, at least, much of the time—come back to haunt you.

What happens to the writer's credibility when readers absorb the two following paragraphs and think about the apparent contradiction?

> James Brown, who is perhaps the world's greatest authority on feeling good, relived the experiences and rhythms of his song as he toured his 62-acre Beach Island, S.C., spread, taking in sights and sounds denied him during the hard time he served in a South Carolina prison.

Brown served 26 months of two concurrent six-year sentences for failing to stop for police, aggravated assault and weapons violations.... (*Renee D. Turner, "The Ordeal of James Brown,"* Ebony, *July 1991, 40*)

On their face, these paragraphs indicate James Brown is a pretty good authority on feeling bad times, as well as feeling good. After all, 26 months in prison cannot have been fun. In this example, the writer is making a play on words that doesn't communicate and, indeed, comes across as a sweeping and contradictory generalization.

Here is a generalization, which we're sure even the writer didn't care for when it appeared in print:

When sportsmen aren't pursuing game in field and stream, they are likely to be reading about it in their libraries. Sporting books are widely collected.... (*"Reading Crop,"* Connoisseur, *July 1991, 101*)

Well, many hunters we know don't have libraries, aren't particularly avid readers, and are busy with jobs, household chores and so forth. Get our point? You may *talk* across the kitchen table in such generalizations, but they don't communicate well in writing for readers who seek literal information.

Here's what can happen if you write before you think:

If you follow Highway 72 through northern Alabama, it will take you to Florence, home of William Christopher Handy, "Father of the Blues." (*"Alabama,"* American Visions, *June 1990, 7*)

Now, what's wrong with that example? *Think.* Highway 72, like many highways (we'd say *all,* but you know how we feel about such generalizations), runs two ways. Depending on where you are when you set out, following in one direction takes you toward Florence. The other, of course, takes you away from the city.

Acknowledge Your Limitations

How many times have you or a friend described someone as a "know-it-all"? It's a massive put-down, and a signal to all that the person's credibility is questionable.

In your writing, don't label yourself a know-it-all. It's a terrible self-inflicted wound—and so easy to avoid.

If you don't *know* and are relying on memory, say so, as this writer did in 1991 when recalling an incident in 1955 during the civil rights campaigns in Alabama:

That strategy session at Mrs. Robinson's house remains one of my great memories as a journalist.... (*Carl T. Rowan, "Marching Toward Freedom,"* Vogue, *Jan. 1991, 182*)

If you're unable to sort through conflicting data to reach a conclusion for your readers, say so. This writer did in an article on coffee drinking:

Frank evaluation of its hazards is not easy. There is a vast literature on the effects of caffeine on the body, and for every study reaching one conclusion, seemingly there is another that contradicts it. Although most major health risks have been ruled out, research continues at a steady clip. I'll summarize here the work done recently.... (*Corby Kummer, "Is Coffee Harmful?"* The Atlantic Monthly, *July 1990, 92*)

If you think you know Washington's policy, but aren't sure, insert a qualifier. Often, it takes only a single word:

The Bush Administration *appears* to be about to offer the Soviet Union a much more important helping hand.... (emphasis added) (*"What's Ahead for Business," Howard Banks, editor,* Forbes, *8 July 1991, 35*)

Finally, Check—And Check Again

The accuracy of everything that flows through your keyboard and into print is your personal responsibility. That includes the facts of your building blocks—the Five W's and How—and the overall structural integrity of your story. So, when you've written and rewritten, polished and improved, check again whether you've got it right.

We can't emphasize it enough: Strong reporting and a passion for accuracy often will compensate for some weaknesses in writing skills. But not for long will even the most brilliant writing style cover inaccuracies and reporting weakness. We know professionals who fashion fine magazine careers with only so-so writing ability because they understand what is and isn't a story and know how to get it and get it right. Conversely, we have seen fine writers nose dive into career ruin because they consistently made factual errors.

When you make it big in magazine writing—at *Newsweek*, *The New Yorker*, *Vanity Fair*, for example— you'll have fact checkers to help you sort out, among other things, where Highway 72 leads in northern Alabama. Even then, however, what appears under your byline is your responsibility.

A study of fact checkers at three national weekly magazines gives you clues on where in your writing to double-check for errors. The study, done by Susan Shapiro and published by the Gannett Foundation Media Center (now the Freedom Forum Media Studies Center), breaks out types of content that gave fact checkers "pause," or reason to check for inaccuracies:

- "Clearly objective matters," such as proper noun, title and spelling, created 16 percent of pauses by fact checkers.
- "Relatively objective questions," such as whether location and date or quotes are correct, created 35 percent.
- "Less objective questions" caused 24 percent of the checks. These involved whether an event happened as described, for example.
- "Subjective questions" created 25 percent of pauses. These involved characterization by writers of someone's intent or belief, for example, and references to what is likely to happen in the future, or generalizations.[6]

Of course, there comes a time when you (and, certainly, your readers) need to relax a bit with a lighthearted piece that isn't factual and doesn't pretend to be—one written just for fun. When that time arrives, you might want to open with a disclaimer, as Stanley Bing did in telling his *Esquire* readers how he researched a story on men who lust after women other than their wives:

> The following anecdotal material is gleaned from men I know who are not myself, and even the fake names I usually employ to protect their bogus identities have been changed. That's how dangerous this stuff is.... (*Stanley Bing, "What's Your Line?"* Esquire, Oct. 1989, 111)

SUMMARY

You must prove to editors that you are a reliable, accurate, credible writer, or those gatekeepers won't open their pages to you. Readers demand authoritative, information-packed writing.

Writing authoritatively requires reporting with precision the basic building blocks of your story—names, ages, titles and so forth. You also must write with integrity and balance, ensuring your story, broadly and as a structural whole, is truthful.

One way to build credibility and authority into your writing is to make the Five W's and How work harder for you. Don't jam them tightly in the first few paragraphs, as in basic newswriting. Rather, weave them gracefully and subtly throughout your story fabric.

The *who* or human element is extremely important in magazine writing. Deftly build your writing around it. The "what" element of newspaper writing sometimes is too superficial for magazine writers. Go behind it to investigate the "real what"—not only what happened, but what it means.

Where is essential to any story, of course. In magazine writing, you should insert it with a ring of authority and make it do something special for your story.

You cannot match the immediacy of newspaper or TV writing, so give particular care to the *when* of your story. Insert it to give readers some sense of time, even in seemingly timeless or old stories. But do so without unnecessarily diverting your readers from the narrative path or dating your story.

Why and *How* are your challenge to give readers a dimension of background they cannot get from spot-news media. If you succeed, you can advance reader understanding beyond what they get from newspapers or TV.

Inserting believable detail gives your writing a ring of truth. Draw from your own experiences or on-the-scene reporting. Weaving in facts and figures is extremely important. Don't fear they will destroy your scene-setting or mood writing. They strengthen it.

By investing money to buy your magazine and time to read what you write, readers appoint you their surrogate to witness events they cannot attend and to report developments beyond their reach. You must serve them with integrity and healthy, balanced skepticism. Look behind the obvious, uncover the bad as well as the good. Carefully qualify information you relay to readers. You're not obligated to discover truth; you *are* obligated to report facts.

Many wounds to your credibility as a writer can be self-inflicted. In reaching for color, you may scoop up too many adjectives, generalizations and wild exaggerations. Don't overwrite.

Acknowledging your limitations can add enormously to your credibility. If you don't know, say so. If you cannot reach a reasonable conclusion for your readers, level with them.

And, finally, before turning in your copy, check it for accuracy—then double- and triple-check it.

RECOMMENDED READING

As you incorporate into your own writing style some of the basics discussed in this chapter it's important that you read widely in the different styles featured by various magazines.

For a relatively hard, straightforward approach to current events, read the newsweeklies: *Time, Newsweek, U.S. News & World Report.* Note particularly their handling of the when, why and how elements. Each magazine has writers who are experts in pitching stories ahead and presenting background and analysis not found in all newspaper or TV writing.

The thought leaders—*Harper's Magazine* and *The Atlantic* among them—provide excellent examples of authoritative, in-depth writing that carries great credibility. *Esquire* and *Rolling Stone* are among our favorites for magazines that present often deeply analytical writing in a much more "swinging" style. Much of the writing in *Esquire* is a joy to read.

The complexity of public attitudes toward media credibility is discussed thoughtfully in "The People & The Press," a continuing study published by Times Mirror Center for The People & The Press, 1875 I Street NW, Suite 110, Washington, D.C., 20006. Other insights into public attitudes are in "Relating to Readers in the '80s," a survey commissioned by the American Society of Newspaper Editors and conducted by Clark, Martire & Bartolomeo, Inc., May 1984, and "Newspaper Credibility: Building Reader Trust," ASNE Research Report, 1985, P.O. Box 17004, Washington, D.C., 20041. Both concern primarily newspaper credibility problems, but nevertheless contain many valuable hints for magazine writers.

NOTES

1. Jennifer Conlin, "Coming to America," *Newsinc.*, Jan. 1991, 18.
2. Dominick Dunne, "Khashoggi's Fall," *Vanity Fair,* Sept. 1989, 245.
3. Robert Scheer, "The Further Adventures of Paul Newman," *Esquire*, Oct. 1989, 164.
4. Lisa Gubernick, "A Piece of Madonna?" *Forbes*, 22 July 1991, 16.
5. Julie Pitta, "Second Time Too Rich," *Forbes*, 5 Aug. 1991, 94.
6. Susan P. Shapiro, "Caution! This Paper Has Not Been Fact Checked. A Study of Fact Checking in American Magazines," Gannett Foundation Media Center, 1990.

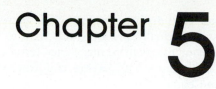

Chapter 5

Selecting and reporting your story

The moment of truth is here: It's time for you to start writing for publication, time to select a story idea, then report and shape it for a magazine.

In this chapter we'll give you some hints on taking your steps toward getting published. As we move ahead, keep in mind a couple of points.

First, this book and theoretical discussions of writing cannot make you a writer. *You* must make you a writer. You must generate story ideas, select target magazines, then gather, sift and evaluate information that will make your writing resonate with strength. Then, you must submit your story, that precious baby you've brought to life, to the judgment of editors.

Second, if you find all that daunting, remember that every professional writer (including the co-authors of this book) began right where you are—uncertain, not knowing where or how to start and perhaps even a little fearful of submitting to the critiques (and, maybe, humiliation) of editors. We could tell you not to worry about that, but we know you will, just as we did. Rather, we advise you to plunge into serious writing and try to get published despite the ego hits you're certain to receive. You'll be a better writer for it.

Whether you start as a free-lance writer or magazine staffer, you should recall fundamentals we discussed in the first four chapters of this book. Ignore them and you'll "write for the spike"—industry parlance for creating copy that editors are certain to kill or reject. Recall from Chapter One that somewhere in the incredibly diverse magazine industry is a publication for virtually any topic you want to write about. Remember, also, that readers seek many things from magazines but are particularly hungry for factual information on how to cope with careers, children, money, crime—life in general—as we discussed in Chapter Two.

And, as you create your strategy for getting published do remember the lessons of Chapters Three and Four: Whatever your story idea, your writing must be colorful, strong in its fundamentals and *engaging*. Unless you write with authority and credibility—possible only with careful reporting—you will be dismissed by readers and editors alike. Cover, as you must in basic newswriting, the *who, what, where, why, when* and *how*. But strive for the added dimension and grace that can make magazine copy sparkle.

Let's start with how you can select a story idea that's good for you and relevant to your target magazine. Then, we'll cover gathering information and interviewing sources to build the core of strong reporting that's so crucial to all successful writing.

HOW TO GENERATE STORY IDEAS

You don't know where to start searching for story ideas? Marshall Loeb, *Fortune*'s managing editor, provides a clue on where he gets some of his: "A good editor is a great thief, creatively appropriating ideas from just about anywhere."

Mind you, Loeb isn't suggesting plagiarism, and we certainly aren't, either. Rather, we are suggesting that even the glimmer of an idea arising from a book, a newspaper, a magazine article or a conversation with a friend can be expanded, adapted and shaped into your own publishable story idea.

Loeb's quote comes from an open letter he wrote to *Fortune* readers, explaining how his magazine came to do a stunningly effective piece, "The S&L Felons." The article profiled individuals who were involved in savings and loan association frauds and published their photographs. Loeb explained:

> When Executive Editor Allan Demaree wished aloud that he could see the faces of the villains in America's savings and loan debacle, he had in mind *Life* magazine's famous 1969 pictorial of the faces of one week's dead in Vietnam, and last year's stunning gallery in *Time* of a week's toll from guns in the United States. There's no comparing lost lives to stolen money, of course, but "The S&L Felons"—beginning on page 90—puts a human face on what may have been the white-collar crime wave of the century.[1]

So, do as the pros do: The moment you've finished reading this chapter (but not before, please!) find the largest magazine sales rack in town. Stand before it, study all those colorful covers clamoring at you, flip through many magazines—and let the story ideas flow.

Which magazines catch your attention?

Are you drawn to entertainment magazines because you're a rock music fan?

Do motorcycle magazines stand out because you ride a Honda?

Have you plucked a sports magazine from the rack because you're a sports nut?

You can match your personal interests and hobbies with specific magazines among the more than 11,000 in the marketplace. This is a *journey of self-discovery*—an exercise in thinking deeply about yourself, your strengths as a reporter and writer and your weaknesses (we all have them). The goal is to find subject areas where your current background knowledge and writing abilities can be best put to work.

This journey of self-discovery is one every successful writer must make. One of this text's co-authors made the journey 35 years ago when possessed by love of flying and writing. He has been doing both ever since, as a reporter and editor in chief of *Aviation Week & Space Technology*. It's the happiest of all circumstances when you tie your personal passions to your writing.

First Lesson: Explore Familiar Territory

For beginners, the first lesson in generating story ideas: Explore familiar territory. Don't try, first time out of the gate, for a story that will advance the world's understanding of, say, nuclear physics. If rock music is your thing, consider stories about that; if you are a fan of football, or chess, or jogging, or amateur theatricals—or whatever—think about how you can write on those subjects.

Be realistic about the salability of your expertise and the depth of your writing background.

For example, although you may have been a rock music fan since childhood, you may not be ready to knock *Rolling Stone* on its ear with the definitive story, written from University Town, U.S.A., about the worldwide evolution of rock music! *However,* you *may* be positioned perfectly to do a story for a local city magazine on how music interests are changing among your fellow students on campus.

Although you may not be ready to write for *Sports Illustrated* on the status of college football nationwide, you may be ready to write about *your* college's football team for the magazine section of a leading daily newspaper in your state.

Of course, it may be possible to score with a national magazine even as a beginner. Look for a local story angle that's yet unexplored by other writers or one that might signal a trend with nationwide application.

For example, there may be nationwide interest in your university's football scholarship program *if* your reporting uncovers new developments in how scholarship money is raised and spent—and *if* your writing highlights the meaning those developments have for universities elsewhere.

Perhaps you can stir wide interest in a story about how women at your university practice sports medicine in team sports, such as football or baseball, traditionally played by males. It may be a winning idea *if* this is a trend certain to spread to other universities.

How about a story on drug use and drinking at your university as a signal of changing habits among young people at universities everywhere? Is drug use, the terror of a generation of students and parents, down while drinking is up? If so, you may have a national story.

Second Lesson: Let Your Imagination Run

When hunting for story ideas we spend much time in front of magazine racks (our store manager doesn't mind; yours won't, either.) Come along with us on a hunting expedition.

Ah, there's an issue of *Fortune.* We flip through its pages and see a major piece, "How to Manage in a Recession." It's obviously aimed at business executives and doesn't offer much for a beginner writer at the university level. Right?

Well, don't be hasty. Let your imagination run. It's the "how-to" angle that catches our attention.

Let's see, if *Fortune* can offer how-to guidance for business managers, why can't you do a piece on … "how to stretch a student food budget," "how to plan a low-cost (but still enjoyable) spring break," "how to handle a disastrous love affair" (a *sure* winner).

Now you're rolling! Suddenly, a *Fortune* article aimed at a business audience probably foreign to you can help you generate local stories for an audience you know—your fellow students.

A bit deeper in the same *Fortune* we encounter "Why Washington Dismays CEOs." Not much for students in this article about chief executive officers, unless … "Why Our University Has a New Admissions Policy," "Why the Athletic Department …" or "Why the University Health Services. . . ." That is, take your lead from *Fortune* and ask "why" about any campus institution or policy important to a large number of students.

Still deeper in the same *Fortune* is "The Inside Story of the AIDS Drug." How about the "inside" story of university grading policies? Or, how (or whether) graduate teaching assistants are trained for the classroom? Still in the same *Fortune,* we encounter "Survival Tips for Travelers."[2] How about survival tips for students newly arrived on campus or how to survive when living alone for the first time in an off-campus apartment or how to survive exam pressure?

Hey! There's *Architectural Digest.* What ideas possibly could spin out of that magazine? Well, we see that writer Artemis Cooper visited actress Jane Seymour in Britain and lets us peek inside her fabulous country home.[3] How about a story for a campus magazine on the home of your university president? Or, how about visiting an old off-campus home (or store or farm or factory) for a piece for your local city magazine?

In the dentist's office, of all places, we pick up *McCall's* and see, "Ten Easy, At-Home Ways to Make Learning Fun," a story on how parents can enrich a child's formal education.[4] Nothing there for you, obviously. But wait. Do you realize how much parents worry about children being away at college, away from home for the first time?

How about an article, written from the student perspective, on 10 ways parents can prepare children to leave home? How about 10 hints on what clothing and appliances students will need at college? Or, how about 10 things parents should tell children about sex, drugs, alcohol and money before they go to college?

When you've looked at all the magazines on the sales rack (or when the store closes) you can turn your hunt for story ideas in other directions.

First, think deeply about what interests you. Success in school, love, job; good health, good grades, good eating; a high salary and low cost of living: If it interests you, it almost certainly interests others.

Second, listen to friends, classmates, strangers on a bus. What are they talking about? Do as the pros do: Key story ideas off the hopes, fears, dreams and interests of people around you. Magazines spend hundreds of thousands of dollars for reader research; you can do valuable audience research by listening.

Third, look for story ideas in contrasts: the oldest and youngest students on campus; the newest and oldest buildings; beauty and ugliness; good guys and bad guys; the expected and unexpected. Readers lust for something different, off-beat.

Fourth, remember the basic definitions of news: People are interested in timely writing about personalities, issues and things—conflict and events—that have impact on their lives. And look for *cruciality* in all that. News from afar about esoteric topics may be nice to have; information for your readers on how they can live better lives tomorrow—how they can survive in class, at work—can be crucial.

Fifth, look for the unusual, happy, even silly story about cute kids, pets (the "fuzzy puppy story"), people who succeed, people who make you laugh. Your readers, inundated by gloomy news, will bless your byline if you give them a good-all-over feeling, even if just for a few minutes!

FINDING A HOME FOR YOUR IDEA

When you've precisely shaped a story idea you must be equally precise in locating the right magazine for it. It's strange (*absurd,* really), but many writers don't do that.

Many writers refine a story idea from *their* standpoint and submit proposals that ignore the needs of the target magazine and its readers. Next stop: wastepaper basket.

You can get a quick idea of a magazine's content and, thus, how its editor likely will regard your idea by reading *Writer's Market,* published annually by Writer's

Digest Books, 1507 Dana Ave., Cincinnati, Ohio 45207. This reference work lists hints on how to sell book ideas, screen scripts and poetry as well as magazine pieces written for consumer magazines, special interest or trade journals and technical/professional publications. *Writer's Market* lists a publication's content, what its editors are looking for, how to submit story ideas and so forth.

Even better: carefully study your target magazine.

Study the Target Magazine's Audience

Some editors publish articles *they* like. Successful editors publish articles their *readers* like and need.

So, the more you know about your target magazine's audience, the better your chances of meshing successfully with its editor. There are two principal ways to get a fix on audiences.

First, examine the magazine's own audience research. This normally is in advertiser-oriented material variously called a media kit, marketing kit or advertiser's kit. The kits profile readers' ages, education and income levels, hobbies, consumer habits and so forth.

Second (and most importantly), examine the target magazine. Careful study of content will provide strong signals on which types of stories are covered and how they are angled or "pitched" for readers. Be certain your study goes beyond the obvious.

For example, all travel magazines don't have the same audiences and thus aren't markets for the same types of articles. A travel magazine that covers low-cost weekend trips or how to camp outdoors in a state park probably has an audience of relatively low-income readers. For them, you might write a story about piling the kids into the station wagon and enjoying a low-budget holiday.

A magazine featuring adventure travel in the Arctic and $50,000 African safaris probably has readers who are considerably higher on the income scale. Don't write for them an article on how to pitch a tent under the stars to save money.

Now, you might say all that is painfully obvious. Yet, editors receive many story proposals that are so ludicrously wide of the mark that it's clear the writers haven't even looked at the target magazine.

It's best to read a magazine for an extended period to develop a feel for its coverage. But simply flipping through back issues or tables of contents can give you enormously important insights into how editors judge their audiences' needs and desires.

Some magazines publish in their tables of contents explicit guides to their publishing strategies. Note how as a writer you can draw precise guidance on audience needs from this "Statement of Purpose" published by *Trilogy*:

> TRILOGY is an outdoor magazine that takes no editorial stands, promotes no single policy or idea over another, and has no axes to grind.
>
> Our goal is producing an interesting and informative magazine by providing glimpses of the outdoor world's delights and by creating a forum to air the wide range of ideas which provoke intense debates concerning the preservation and enjoyment of that outdoor world.
>
> The Recreation section focuses on outdoor adventures, travels, and travails on land, sea, and river. Challenging wild country can profoundly affect one's life. Probing the personal and spiritual rewards the outdoors can offer is key to this section.
>
> Information about preparing for outdoor treks is featured in the Green Pages, a catalog of experienced guides, outfitters, outdoor retailers, and other information geared to helping you make the most of your outdoor endeavors.
>
> Making sure there will be enough of the great outdoors to enjoy is the focus of three sections: Industry, Environment, and Opinion, where the TRILOGY forum truly comes to life.

Corporate America has had and continues to have a profound impact on the natural world. This section gives business a chance to explain, often in its own words, how it has or can promote or protect the outdoors.

The Environment section is as varied as its title has come to imply. Personal experiences and insights from outstanding non-profit organizations give readers colorful, detailed information about the day's pressing environmental issues, problems, and solutions.

The Opinion section gives everyone their due, whether it's an Earth First! member or the CEO of a major corporation.

Thus, TRILOGY seeks to give voice to those deeply concerned about the outdoor world we all enjoy, cherish, and want to pass on to future generations.[5]

Note that *Trilogy* obviously is a market for articles on environmental preservation, camping and adventure travel and the equipment used in hiking, climbing or boating. Close reading of similar statements of purpose or an editor's open letter to readers can provide helpful hints on how to market your story idea.

Do an article search in your library. The reference desk will show you how to use computerized systems for a quick rundown on subject matter published by major magazines. Learn whether your target magazine and its competitors have published stories similar to the one you have in mind.

Remember throughout this process that you must find a magazine audience whose needs and desires you reasonably can meet with your current reporting strengths and writing skills. Are you qualified to write for Arctic travelers who probably earn $100,000 or more annually? Or, should you start by writing for those weekenders on how you camped out under the stars in state parks, and how your readers, like you, can enjoy such inexpensive vacations? Be certain, also, to select stories you reasonably can research and report. Interviewing the state park ranger outside town is one thing; reaching the Arctic for firsthand reporting is quite another.

Study the Magazine's Writing Style

Look for two other things when studying a target magazine: (1) the story structures that published writers use, and (2) the overall tone of the magazine and its writing.

In sum, study the target magazine's writing style and consider whether your story idea and writing abilities seem compatible with published content.

For example, do the magazine's writers use many first-person structures ("how I backpacked through Montana")? Are there many how-to structures ("how you can backpack through Montana")? Are story structures "soft" or "featurish" and obviously designed as human-interest stories? Or are published stories "harder," close to the news and, really, expanded versions of the old standbys in newswriting, the Five W's and How?

Do published writers structure stories primarily around people or things? Are personality profiles featured? Or do writers more frequently profile products, services and corporations?

What length stories normally are published? Do stories normally stand alone, or are they often accompanied by graphs, charts and other sidebar material? Pay serious attention to how writers lace their stories together.

To understand a magazine's tone, search for subtleties, such as whether language is formal or informal. In use of vocabulary and technical terms, are writers pitching at an upscale audience? Or is the reader "Joe Sixpack"? Both are important audiences for magazines, and your challenge is to get on the right wavelength.

Let's look at the tone of stories we cited earlier in this chapter. First, note the intro of *Fortune*'s "Survival Tips for Travelers":

Peter Mayer, chairman of publisher Penguin Group, recently booked an overnight flight from New York to Paris on Air France, just so he could attend a meeting the next morning. Then, he says, "my secretary made reservations with two other airlines that were leaving about the same time." When he got to New York's JFK airport, he paid the cabdriver to wait outside a few minutes so that if a problem arose he could get to another terminal quickly. Good thing. The Air France plane was delayed five hours. He switched to TWA and made his meeting with time to spare.

Mayer's strategy is not one the airlines smile upon, but it represents the kind of extra steps managers are taking these days in a world of more—and often more hectic—business travel. Corporate travel has increased 48% in the past five years; the bill last year was $95 billion. Combine all that to-and-froing with airline deregulation around the world, and you can understand why executive travelers are developing new ways to cope with restrictive ticketing policies, increasingly congested airports, and what many consider a general deterioration of service. . . . (*Karen Freifeld, "Survival Tips for Travelers,"* Fortune, *5 Nov., 1990, 155*)

In the *Fortune* piece, the Peter Mayer vignette, though well crafted, is almost a, well, grudging concession to readability. It's terse, jammed into one paragraph. It almost shouts, "Let's get through this quickly and into the stuff that counts, the second-paragraph discussion of dollars and percentages."

Lesson: If writing for a magazine that features *Fortune*-type writing, strive for human-interest intros but quickly get into businesslike discussion of details that are operative for executives.

Next, consider the tone of the *McCall's* story on home learning:

Relax. This is one list of ideas for ways to enrich your child's education that has nothing to do with flash cards, spelling bees or turning the dining room into a classroom. You will find no schedules, no charts, no goals and objectives here.

What you will find are creative and enjoyable ways to inspire your child with the love for learning. . . . (*Anita Diamant, "Ten Easy, At-Home Ways to Make Learning Fun,"* McCall's, *Sept. 1991, 70*)

Notice the informal tone ("Relax.") and how the writer uses "you" to establish rapport with her readers. Lesson: If you write for *McCall's* you should strive for an easy, flowing style that makes even the most technical information *palatable* for readers.

Now, read the following from *Boating* and decide which writing style you would need to appeal to the magazine's editors:

I guess the guys standing out in front of the Dockside Marina Ship's Store in Morehead City, North Carolina, were impressed with one thing more than any other—speed. The new Fountain 47' Sport Cruiser is fassssssssst. When, in response to the single most often asked question associated with high-performance-Boat-Test confab, I told them I'd just measured a two-way average top end of 70 mph, you could taste the silence, it was so dang piquant.

Didn't last long, though. A grandfather-type, with a bluewater tan and an RC Cola clutched in a massive fist, emitted a low, long whistle of astonishment, the sound of which had a dual effect: 1) It emphasized, in a guys-hanging-around-a-dock sort of way, just how much full-throttle excitement Reggie Fountain is capable of building into his boats and 2) it caused Bob, a middle-aged coonhound strolling by at the time, to short-circuit his ramblings and add his sloppy grin to the assemblage. . . . (*Bill Pike, "Triple XXXtasy,"* Boating, *Oct. 1991, 56*)

Boating editors obviously like first-person "I" stories written with a slangy, irreverent tone ("I guess the guys," "an RC Cola clutched in a massive fist," etc.) But beneath the wise-guy surface of this story is a serious undercurrent: A new Sport Cruiser has been tested at high speed and reported on with precise technical detail. (Question: What do you think about writer Pike's use of "piquant" in his first graf? Yes, we know you understand the word means "agreeably stimulating to the taste" or "pleasantly biting." But, do you think *Boating*'s readers generally know that? And, do you find that rather, well, elegant word somewhat out of place in the story's overall slangy environment?)

Okay. You've refined a story idea, selected a target magazine and studied that magazine's content and style. What's next? You should contact the magazine's editor. If your idea is unacceptable, you can quickly get on to something else—another story idea or editor. If your idea is acceptable, the editor will want to help you shape it, specify length and so forth. This process of approaching editors is so important that we must devote all of Chapter Nine to it. So, let's move to researching a story.

RESEARCHING YOUR STORY

A common error among beginner writers is believing good writing is mainly flashy writing. It's not.

Above all, good writing is clear, straightforward presentation of accurate, well-researched information that's important to your readers. Good writing communicates effectively.

Of course, writers who handle the language with skill and subtlety, who weave in color, who sketch vibrant and lasting word pictures—these writers communicate most effectively because they make it easy, even fun, for their readers to absorb and understand information. So, whether you intend to communicate facts, ideas, moods or whatever, in "hard" or "soft" stories, you'll do your job best with graceful writing that takes full advantage of the beauty and the majesty of our language.

Beneath it all, however, must be factual substance based on thorough reporting and research.

Even Tom Wolfe, a great stylist, says reporting is "the most valuable and least understood resource available to any writer with exalted ambitions. . . ."

Wolfe, author of many magazine articles and books, puts it this way: "I doubt that there is a writer over forty who does not realize in his heart of hearts that literary genius, in prose, consists of proportions more on the order of 65 percent material and 35 percent the talent in the sacred crucible."[6]

Organizing the Hunt for Substance

Two realities must guide your research and reporting.

First, your problem is not finding information. The writer's world is awash in information. Your problem is locating the right information, separating what is *crucial* to your readers from what is not.

Second, a writer's most important expendable asset is *time*. Don't waste it in a disorganized, helter-skelter pursuit of information.

In organizing your research strategy, think through what you've already learned about your target magazine. If its content is technical (*Boating*), you'll obviously need to research detail such as engine specifications, speeds and so forth. If your target magazine features musings on the great outdoors (*Trilogy*), you'll perhaps need to focus research in other directions.

Warning: Don't focus so precisely in advance that you overlook or ignore new, unexpected information you will inevitably encounter in your reporting rounds. Cast your reporting net more widely and you often will end up with a story quite different from—and better than—the one you started out to get.

Jot down answers to these questions:

- What core ideas do you envisage developing in your story (for example, 10 things freshmen should know about drugs, sex and alcohol on your campus)?
- What information do you already know you will need to build those core ideas (statistics on drug use, or the incidence of sexually transmitted diseases)?

- What obvious local sources are available for such information (for example, campus police on number of drug busts and your university health center on incidence of sexually transmitted diseases)?
- What is the wider context of your story (nationwide patterns of drug abuse, or national figures on sexually transmitted diseases among college-age people)?

In the scenario above, start your research by building a wider context of national statistics. It's obvious, isn't it: Unless you understand nationwide trends you cannot understand the significance of a six percent increase on campus. And unless your writing casts your story against national averages, your readers won't know the importance of what you report about your campus. Note, also, that when you establish a nationwide context you have a good story regardless of what is happening locally: The incidence of on-campus disease will be higher, lower or the same as national averages, and that's a story!

Now, how can you locate the statistics you need?

Ask somebody!

It's not that the figures aren't on paper somewhere or readily available in some university or government computer. They are. But where among the library's millions of books and documents? In which of the thousands of state and federal computers?

Ask the authoritative source where to begin your search: the health service director or your library's research desk, for example. Even if those sources don't know, they can direct you toward someone who does, and perhaps in minutes, not hours or days, you'll be telephoning the Federal Centers for Disease Control in Atlanta, where nationwide statistics are compiled, or leafing through the *Statistical Abstract of the United States,* the Census Bureau's annual report on an astonishingly wide variety of facts about America.

The Library: A Writer's Best Friend

Good writing obviously must take readers beyond what they already know as well as beyond what already has been written.

Your initial research, therefore, must have *two* missions: (1) building the wider context, and (2) acquainting you with what other writers have done on the subject so you can use their work as a platform to leap ahead into new territory. Inevitably, all this will pull the serious writer into a library.

In books, periodicals and computerized services, your library has a treasure of research materials. Some essential ones include:

1. *Readers' Guide to Periodical Literature.* This lists recent articles in well over 100 periodicals.
2. *The Encyclopedia Britannica* or *Encyclopedia Americana.* Authoritative sources for getting quickly up to speed in a multitude of subjects.
3. *Statistical Abstract of the United States*
4. *Information Please Almanac* and other almanacs are mostly published annually and will give you current figures in many subject areas. Note specialized publications, such as *Almanac of American Politics.*
5. *The National Newspaper Index.* This lists articles in a number of major newspapers, including *The New York Times* and *The Wall Street Journal.* Note also individual newspaper indexes; *The Times'* is superb. Newspapers generally are stored in microfilm.
6. *Magazine Index.* An index of nearly 500 magazines. Periodicals are on microfilm.
7. *Nexis.* A computerized database providing, among other things, timely access to current articles from newspapers, magazines, newsletters and news

services. Other databases are accessible via *CompuServe, Dialog, Newsnet, Dow Jones News Service* and similar computerized services.

8. *Facts on File: A Weekly World News Digest.* For the off-beat, don't overlook such reference works as *Guinness Book of World Records.*

9. *Who's Who.* Gives you the names of sources on an international, national or regional level—or by expertise. This is a *must* stopping point before you interview important sources. Also check *Current Biography.*

10. *Directories in Print.* So many directories are published that you may need this guide to find those pertinent to your research!

11. *Index to U.S. Government Periodicals.* Points you to hundreds of reports, research articles and newsletters issued by the federal government. Periodicals are available through the Office of the Superintendent of Documents, U.S. Government Printing Office, Washington, D.C.

12. *The United States Government Manual.* Lists federal agencies, boards, committees and so forth, with descriptions of activities and key officials.

13. *Standard & Poor's Register of Corporations, Directors and Executives.* Your starting point for researching corporate America.

14. *The Encyclopedia of Associations.* Lists organizations (including some dealing with drug abuse and sexually transmitted diseases).

A few more research hints:

- Most universities have specialty libraries for science, law, medicine and so forth. Use them when your research focus takes you deeply into subject specialties.

- Stay current on what your library is doing to make data available via new on-line computer services (which report now what was reported by news services just seconds ago) and on CD/ROM, or compact disc/read-only memory. CD/ROM technology makes huge volumes of data available on single discs and enables you to summon in seconds on a computer screen what otherwise might involve hours in library stacks.

- Learn to leap ahead, not toddle, in your research: Use almanacs or directories for clues, for example, encyclopedias for background, then move quickly to *Readers' Guide* or *Nexis* to learn what's been written on your subject and *Who's Who* to locate sources for interviews. Conserve that valuable asset, time.

Now It's Time to Reassess

With basic library research completed, you must consider two factors.

First, has your original story idea been proven valid? Or did your research reveal another writer already exploited it? Did your idea prove weak, insufficiently interesting or lacking current developments you can carry ahead? If so, kill the idea. Don't waste your time or an editor's on an unpromising idea.

Second, if you are still "go" on every aspect of your original idea answer this checklist:

- Is the original idea precisely one you still want to pursue? Or did your research show a story on drug abuse and sexually transmitted diseases would be too broad? Should you refocus your idea to concentrate on, say, drug abuse alone?

- Does it appear the story approach you envisaged (10 things freshmen should know) still is elusive? Was your approach featured recently in both *McCall's* and *Time*? If so, change your direction.

- Did your research reconfirm your original belief that certain core ideas must be treated in your article? Or should the internal dynamics of your story be adjusted to cover other issues as well?

- Has your research widened your understanding (through national statistics on drug abuse, for example) of your topic? Will you be able to evaluate local input in proper perspective?
- Did your research into background information and existing published articles provide a platform from which you can leap ahead, into new, unexplored territory? Can you now identify new developments to explore? Can you see new angles that will give your article special sparkle?
- Can you list issues yet to explore, questions to ask, sources to contact—and sketch all that out in an orderly, efficient plan?

If you answer affirmatively to the checklist above you're ready for the next—and most important—tool in any writer's research.

INTERVIEWING: YOUR TOOL FOR SUCCESS

Whatever your topic, no matter what your library search reveals, you can't make your writing really sing without presenting original, firsthand information. There are two principal ways to accomplish this.

First, you can write in real-life, first-person detail about your own experience or what you witness. Whether it's how you shot the rapids, broke a drug habit or were converted from rock to country music, telling your own story can lend enormous strength to your writing. Problem: Most of us have few firsthand experiences of compelling interest to readers (other than our mothers). So, unfortunately, you're limited in how many times you can use the how-I-did-it or how-I-survived-it formula.

Second, however, you can structure writing with great appeal by extracting authoritative detail or describing human drama from the lives of others. That means developing the ability to locate people sources, then persuade, cajole, sweet-talk and sometimes manipulate them into revealing information you need. (Interviewing also is essential, obviously, when you're writing personality profiles. More on that in Chapter Six.)

How important is interviewing? We say without reservation that it's a major difference between an amateur and a professional, between success and failure as a writer. If you don't like talking to people, if you cannot—or do not want to—interview people, you're in the wrong business.

But, how to get people to talk to you?

How to Develop Sources

Anybody can be an important source, of course, and many successful writers have war stories about how they unexpectedly received crucial information from the most unlikely sources. Lesson: Regard everyone you meet, even casually, as a potential source.

Realistically, however, you must develop sources and you have limited time to do so. Work smart; go about the task with great care. Your primary goal must be to develop not just any sources but, rather, those who are authoritative and positioned to know what you need to know.

Locating sources is relatively simple if you're a magazine staffer assigned to a beat or are a free-lancer specializing in one or two subjects. Over time, you'll discover who really has expert knowledge in your field and who has power over money, people, events, ideas and so on. But don't seek sources in only the obvious places, among presidents, vice presidents and others with titles on their doors and rugs on their floors. Look for *assistant* vice presidents, clerks, secretaries—anyone in a position to know what's happening. Watch particularly for whistle-blowers, disaffected or public-spirited persons who want to expose hidden news.

Cultivating sources can be harder than locating them. It takes planning and expert people skills. We think these factors should guide your "care and feeding" of sources:

First, you must be willing to devote time and energy to personal contacts, to work at the task, even if that involves drinking a lot of poor coffee (leisurely, without signaling impatience) and listening to lousy jokes. If reporting is most of what successful writers do (and it is), developing sources is mostly what reporting is about.

Second, you must demonstrate professional credibility as a serious writer who knows a subject—or is willing to learn. Whatever their specialty, the sources you need are serious about it. Talk flippantly about science, and you can strike off scientists as sources; write inaccurate, unbalanced articles about sports, and coaches and players alike will dry up; write superficially about politics, and serious politicians will avoid you.

Third, you must demonstrate you are personally honorable and reliable. That means never breaking your word to sources, never betraying a confidence, never promising anonymity and then naming your sources. If word gets around that your promises are worthless, you are dead. (And don't lightly promise anonymity. You may have the choice someday, in a libel suit, of breaking that promise or going to jail under a contempt citation. More on this later.)

Fourth, keep your source relationships on a professional level. Don't forget why you contact and "stroke" them: You are after information. Get too friendly with sources, and you may start subconsciously pulling your punches to avoid embarrassing them in print.

When you develop sources, keep their current addresses, telephone numbers and subject expertise in a source notebook. It can become one of your most valuable assets throughout your career. Assistant secretaries, who may not generate news, grow up to be cabinet secretaries, who do; assistant coaches, who don't draft game plans, sometimes become head coaches, who do. If you maintain source relationships, many can be "activated" and become valuable years later.

You face a tough challenge in moving "cold" into a new subject area, trying to find sources among experts who don't know you.

Often, library research will at least give you names to pursue. Don't overlook other sources, such as university information bureaus, which often keep lists of campus experts willing to talk with reporters on a variety of topics. Dealing through public relations offices may be necessary. But remember: Some PR executives make a living steering reporters *away* from controversial news, sanitizing it or offering up spokespersons who can present it in the "best" terms.

Some PR officials can be helpful, but if you talk with enough people, you usually can go directly to the sources you need. Good telephone openers: "I'm calling at the suggestion of Prof. John Jones who says you're an expert in . . ." or "I'm writing an article for *City Magazine* and would like to talk to you about. . . ."

Even if you're unknown to the source, Prof. Jones' referral or *City Magazine*'s credibility may give you something you can ride into an interview.

Persuading reluctant sources to submit to an interview and share their expertise is an art you can develop only with experience. Here, for starters, are a few techniques we've used:

- If the source is involved in controversy, the get-on-the-record argument: "I have the viewpoints of those who disagree with you, and I want to put your position on record."
- The you-owe-it-to-your-art argument: "Biology (or modern dance or higher education or whatever) is under attack these days and you could help me give the public the other side."

■ The help-me-before-I-make-an-error argument: "Your specialty, biology, is complicated and, frankly, I need your help on a couple of points to make sure I don't misrepresent your discipline (and, by extension, you) to the reading public."

You'll need to visit the source. Trying to get meaningful information from a "cold" source via telephone won't work most of the time. The source may set time and place—probably an office—for the interview, of course, but if you have a choice, opt for a site (such as the source's home) and a time (maybe a weekend) that promise a long interview, if you need it, in relaxing surroundings. Interviewing sources in a bouncing taxi speeding to the airport or while gobbling a 15-minute lunch may be necessary, but often is unrewarding.

"Psyching Up" for an Interview

Going into an interview confident, well prepared and emotionally "up" is crucial to your success. To gain confidence, you can do several things:

First, prepare. Then prepare some more. Learn all you can about the subject *and source.* Check *Who's Who* and sources who know the source. Look for insights into professional credentials and personal background. You gain enormous advantage by knowing more about the topic than the source thinks you know. And consider your advantage if you know the source is a fanatic Chicago Cubs fan—and you are one, too (or can quickly become one!).

Second, plan an interview strategy. Keep these factors in mind:

■ Prepare more questions than you think you'll need. A 30-minute appointment can turn into a two-hour session. Go equipped with a list of things to talk about.

■ Ruthlessly eliminate from your list questions you should answer in the library. You'll antagonize expert sources by wasting their time asking elementary questions (such as asking a broker what "equities" are or a coach what "red-shirted freshman" means.)

■ Jot down topics you can explore for *news,* for fresh developments that will carry your writing into unexplored territory. How can you go beyond what's already published? Prepare to stimulate, lure, entice, even anger your source into revealing what you need.

■ Plan carefully the order for asking questions. Plan to first throw a few gentle softball questions to warm up the source, then to edge into hard-news or controversial areas before finally moving into questions that might upset the source and terminate the interview. It's an old rule: Save the toughest questions until your notebook is chock-full of most everything you need.

■ Whatever it takes to get yourself ready for a challenge, do it. Drink black coffee, recite your mantra, jog around the block—psyche up to *win.*

How to Win at Interviewing

The initial moments of an interview are crucial to your eventual success. Be particularly alert in two areas.

First, read carefully any signals on how comfortable your interviewee is with the process. "News-wise" sources, such as politicians or others used to being interviewed, may signal, "C'mon, let's get started." Other people, however, are literally terrified at being quoted in a magazine, and with them you must proceed ever so gently.

Second, you must use the early minutes to establish the ground rules and take command of the interview. We suggest this approach for openers:

- Open low-key (chat about the Chicago Cubs, for example) until you sense your interviewee is relaxed or ready to proceed.
- Quickly weave in your purpose: "I'm doing an article on student drug abuse for *City Magazine,* as I explained on the telephone, and I understand you are an expert I can quote." There! This interview is on the record and the interviewee will be quoted.
- Keep notebook and pen out of sight until the conversation develops an important fact or quotation, then say something like, "Let me be sure I get that down accurately." You now can bring out the tools of your trade in a non-threatening manner and also show you're a serious journalist who wants to be accurate.
- Many writers use a tape recorder to catch complicated material in lengthy interviews. But remember that although a tape recorder might not frighten some sources who are interviewed frequently (indeed, officials might bring their own), that little black box could frighten some unsophisticated sources witless. If you use a tape recorder, pull it out with another statement of your professionalism: "Let me use this just to make sure I quote you accurately."
- Take control of the interview. You can't do this by sinking your head into your notebook, breaking eye contact and furiously scribbling notes on everything said. That makes you a stenographer, not a reporter, and you'll walk out having only listened. You must learn to direct the interview through questions, breaking eye contact only to write down key facts or quotes.

Juggling questions, answers, note-taking and simultaneously adjusting your interview strategy can be learned only through experience. You may do miserably first time out; almost everybody does. Be of good cheer. You'll learn.

Broadly, you can use these types of questions:

Open-ended questions are general and designed to let the interviewee ramble a bit: "Tell me your views on the city's drug-abuse program" or "Explain how you feel about current trends in drug abuse on campus." The strength of such questions is that the interviewee may respond with new, important information you didn't expect. The weakness is that the interviewee can talk non-stop unless you regain control.

Closed questions are designed to elicit specific information and reassert your control: "Will you testify Wednesday in the City Council's hearing on drug abuse?" or "In which year did you detect the new trend in drug abuse?"

Follow-up questions are aimed at probing more deeply into a topic: "Exactly what do you mean by that?" or "Please give me details on that."

Yes-or-no questions will pin down the interviewee: "But isn't that contrary to what you testified last week?" or "Do you believe, yes or no, in legalizing marijuana?" Warning: Even though you ask yes-or-no questions gently the interviewee might perceive them as entrapment—and your interview might be terminated.

Be careful, also, with two other types of questions: *leading questions* ("Don't you agree Smith is wrong?") and *loaded questions* ("Is Smith a fool?") Both can be unethical and, because they easily anger people, counterproductive. Obviously, however, leading and loaded questions sometimes can be used to prod a reticent source into "opening up."

Throughout, watch for audible and body language signals from the interviewee. A quick shift in tone of voice or the conversation or shifting in the chair may indicate the interviewee is attempting to avoid a controversial topic. Conversely, some interviewees signal they *want* you to ask certain questions. It's curious, but even people who desperately want to reveal information sometimes don't feel right about simply volunteering it. They want you to ask.

If the subject evades your question or the answer is inadequate, circle the point—ask the question another way or come back to it later. Even a question that's evaded can start the interviewee thinking, and you might get what you need next time around. For this reason, always conclude an interview by asking, "Is there anything else you want to tell me?" or "Is there anything else I need to know for this story?" Finally, get the source's permission and telephone number for a follow-up call if you later discover you need additional information.

Two Tough Questions for You

This is how it happens: You're shaking hands, thanking the interviewee for his or her time and heading for the door, secretly gleeful because you've just tucked a dynamite story into your notebook. Then, the interviewee asks:

"This interview is off the record, isn't it?" or "You'll let me see the article before it's published, won't you?"

You now can stand on principle, say "no" and continue heading for the door. After all, you laid down on-the-record ground rules at the beginning of the interview and you have every right to insist they be followed.

Of course, anybody who has ever reported and written for a living will tell you such an abrupt "no" likely will cost you a source—perhaps a valuable source who could be used repeatedly in the future on more important stories. So, we suggest diplomatic efforts to disentangle yourself:

- First, try the smile-and-kidding approach: "C'mon, you know we agreed this is on the record."
- If that doesn't work, consider just how valuable this source is, and perhaps offer a compromise: "I'll give you a call and check any direct quotes or important facts to make sure I got everything down accurately," or "I'll let you read for factual accuracy."
- If this valuable source still insists, you might have to cave in. Many writers (we are among them) will acknowledge they've been trapped that way. But you shouldn't let the same source do it to you twice.

However you resolve such a dilemma, we recommend against letting the source censor your copy before publication. If you do, you've lost control of your own keyboard.

ORGANIZING YOUR INFORMATION

If you've researched and reported your story properly and interviewed enough sources, you'll have much more information than you can jam into any single article.

Don't panic.

With experience, you'll learn to sift and evaluate information, assigning priorities and holding it in an accessible system for later use. Some writers transfer salient points to index cards; others fill boxes or computers with interview transcripts and background files.

Of course, over time you'll develop your own system, as do all writers. We have a few hints.

First, never leave an interview or the library without quickly evaluating salient points that stick in your mind. Trust your instincts. Write down the three or four most important facts you've uncovered. What's important to you likely will be important to readers. Discard or file away secondary material.

Reevaluate your priorities the next day, and juggle the list in accordance with what, in the light of a new dawn, now seems important. What facts are missing? What holes remain in your research?

Periodically throughout the research process, evaluate each day's yield and reflect on what is emerging as most important overall. Begin shaping in your mind how you must structure your article to transmit core ideas to readers. Do you have a people story that will need a human-interest approach? Or, must this story hang on cold, dispassionate facts and figures?

If you've researched your topic fully and thought deeply about information that you have, the story structure you need will begin to emerge almost automatically in your mind. We turn to that in Chapter Six.

SUMMARY

To get started writing for publication, see if you can match your personal interests with magazines on your supermarket's sales rack. Leaf through those that interest you—entertainment magazines if you like music, motorcycle publications if you ride a Honda—and let your imagination run. Story ideas will pop out.

Explore familiar territory, such as stories you can do on campus for local magazines and audiences you understand. Consider what interests you. Success in school, love or job; good grades, good eating: If it interests you, it likely interests others. Listen to what friends talk about and look for stories in contrasts—old versus young, beauty versus ugliness, good versus bad. Remember that readers like timely writing about personalities, issues and things—conflict and events—with impact on their lives.

Finding a home for your story idea involves carefully studying target magazines. Read a magazine's media kit for insights into its audience, and examine which types of stories it publishes and how they are angled.

Note particularly a magazine's story structures and overall writing tone. Learn all you can about a magazine before submitting your idea to its editor.

Beginner writers sometimes believe good writing is mainly flashy writing. It isn't. Above all, good writing is clear, straightforward communication of accurate, well-researched information that's important to readers.

Researching is a hunt for substance. That requires sorting through a sea of information for facts crucial to readers. Plan your search to avoid wasting your most important expendable asset, time.

The library is a writer's best friend. Use it to research a wider context for a local story—collecting, for example, national figures on drug abuse as background for a story about drugs on your campus.

After initial library research, reassess whether your original idea still is valid. If not, kill the idea.

If the idea is valid, consider whether it must be refocused. Do you need to change directions? List core ideas to be explored, obvious sources to contact, questions to be answered.

Successfully interviewing sources is key to any writer's success. You can extract authoritative detail and human drama from the lives of others to strengthen your writing.

Writers must spend lots of time developing sources, then polishing their interview skills. It's important to go into an interview knowledgeable about the topic and interviewee. You need a carefully drafted strategy ensuring that you, not the interviewee, will control the interview.

If you've done your reporting and interviewing properly, you'll have much more information than any article can contain. Carefully evaluate the yield of each day's research and assign priorities to the four or five most important facts you've uncovered. You then are ready to structure your article.

RECOMMENDED READING

To learn how professional reporters pry news out of sources, watch televised news conferences and read transcripts of conferences published in *The New York Times* and other newspapers. Note the subtleties of question asking: Some reporters score with indirect, soft questions; others extract news with direct, aggressive questions. Note particularly how follow-up questions often yield important information that doesn't come out of responses to initial questions.

An excellent text on how to research an article is Lauren Kessler and Duncan McDonald, *The Search: Information Gathering for the Mass Media* (Belmont, Calif.: Wadsworth, 1992). Note also, Shirley Biagi, *Interviews That Work,* 2d ed. (Belmont, Calif.: Wadsworth, 1992).

One of the strongest presentations of reporter techniques is John Ullmann and Steve Honeyman, *The Reporter's Handbook: An Investigator's Guide to Documents and Techniques* (New York, N.Y.: St. Martin's Press, 1983).

NOTES

1. Marshall Loeb, "Editor's Desk," *Fortune,* 5 Nov. 1990, 4. The story, "S&L Felons," by Alan Farnham, appeared on page 90 of that issue.
2. All articles cited were in the 5 Nov. 1990, issue of *Fortune.*
3. Artemis Cooper, "*Architectural Digest* Visits: Jane Seymour," *Architectural Digest,* Jan. 1991, 112.
4. Anita Diamant, "Ten Easy, At-Home Ways to Make Learning Fun," *McCall's,* Sept. 1991, 70.
5. Table of Contents, *Trilogy,* Nov./Dec. 1991, 5.
6. Tom Wolfe, "Stalking the Billion-Footed Beast," *Harper's Magazine,* Nov. 1989, 45.

Chapter 6

Story form
and
structure (I)

Well, you've selected and researched your story idea, interviewed sources, and your notebook is full.

What now?

You could start writing, of course. But if you did, which direction would you take? Which story form or genre would best tell your tale? How would you shape the structure of your story?

Obviously, you've got some heavy planning to do *before* you start writing. Consider:

- What type of information must you communicate? Hard facts? Or soft, entertaining information?
- Who is your audience? Experts seeking quick transfusions of how-to-cope information? Or casual—even reluctant—readers who must be wooed into your story?
- Frankly (*very* frankly), are your writing skills strong enough to handle a highly complex story form, or at this stage in your growth as a writer should you stick with something simple and straightforward?

Only when you answer those questions can you decide which story form and structure will best help you reach that wondrous goal of communicating clearly and effectively with readers.

In Chapter Six, we turn to some of the story forms and structures available to you. There are many, of course, and we think you'll be able to find several suitable for your current writing abilities.

Caution: Don't feel limited to the genres and structures we describe in pages ahead. For certain, don't take too literally our sketches illustrating various structures. They're merely our attempt to help you generate your own ideas for structuring an article. We suggest you follow only one rule in designing a story structure: If it works, use it!

THOUGHTS TO STRUCTURE BY

Whatever your audience or the information you must communicate, structure your story with several thoughts in mind.

First, in writing for general-circulation consumer magazines your structure should emphasize people—what they do, what is done to them. Good science writing for those magazines isn't about science; it's about people in science and how science affects people. To communicate sports news or the most esoteric economic or business information, find the people and structure to highlight them. (A depersonalized "nuts-and-bolts" approach may be appropriate for technical magazines. More on that later.)

Second, imagine how you would tell your story to a friend. The admonition to "write like you talk" is nonsense, of course. You need only listen carefully to how many people talk to understand that precisely replicating conversational structure in writing would leave magazines a jumbled, disjointed, slangy mess. Nevertheless, the conversational flow of "telling" your story may help you identify the most logical structure for your writing.

Third, design your story so you carefully parcel out facts, figures, technical terms, concepts and characters that readers might have difficulty absorbing. Push too much difficult information at readers too quickly and they'll choke—or stop reading. But parcel out manageable bites and you'll pull readers deeply into your story. And do remember that your research probably has turned you into something of a semi-expert in the subject. What to you is a manageable flow might overwhelm readers being introduced to your subject for the first time. Pace your writing to match *their* likely ability to absorb facts, not yours.

Fourth, structure to highlight clearly the core ideas your research showed are essential. That means ruthlessly discarding bits of secondary information that will camouflage your central meaning if left draped all over your story structure. To communicate particularly difficult ideas you can structure in a bit of circularity, returning to the same issue several times and explaining it differently. This requires delicate handling, obviously; glaring repetition will bore readers.

Let's look at various story structures that will accomplish all that.

The News/Informational Structure

In writing for some trade magazines or newsweeklies, you'll be working close to breaking news, although not as close as in daily newspaper or broadcast writing. And your readers will expect story structures that enable them to get to the news quickly and absorb it easily.

In basic newswriting, the solution to that challenge, of course, is the old standby, the inverted pyramid. You'll recall it looks like this:

FIGURE 6–1 Inverted-Pyramid Structure

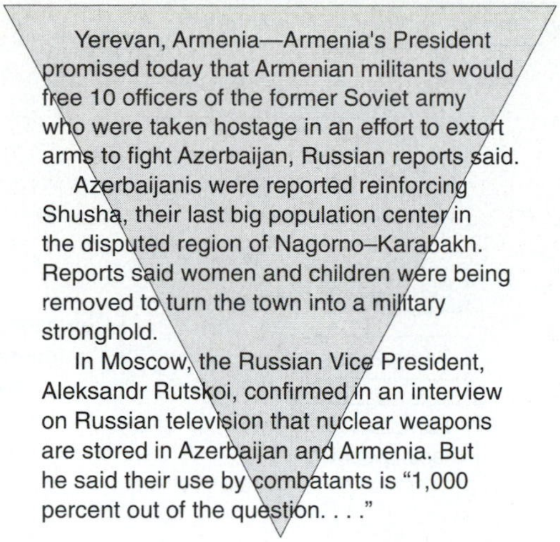

Yerevan, Armenia—Armenia's President promised today that Armenian militants would free 10 officers of the former Soviet army who were taken hostage in an effort to extort arms to fight Azerbaijan, Russian reports said.

Azerbaijanis were reported reinforcing Shusha, their last big population center in the disputed region of Nagorno–Karabakh. Reports said women and children were being removed to turn the town into a military stronghold.

In Moscow, the Russian Vice President, Aleksandr Rutskoi, confirmed in an interview on Russian television that nuclear weapons are stored in Azerbaijan and Armenia. But he said their use by combatants is "1,000 percent out of the question. . . ."

The Associated Press dispatch for morning newspapers, March 12, 1992.

As you'll note in Figure 6–1, the inverted pyramid presents crucial facts in the first paragraph, then laces others together in descending order of importance in subsequent paragraphs. This hard-news structure, one of the oldest in journalism, remains popular with newspaper editors because it permits them to "chop from the bottom" if, under deadline pressure, they must trim stories to fit the available "news-hole."

We don't use the inverted pyramid much in magazine writing because, obviously, a weekly or monthly periodical mostly trails daily newspapers in reaching readers with hard-news facts. That requires us to write differently, to overlay the news in our stories with analysis and interpretation, and the inverted pyramid isn't the best structure for that. But the inverted pyramid isn't popular in magazine writing for another reason: Its straightforward nature virtually eliminates any possibility of achieving the flowing grace and rhythm that must differentiate magazine writing from the frequently breathless, bang-bang writing of daily journalism.

Nevertheless, you can use news/informational structures for close-to-the-news magazine articles like this:

Spinoffs are fast becoming the way to boost magazine franchises and introduce new magazine ideas during the recession.

With Hearst Corp., K-III Magazine Corp., Meredith Corp., The New York Times Co. Magazines, Time Inc. Magazine Co. and Walt Disney Co. all joining the trend, the proliferation of spinoffs underscores the new cautiousness in publishing.

Most such line extensions are introduced as one-shots or annuals, so publishers can make them disappear fairly quietly if unsuccessful. And they're less expensive to produce.

Also, with the link to an established book, it's easier to gain advertiser support for a spinoff.

"The cost of the raw start-up is very high, and the willingness to gamble on that in October of 1991 isn't as exciting as it was two years ago," said John Mack Carter, director of magazine development at Hearst. . . . (*Scott Donaton, "Magazine Spinoffs Take Off," Advertising Age, 28 Oct. 1991, 20*)

The structure of this story could be sketched not as an inverted pyramid but, rather, like Figure 6–2.

Note the Figure 6–2 structure is perfect for a survey or trend article, for pulling together informational bits and pieces that are developing independently. When as-

FIGURE 6–2 Possible Structure for a Survey or Trend Article

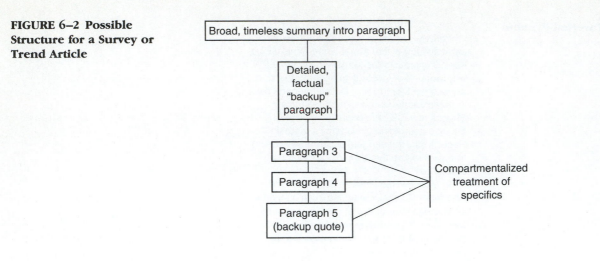

sembled in one piece, they show a meaningful trend is under way—in this case, that spinoff magazines are being launched.

Basic elements of a survey article include:

1. A lead that pulls together pieces of a developing puzzle or spotlights a trend. In the *Ad Age* example, it's likely each magazine company announced independently it was launching spinoffs; writer Donaton alertly puts those announcements together and brings to his readers news of a trend. A survey lead often is timely but timeless—that is, close to new developments and written in present tense but not "pegged" to a specific time element ("... sources said today" or "... it became apparent on Tuesday").

2. A detailed backup graf or two to support the lead. You've cheated your readers if you don't give them evidence of the trend or development you've highlighted in your lead (in the *Ad Age* lead, "Spinoffs are fast becoming"...). Note: The backup graf doesn't work if inserted deep in the story. It must be high, close to the main thrust of the lead.

3. Substantive specifics, high in the story, of the lead's core thought. Writer Donaton provides that, in part, with John Mack Carter's quote. And in subsequent grafs, which we don't have space to reproduce, the writer quickly inserts other specifics, including plans by *Country Home* to spin off two magazines, *Country Gardens* and *Country Traveler*.

You'll recognize, of course, that facts are stacked in descending order of importance in the preceding *Ad Age* story. Thus, the story, like an inverted-pyramid story, can be trimmed from the bottom. That's why some trade magazine editors, often rushing against weekly deadlines, favor that story structure. They, like their newspaper colleagues, sometimes must chop from the bottom.

The news/informational structure can be particularly valuable if you're writing on timely topics for the weekend or Sunday magazine section of a local newspaper or for a monthly magazine.

For example, the structure is perfect for pulling together bits and pieces of campus crimes or accidents in recent weeks. Let the campus daily paper report each crime as it occurs; you then can move in with the news/informational structure, pull together, say, a month's worth of bits and pieces—and illustrate for readers patterns developing in crimes against students.

If you can see patterns in pieces of a puzzle, then interpret and analyze the broader picture, you can have great success writing close to the news and using the news/informational structure.

The "Neck-of-the-Vase" Structure

This structure is used often by magazine *and* newspaper writers (*Wall Street Journal* page-one writers employ it masterfully) because it lends itself so well to beautifully crafted writing.

The structure has three essential elements:

1. An intro that plucks from a multifaceted, highly complex story a single element—a person, a situation—that readers can comprehend as they are led, ever so gently, deeper into a web of details.
2. A quick transition into the body of the story, into its wider dimensions and the true meaning the writer is attempting to illustrate.
3. A "kicker" or exit from the story, often employing in the conclusion the same person or situation used in the intro.

Here, a *Life* writer uses the neck-of-the-vase structure (Figure 6–3) to achieve enormous impact. This is part of the neck of a story about people who have near-death experiences:

> "I was deathly ill, shaking with fever, when I arrived at the hospital," the woman remembers. "My temperature was almost 106 and I was having cardiac arrhythmias. I felt an incredible pain. The wall of my uterus was ripping apart. I was in septic shock, going into labor. As I lost consciousness I heard a voice shouting, 'I can't get her blood pressure!'
>
> "And then, within the tiniest fraction of an instant, I was out of my body and out of pain. I was up on the ceiling in a corner of the room, looking down, watching doctors and nurses rush around frantically as they worked to save my life. Then one of the doctors, really upset, yelled, 'Shit!' And that somehow turned me over. Now I was in a sort of a tunnel, a cloudlike enclosure, a grayish opalescence that I could partially see through. I felt wind brushing against my ears, except I didn't have ears. I was there, but my body wasn't. . . . "

Gripping stuff, so the writer wisely carries the quotation forward for several hundred words, then *ends the neck*:

> "I have kept this experience to myself, but I go over it in my mind every night, and it has taught me three things. First, I know that death is not painful. I will never be afraid to die. Second, I know that it's important to be true to myself and to others, because I will be accountable for my life when it's over. I'm talking about eternity, something I'm going to experience for all eternity. And the third thing I know is that when you die you're not snuffed out. I know that I'm more than my body. There's a soul that's me. And I know that I, my soul, will always be there. I know for certain that there is life after death."

Now, with readers hooked, the writer moves from the neck to the body of the story—from a woman's single recollection to a wider discussion of near-death experiences reported by many people. This is the transition paragraph:

FIGURE 6–3 "Neck-of-the-Vase" Story Structure

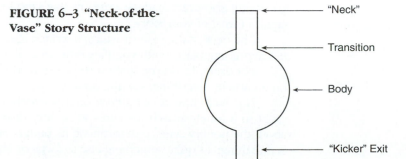

Strange and powerful though it was, the experience that 12 years ago transformed a Philadelphia nurse named (Jane Smith) was far from unusual. All through history, people who have approached the border of death's kingdom have returned with eerily similar visions. But it was not until 1975 that knowledge of near-death experiences became a mass phenomenon, a subject of both scientific study and public controversy. In that year psychiatrist Raymond Moody wrote *Life After Death,* the first commercially published book to compile anecdotes about near-death experiences, or NDEs. In the intervening years, *Life After Death* has sold seven million copies and given birth to an industry. Now the increasingly open discussion of these visions has begun to change the climate of dying in America. . . .

With the preceding paragraph, readers now have moved from the neck into the body of the story and what all along was the writer's main goal: a wider discussion of research into such experiences. For several thousand words, the writer describes the views of physicians, theologians and others (and gives the narrative superb boosts along the way by recounting near-death experiences of other persons).

Then, the writer exits the story with this:

"Death meets us everywhere," wrote the 17th century divine Jeremy Taylor, and "enters in at many doors." In the 20th century, this seems like an archaic view because modern medicine has so dramatically improved the length and quality of life itself. But modern medicine has not eradicated what Sir Thomas Browne, a contemporary of Jeremy Taylor, called "the incessant Mortality of Mankind." Whatever else near-death experiences may be, they are grounds for hopeful meditation.

"Many things," said Browne, who was both a physician and a man of faith, "are true in Divinity, which are neither inducible by reason nor confirmable by sense." He also said, "I love to lose my self in a mystery." And every mystery—even NDEs—offers the hope of a future resolution. (*Verlyn Klinkenborg, "At the Edge of Eternity,"* Life, *March 1992, 64*)

Compare the strength of the neck intro above to a lead like this:

Thousands of Americans report "near-death" experiences, and researchers are at a loss to explain them.

You can see how an anecdotal neck intro, by focusing on one person's dramatic story, can hook readers much better than a general (and dull) lead.

Caution: Effectively employing the neck device requires you to develop the single person or event fully in your first few paragraphs. In the *Life* story, for example, the neck would be weak if limited to a quotation of just a few words. Readers would not identify with the nurse or get pulled deeply into the story. *However,* the story structure would be equally ineffective if the nurse episode ran on for thousands of words. The story then would be about a single person, not about near-death experiences in general.

Write and rewrite, experiment and polish to get exactly the right balance between the anecdotal neck and explanatory body. Fashion a neck that's too brief and you might not attract readers; write one that's too long and you'll divert them from the central thrust of your story.

The neck-of-the-vase structure, if written carefully, will enable you to lure readers into going places with you they otherwise wouldn't dream of visiting.

For example, do you think you can sell readers or editors of a campus magazine on an article describing, say, the poultry science department of your university?

No? Well, how about a neck on a researcher who labors in the lab until midnight in a lonely search for cures to poultry diseases? Note the difference: A story about the poultry science department, its budget and what department members do is one thing; it's quite something else to focus on the lonely and very dramatic search by a single individual for answers to a scientific mystery.

Are readers interested in a story on, say, garbage collection on campus? No? How about a neck on John Jones, for whom fall Saturdays are very bad days: He and his janitor colleagues must pick up tons of litter dropped by football fans.

Use the scientist and janitor in brief vignettes to pull readers into larger (and meaningful) stories.

Let's look now at a story structure you can build entirely around a single individual.

The Profile: A Winning Form

Listen to your friends (writers must be good listeners) and at day's end make a list of subjects they discuss. Unless you move in an unusual crowd, *people* will be high on your list of subjects most discussed. People love to talk about people, and that very human characteristic can hold a strong writing peg for your stories.

For example, would you like to read a story about corporate takeovers of airlines? Not particularly? Well, do you find the following *Vanity Fair* story any more appealing?

> When he smiles, Frank Lorenzo has the look of an extraordinarily happy little boy flooded by some sudden joy. It is a huge grin, a true ear-to-ear affair that moves his features in great, broad shifts. But when the smile goes and the face falls to its natural aspect, the result is a rather unnerving transformation. Now the dark, slightly bulging eyes, the sunken cheeks, the deep downward creases along the mouth suggest something menacing, the look of a vulture circling lunch. This is the face that America connects with the name Frank Lorenzo. This is the face of the man Barbara Walters called "the most hated man in America."

Is that powerful writing more interesting than airline takeovers? Yes? Wrong. The story *is* about airline takeovers. Here is the second paragraph:

> Lorenzo has been called worse. "Typhoid Mary," for example. "Adolf Hitler." "Slimeball." Such is the language of fanatical passion, the sort of passion that Lorenzo has inspired in a seventeen-year career in the airline industry, a career in which he has fashioned a huge empire from virtually nothing, along the way busting unions, firing thousands of employees, putting two airlines—Continental and Eastern—into bankruptcy, and introducing the industry to the ungentle art of hostile takeovers . . .

Welcome to the personality profile, one of the most effective story forms you can use. Whatever your subject, however complex the material you must communicate, you can create appealing and informative copy by using a personality as a vehicle to pull in readers. This writing approach exploits the interest all readers have in other people and, when well done, attracts them to stories they otherwise wouldn't give a second thought.

The *Vanity Fair* story, for example, isn't really about Frank Lorenzo. Rather, it's a hard-core story about a wave of corporate maneuvering that afflicts the airline industry, and one man at the center of that. But once the writer introduces you to the *man* in the first and second paragraphs, how can you ignore the *story*? Suddenly, a dry-as-dust subject comes alive and, if you're like us, you're wondering, "What would it be to meet a man like that?"

Now the writer really sets the hook with this third paragraph:

> It is this menacing figure that I expect to find behind the door of Lorenzo's rather modest office at Texas Air headquarters in Houston. He had not been eager to sit for an interview—he never is—and had expressed his sentiment through aides in the bluntest fashion ("The magazine is a piece of shit"). Lorenzo prefers to operate as invisibly as possible, a style that his friends and family attribute to an almost pathological shyness but that has the effect of reinforcing his image of arrogance. He has paid a price: an extraordinary public malediction even in an age that finds its heroes in the likes of Donald Trump. The vilification of Frank Lorenzo is not confined to the airline unions; it extends

to all of organized labor and even beyond to the general public.... (*Peter J. Boyer, "Frank Lorenzo,"* Vanity Fair, *Dec. 1989, 238*)

Although the personality profile is an enormously strong story form, you must use it selectively and fashion it with care.

For example, a profile often isn't appropriate for a timely, breaking news story. If you have an exclusive, important news story for, say, a newsweekly, use a straight or hard-news structure. Get to the news quickly. Don't wander around, describing how somebody grins. Peter Boyer did that so effectively in the *Vanity Fair* story because his was a timeless roundup or summary story.

Also, to be effective, the personality profile must be drawn with great precision and in a manner consistent with the central message of your story.

If you are doing profiles designed to be no more than pictures of interesting figures, simply weave in lots of descriptive detail—including how they look, walk, talk and so on. Draw complete pictures of the individuals and your stories are complete.

However, if your goal is to tell a deeper story (airline takeovers, for example) you must carefully restrict the amount of descriptive detail on the personality so it doesn't overshadow the wider story. In some stories it's effective to use a personality only very briefly in your lead to merely pull readers into a wider story. Here is an example:

> Stepping brightly into a cramped, windowless cubicle in New York's Rockefeller Center, Mirjana Popovic introduces herself. *"Drago mi je,"* she says pleasantly. When I don't respond, she repeats herself, speaking crisply and gesturing for me to mimic her. Then she begins pointing to various objects and pictures in the room. *"Ovo je olovka,"* she says, holding up a pencil. After several attempts, I'm able to say "This is a pencil" in passable Serbo-Croatian, earning a smile from my Yugoslavia-born teacher.
>
> Such is the renowned Berlitz technique: Get the student thinking, not just speaking, in any of the 45 major languages Berlitz International teaches. Berlitz also sells phrase books, home-study courses and pocketsize electronic translators. For this polylingual work, Berlitz is estimated to earn around $26 million this year, on revenues of $290 million.
>
> Founded in 1878 in Providence, R.I. by German immigrant Maximilian Berlitz, the company is an old hand at the language training game.... (*Seth Lubove,* "Ove Je *Line Extension,"* Forbes, *22 July 1991, 64*)

As you can see, this profile of a person (Mirjana Popovic) quickly turns into a profile of a company (Berlitz). But even though brief, the personalized lead succeeds much better than would a lead that started with, say, third-paragraph information: "Founded in 1878 in Providence...."

Two lessons:

First, it's a judgment call on how far to go in a profile in describing the personality. In some stories, the personality can be the thematic continuity that carries readers all the way through your story, exposing them to other informational elements you need to present. Recall in the Frank Lorenzo story how the writer exposed you to other elements—airlines, unions, bankruptcy—while all the time you thought you were reading about a personality! In other stories (Berlitz, for example) the personality can be used only briefly in the lead, then discarded on the assumption readers already are hooked and will dutifully plow deeper into the business news elements of the narrative.

Second, the profile can be used on things other than personalities—companies, for example, or products or services. Here's a profile of an industry:

> With mega-carriers dominating the skies, you might think mini-carriers had disappeared in the wide open spaces of deregulation.
>
> In fact, commuter airlines are flying high as executives shuttle in and out of some 40 hubs across the nation. And with big business relentlessly moving offices to the boonies, you're more likely than ever to have a close encounter with a commuter carrier.

In the past five years, commuter traffic has jumped more than 50 percent—from 4.4 billion passenger miles in 1985 to 6.8 billion last year. Some 65 percent of the passengers are business travelers, according to the Regional Airline Association in Washington D.C.... (*Paul Burnham Finney, "Commuter Airlines Are Flying High,"* Travel & Leisure, *Feb. 1990, B-1*)

After those first three paragraphs, the narrative could go in any of several directions. It could move more deeply, for example, into profit levels and other information of interest to investors who buy airline stocks. Or the writer could head into territory more appealing to those who fly on commuter airlines. Now read the story once more and guess which way it actually went. You cannot tell from these paragraphs, can you? A clue: Note where the story was published: *Travel & Leisure.* Written for a travel (not investment) magazine, this industry profile naturally moved deeply into discussing flight safety, commuter fares and other subjects interesting to travelers, not investors.

You'll recognize immediately the many ways you can use the profile to get started in magazine writing. Your campus abounds in interesting personalities, from the president to that new assistant professor from Albania. Find a personality and profile him or her for a magazine on or off campus. Interviews (the more the better) are key to writing interesting personality profiles. Let your subject talk, talk—and ramble. This often uncovers fascinating personality characteristics that will strengthen your profile.

You also can use a personality profile to lure readers into a broader story—profiling your football coach, for example, or a new quarterback as a way of examining the team's chances next fall. Or, you can profile your college's vice president for finance as a device for getting readers into a discussion of your university's budget or financial situation.

Try your hand at personality profiles. They're fun for writer and reader alike.

The "How-To" Form

Help! I need help to cope!

That plea is heard frequently in research into what American readers need from magazines. Many people feel overwhelmed by the complexity of life and how best to live it. To lend a helping hand, use the "how-to" story form.

This form works best when your goal is more than merely alerting readers that a problem exists and you want to provide a step-by-step explanation of how they can solve the problem. For example, a news/informational structure might be best for reporting new strategies auto dealers are using to inflate car prices and pressure buyers into taking optional equipment they don't need. A how-to story should educate readers on how to resist sales pressure and get the best possible deal.

When you consider using a how-to form, you should keep several points in mind.

First, you'll have a wide audience if you use this form on developments that affect many people. Writing on how to buy a car or finance a new home speaks to more readers than does a story on, say, how to build low-cost birdhouses for blue jays.

Second, your story should quickly and briefly summarize the problem: greedy salespeople, tricky language in mortgage agreements or whatever.

Third, your story then should move deeply into a step-by-step explanation of what to do about the problem. That means, of course, that you must gain deep personal insight into the problem and its solution through investigative reporting plus interviews with experts and that you must translate difficult concepts and technical terms into language your readers can easily comprehend.

Fourth, your writing must be engaging, attractive, readable. Even if you promise help in making or saving money, readers will dismiss your writing if it is wooden and difficult to understand. Successful how-to writing must be crafted carefully by writers who regard themselves as helpful guides leading readers through unknown and often hostile territory.

The how-to genre is strong in the form depicted in Figure 6–4.

Let's look at how an *Inc.* writer uses this form for an article on how to decide whether you should start a business. First, a catchy lead directed at "you," the reader:

> As honestly as you can, answer the following questions: Were you a high achiever in high school? Do you like team sports? Are you prone to optimism?
>
> If your answers to the above questions amount to a resounding "who cares?" you may indeed have what it takes to start a business. Because the hard truth is that no quick quiz can answer the tough questions you have to ask yourself before setting off on your own. And even if a test confirms you have the traits of a risk taker, that still says nothing about those other prominent predictors of entrepreneurial survival: your skills, your idea, your financing, your motivation.
>
> Those are just some of the difficult issues you need to contemplate before you make any moves.

In the sixth graf, the *Inc.* writer summarizes the problem people face in deciding whether to start a business:

> No one is suggesting that to start a company, you should think every ramification through to its potentially paralyzing conclusion. But the clearer your reasons for being in business, the better you'll feel about navigating the inevitable storms—a vaporizing client, the defection of a key manager, a softening economy.

Now, the writer enters the most crucial dimension of the story—providing a step-by-step solution to the problem of how to decide whether to start your own business. This is the transition graf into that dimension:

> These days, it seems, more and more people are thinking about entrepreneurship, from middle managers ousted from large corporations to graying baby boomers. With that in mind, here are some of the broad questions many company founders thought through—or wish they had—before they set down the first syllable of their business plans. . . .

FIGURE 6–4 Structure of the How-To Story

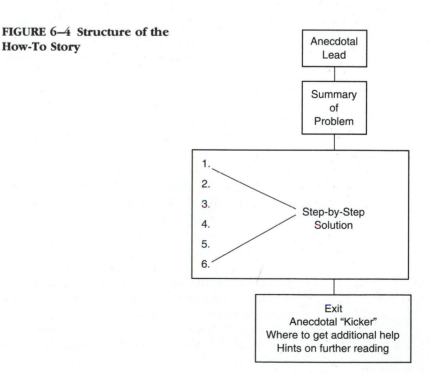

The step-by-step process is examined by listing questions decision makers must ask themselves. The writer skillfully answers each with several hundred words quoting successful entrepreneurs on how *they* answered it. The questions:

Is my idea good enough?
Do I have the management skills I'll need?
How important is money to me?
Can I live with the risk?
What do I tell my family?

The writer now exits the story with an anecdotal kicker on how some entrepreneurs don't let owning their businesses infringe on their private lives:

> On a trip to New York City last fall, (Fred Smith) was asked by a client if he could stay overnight so they would have more time the next day. (Smith) was tempted; with revenues shrinking, he really needed the business. But he had also promised he would be back home in California the next day to see his children's Halloween costumes and to take them trick-or-treating. Off to the airport he trudged. The next night he was roving the neighborhood. "I didn't make any money out of that deal," admits Smith with a sigh. "But I got a Snickers bar." (*Joshua Hyatt, "Should You Start a Business?" Inc., Feb. 1992, 48*)

You have virtually unlimited opportunities to use the how-to form in getting started as a magazine writer while still on campus. After all, your primary audience—the student body—is spending years on campus learning how to do something.

Note these possibilities: how-to stories on applying for scholarships, interviewing for jobs, registering for classes, getting maximum weekend entertainment for minimum dollars, studying efficiently.

Next, we explore a close kin of the how-to structure.

The "How-I-Did-It" Form

Some of the most powerful writing in magazines is woven around the "how-I-did-it" form. There are two principal reasons the form can be strong for you.

First, newspapers traditionally avoid first-person writing on grounds that inserting "I" leads to subjective writing, which impairs efforts to be objective (which may be an unattainable goal, anyway). In any event, the how-I-did-it genre is all but exclusive to magazine writers. That means you can give your reader something refreshingly different from the cold, dispassionate, distant writing featured in so many newspapers.

Second, you can pack enormous drama into the how-I-did-it form, dragging readers along on your personal adventure, letting them see through your eyes, experience your thrills, chance your dangers—helping them live without leaving their arm chairs.

Important: You need not wait until you can trek through the Himalayas or skin-dive off Bermuda before you employ a "how-I-did-it" structure. You can use it on adventures many people have experienced, at places near home—an airport just outside town, for example. Note:

> On a recent trip to Los Angeles I blunder into a dangerous conversation without realizing what is happening.
> I am at dinner with Tony Bill and his friend Helen at a restaurant in Venice, California, and although Tony is an actor/director/producer ("My Bodyguard," "Five Corners") and I'm a screenwriter, the talk tonight is not about movies but Tony's impending examination for a pilot's rating.
> "Tony's a marvelous pilot," says Helen. "You'd love flying with him."
> "How about tomorrow morning?" Tony suggests.
> "Great," I say.

" We'll take an open-cockpit biplane," he says, "and we'll do aerobatics. Would you like to do aerobatics?"

"Aerobatics?" I say. "Uh, well, sure."

Why do I, a guy whose knuckles whiten when the airliners I ride go through minor turbulence, reply "Uh, well, sure" to an invitation to do aerobatics in an open-cockpit biplane?

Well, for one thing, I don't wish to seem a wimp. For another, I happen to be afraid of most everything in life, so by doing really dangerous things I can put the others in proportion better. Also, doing dangerous things is kind of fun.

"Meet me tomorrow morning at the Santa Monica airport," says Tony as we leave the restaurant. "At California Aviation, Hangar 7."

"Hanger 7," I repeat.

"Don't eat breakfast," Helen advises darkly.

Don't you find that present-tense, first-person intro above nearly irresistible? It's from a *Mirabella* story by Dan Greenberg on how he got himself suckered into an open-cockpit plane with an aerobatic pilot. Note the charming touch: Greenberg sets himself up as the goat of this piece.

Starting the next morning, when he awakens "to overcast skies," writer Greenberg takes us minute by minute into the cockpit and toward his rendezvous with destiny. He neatly escalates the tension:

At the top of the dashboard I read an unnerving little plaque installed by the fellow who built the plane. . . . It reads as follows: "Passenger warning: This aircraft is amateur-built and does not comply with the federal safety regulations for 'standard aircraft.' In my opinion it exceeds them."

I do not find the last sentence reassuring. I find it smug and defensive.

Tony slips something over my head and shoulders and buckles it around mé.

"What's this?" I ask.

"A parachute," he says.

"A parachute," I say.

"It's highly unlikely you'll have to use it," says Tony.

"Where," I ask, "is the rip cord? And how do I pull it?" These are not questions I am glad to be asking.

"Look down at the left side of your chest," he replies. "See the flattened steel ring with the piece of yellow tape on it?"

"Yes."

"That's the rip cord. You pull it straight out from your body. With both hands."

"Yes."

I visualize pulling the rip cord straight out from my body with both hands after extricating myself from the cockpit, clutching an overhead wing strut with one hand, placing my feet carefully on the fuselage so as to be able to jump clear of the plane, as the wind buffets me about and the plane screams downward in a sharp nosedive and the ground rushes up to greet me. . . .

Writer Greenberg uses unconventional writing to convey to readers what it's like to do high-speed rolls and loops at 4,000 feet:

The sensation is: Oh-no-Oh-my-God-we-are-turning-over-we-are-actually-turning-over-we-are-out-of-control-I-am-going-to-fall-out-of-the-damned-plane-Oh-please-please-stop-There-goes-my-stomach-thank-heavens-I-didn't-eat-breakfast-Wait-we're-coming-out-of-it-Oh-thank-God-we-didn't-die.

It is not a natural feeling. Your body fights it, your shoulders strain against the harness, your intestines slide around inside you in panic, you feel dizzy and queasy and disoriented. . . .

From that stomach-wrenching high, writer Greenberg gently de-escalates tension (as his plane descends for landing) and exits with a kicker:

"So," asks Tony, after I have disengaged myself from seat harness, parachute, helmet and headphones, "think you'd like to do it again sometime?"

"Uh . . . yep," I say. (*Dan Greenberg, "A Wing and a Prayer,"* Mirabella, *Nov. 1991, 112*)

We think two things particularly are remarkable about the preceding example.

First, there's nothing new about the subject matter. We've seen other stories by people who fly with aerobatic pilots, get airsick and write about it.

Second, however, writer Greenberg *writes the hell* out of that story. He brings new vigor to an old idea. His self-deprecating humor is terrific (we suspect readers love writer-goats more than writer-heroes). Greenberg's verbatim dialogue is precise. His pacing and build toward climax are beautiful.

Remember all that when searching on campus and off for ways to use the how-I-did-it form. How about a humorous walk for campus magazine readers through the bureaucratic tangle of registration? Maybe "How I Survived Exam Week"? Perhaps "How I Got the Job (or scholarship, or loan, or good deal on a new car)"?

The Narrative Form

Arguably, this section should be headed, "The Form*less* Narrative." That's because we deal here with a story concept rather than structure, more a catchall form than a narrowly focused story type.

Within this broad meaning, the narrative we want to discuss is, simply, a heck of a good story told through superbly colorful and detailed writing. This type of story is, above all, just plain good reading.

Not to say, of course, that serious topics aren't covered in this form of narrative. They are. In fact, writers are most successful when they can combine a serious topic with beautifully crafted writing. Note:

> On the undulating approaches to Hugh M. Hefner's Los Angeles mansion, squirrel monkeys, peacocks, flamingos and an occasional jogging Playmate parade. A paved drive-way loops up past a grotto filled with Japanese koi fish and ends at the portals of the mock-Tudor retreat of Playboy's reclusive 65-year-old founder. Thirty-eight years after he started Playboy and two years after he married a Playmate less than half his age, Hefner still lives his fantasies.

That intro is from a *New York Times Magazine* piece by Roger Cohen on how Christie Hefner took over management of Playboy Enterprises. Throughout, Cohen weaves operative business information into strikingly effective writing certain to attract non-business readers. Note:

> With hemlines that do not budge far from her knee and a hair style that is quietly conservative, Christie's scrubbed-clean look is the image of Midwestern decency. If Hefner is Los Angeles baroque, luxuriating in a mansion that costs the company $3.7 million a year, Christie exudes the briskness and pragmatism of her hometown and favorite city, Chicago, and has a surface manner so steel-like it is hard to gauge what lurks underneath.
>
> Overall, she is as comfortable in the gray-suited business world as her dad once was hosting all-night bashes. Where Hefner "leveraged," to use Christie's favorite word, his fantasies into a thriving business that helped change America's sexual mores and then used his own unbridled sexuality to feed *Playboy's* myth of the eternal bachelor, she maintains a strict division between business and pleasure and an even stricter eye on the bottom line.
>
> "Hef," she says, "is a man of the big picture. He is a creative force. I try to insure that he does not have to worry about our business performance. So I manage very closely." Then her voice takes on a sharp edge as she adds: "You can't delegate turning a company around." (*Roger Cohen, "Ms. Playboy,"* New York Times Magazine, *9 June 1991, 32*)

The segment above illustrates perfectly the best characteristics of this type of narrative writing: The writer has a keen eye for detail (hemlines and hairstyle) plus a sharp ear for meaningful quotes ("Hef," she says, "is a man of the big picture . . .").

Some writers with such superb reporting skills take their inspiration from what Tom Wolfe described in his book, *The New Journalism*, as a writer's responsibility to use detail and dialogue to create scenes that take readers inside the story, its characters and situations. *New York* magazine and others developed this approach in the 1960s.

Unfortunately, some writers use the "new journalism" of the 1960s as a means of rejecting traditional efforts to be objective. Instead, they use fiction-like writing devices for inserting subjective judgments and even composite (or phony) characters into a story.

Principled writers reject those worst elements of new journalism. But even writers with a reputation for factual reporting sometimes get dangerously close to injecting subjective, highly personal views into their writing as they strive for color. In Roger Cohen's *New York Times Magazine* story, for example, note "Christie's scrubbed-clean look is the image of Midwestern decency." Surely, there's a bit of the writer in that description, along with objective fact!

Nevertheless, it is an incredibly alert reporter's instinct combined with a rollicking writing style that can make this narrative form so attractive. Witness:

> On a wintry evening early in 1988, a silver-haired man in his forties entered the main dining salon of the Russian Tea Room and was greeted by the furious cold eyes of a well-dressed young woman who was seated alone. When the man pulled a chair out to join her, she got right to the point. "I trusted you, John!" she said. "How could you have done this to me? You've devastated me!" (*Christopher Byron, "Other People's Money,"* New York, *17 Sept. 1990, 39*)

> It's after school and students are sitting in the pizza parlor across the street from the main classroom building, eating slices, discussing homework assignments—and reading *Women's Wear Daily*. Clearly, these are not your typical undergraduates; they're design students at New York's Fashion Institute of Technology. Sometimes referred to as "the victims" by those in other departments, they're easy to spot: no detail of their appearance goes unstyled. It's little wonder that photographers from *WWD,* the garment industry's daily newspaper, regularly roam the campuses of FIT and the Parsons School of Design to record what the students are wearing. Schools like these are the incubators of future fashion talents.... (*Sarah Ferguson, "Studying Style,"* Elle, *March 1991, 200*)

> If you subscribe to the generally useful notion of success as a bitch goddess, then Kevin Kline has neither won her nor even wooed her with much devotion. His name doesn't leap to an adoring nation's lips, like that of the other, newly totemic Kevin (that's right, Kevin Schwarzkopf); he can't command the riches heaped on Tom Cruise (who'll command them only so long as his movies keep making heaps). But if you think of success as the blessed state of doing what you love to do superbly well, then Kevin Kline has hit it as big as anyone in Hollywood or anywhere else. He's a star who moves freely between stage and screen, an actor of extraordinary verve and skill, a thinking woman's heartthrob who plays physical comedy with a modern touch.... (*Joe Morgenstern, "Kevin's Choice,"* Connoisseur, *July 1991, 39*)

As the final three examples illustrate, fast-moving, *hip* writing can turn a so-so story into a great narrative.

This style is for insiders (you mean you don't know of New York City's famous Russian Tea Room?). It's for readers on the cutting edge of change (*Women's Wear Daily is* the edge in the fashion world). This style is for those who know and care about Kevin Kline.

Try your hand with a swinging approach to insider narratives on campus life. Touch the light and fancy-free story. Neither you nor your readers should be serious *all* the time!

We won't attempt to sketch the narrative form for you. It's hard to find two of this type that look alike, and we hazard a guess that you won't write two that are structured alike, either. Rather, in planning this type of narrative you should jot down the central themes you want to stress and the main goal of your story, so you'll know generally where you want to go. Then, plunge into the writing with fervor. Let it lead you where it will, and rewrite and edit to tighten up.

SUMMARY

After your research and interviews, but before starting to write, you should plan the structure of your story.

Structure to emphasize people—what they do, what is done to them. To communicate effectively, highlight the people in the story.

Imagine how you would tell your story to a friend. Don't write as you talk—that's nonsense. But "telling" the story will help you structure it logically.

Also structure so you carefully parcel out complex facts, figures, technical terms, concepts and characters. Push too much difficult information at readers too quickly and they'll choke.

Structure to highlight clearly the core ideas essential to your story. That requires ruthlessly discarding secondary information and not draping it all over your story structure.

The newswriting's traditional inverted pyramid story structure doesn't often work for magazine writing. But you can use a similar news/informational structure for stories that are close to the news.

The neck-of-the-vase structure is extremely valuable because it helps you extract a single element or personality from a multifaceted, complex story, then use it to lead your readers ever so gently into a web of details.

The personality profile is a winning structure. People love to read about people, and you can use that interest to pull readers deeply into your stories. You can write stand-alone profiles about personalities, or use the profile as a device to attract readers to other subjects.

Reader research hears the cry, "I need help to cope!" Answer that cry with the how-to structure, a story form you can use to show people how to solve problems.

A close kin is the how-I-did-it structure, a form used for some of the most powerful writing in magazines. Newspapers generally avoid first-person writing, which means the structure is virtually exclusive to magazines. Also, this structure permits you to pack enormous drama into your writing, letting readers still in their arm chairs experience with you a personal adventure.

The narrative structure of many magazine articles flows from 1960s "new journalism." It requires a sharp reporter's eye for detail and an ear for meaningful quotes. One goal is constructing vivid scenes that take readers inside a story, its personalities and events. For unprincipled writers, new journalism can mean inserting subjective, highly personal views into their copy and constructing composite (phony) personalities.

RECOMMENDED READING

Reading other writers is your best bet for learning how to structure stories. Sample widely the structures published in a variety of magazines. Note particularly how (or if) writers link story structures to the complexity of their material and the presumed interests and comprehension levels of their audiences.

For general writing strength, see feature copy in *The Wall Street Journal* (particularly front-page neck-of-the-vase stories) and *The Los Angeles Times*. Many of the writing techniques in those newspapers (and *Washington Post*, *New York Times* and others) are fully applicable to magazine writing. For a look at many newswriting structures, see Conrad C. Fink, *Introduction to Professional Newswriting* (White Plains, N.Y.: Longman, 1992.) Also note magazine-like writing in Roy Peter Clark, *Best Newspaper Writing* (winners of American Society of Newspaper Editors competition, published annually by Poynter Institute, St. Petersburg, Fla.).

Also note William E. Blundell, *The Art and Craft of Feature Writing* (New York: New American Library, 1988) and read everything Tom Wolfe and John McPhee write.

Chapter 7

Story form and structure (II)

Although among the strongest story forms, those we studied in Chapter Six are not the only ones you can use to communicate effectively. Far from it.

In magazine writing, the limits of your imagination are virtually the only limits on how you can structure a story. We urge you to approach each story you write as a personal challenge to cross new frontiers in writing, to reach for different and exciting ways to express yourself.

In Chapter Seven, we'll discuss a variety of forms and structures available to you. Again, we caution you to view our suggestions only as rough guidelines for your personal creative efforts.

Ahead are service articles, personality interviews, question-and-answer stories and other useful writing approaches.

WIDENING YOUR WRITER'S OPTIONS

A danger for beginner writers lies in finding a comfortable niche—a form, structure and style you can handle easily—and settling permanently into it. That's a trap you should avoid.

As you gain experience and confidence in your ability you should strive to create your own unique style. With time and lots of effort, a style can become distinctly yours, recognizable to readers and writer colleagues alike. When the mere sight of your byline alone draws readers familiar with your style you will have "arrived" as a writer.

As you cast about for a style distinctly yours, try different, even offbeat story forms and structures. Let's look at alternatives.

The Service Article

Writers fashion service articles so many different ways that we're a bit uneasy discussing any of them as a specific story "form." The only commonality in their use, really, is in what they are designed to do: introduce readers to a new product, service or way of doing things. Nevertheless, many well-written service articles *do* have certain characteristics:

- A broad, often anecdotal and neatly crafted intro that will catch readers' attention.
- A quick technical or meaningful explanation of why the product or service is important.
- Elaborate specifications of the product or service, including why it is superior (or inferior) to others, its price, availability and so forth.
- Throughout, evidence you've researched the article thoroughly, consulted experts and, simply put, know what you're writing about.

The priorities, if not actual structure, for presenting that type of information look like the sketch in Figure 7–1.

The structure outlined in Figure 7–1 was used by Jane Michaels for a *Woman's Day* article on "nine tried-and-true ways" readers can avoid or resolve problems with co-workers. Her anecdotal intro:

> Marcia was a junior sportswear buyer for a large department store. Her future couldn't have looked rosier until Stan was hired as a junior haberdashery buyer. He moved into her office and immediately made a move on her. After weeks of ignoring his innuendos and fending off his passes, her nerves were shot and her work was suffering. One day at lunch she overheard two colleagues discussing how Marcia's affair with Stan was affecting her work.

FIGURE 7–1 Basic Structure of a Service Article

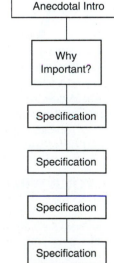

Down the hall in the accounting department, Susan was cleaning out her desk. She had been fired for moonlighting—something her boss would never have learned about if a clerk hadn't turned her in. "Why did you do that," Susan asked, "when you had nothing to gain from telling?"

"You're just so unfriendly, Susan," the clerk answered coldly. "You never even say 'Good morning' ". . . .

Now, writer Michaels moves out of her three-graf anecdotal intro and into the second phase of her story—why problem solving in the office is important:

Bosses who make impossible demands aren't the only reason people want to pull the covers over their heads when the alarm goes off in the morning. Co-workers are far more numerous than employers, and each one presents the potential for trouble. . . .

Wherever you work—in an office, a factory, a store—being competent involves more than doing your work well. It also requires an ability to deal effectively with uncooperative or even job-endangering fellow employees.

With the scene thus set, writer Michaels goes to the third (and most important) phase of her article—nine specific suggestions on what to do about personal problems:

1. Store up a reservoir of good feeling. People who are courteous, kind, cooperative and cheerful develop the most valuable aid to workplace well-being—friends and allies. . . .

2. Be intelligently paranoid. Newcomers should move with caution; make sure you know the turf before you start to dig it up. . . . (*Jane Michaels, "You Gotta Get Along . . . to Get Ahead,"* Woman's Day, *3 April 1984, 58*)

Suggestions simply are numbered and dealt out in accord with writer Michaels' sense of their importance. The article ends abruptly with No. 9 ("Recognize that most office problems are minor.") There is no "kicker," no attempt to "dress up" the article beyond what it is—a list of helpful hints.

Jules Older, writing for *USAir Magazine,* uses the same general structure for discussing a product. His intro:

Should you ever doubt the existence of modern miracles, consider the fax. A letter that takes three weeks to reach London by sea mail, one week by air, or one night (and $25) by courier service takes less than 30 seconds by fax. It costs about two bucks.

Next, Older's technical description and justification for the importance of his article (and note his writing):

"Fax" is shorthand: It's a verb meaning to send a document from one facsimile machine to another, a noun meaning the document sent, and another noun for the machine itself. The facsimile machine is simply a photocopier that knows how to use the phone. So you can fax a fax from your fax to any other fax in the world—a miracle indeed. . . .

Now, the author launches into specifics on making a choice:

For many businesses, the question of whether to invest in a facsimile machine has been surpassed by the question of which one to buy. With changes in technology coming so rapidly, that's become a vexing question—a wrong choice can mean inconvenience and unnecessary operating expense. . . . (*Jules Older, "A Matter of Fax,"* USAir Magazine, *Aug. 1991, 39*)

Two things impress us about the fax story.

First, author Older lays a nice writing touch atop what a lesser writer might have dismissed as a mere nuts-and-bolts story. Remember that even though you offer a service article chock-full of information crucial to your readers, they will not accept dull, wooden writing.

Second, deeper in his story (which we don't have room to reproduce), Older provides much that a prospective buyer needs to know: performance specifications of different types of fax machines, prices and addresses and telephone numbers of manufacturers. A service article must be a complete guide readers can follow toward news they can use.

The service article can be nicely adapted to on-campus magazine writing. Why not try one on, say, nine easy steps that (counselors say) students can follow to ease tension with dormmates? Or, how about a service article on five steps students can take to avail themselves of university-provided career counseling, or how to use a new computerized library system, or buy the right personal computer?

Like all magazine articles, service articles are strengthened by clever, colorful writing. Their central purpose, however, is effective communication, via clear language and explicit detail, of information operative to readers in their daily lives. Let's look at another story form with that mission.

The Digest (or Summary) Article

Like newspaper editors (at *USA Today*, for example), magazine editors increasingly are responding to reader demands for information that's tightly packaged and easily accessible. Enter the digest or summary article. It's a story form often devoid of writing flourish and, rather, simply structured to deliver at-a-glance facts and figures.

For writers, this story form can be less than fulfilling. You are *required* to put aside your hard-won skills in being subtly engaging, pleasantly indirect, metaphorically colorful—and to give 'em the facts straight and hard. Nevertheless, this form can give you the enormous satisfaction of delivering information to readers who need it, sometimes desperately, and who don't have time to work through a long, convoluted story to find it.

As you might guess, the digest is highly favored among editors of magazines directed at professionals and others who lead frenetic lives at work, home or play.

For example, *Lear's,* read by many professional women, offers "Money & Worth," a regular feature that often compresses onto a single page a summary of important financial advice on stock market investing, handling a threatened lawsuit, shopping for auto insurance and so forth. To facilitate quick understanding, the feature is written in basic, simple language and frequently contains lists of important facts or definitions (e.g., What is a blue-chip stock? A dividend?).

Esquire developed an attractive one-page feature, "Smart Money: Real Estate," that examines a single representative home in this form:

The Place:	Montclair, New Jersey . . .
The Architecture:	Shingle style . . .
The Market:	Houses range from "modest" $175,000 homes . . . to $2.8 million . . .
The Outlook:	(for growth in value)
The Pros:	Good schools . . .
The Cons:	Taxes—good schools and services aren't cheap . . .[1]

At a glance, *Esquire* readers can decide whether to pursue real estate opportunities in Montclair, N.J. *Always,* summary articles should contain addresses, telephone numbers and other references readers can use to obtain further information.

Modern Maturity, published by the American Association of Retired Persons, adds a list of books and other suggested readings to a story on how to handle estate planning and wills. Another sidebar, or accompanying story, is a list of seven steps to take in finding the right lawyer to handle estate planning.[2]

One useful digest form is a series of compressed reviews of books with a common theme. For example, writer Meryl Gordon does that for *Lear's* in a book roundup. In about 200 words each, she digests seven books under this introduction:

> As the 1980s draw to a close, one thing seems clear: Historians will look back on this decade as one of unparalleled American prosperity. But there has also been a dark side—the illegal dealings of financier Ivan Boesky, the Exxon oil spill, the alarmingly large U.S. trade deficit, to mention a few examples. Some of the ups and downs of the era have been captured in a grab bag of newly published books.
> Turning first to Wall Street.... (*Meryl Gordon, "Silk Purse Manual,"* Lear's, *July/ Aug. 1989, 21*)

Now, the *reporter* in us stresses the goal of communicating facts in a digest or summary article, but the *writer* in us can't leave the subject without emphasizing that you can create enjoyable reading out of even a list. For example, *Forbes FYI,* read by wealthy, busy business executives, commissions Alex Beam, a *Boston Globe* columnist, for an article titled, "Dad's Survival Guide to Disney World." It's a collection of lists and sidebars on what parents can do with their children in the Magic Kingdom and how much it will cost. And, does Beam have fun! One of Beam's lists is "All You Need to Know About Disney World in Ten Easy Lessons." His first lesson:

> 1. Take your children out of school and visit between Labor Day and Thanksgiving. It's illegal in most states, but get a load of these attendance numbers: up to 70,000 a day per park during school vacation weeks, 20,000 a day from mid-September until mid-November. Tell the principal you're off fossil-hunting in Montana.... (*Alex Beam, "Dad's Survival Guide to Disney World,"* Forbes FYI, *April 1992, 66*)

The Interview or Conversational Form

Many people read magazines for information on coping with the demands of daily life, but there is a huge audience for you among people who want to escape them for a few moments. For the escapees, the interview or conversational story is perfect.

Contrasting with the direct, punchy service article or digest, the interview story has a greater chance of succeeding if you let it wander pleasantly a bit, poking here and there in a shoes-off, laid-back way.

You can structure interview stories for many purposes. Two ways are most popular:

- To reveal insights into individuals while simultaneously delivering meaningful information about, for example, their careers, art or businesses. This might involve interviewing an actress and writing about her as a personality but carefully weaving in serious commentary on her acting abilities, her filmmaking philosophy and so forth.
- Or, simply put, you can use the interview story to serve the voyeur in all of us by providing a lighthearted peek into the private lives of famous people. This might involve interviewing an actress about her loves and hates—but not getting too serious about her art. This type of interview story might be described less kindly as gossipy, although it entertains millions of readers.

Obviously, you must go into any interview well prepared with background on the personality involved and the wider dimension of the subject you want to explore—acting, business or whatever. Tape recorders are extremely valuable here. A single article can require hours of interviewing and you're better able to hold a "conversation" and steer it in rewarding directions if you don't have to take notes. It can take several sessions to get the interviewee to relax and talk in revealing terms.

Charles Michener obviously had Glenn Close's confidence when he interviewed her for *Esquire.* He got terrific quotes.

"A few years ago I was on a very jammed New York subway, and I saw this girl looking at me. I thought, Here it comes, and sure enough, she said, 'Aren't you Meryl Streep?' I said, 'No,' and she looked at me harder and said, 'Oh, uh, I don't mean Meryl Streep. I mean Glenn Close.' I said, 'Yeah, I *am* Glenn Close.' And she said, 'What are you doing *here*?' "

The preceding quote was selected carefully. It is meaningful to film fans who know of a rivalry between Streep and Close. It is followed immediately by scene-setting detail that writer Michener uses to invite his readers to sit in on the interview:

I can imagine other celebrated actresses telling this story indignantly—or not telling it at all. Glenn Close is sitting under a tree in the leafy backyard of her house on a country road, an hour out of New York, barefoot and dressed in old overalls and a T-shirt, and her tone is light, dry, and amused. It is a story rich with suggestions: of rivalry with another, even more celebrated actress of her generation; about the cost to one's privacy imposed by stardom; about the ambiguous nature of *her* stardom. But Glenn Close does not say, "What do you think?" Instead, she looks away, smiles, and then breaks out in an amazing laugh—a laugh that is half giggle, half guffaw, a laugh that makes you think, once again: this is a woman of many unexpected parts.

Now, in his third graf, writer Michener establishes Close's credentials as an actress. It's an essential element in an interview structure: Why are we talking to this person? Note how Michener fills in the uninformed among his readers ("five Oscar nominations") but does so with a kind of insider tone that doesn't insult the movie-moxie of dedicated filmgoers in his audience:

It is not a question we ask of the great movie stars who feed our fantasy of *knowing* them every time they appear on-screen. Glenn Close has been brilliant in five of the most successful dramatic films of the '80s, for which she has won five Oscar nominations. (She also won a Tony for her 1984 Broadway hit, Tom Stoppard's "The Real Thing.") And still she hovers beyond our fantasies—unrecognizable at first glance on the subway.

For the next 300 words or so, Michener comments on roles Close played in various movies, suggesting they required her to "go from sexual glutton to homicidal maniac." Michener asks, "But who is she?"—which serves as transition back into the interview:

I first met the "real" Glenn Close when she entered the Royalton Hotel in midtown Manhattan, concealed behind black sunglasses, to join me for lunch. . . .
I had read accounts of her childhood. . . .

Another essential element in the interview story: lots of one-on-one quotes—I said, then she said, then I said.

Writers who labor for years to develop skills in absorbing information, then spinning it back out in their own words, sometimes forget the magic of lengthy, direct quotes. Carefully chosen and spaced, they can transport readers into the interview in a way that paraphrasing cannot. Sometimes you should step out of the way and let quotes tell the story.

But, of course, to let quotes ramble and overwhelm your story is to lose control. Michener doesn't let that happen. Midway through his story, between quotes from Close, he inserts this:

It came: the laugh I was to hear over and over again, always unexpected—a laugh suggesting that there was both an awkward little girl and a raucous, earthy woman inside this quietly self-possessed beauty.

That insertion serves two purposes.

First, it continues the word picture Michener is drawing for us, expanding our understanding of the actress.

Second, and importantly, it ties back to the "amazing laugh" reference in the story's second paragraph. Lesson: The interview story tends to sprawl, to take off in several directions—unless you maintain control. One control device is to establish *thematic* continuity, referring several times throughout to a personality trait or habit —a laugh—that serves to tie together the bits and pieces of a wide-ranging conversation.

Above all in an interview story, however, when you get good quotes *let them run*. Michener carries Close's all the way to the end, exiting with this:

> . . . I asked her how far she felt she had traveled as a woman and an actress. Her answer was completely in character:
>
> "Now," said Glenn Close, smiling, "I'm just getting interesting . . . just." (*Charles Michener, "She's Not Meryl Streep, But She's Close,"* Esquire, *Nov. 1989, 137*)

Now, let's look at a close cousin of the interview story.

The Q-and-A Form

The "Q-and-A"—the question-and-answer story—has long been a fixture in American journalism for interviews or for examining, point by point, an important subject.

This form normally features a short introduction of the personality being interviewed or subject being discussed. A simple arrangement follows: one after the other, your questions and the answers.

The form's basic strengths are:

- You arrange, in open and accessible form, a series of questions your readers presumably would ask if they could sit in on the interview.
- Interviewees can present their views in their own words and in longer direct quotes than possible in a typical interview story.

The Q-and-A's basic weakness is that it forces readers to perform a task many don't have the time, reportorial training or inclination to do: plow by themselves through lengthy quotes, attempting to sort out and understand what's important. The Q-and-A structure gives you little opportunity to use your skills in interpretative or analytical writing. Your guidance to readers is limited to ensuring you ask the right questions and arrange them and the answers with some sense of priority according to importance.

Following is a Q-and-A Frank Spotnitz developed with filmmaker William Friedkin for *American Film*. The scene is set with about 350 words on Friedkin and his filmmaking background. The first two paragraphs make clear we're about to be taken into a Q-and-A on filmmaking, *not* a personality:

> Simple answers are hard to come by in a William Friedkin picture. Whether it's the detective whose tactics are tougher than the bad guys' in "The French Connection" (1971), the priest with his own secret guilt in "The Exorcist" (1973) or the cops crossing the line in "Cruising" (1980) and "To Live and Die in L.A." (1985), Friedkin refuses to let his heroes take the easy way out. All of us have darkness in our hearts, the filmmaker tells us. We care about his heroes because they must overcome not only the evil around them, but the evil they find in themselves.
>
> For a man whose movies bristle with ambiguity, Friedkin is remarkably single-minded when it comes to filmmaking. The 51-year-old director is passionate about the need for risk-taking, dismissing much of what's made today as technically brilliant but soulless. . . .

The questions Spotnitz asks Friedkin are equally penetrating. Answers run into *hundreds* of words. The first two questions:

> Question: You give such life and credibility to all of your images. Is that because of your documentary background or is it a conscious effort on your part?
> Friedkin: I think it's both. . . .

Question: You said once that your approach to film hearkens back to something that you learned from David Wolper: Show something, but never tell them what you're showing them.

Friedkin: Yeah. A lot of filmmaking is show-and-tell. . . . (*Frank Spotnitz, "Dialogue on Film,"* American Film, *Sept. 1990, 16*)

For film buffs (who make up *American Film*'s audience), it's no hardship to read Friedkin's full answers, dealt out in his own language, at his own pace. These readers want to search for themselves among the nuances and subtleties of Friedkin's mind, looking for clues to his artistic sense. For the buffs, it's a relief on occasion to discover for themselves, not to be told by you, the writer—and that applies to all magazine writing specialties, including sports, business, whatever.

However, there *is* a Q-and-A form that involves *only* the writer. In this form you create the answers as well as questions, choosing topics you know will interest your readers and using the Q-and-A format, not the narrative, only because it's so open and easily read.

Eve Smith uses this form—in essence interviewing herself—in an article for *Lear's* titled, "Collectibles: The Fine Art of Buying What You Love." Without introduction or scene-setting detail, Smith plunges into asking herself questions—and answering them. Examples:

There's been a real boom in collectibles in the past few years. Why?

In part the boom has to do with the old-fashioned joy of seeking out and bargaining for unusual objects. . . .

What are collectibles anyway?

Books, toys, tinware, tapestries, old Elvis records—basically anything that people are eager to acquire and keep or trade. . . . (*Eve Smith, "Collectibles,"* Lear's, *June 1991, 38*)

The "As-Told-To" Story

Skilled writers can take the Q-and-A into a higher form, the "as-told-to" story. This often involves interviewing someone who has an interesting story to tell but who is incapable of or unwilling to write it.

For example, the as-told-to form is perfect for interviewing, say, hospitalized survivors of a disaster and presenting in their own words the horror and drama of what they've been through.

To properly write an as-told-to story, you must have a keen ear for quotes, precision note-taking abilities (or, better, a tape recorder) and an ethical determination to catch the interviewee's story accurately, in their language, with their rhythm and pacing. That includes catching faithfully even grammatical errors . . . the stops . . . the starts . . . the repetitions that mark everyday speech.

Because you, the writer, are behind the scenes, telling someone else's story, you also must faithfully inform your readers of how the as-told-to story evolved. *Forbes* did that in dramatic detail when explaining how it obtained "My Story—Michael Milken, as Told to James W. Michaels and Phyllis Berman." It is the story of a Wall Street giant jailed for violating securities laws in the junk bond era.

First, Michaels, editor of *Forbes*, "talks" to his readers in a lengthy open letter that says, in part:

Berman and I each visited him in the drab former Army facility that serves as a minimum security prison in Dublin, near Oakland, Calif. In addition, *over a period of four months we traded questions and answers on the telephone with Milken.* At first he would deliver rambling statements about his philosophy, rolling right over our attempts to ask questions and fighting to dominate the conversation. He clearly wanted to do the interview his way, but as time wore on he opened up and began to answer questions directly, naming names and citing dates. . . . (emphasis added)

As a condition of Milken's speaking freely, we agreed to let him and his lawyers read direct quotes before they were printed—lest he say something that would complicate his massive legal problems. This led often to further discussions that prolonged the interviewing but produced additional information and refinements. The process left us convinced that Milken had dropped his efforts to take control of the article and was responding honestly and sincerely to our questions—the friendly and unfriendly ones alike. Mike Milken is a chastened man.

He deserves a fresh hearing in the court of public opinion. . . .

The editor's note informs readers that what follows is not a simple interview but, rather, the result of discussions over *four months*. Obviously, this must be an as-told-to story, not a simple Q-and-A. Writers Michaels and Berman then set up the story with a lengthy introduction:

A few years ago the most powerful man on Wall Street, Michael Milken, 45, is now in federal prison, having pleaded guilty to violations of the securities laws. To the media he has become a symbol of everything that was wrong in the Eighties—greed, manipulation, disruptive hostile takeovers, the S&L losses. A *Wall Street Journal* editor has written a best selling book, *Den of Thieves,* which places Milken at the center of a criminal conspiracy.

Our crook-sniffing equipment is sensitive and we can usually smell a phony a good way off. We do not believe the conspiracy theories. Milken was ruthless and sometimes grasping, but we have seen no evidence that his legal transgressions were other than of the relatively technical variety to which he has pleaded guilty. None of these illegalities even remotely accounts for the man's astounding success. . . .

The scene-setter includes this warning to readers:

Wherever possible we verified his statements with people involved, and in most cases the statements checked out. We emphasize, however, that the version of events is largely Milken's and may not agree with other people's.

Then, writers Michaels and Berman move to a Q-and-A format which is standard—except, of course, that it's obvious the material was gathered in different interviews, then arranged in a single article in accord with *Forbes*' own sense of news priorities.

The questions get very tough. When Milken protests he has been portrayed improperly, Michaels and Berman shoot this question: "But you did deal with the crook (Fred Smith)?"

Milken responds, "It was obviously a terrible mistake ever doing a single trade with him. . . ."

In maintaining the integrity of the as-told-to format, the writers let Milken's responses run long. After a lengthy but unclear answer, they give him opportunity to continue: "Elaborate, please."

The writers also go to great lengths to level with their *readers*. They publish this footnote:

Milken had thought that by the time this article appeared Federal Judge Kimba Wood would have ruled on his appeal for reduction of his ten-year sentence. However, the ruling has taken longer than expected. Milken, therefore, asked us to postpone the article. This *Forbes* declined to do. (*"My Story—Michael Milken, As Told To James W. Michaels and Phyllis Berman,"* Forbes, *16 March 1992, 78*)

A few things strike us about the Milken article, which ran 17 full pages in *Forbes*.

First, it is Milken's first detailed explanation, outside a courtroom, of how he views one of the biggest financial stories of our time, the junk bond crisis. That is, *news* is the core of this story's appeal, and journalists dug it out. Again: Don't confuse successful magazine writing with flashy writing only; good writing also communicates important information.

Second, the editor's note, story and footnote present a total picture that's fair to Milken and to *Forbes'* readers. Milken gets space to tell his story; readers get details on ground rules and how the article evolved.

Third, this as-told-to story, particularly *Forbes'* subjective interpretation of criminal evidence, isn't a model for beginners. Use the easily manageable Q-and-A for campus-related stories, then work into the more complicated as-told-to form when you're more experienced.

The "Come-Along" Story

Sunday, April 21, 6:00 a.m., Reykjavik, Iceland: I know nothing about glaciers. I know very little about Iceland, the geography, the terrain, or the weather. I especially know nothing about the people. All this is about to change.

Sunday, 9:00 a.m.: We start our engines, a caravan of enormous 4 x 4s loaded with equipment. Most of it I can't figure. Why the 10-foot lengths of 4 x 4 beams with holes drilled in them? Why are we carrying skis and long lengths of rope? Why are so many wives and children here to say goodbye to us? Why is Channel 2 sending a newsman to do standup interviews in the parking lot?

I am surrounded by Icelandic-speaking people, and because neither I nor Feature Editor Peter MacGillivray comprehend the language, we are somewhat in the dark about the details of our departure. I find myself thinking back to the moment we agreed to take part in this expedition, and how it all came to this. . . .

Intrigued? Want to know what this is all about? Read on:

Nearly a year ago, we were approached with a wild idea. The goal would be to drive to an enormous glacier, scramble on top of it, and drive to the highest point in Iceland, a volcanic mountain that few have ever visited. From a base camp at the foot of this frozen volcano, we would drive, push, and winch to the top. Conditions would be challenging; driving would be hard, weather would be cold, there would be some danger and some potential for hardship. We would have serious winch work to do in cold conditions and bad weather. But we would be accomplishing something that no one had ever done before. . . . (*John Stewart, "Iceland Expedition '91,"* Four Wheeler Monthly, *Oct. 1991, 26*)

Now readers can scramble across an Icelandic glacier without leaving their comfortable chairs—courtesy of the come-along story. This form is superb for involving readers emotionally in an adventure or unusual experience as a means of leading them into a special topic.

As you can guess from the citation following the excerpt, the story isn't about writer Stewart's personal adventure or about Iceland's glaciers. Rather, it's about performance of four-wheel drive, all-terrain vehicles. By opening with an anecdote about Reykjavik at 6 a.m., however, Stewart sets a nearly irresistible trap for his readers—they've almost got to continue reading.

Writing for *Smithsonian,* John Skow edges us more gently into adventure:

Shoreward from the barrier reef, south along the coast from the port settlement of Dangriga to Monkey River Town, then inland toward the Maya Mountains, up the Monkey River to its source at the confluence of the Bladen Branch and the Swasey Branch, gaining altitude westward beyond the last big banana plantation and the last tiny slash-and-burn milpa on the coastal plain. Michael Stewart spots a king vulture. He banks the Cessna for a look. . . .

We are flying now below cliff tops that reach to about 1,500 feet, threading the mountainous, upstream course of the Bladen Branch into a region nearly impenetrable on the ground. High, tumbled, white rock faces scar the riotous upland rain forest. . . .

This is an unplanned side trip; Stewart's volunteer mission today is to fly a survey for two Belize government fisheries biologists who are monitoring the run-off of soil, pesticides and fertilizer from large citrus and banana plantations into the waters around the coastal reefs. . . . (*John Skow, "Everything Looks Different When You Are Up in the Air,"* Smithsonian, *Nov. 1991, 86*)

Note the two preceding stories share these characteristics:

■ First-person or you-are-there detail in anecdotal intros that lure readers into involvement in the story with the writers. Note how writer Skow has you winging across mountain and valley before gently introducing you to the thrust of his story: environmental concerns about the tropical forests of Belize.

■ A *transition graf*—the third in both stories—to move readers from an anecdotal intro into a bit of background on the subject at hand, before resuming the come-along anecdotal style. This graf is variously termed the "nut" or "capsule."

■ A chronological flow, explicit in the Iceland story ("6:00 a.m.," then "9:00 a.m.") and more subtle in Belize ("He banks the Cessna for a look" and, later, "We are flying now").

The "come-along" form is perfect for your magazine writing while on campus. Walk your readers through, say, a day in the life of your university president (starting at breakfast!) Or, recount your own minute-by-minute adventure in getting through registration. Or how about inviting readers of a city magazine along on a room-by-room walk-through of a famous old house?

Briefs and Brites

You may feel the urge to strive for long stories, to equate length with substance. Certainly, the story forms we've studied can tempt you to "write long."

But, we urge you to think short on occasion, too.

For one thing, editors get desperate for briefs, stories of a graf or two that they can use to complete page layout. Bits and pieces sometimes lend welcome variety to a magazine. But, also, you can turn a nice phrase with a tight little brief, particularly if it is a "brite" or humorous piece. This was in *Fortune*, among briefs recounting the arrest and sentencing of white-collar thieves.

> (Fred Smith), 51, president of a chocolate company, borrowed $1 million from thrifts and banks by overstating his net worth. . . . (Smith's) just desserts: six months. (*"Crime,"* Fortune, *5 Nov. 1990, 101*)

Don't you wish you had written that?

SUMMARY

A danger for beginner writers lies in finding a comfortable niche—a structure and style you can handle easily—and settling permanently into it. Avoid that trap. Create your own distinctive style by trying different story structures.

Your options include the service article. It can be structured different ways, but should introduce readers to a new product, service or way of doing things.

The digest or summary article is increasingly popular among editors responding to reader demands for information that's tightly packaged and easily accessible. It often is devoid of writing flourish and, rather, structured to deliver at-a-glance facts and figures.

The interview or conversational structure, in contrast with the punchy service article or digest, succeeds best if you let it wander a bit in a shoes-off, laid-back way. Structure this type of story to reveal insights into individuals and simultaneously deliver meaningful information about their business, careers, art or whatever. Or, you can use the interview story for a lighthearted peek into the private lives of famous people—and never mind art.

The Q-and-A structure, long a fixture in American journalism, can be used for interviews or for examining, point by point, an important subject. Its features are a short introduction, followed by simple arrangement of questions and answers.

The as-told-to story is perfect for interviewing, say, hospitalized survivors of a disaster and presenting in their own words the story of what they've been through. Using this form takes a keen ear for quotes, precision note-taking and ethical determination to recount the interviewees' story accurately.

The come-along story is wonderful for involving readers emotionally in an adventure as a means of leading them into a special topic. The structure can include an anecdotal introduction, then a transition (or "nut") paragraph of essential background, followed by chronological recounting of how you moved through the adventure.

Briefs and brites shouldn't be ignored. Short, tight items are needed for magazine layout—besides, you can have fun turning a nice phrase with a brite or humorous piece.

NOTES

1. This example is "Smart Money," *Esquire*, Nov. 1989, 89.
2. Armond D. Budish, "The Multipurpose Trust," *Modern Maturity,* Aug.–Sept. 1991, 44.

Chapter 8

How to attract and hold readers

Here's a shocking scenario for you:

You've spent days (weeks?) reporting your story and interviewing sources.

You've laboriously arranged research and background material in logical, accessible form.

You've sweated over choosing just the right story structure.

Now, you've got to figure out how to write a lead for your story that will catch readers' attention in just seconds.

You now must devise a way of waving at the passing parade of readers, pulling them toward you despite competition from life's barking dogs and crying children—the clamorous, hectic pace of everyday living that wrings magazine readers dry of the time and attention they have for you and your story.

You also must compete against everything else in the *magazine,* writing something that shouts, "Hey, over here!" as readers flip through the pages, glancing here, gazing there, then moving on.

So, we turn in Chapter Eight to writing leads. It's an art form much studied by even highly successful writers and editors for two reasons.

First, the pros know readers are a busy, distracted and sometimes fickle lot who must be romanced by the first few grafs into reading a full story. It's not enough to collect important—even crucial—information and simply push it forward in colorless, lifeless writing. You must write from the start with strength and attractiveness. There is so much good writing out there—even excellent writing—that your story must stand out or all that fine material you've researched and collected is wasted.

Second, writers look upon lead writing as the arena where amateur writers are separated from professionals, the showcase where true wordsmiths can demonstrate their creativity and ability. Maybe we shouldn't judge writers by their leads, but we often do.

In the pages ahead, we'll look at a variety of leads and discuss some things you can do to strengthen your writing's appeal, as well as some traps to avoid.

LEADS THAT DO—OR DON'T—WORK

So great is the reputation of some writers that their byline alone attracts readers.

"By Tom Wolfe," for example, never fails to draw a crowd, regardless of what's under the byline. "By Frank Deford" is enough for sports readers.

'Twas always thus: "By Ernest Hemingway" has lured generations of readers into plowing dutifully through even some awful stuff, as well as truly great writing.

We wish for you eventually the same byline recognition. Until then, however, you might want to work very hard on your writing—particularly leads, or introductions, and the first 150 or so words of your stories.

Some general guidelines:

- Carefully pick the tone and angle of your introduction to reflect the basic material and core ideas of your story. It's obvious, isn't it: Cancer, child molestation or environmentally poisoned streams aren't funny, so don't write flippant leads for such stories. On the other hand, never miss an opportunity to write a humorous lead for a truly funny story.
- Think deeply about your readers' expectations, needs and, importantly, their likely level of expertise in your subject. Write over their heads with terms and concepts they don't understand, and they're gone; write down to them, beneath their understanding, and they're gone. Don't use imagery or personalities without being certain they're familiar to your readers. You know who Michael Jackson is; some older readers may confuse him with a basketball player. A lead pegged to lyrics of a popular song may instantly create a mental picture for you, but leave readers mystified. And remember: Readers don't always remember. A Times Mirror poll in November 1991 found only 66 percent of 2,020 adult respondents remembered that the Persian Gulf War ended in 1991; the rest either didn't know or said it ended in 1990.[1]
- Practice lead writing. Write, rewrite, then rewrite again. Take a hint from Pam Houston, who sold a story to *Mirabella* and was asked by its editors to comment on her writing experience. Said Houston: "I've been writing—something—since I was twelve."[2] Why don't you start writing—something—now? For starters, we'll discuss some of your lead-writing options.

"Grabber" and "Shocker" Leads

One way to get heard in a crowd is to shout. One way to get noticed in a crowded magazine is to reach out and, figuratively, grab readers. Like this:

> *This* is what it is like to be the sexiest man alive.
> People gawk. Women smile and edge closer to get a better look. Men watch enviously from the corners of their eyes. Some are startled, first goggling, then turning

away abruptly lest they be caught staring at the man in the *rosso chiaro*—in English, "brilliant red"—Ferrari Testarossa.

"It's funny, the effect this car has on people," says (Fred Smith), Ph.D., the man behind the wheel. "In Washington, people fall off the curb when they see the Testarossa. But in Philadelphia's Main Line it's completely different. Either it doesn't draw attention, or people pretend they don't see it".... (*Jack Smith, "A Vroom of One's Own,"* Town & Country, *Jan. 1992, 76*)

Compare that lead with this:

Driving a $200,000 Ferrari Testarossa can really get you noticed!

No contest, right?

Now examine the elements of *Town & Country*'s "grabber" intro:

- The first graf indeed is a grabber. It's simple (just 11 words), direct and powerful—likely to catch the attention of many readers, whatever their gender.
- The second graf carries forward the first-graf theme of excitement. Don't leave a single-sentence grabber lead out there all by itself; back it up.
- The third graf is a *quote from an authoritative source* (a man who owns one of the cars) that backs up both the first and second grafs, presenting readers with a tightly woven intro of 101 words in one manageable, three-graf package. The story then goes on over three pages of text to discuss other costly sports cars and people who drive them.

Here's another grabber:

There's always something crazy going on in the Motor City. On July 20, it was the discovery of the body of a 15-year-old girl, on fire, in a city trash bin. The girl, a cheerleader at East Catholic High in Detroit, had allegedly been strangled and torched by a 19-year-old friend, who was charged with first-degree murder.

Dave Bing, the former Detroit Piston guard who was elected to the NBA Hall of Fame in 1989, shakes his head and clenches his jaw as he ponders the news. Bing, 47, now the CEO of Bing Steel and two other Detroit companies, is seen as a knight of hope in a city that needs hope as badly as a desert needs water. Societal forces and global business trends have conspired against Detroit. White flight to the suburbs after the 1967 race riots, the decline of the U.S. auto industry, the collapse of the city's housing market, the twin whipsaws of drug use and the disintegration of the black family—all have helped turn Detroit into a sinkhole of chaos from which little escapes. "America is in bad shape," the city's mayor, Coleman A. Young, has said. "Detroit is in worse shape." Indeed, a recent story on the city in *U.S. News & World Report* reported that in Detroit "spectacular crimes have become a kind of civic tradition".... (*Rick Telander, "The Black Athlete Revisited: Life Lessons From a Man of Steel,"* Sports Illustrated, *19 Aug. 1991, 48*)

Note that the lead graf is longer (62 words) than the sports-car lead but also opens with a strong single-sentence "grabber" (... "something crazy going on" ...). But this opener contains gruesome details that really are written to shock more than gently grab.

Note how the author structures the Detroit intro: Catch attention with the first sentence, back that up with additional, shocking detail, then go to quotes (Young and *U.S. News*) for extended backup—the same one-two-three arrangement featured in the sports-car story.

Want to know what the Detroit story really is about? It's about Dave Bing, former National Basketball Association star who became a successful businessman in Detroit, despite obstacles there. It's an inspirational story certain to motivate youngsters—if they can be lured into reading. We think writer Telander and *Sports Illustrated* do a superb job of luring readers, which is the goal of grabber and shocker leads.

You need not always stretch so imaginatively to grab and shock, as do writers of the two preceding examples. Sometimes, straightforward statement of fact is enough. Like this:

Alcoholism is an intimate experience for 43 percent of U.S. adults. About 76 million Americans have been exposed to alcoholism in their family, according to the National Center for Health Statistics. These people grew up with or married an alcoholic or a problem drinker, or had a blood relative who was an alcoholic or problem drinker. They are 46 percent of women and 39 percent of men. . . . (*Joe Schwartz, "Everybody Loves a Drunk,"* American Demographics, *March 1992, 13*)

Sometimes a little play on words does the job. Here's how an *Economist* writer handles what you might think is a hopeless task of enticing readers into a story about the Federalist clique in British politics:

It may not be pornographic but the f-word certainly stirs up the British. This is the second time that federalism has divided parties and agitated polemicists. For the half century from 1880, few topics stirred stronger passions. The issue then was not Europe—a far-off continent about which the British knew little—but the Empire. . . . (*"Federal Follies,"* The Economist, *14 Dec. 1991, 62*)

"I"-and-"You" Leads

You can achieve special intimacy with readers by crafting leads that flow with the rhythm of one-on-one personal conversation. Use "I," the writer, to reach out to "you," the reader.

The "I" approach can be effective even when your intro is nothing more than a humdrum picture of your everyday life:

Thursday, January 2, 8:30 a.m.: I wake up to find, or should I say *not* find, my husband The Banker. I do have a vague memory, now hours old, of his tiptoeing around the house to shower, shave and dress, then surging out the door. I have an even vaguer recollection of his muttering something about having to make his own breakfast.

That evening, at 8:30, The Banker arrives home, still full of vim and vigor. . . . (*Jane Wilkins Michael, "The Winter of Her Discontent,"* Town & Country, *Jan. 1992, 37*)

Why is writer Michael effective with such a low-key (almost dreary) word picture as the one above? Because she offers a comfortable, non-threatening invitation to readers who want to peruse her story (about beauty and fitness hints) without being pushed too hard intellectually. Michael offers bathrobe-and-coffee talk over the kitchen table with a friend.

In contrast, get ready for rigorous adventure with this "I" lead:

Almost 4,000 meters below the surface of the Pacific Ocean, Dudly B. Foster switched on the *Alvin* submersible's external lights. Janet A. Haggerty and I peered through our four-inch portholes, looking for the first glimpse of the seafloor. A couple of minutes later we settled on a lightly sedimented incline amid a cluster of small, white-streaked, green boulders. For the next five hours, cold and bent in fetal positions, in the cramped interior of the *Alvin,* we completely forgot physical discomforts as we explored a mountain of green mud 80 kilometers west of the Marianas Trench. . . . (*Patricia Fryer, "Mud Volcanoes of the Marianas,"* Scientific American, *Feb. 1992, 46*)

Sometimes, you can speak successfully to *and for* your readers and build a special bond with them. Lisa Grunwald does that for *Esquire* in an article on how people get ground up in striving for career success:

Four o'clock in the afternoon.

The twitching hour.

A pounding starts in your head that is both painful and numbing and, for the purposes of this article, completely metaphorical.

This pounding represents the cumulative effect of too many challenges, contests, ambitions, doubts, failures, frustrations, successes, lapsed mentors, lapsed ideals, and lost expense-account slips. It represents, in short, what you've been doing with your work life, and what your work life has been doing to you.

Your eyes glaze and wander and find, with chilling accuracy, the least interesting stain on your office wall. You fidget. You untangle the phone cord or, worse than that, make a mental note to get around to it.

It's not that you're unhappy. You probably have too much pride for that. It's just that you can't help wondering what the hell you are doing here. . . . (*Lisa Grunwald, "Is It Time to Get Out?"* Esquire, *April 1990, 130*)

Obviously, when you start "talking" intimately in your leads to but also *for* readers, you must be certain of your audience. For example, it's a good bet that enough career-minded people read *Esquire* to ensure sufficient numbers will identify with "the twitching hour" in the last story.

However, do you think enough magazine readers *actually see* the following scenario every afternoon?

Every afternoon, you see them—running off to soccer practice or toting a tiny violin off to Suzuki class. These days, a child is likely to fill at least some afternoons each week with special classes and sports activities. . . .[3]

Do you think readers might peruse the following, then mutter, "No, frankly, I'd never expect that. . . ."

You'd expect the world's most famous innkeeper—who hosts more than 40 million guests a year—to be eager to talk about the rough-and-tumble hospitality business, often peppering his conversation with such industry buzzwords as "average daily room rate" and "occupancy figures."
But not Baron Hilton. . . .

The "you" lead doesn't work well if it places unreasonable expectations on readers—like expecting them to have thought deeply about what Baron Hilton might say on the hotel business.

Here's an I-and-you lead we really liked at first glance because of its warm, chummy opener:

I don't know about you, but I spent too much of the '80s believing that the reigning spirit of the decade was greed. The greed was there, all right, naked and exhibitionistic (Trump's priapic tower, Imelda's yonic shoes, the seven-figure birthday orgies of Saul Steinberg and Malcolm Forbes). But until I stopped obsessing about the lifestyles of the rich and heinous, I could not see that greed was just an epiphenomenon—the showy surf of a deeper current. . . . (*Patricia O'Toole, "Silk Purse Chronicles,"* Lear's, *Dec. 1989, 27*)

Do you know why our initial exhilaration over the last lead disappeared quickly? Because we had to use a dictionary to understand it—to look up "priapic" and "yonic" (two words we *swear* we've never seen before). Should writer O'Toole assume *Lear's* readers know these words? Will you attract and hold readers if they must use a dictionary to work through your story? If you wonder how readers will react, reflect on what *you* probably are thinking right now: Is it worthwhile to get up, find a dictionary and look up "priapic" and "yonic"? Or should you just move on to something else?

Smooth your readers' path—don't litter it with obstacles.

For certain, don't create an obstacle by asking your readers to imagine themselves looking for lodgings in the Loire Valley 500 years ago, then pull them forward to looking there for a bed today. A *Travel & Leisure* writer asks that of readers and, we think, fails:

Five hundred years ago, attractive lodgings in the Loire Valley were plentiful—if you knew the right people. Francois I, for example, built a chateau at Chambord with no fewer than 440 rooms, enough to entertain scores of demanding houseguests in 16th-century splendor.

Today, you don't need introductions to royalty to find a bed along the Loire. . . .[3]

A variation of the I-and-you lead is one that introduces "our" (writer and reader) concerns or interests. An example:

> During the past decade, there has been much said about our concern for the customer. Still, the customer may wonder how this consideration is being translated at the store.
>
> Sales, marketing and collaterals are all methods of communication. They are meant to motivate the buyer to a new or different mode of behavior. . . . (*Sandra Tenney Myklebust, "Image in the Bag,"* Retail Store Image, *Jan. 1991, 16*)

You'll note that this lead works only because the writer is absolutely certain her readers truly share "our" concerns over retail store customer relations. How can she be so certain? She's writing for *Retail Store Image,* a niche trade magazine for a very specialized, homogeneous audience of readers who work in the retail industry.

Leads That Put Readers to Work

When they pick up a magazine, readers become active seekers of information and entertainment. This gives you a perfect peg for leads that make readers work a bit.

Two forms are particularly successful: the question lead and the "picture-this-scenario" lead.

In writing question leads, remember your basic task as a writer is to answer questions, not leave them dangling unanswered. So, *rush* to answer any questions posed in your lead. You can provide your own answer:

> Will this year's tax cut bring back real estate tax shelters?
>
> At first glance, the answer is no. . . . (*Laura Sanders, "A Done Deal,"* Forbes, *2 March 1992, 44*)

You can also provide the answer from an authoritative source you've interviewed:

> How does a company achieve economic success in today's global marketplace?
>
> "You need to listen to your customers," explains Masaharu Matsushita, the 78-year-old chairman of Matsushita Electric Industrial Company, Ltd., the world's fourth-largest electronics company, and one of the most highly respected corporate executives in Japan.
>
> "It's extremely important to listen to the people who buy your products and to the people who sell them. . . . (*Mike Sheridan, "Masaharu Matsushita,"* Sky, *Oct. 1991, 44*)

Picture-this-scenario leads make readers work (not too much, of course) and, if written properly, create a special, intimate involvement. Note:

> Picture a quiet street in some prospering English town, a nineteenth-century residential row of brick walls, garden gates, peaked roofs and mellow tranquillity. Now move it all—peace and quiet intact—to the heart of London. The Kensington address of William E. Wiltshire III is such a haven, and although guests may enter reeling from the vehicular battles of the London streets, they recover quickly under the spell of an extraordinary house.
>
> "It's a collector's home, and a place for entertaining," says William Wiltshire, a Virginia-born art dealer and collector, of his renovated 1860 residence. . . . (*James S. Wamsley, "A Kensington Collection,"* Architectural Digest, *Sept. 1991, 38*)

Now, *imagine* you're in Taos Ski Valley (sounds good to us!):

> Imagine a ski resort offering some of the world's most challenging slopes, 5-star cooking and deluxe rooms, but without any long lines, paparazzi or attention-seekers sporting the latest and loudest ski wear. That's what Ernie Blake had in mind when he founded Taos Ski Valley in the fifties, styling his New Mexico resort on the low-key Alpine villages of Switzerland. . . . (*Brooks Peters, "Travel Debriefing,"* Mirabella, *Nov. 1991, 183*)

Obviously, you'll not succeed with picture-this-scenario leads if you ask readers to stretch their imaginations too far. For example: "Picture yourself sticking up a bank in midtown Manhattan ..." or "Imagine yourself talking to moonmen who landed by spaceship in your backyard...." Get the picture?

The following lead, published in 1991, starts off well, asking what appears to be a reasonable question: whether readers remember 1989. But, even though this lead is for an investment-oriented *Money* audience, do you think the scenario works?

> Remember the good ol' days of 1989? Of course you do. Who could forget that a little over two years ago the average money-market mutual fund yielded a robust 9.2%? Savers then could hardly go wrong. . . .

In this lead, the writer assumes (correctly, we think) that anyone who could read in 1991 will remember 1989. We're not certain, however, that everyone will remember that 1989 was the year "the average money-market mutual fund yielded a robust 9.2%." Again, don't write leads that lay heavy expectations on readers.

The Quote Lead

Can you resist the following?

> "My wife says I look at buildings the way other men look at women, and I think maybe I do," concedes Paul Buchanan as he emits an explosive little laugh and chomps down on the unlit cigar that stays parked in the corner of his grin. His interest is professional. And it is said that among the handful of people in this country who "read" old buildings, Buchanan's memory, his analytical skill, and his ability to re-create the logic of long-forgotten builders are unmatched.
>
> Buchanan's trademark cigar, rumpled clothing, unpretentious manner, and unfailing courtesy suggest television's ace homicide detective Columbo, and like Columbo, Buchanan pursues investigations with a singleness of purpose. He hates cocktail parties, loves Big Macs, drives an ancient Ford, avoids paperwork, and obviously relishes the footwork of his profession—scrambling through attics and basements, caressing a moulding, raking a strong light across a plaster wall, and constantly scrutinizing artifacts and mentally filing relevant information.
>
> Consultants such as Buchanan typically are asked by the owners of a house or a house museum to examine an old structure and determine the period in which each of the various components was built, thus establishing a structural chronology. The clients can then determine, perhaps with the advice of the consultant or an architect, how to restore or otherwise modify the house. . . . (*Allen Freeman, "Paul Buchanan, House Detective,"* Historic Preservation, *Jan./Feb. 1992, 31*)

There's wonderful imagery in the intro above. The "cigar that stays parked in the corner of his grin" and comparison with detective Columbo create instantaneous images in readers' minds.

But what makes that intro work? The opening quote. What a wonderful way to lead readers into a story about old houses!

Lesson: When you get a good quote, use it. *But* back it up with complete and colorful description of the person who uttered it; weave quote and imagery into a seamless whole, then escalate the reader—ever so gently—toward the core of your story. That is the way to write effective intros.

Here is an example of how leaning on a weak quote for your lead can result in a weak intro:

> "I love my life," the actress Lorraine Bracco said. "Even though you'd call me a late bloomer, because as a kid I was so discouraged, I never thought I'd achieve *anything.*"
>
> We spoke in a dust-covered jeep en route from a remote jungle film location base camp in Catemaco, Mexico, where Bracco was filming "Medicine Man," co-starring Sean Connery. . . .[3]

The preceding quote lead, from *Parade,* fails, in our opinion, because it's so typical of the meaningless froth that bubbles out of so much Hollywood writing. It's a quote that could be placed in the mouths of countless actresses or their public relations agents.

Lesson: Don't tie stories to weak quote leads.

Also avoid quotes that require three readings before comprehension dawns:

> "Spaniards are not particularly monarchist," King Juan Carlos I once remarked. He then added: "but they are becoming Juan Carlist."
>
> The monarch's first statement was a realistic assessment of the erratic fortunes of the Spanish royal household over the past 200 years. He knows better than anyone that the Spanish monarchy has not enjoyed the rocklike solidity of, for instance, its British counterpart....[3]

The preceding quote lead, from *Town & Country,* fails because it requires readers to understand the difference between a Spanish monarchist and a Carlist, and how all that relates to the British royal household. The lead quote demands too much from readers.

Counterpoint Leads

Successful lead writers achieve a flow and rhythm that, like good music, seduces readers into flowing right along with the words. Once you have readers moving in one direction, you can achieve special effect by jerking them back in another direction. In music, that's called counterpoint.

Here's an example:

> Pity poor Travelers Corp. Its once-unshakable signature umbrella has been tattered by a combination of reckless real estate lending and a dismal five-year underwriting cycle. With the industry riven by consolidations, buyouts and failures, Wall Street analysts don't know what will become of 138-year-old Travelers, one of the weakest of the wounded giants. They have driven down Travelers' stock to less than half its stated book value.
>
> But not everybody is writing off the insurer. In fact, the blanket of bad news may provide a perfect cover for some savvy shoppers who realize all is not bleak in Hartford, the Connecticut city that Travelers calls home.... (*Adrienne Linsenmeyer, "Battered Bumbershoot,"* FW, *3 March 1992, 18*)

Note how the writer takes you in one direction in the first graf ("Pity poor Travelers Corp."), then suddenly, in the second graf, reverses course ("But not everybody is writing off the insurer.").

Next, a writer takes you in one direction ("image"), then pulls you in another (with "reality"):

> Judging by the U.S. media's coverage, the mood in Hong Kong is one of gloom and despair, with most of the colony's residents trying to flee before Beijing takes over in 1997. That is the image. Here is the reality:
>
> In 1991 Hong Kong's stock market outperformed every other major market in the world as the Hang Seng Index climbed 42% (measured in U.S. dollars). This year the index continues to test new heights.... (*Andrew Tanzer, "Cantonese Conquistadors,"* Forbes, *2 March 1992, 56*)

Following are two examples of how you can achieve special effect by taking readers backward in time, then using "counterpoint" to jerk them forward to the present:

> Seven years ago (Fred Smith) answered an ad for a commercial diving school in Houston. The ad promised travel, high pay and adventure, and it wasn't kidding. Now 32, Smith makes about $55,000 a year managing a team of divers who specialize in servicing nuclear power plants.... (*Christopher Palmeri, "Somebody's Got to Do It,"* Forbes, *2 March 1992, 45*)

For every season there is a financial fashion. In the 1980s debt was in vogue and the smart people on Wall Street made fortunes trading debt for the public's equity. Now debt is passe and equity is all the rage, and the same smart people are making second fortunes by selling equity back to the public, at much higher prices than what they paid just a few years ago.... (*Richard L. Stern and Tatiana Pouschine, "Junk Equity,"* Forbes, *2 March 1992, 40*)

Now, glance once more at the sources of the last three examples. Note anything special? All three counterpoint leads were published in one issue of *Forbes,* between pages 40 and 56. Is *Forbes* using too much of a good thing? Is it succeeding so well with counterpoint leads that it's using too many? If you find a certain lead structure and rhythm work for you, use them—but not too often. Don't get into a writer's rut.

Leads to Use for Variety

There's an easy way to check whether you've fallen into a writer's rut or other bad habits in lead writing (besides listening to editors). Keep all your clips in a single chronological file, then flip back through them occasionally to see if you've been overworking the I-and-you lead structure or writing too many counterpoint intros.

If you see a pattern developing, try other forms for variety.

The "Dramatic-Moment" Lead

Orange County Deputy (Fred Smith) was the first to arrive. He parked his cruiser in front of (the house) just after 11:30 p.m. on Sunday, October 13. As (Smith) got out of the car, 39-year-old (Jane Doe) stepped into a circle of light on the porch. "I'm crazy," she said, trembling. "I shot my daughters." Blood trickled down the right side of her face.

The first floor of the house lay in darkness. Lights burned upstairs. (Smith) made his way to the master bedroom in the rear. "Get in here, now!" he hollered at another deputy coming up the stairs behind him.

The scene was one from every police officer's nightmare. Four-year-old Stephanie (Doe) lay on the bed in her pajamas, her hair matted with blood. She wasn't moving, but she had a pulse, and her eyes were open. (Smith) found eight-year-old (Alice) on the floor, dead. "There's the gun," (Smith) said, nodding toward a .38-caliber pistol that lay about six feet from the bed.

(Jane Doe) had turned that gun on herself just before calling 911.... (*Peter Wilkinson, "She Shot Her Little Girls,"* Redbook, *Feb. 1992, 79*)

This story is about a woman who cracked under the strain of being a "model mom." Think how writer Wilkinson could have *ruined* it:

Being a "model mom" proved too much for Jane Doe, as it does for many women. Doe cracked under the pressure and committed a horrible crime.

Lesson: When you come upon the "dramatic moment," use it.

The "Warning" Lead

In the golden days of radio, an announcer made quite a hit by warning listeners not to change to another network: "Ah, ah, ahhhh!" he would intone, "don't touch that dial!" A writer's version of that warning:

Before you turn another page of this magazine, consider your actions carefully. Every time you wish to grasp a page, you must place one finger above the paper and another below so that the distance between each finger and the paper is about equal to the diameter of an atom. At that point, the electrons at the surface of your fingers repel the electrons on either side of the page. This slight redistribution of charges produces an electric field that is strong enough to allow you to squeeze the page between your fingers. Remarkably, by applying electric forces at the atomic scale, you can hold onto objects that are, on the whole, electrically neutral. . . . (*Steven Chu, "Laser Trapping of Neutral Particles,"* Scientific American, *Feb. 1992, 71*)

Isn't that lead a cute way of luring you into reading about electrons?

Here is a version of the warning lead that makes an amusing play on the subject of the story, time management:

> We don't want to waste your valuable time, so we'll get straight to the point: on the following pages two CEOs who have built businesses on the concept of time management explain how and why their daily planning systems make them, and their companies, more productive. We're presenting two rather different perspectives on the subject because, according to time-management experts, there's no one right way to manage time. . . . (*Terri Lammers, "The Custom-Made Day Planner,"* Inc., *Feb. 1992, 61*)

The "Double-Take" Lead

This structure achieves impact through understated, matter-of-fact recounting of something very dramatic. It makes readers say, "Whaaaat? Give me that again!" Example:

> Susan Perkins is a busy woman, but then, stepping out of a plane at 5,500 feet, she has a lot to do.

With that single, understated sentence above, the writer firmly hooks his readers. Could *you* stop reading? No? Well, we'll take pity on you. Read on.

> Almost immediately her parachute fills with air above her. Clad in the pink-and-blue jumpsuit of the Misty Blues All Woman Skydiving Team, Perkins descends to 3,800 feet, getting set up and in position over the landscape and the audience below.
>
> Then the ride really begins. Cutting loose one side of her chute, Perkins promptly goes into a spin. With the wounded canopy flapping wildly overhead, she gyrates 25 times while plummeting close to 1,000 feet in less than half a minute. But the centrifugal effect takes its toll, and the ground is getting close. So Perkins quickly cuts the remainder of her useless chute, stabilizes and freefalls for an instant, and then pops a fresh pink-and-blue canopy at about 2,500 feet up.
>
> And the crowd goes wild. . . . (*Neal Santelmann, "Oh, Chute!"* Forbes FYI, *30 Sept. 1991, 71*)

An important point about this lead structure: The first graf promises readers an interesting tale about what a woman does when she steps out of a plane at 5,500 feet—and the writer immediately delivers details in the second and third grafs. Quickly deliver on your first-graf promises, or readers will wander away feeling cheated.

The "Ring-a-Bell" Lead

Lead writing to a large extent is a search for memories, images, sounds, sights, smells and names that will "ring a bell" with readers and pull them into your story.

Can you resist a combination of the following names *and* sex?

> Lately everyone is doing it. Christie Brinkley is doing it, Mick Jagger is doing it, even diehards like Hugh Hefner are doing it. *It* is Hot Monogamy—fidelity with the electricity turned way up, passion that renews itself over the years. It's relationships where husbands and wives are eager lovers as well as parents and friends. It's marriage as an erotic adventure.
>
> Helen Singer Kaplan, M.D., Ph.D., head of the human-sexuality program at the New York Hospital-Cornell Medical Center in Manhattan, coined the phrase Hot Monogamy. She says nineties couples want the marriages their grandparents and parents had. The emphasis is on stability, children, family togetherness—plus something more: great sex. . . . (*Ronnie Landroff, "Hot Monogamy,"* Redbook, *Feb. 1992, 63*)

Note above how quickly writer Landroff moves from the "I-gotcha!" lead into serious discussion of the subject, marriage, by an authoritative source. Well-known names are used only to catch your attention.

Now, what do you think about the following ring-a-bell lead?

> Eleanor Roosevelt would have felt at home with them. Like her, they are women who care more for issues than for image or even, in a narrow sense, for self. They spend long—usually unpaid—hours working to aid the poor, shelter the homeless, educate the illiterate, and empower the disenfranchised. They tend not to sit still for long. They wouldn't know what to do with a publicist if they had one. And they don't "do" lunch. . . .[3]

You probably at least recognize Eleanor Roosevelt as wife of President Franklin D. Roosevelt. But she died in 1962 and, although she was a great woman in her own right, do you know enough about her to understand what image the writer is trying to invoke with her name?

Lesson: Don't reach too far back in time for names, images or memories that, even though familiar to you, might not ring a bell with your readers.

The "Tell-Me-a-Story" Lead

"Once upon a time. . . ." As children, we thrilled to that "lead." Below, a writer finds a perfect way to invoke memories of that:

> This is the story of a fabled Scottish castle perched high on a hill on the Atlantic coastline, and of how I, a Yank from Grosse Pointe, Michigan, became its eighteenth laird. The castle's history is one richly textured with tales of property battles, a celebrated love affair, ghosts, intrigue—even a curse. And it is a history to which I—much to my surprise—now find myself adding a chapter. . . . (*Spencer Boyd, "One Man's Castle,"* Historic Preservation, *Jan./Feb. 1992, 22*)

GETTING "SPARKLE" IN AND "HO-HUM" OUT

Writing can be an exasperating business.

Sometimes, you find exactly the right word or phrase to make a sentence or paragraph sparkle, and you're on your way, swinging merrily through a fine piece of writing.

Other times, however, words and phrases clunk down woodenly on paper. Paragraphs just squat there, defying you to make something of them. Result: ho-hum writing.

When writing goes badly, it's a cop-out to shout, "writer's block!" and flee the typewriter. You must keep at it, striving to put sparkle into your writing. Merciless self-editing and rewriting is the way to get the ho-hum out.

Let's look at examples of writers who obviously worked hard—but in subtle ways—to get the sparkle in.

Reaching for Something Fresh

Do you see in the following that little something extra, the author's reach for something fresh?

> (Fred Smith), 43, a short, slight lawyer with graying black hair and a gold pinkie ring, moved to Tampa, Fla., two years ago from Louisiana just to take advantage of the bankruptcy business. "This is bankruptcy heaven," he says. . . .

Yes, it's "gold pinkie ring" that caught our attention above. That little touch brought alive what could have been a ho-hum lead on a story about bankruptcy. Throughout the four-page story the writer inserted other little tidbits of color that boosted our interest and kept us reading. For example, several hundred words into the story we found this colorful "booster":

> Here is a (Smith) client: Connie, a well-coiffed blonde of 61 who wears white pumps and a necklace of white beads the size of quail eggs. This is an emergency appointment. She has just been down to the bank and discovered that the Internal Revenue Service has frozen her account to collect a 2-year-old tax bill for $1,500. . . .

Now, frankly, we didn't really want to read a lengthy story about bankruptcy. But the writing was enticing and, without realizing it, we read all the way to the end. There, we found a colorful exit—a vignette about the lawyer mentioned in the first graf.

> In his office on a slice of strip mall development in suburban Tampa, (Fred Smith) gently eases 36-year-old Nancy Ann into bankruptcy. Her $195-a-month minimum credit card payments and the $175.36 payments on her 1989 Mitsubishi are eating too heavily into the $750 a month she earns these days as a cosmetologist. Business got slow with the Gulf war, and tears are running down her cheeks.
>
> "I've always paid my debts," she says. (Smith) pushes a roll of toilet paper from the office rest room in front of her.
>
> "You have a good cry now," he says. (*Charlotte Allen,* "The Bankruptcy Boom," Insight, *24 June 1991, 18*)

"Gold pinkie ring"? "Toilet paper"? In a story about bankruptcy? Yes! *Get the sparkle in.*

Now, let's say you want to write something about once-wealthy oilmen who got their comedown during the oil bust in Texas. How about:

> When I lived in Texas at the tail end of the oil boom of the early 1980s, I knew many once-wealthy oilmen who had gone bust.

Awful, right? Now, how about this:

> I lived in Texas at the tail end of the oil boom of the early 1980s; I got there just in time to watch the great boom turn into the great bust. I met oilmen who had once thrown money around with abandon—renting helicopters to fly to, say, lunch—and who were now in Chapter 11; watched dentists who had quit their practices return sheepishly to drilling teeth instead of wells; walked through gleaming new corporate headquarters, filled with the handsome furniture that had become every geologist's due, except that there weren't any geologists. They'd all been laid off. . . . (*Joseph Nocera,* "Wall Street, Texas, U.S.A.," Esquire, *Sept. 1990, 93*)

Renting helicopters to fly to lunch? Dentists back drilling teeth? Now, that's sparkle!

Other sparklers we like (we'll add emphasis):

> His is the face of today's Labour Party. No one exemplifies Neil Kinnock's claim to lead a competent, serious party of government better than Gordon Brown. *His permanent pucker of concentration* will loom often across millions of television sets in the months ahead. Know him, and you know Labour. . . . (*"A Study in Brown,"* The Economist, *11 Jan. 1992, 56*)

> Los Angeles, say what you will about it, is a great place to drive in *and drive away from*. Of course, driving in L.A. usually means traveling the freeways, which can be a pleasure when the sun shines and traffic moves and you have the good fortune to be in a car with a sunroof that's open or a top that's down. This kind of driving is why Henry Ford invented the Model T and old Cadillacs have fins. But when you're caught in the middle of an inappropriately named "rush" hour and traffic hasn't moved 50 feet in ten minutes—not because of an accident *but because there are so many damn cars*—the pleasure turns to nightmare. That's why knowing your way around well enough to escape

the freeways and take the back roads is so important here in L.A. . . . (*Eric Goodman, "Driving in Place,"* Lear's, *July/Aug. 1989, 36*)

> For every individual made happy, secure, or powerful by money, there are probably two *who are rendered crazy by the stuff.* So many illusions emanate from money's spell that those with plenty of it often can't enjoy it, and that many of those who, otherwise blessed with the capacity to collect enough of it to at least feel free, are taunted by it. (*Donald R. Katz, "Money Hell,"* Esquire, *Oct. 1989, 89*)

Note the slangy reference in the last example to money ("the *stuff*"). When appropriate, use a slangy, swinging style. For example:

> Okay, first Donald left Ivana for Marla, right? Then he dropped Marla for Carla. And then he shunned Carla for Marla. Wait a minute. Who's on first? Call Abbott and Costello. Or call Marla Maples and Donald Trump. The last time anybody sorted it all out, it seems that they were engaged to be married—to each other—and Marla was sporting a sparkler as big as the Plaza. . . . (*"Return Engagement,"* People, *22 July 1991, 58*)

And if you don't think you can get sparkle in *any* story, note these two superb efforts:

> They last from a fraction of a second to a minute or two. They are evenly spread across the sky. They are never seen in the same place twice. *You now know almost as much as anyone does about gamma-ray bursts.* . . . (*"What in Heaven?"* The Economist, *18 Jan. 1992, 87*)

> *While their colleagues look up, the neutrino astronomers look down.* For those who hunt these elusive particles, the clarity and dryness of the Antarctic skies are of no consequence. The pure ice a kilometer below them, though, is just what they want. . . . (*"Eyes Down,"* The Economist, *Feb. 29, 1992, 92*)

Avoiding Something Old

As you strive to enliven your writing with freshness, so must you avoid old, hackneyed ho-hum words and phrases that will deaden even the most interesting story.

We think a *Fortune* writer should have tried again when this opener popped to mind: *"It's broke and needs fixing.* America's aging infrastructure, that is. . . ."

We did exactly what a *Broadcasting* writer told us to do: *"Don't look now,* but there's another new technological abbreviation coming from Europe to U.S. radio. . . ." (We *didn't* look further into the story.)

Surely, a *Forbes* writer could find a better way to say Las Vegas ignored an event: "Las Vegas *yawned* when riverboat gambling was approved. . . ."

How do *you* answer this *FW* lead: "Lives there an investor who has not heard the saga of Michael Dell?" (We answered, "yes," and went to other things.)

Well, you get the point: Even a word or two can deaden a lead. And watch those cliches! They signal amateurism.

Following are other things beginner writers often do—but shouldn't.

Speaking for the world: "Europeans are worried. . . ." Not even *Fortune,* which used that, can speak for all Europeans. Neither can *Architectural Digest* speak for *most* people: "It wasn't long ago that most people would have been able to list only two British interior designers. . . ."

Getting inside somebody's head: "(Jane) and (Fred Smith) of Tulsa had two things in mind when they redesigned their backyard. . . ." *Southern Living* could have fixed that easily: (Jane) and (Fred Smith) *recall* having two things in mind. . . ." *Atlanta Magazine* similarly could have fixed this: "(Fred Smith) never thought he'd be 58 and single again. . . ." (How about ". . . *recalls* never thinking"?).

Getting ridiculously incongruous: "As appealing as an icy drink on a sweltering summer day. As seductive as a lover's whisper in the moonlight . . . That's car leasing these days. . . ." (*That* was placed before readers of a prestigious personal finance publication.)

Punishing readers who have done you no harm:

> Engelhard Corp. produces pigments, additives, and catalytic materials. Centocor, Inc. is in the biotechnology business, developing and marketing innovative health-care products to attack a variety of human ailments. Cascade Corp. manufactures the business end of a lift truck—the forks, hydraulic components, and specialized attachments—that make the basic vehicle a versatile tool on factory and warehouse floors.
>
> Three companies in three very different businesses—industrial chemicals, high-tech research and development, and nuts-and-bolts manufacturing. But they have something in common: all three are American companies that have chosen The Netherlands as a European base of operations. . . .[3]

Learn When to Step Aside

Good writers learn when to step aside and let somebody else tell their story.

We fancy ourselves fairly good storytellers after many years in magazines, newspapers, writers' hangouts and classrooms. But we now conclude this chapter by stepping aside for a superior storyteller, Ross Wetzsteon. He steps aside and lets Mickey Mantle write his lead:

> "I remember this one time Billy an' me went deer huntin' down in Texas. We get up at four in the morning an' drive a couple hours to this friend a mine's ranch near San Antonio an' I tell Billy to wait in the car while I go up to the house to be sure everything's okay."
>
> Mickey Mantle has told this story a hundred times—it's his favorite Billy Martin story, and he's got it down pat.
>
> "So my friend comes to the door," Mantle goes on in his flat Oklahoma twang, "an' he says, ' 'Course, Mick, you can use my land anytime you want. But I wonder if you'd do me a big favor. When you're goin' through the barnyard, you'll see an old mule. Would you mind shootin' him for me? I've got to put him away, and I haven't got the heart to do it myself.' I say, 'Sure,' but on the way back to the car I figure I'll pull one on Billy. So I yank open the car door, pretendin' I'm real mad, an' I say, 'We drive four hours to get here and now this guy won't let us go deer huntin' on his land. Gimme my rifle. I'm goin' to shoot the son of a bitch's mule.'
>
> "Billy, he's real upset; he's tryin' to grab my rifle. 'Jeez, Mick, don't do that,' he's sayin', 'They'll put us in jail!' I finally manage to get my rifle away an' walk over to the barnyard an KEE-UUU, I shoot that mule right in the neck. But just as the mule keels over I hear BAM! BAM! BAM! behind me, an' when I turn around I see Billy standin' there with his rifle in his hand. 'Billy!' I say. 'What the hell you doin'?' An' ol' Billy, he says, 'I shot three of his cows!' "
>
> Mantle grins with the same open-sky boyishness he brought to Yankee Stadium from Commerce, Oklahoma, 40 years ago, wearing a Sears suit and a six-inch wide tie and carrying a cardboard suitcase". . . . (*Ross Wetzsteon, "The Mick Hits 60,"* New York, *30 Sept. 1991, 42*)

SUMMARY

All your research and sweating over just the right story structure will fail unless you write a lead that will catch readers' attention. You have just seconds to catch them; if you don't, they'll flip ahead to something more interesting.

In writing leads, carefully pick a tone and angle that reflect your basic material. Don't write over—or under—your readers' level of expertise. Practice lead writing. Write, rewrite, then rewrite again.

Grabber and shocker leads do just what they say: They are written in aggressive, interesting language that figuratively grabs readers.

I-and-you leads are written one-on-one, from writer to single reader. You can achieve special intimacy through such non-threatening invitations to read.

You can challenge readers through leads that put them to work: question leads, or leads that say, "picture-this-scenario." If you lead with a question, however, be certain to answer it quickly.

Counterpoint leads achieve special impact by pulling readers in one direction, then jerking them in another. For example, take readers backward in time, then suddenly pull them into the present.

For variety, try your hand at leads that recount, in detail, a dramatic moment or that warn readers ("Before you turn another page of this magazine, consider your actions carefully. . . ."). A double-take lead involves writing something very dramatic in an undramatic, matter-of-fact way.

You can "ring a bell" by leading with language that evokes memories, images, sounds, sights and, particularly, names of people your readers probably will recognize.

Sometimes, a single word or short phrase will insert sparkle in a lead. Just as you strive to get that into your writing, so should you labor to avoid wooden, ho-hum language. Reach for something fresh. And, whatever you do, avoid the old, hackneyed language and cliches.

Finally—and this is a lesson hard to learn—when your reporting turns up somebody who can tell a story better than you can, step aside. Let the superior storyteller write your lead: Use full quotes, and let 'em run!

NOTES

1. "The Issue That Disappeared," *Atlanta Constitution,* 13 Jan. 1992, A-5.
2. "Contributors: How They Got That Story," *Mirabella,* Nov. 1991, 22.
3. In chagrined memory of all the lousy leads *we* wrote in unguarded moments down through the years, we'll not identify the writers of these lousy leads.

Chapter 9

Selling
your story—
and yourself

We hope that after reading this far in our book you are determined to progress from amateur ranks to professional writer. The next, crucial step in that process is getting stories into print and getting paid for them.

This is an attainable goal for many college students. The only way you'll find out whether *you* can reach it is to try.

So, we interrupt our "conversation" with you about your writing to turn briefly to hard talk about *selling* your writing—and yourself—to editors. We raise this subject now so your further reading in our book, and work in your writing course, can be done against a realistic backdrop of figuring out how you can get into print.

Getting published doesn't just happen; you must make it happen. Learning to research and report a story, then write it, won't guarantee publishing success. You must also learn to work with editors, understand their needs and write persuasive query letters offering your stories. Then, you can build an attractive clip file that will give you a head start in the highly competitive race for jobs after graduation.

Even if you're not aiming at a writing career, the effort to get published is worthwhile. Seeing your byline in print is thrilling. Being a published author also can open entirely new possibilities for you in other fields.

We turn in this chapter to the strategy of getting published (and a thoughtful strategy is exactly what's required). You'll learn how to open contact with editors and present your story ideas and yourself. We'll also pass along a few hints on how to write an attractive résumé and launch a career.

CONFLICTING EMOTIONS: FEAR AND UNREALISTIC AMBITION

Beginning writers often are plagued by one of two emotions as they consider the leap from classroom to career.

By a wide margin, the dominant emotion is fear of even trying to get published. We remember it from *our* beginner days: a fear that actually is an unspoken dread of seeing your writing criticized harshly and, inevitably, at times rejected—maybe (cruel thought) with unkind words from some brute editor!

Some beginners are driven by quite another emotion, a burning conviction that merely taking a couple of writing courses positions them to sell immediately to the likes of *Esquire, Rolling Stone* or *The Atlantic*—for around $10,000 per article, of course.

Rid yourself of such emotions. They can seriously impair your chance of getting published.

In handling fear, take our word for it: Most of your beginner colleagues share your uncertainty. So, first, don't worry that you're alone. Second, simply steel yourself for taking a lot of hard knocks as a writer. Those who presume to *create* and display the product of their creative effort are certain to suffer plenty of criticism and, yes, rejection at times throughout their careers. Start getting used to it. (Although, to be honest, probably no one really gets used to criticism.)

Instead of aiming at *Esquire* with your first story, be realistic: Write on a local subject you understand, use a story structure you can reasonably master and target a local magazine whose audience you know and whose reading needs you can meet.

Let's walk through the process.

Select Your Target Magazine Carefully

Throughout this book, our discussion of writing stresses the need to angle your story to match the character of your target magazine and meet the needs of its readers. Apply the same discerning judgment to every step you take in approaching a magazine and selling your story.

You must become intimately aware of the types of stories and writing your target magazine features. As discussed in Chapter Five, read back issues for a feel of what it prints. Note carefully the tables of contents to determine the magazine's general editorial tone. Double-check that your story idea hasn't been published already. Offering a story that duplicates one published just months earlier does more than win quick dismissal: It stamps you as an amateur who doesn't care enough to thoroughly research what you are doing.

Understand that every sentence, every word you lay before editors goes into a "mental mosaic" of you that they are building in their minds. They are trying to figure out who you are: ambitious, obviously; intelligent, no doubt; and certainly well-intentioned—but also inexperienced, untried, unproven. Can you be trusted to do accurate and honest research and reporting? Should you be given precious space in an editor's darling magazine and access to its treasured readers? Are you worth an investment of time, effort and money? (See Box 9–1 for a professional's view on mistakes commonly made by free-lance writers.)

Now, allow us to play tough editors here for a moment. We will describe what we'll think when you approach us with a story idea.

BOX 9–1   Common Mistakes of Free-lance Writers

Allison Dollar, managing editor of In Motion, *a film and video production magazine, provides hints on selling your articles to magazine editors.*

By Allison Dollar

Free-lance writers often call me up and say, in effect, "I'm a free-lance writer. What do you have for me?" The response, sorry to report, is usually, "Nothing."

Unfortunately, just as in other fields, being good at your craft is not good enough. You must present your talents, and your case, in a compelling and efficient manner. The worst thing a writer can do is to randomly call a range of publications and hope someone bites. The best thing to do is to target a particular genre of publication, preferably one in which you already have expertise.

For instance, if you have an interest in art, do your homework and develop a working list of all publications in that field. Your list ought to include the address, phone number, fax number, contact person and publication type. Sometimes organizing the material on index or rolodex cards speeds the process. This information can be had through the *Writer's Market,* business reference books and other journals. The library is a great resource—use it!

Once you have a working list, get sample copies of the publications. Usually, a company will send you an entire press kit. Scan through the publications you receive to get the flavor, tenor and slant required by that company. The press kit will give you an idea of the audience. The editorial calendar provides a helpful outline of the stories to be covered; this is where you might be able to sell your skills. In addition, the topics can be used as a brainstorming guide for original story ideas, always in demand.

Hone your ideas into a few cogent thesis statements. Work these into the middle of a short query letter that explains who you are, how you are uniquely qualified to write on these subjects, and what you would like to cover. Wait a decent interval, then call the editor.

You'll be surprised to find how a little organizational magic will win an editor's heart. Keep up the good work when you get the job: call with any questions; follow directions; stick to deadline; provide an electronic copy if possible; and send an invoice.

The money will start rolling in, and you'll meet a lot of interesting people, who in turn will refer you to other potential clients.

- Why should we be interested in your story? Does it complement, advance or more fully develop a pattern of coverage we've already established on a subject in our magazine?
- What makes *your* story different? Is it unique? Exclusive? How?
- Even if we like your idea, why should we invest in you? Do you have personal experience that promises special insights into the subject? Can you perhaps write a fascinating first-person account? If not, do you have academic background and writing experience that indicate you would be thorough, professional and trustworthy on this story? Do you have access to expert sources? What can you show us or tell us to demonstrate you have a determined attitude and can deliver?
- How long will you take to finish the story? Roughly, what will its structure be? First-person account? Personality profile?
- What fee will you accept?

Now, we'll move over to your side again to discuss how you can build "talking points" that anticipate and answer those questions and, importantly, sell your story idea.

Sample Talking Points

Envisage this scenario: A long-established campus newspaper serving your college is challenged by an upstart newspaper, and a hot competitive fight develops over student and faculty readers and advertisers. Such head-on fights are increasingly rare in the newspaper industry, and you smell a story in what's happening on your campus.

How do you find a market for the story?

Writer's Market and *The Gale Directory of Publications* (like other standard media reference works) list magazines published throughout the nation and by content specialty. Your university librarian points you to newspaper industry trade magazines. Journalism professors lead you to *Editor & Publisher,* a weekly trade for newspaper professionals, journalism school faculty members and others.

A quick read of back issues reveals *E&P*'s content ranges widely across newspaper-related topics. Two subjects covered in depth are competitive fights between newspapers and significant developments in campus newspapers and journalism education.

Perfect! Now, in preparation for contacting *E&P,* let's develop talking points along these lines:

First, *E&P*'s editor should be interested in your story because (a) it fits into the magazine's general pattern of covering the newspaper industry, and (b) it meets *E&P*'s goal of covering journalism education. That is, your story idea fits neatly into the *pattern* of *E&P*'s ongoing coverage.

Second, your story is unique because head-on competitive fights rarely erupt these days, particularly in campus journalism. And your story is exclusive because you alone see its news value and offer the story idea.

Why should the editor buy your story? Because you are on the scene, read both papers, study writing and journalism and have firsthand access to sources—on both papers, among student readers, advertisers and journalism professors. Can you be trusted to do a professional job? Weave into your talking points these factors: You're deadly serious about a career in writing. You've taken courses (including this current writing course) that prepare you for this story. Of course, if you've written previously for publication—in either newspapers or magazines—mention that!

You can finish the story within two weeks and fax it to *E&P* in New York City. Your writing angle will be "newspaper feud erupts on campus." You will use a story structure based primarily on interviews with the opposing publishers and editors, plus interviews with readers and advertisers. That is, you've selected reporting and writing approaches that an editor likely will believe you can master, despite your lack of experience. Do *not* overreach by promising, say, a national survey of campus journalism as practiced at 100 universities and colleges. No editor will buy that from a beginning writer.

You feel the story would be strengthened by photos of editors and publishers involved, and you can provide them from each newspaper. You also can obtain from the newspapers camera-ready shots of front pages, and a photographer colleague of yours will provide any action shots the magazine desires. That is, you can assist in creating the totality of presentation that *E&P*'s editor will immediately think about when you mention your story idea.

Now, what fee will you accept? Editors generally offer a fee, but negotiate when you can. At minimum, you must recover out-of-pocket costs, so be certain to build the best possible cost estimate. Of course, in our scenario your costs will be minimal (another advantage of picking manageable stories close to home). A walk across campus, not a flight across the continent, gets you to all the principals. So, it's a case of negotiating a fee with *E&P*'s editor, John Consoli. We telephoned him, explained the scenario and negotiated on your behalf.[1] His response: *If* you can convince him on the telephone that the story has the news value we described above and *if* you deliver a strong reporting and writing job, he'll pay you $250–$300 for your story. By any measure, you should go after this type of assignment. The money, though not great, surely would compensate you for the time involved in reporting and writing. More importantly, you would gain valuable experience and a significant clip from a recognized magazine for your portfolio. (For future reference: Once you've established even a short record of successful publication, don't sell yourself or your work cheaply.

Position yourself as a professional—or, at least, a semi-pro—who expects to be properly compensated for hard work.)

Now you are ready to plan your actual approach.

Approaching Your Target Editor

If your target is a campus magazine or a small local publication, you may be able to wander in and get an immediate interview with the editor. Try for that. Face-to-face selling of your story idea is best.

Be sure to carry along a note pad with answers to the questions we asked in the last section. Check them off during the conversation, and *do* remember that if you are an inexperienced, unproven writer you must use this interview to sell yourself as much as your story idea.

You won't always get immediate access to editors, of course (when you move off campus and target big-league magazines you almost never will). In that case, try to telephone the editor for an appointment. In your initial telephone conversation, be prepared to handle this: "Tell me briefly what your story is about." Again, go to your notes and summarize what you have in mind.

At this point, in an interview or on the telephone, you may wonder whether to describe your idea fully. Will it be stolen and given to a staff writer? Reputable editors don't steal someone else's ideas or work, but not all editors are reputable. How do you, as a beginner, know who is and isn't? You might as well be fully forthcoming and hope you'll be treated fairly and honestly. Beginners don't have enough leverage to do anything else. The editor, after all, controls two things you need to start building your career: ink and paper.

Telephone the editor if your story idea is particularly timely. News is perishable and its value often withers quickly. So, editors of weekly trade publications and other magazines tied to current events often welcome quick telephone advisories.

It's quite possible, of course, that you won't be able to contact an editor in person or by telephone, or you may fear doing a lousy job of presenting your idea and yourself in person. For some beginners, the pressure cooker of an editor's office is hard to handle. So, let's look at selling your ideas and yourself by letter.

Writing Strong Query Letters

Picture a busy editor—on the telephone, desk piled with paper—receiving a letter from someone (you) whose name doesn't ring a bell, written from a town (yours) the editor has never visited and concerning a subject (your story idea) the editor has never heard of.

You have a tough sell ahead.

In just seconds, that editor will decide whether you and your story idea are worth pursuing. Your challenge is to make those seconds work effectively for you. Figure 9–1 shows how you could try to sell to Editor John Consoli a story idea on that campus newspaper fight we mentioned earlier.

Figure 9–1 raises a number of important points:

- Demonstrate, beginning with how you address the editor, that you know how to do research. It's worth a dollar or two to telephone the magazine's switchboard so you can address the editor by name, not blindly as "Dear Editor."
- Be certain that everything in your letter, particularly the editor's name, is spelled correctly. Nothing kills a query letter more quickly than misspellings or grammatical errors, which are self-incriminating evidence of amateurism.
- Include your home address and telephone number so you can be contacted quickly if the editor wants consultation.

FIGURE 9–1 A Sample Query Letter

January 19, 1993
116 S. Basil Avenue
Hometown, Ill. 61701
(309) 542-9874

Mr. John Consoli, Editor
Editor & Publisher
11 West 19th Street
New York, N.Y. 10011

Dear Mr. Consoli:

I want to offer you a story on a hot competitive fight developing here on the campus of Hometown University between a 100-year-old college daily, *The Barker,* and a well-financed newcomer, *The Daily Bulldog.*

This story fits nicely into your pattern of coverage for newspaper professionals and journalism educators, particularly because the competing papers are fighting for advertisers and readers both off and on campus. This is a head-on collision, and I feel the journalistic and managerial tactics employed here would be instructive to editors and publishers of all newspapers, regardless of where they are published.

This story is unique because, as you know, there are few head-to-head fights left in the newspaper industry. I am offering the story to you exclusively.

I can write to any style and length, but envision a story of about 700–800 words, structured around interviews with editors and publishers on both sides, and with advertisers and readers. The story would examine competition for both reader time and advertiser dollar. Already, the newcomer has gained a circulation foothold—and has forced the established paper to cut its advertising rates.

As you will note from the attached résumé, I am a senior at Hometown University and, thus, have access to all principals involved. I am a regular contributor to our journalism school's quarterly magazine and have taken several writing courses that I feel prepare me to handle this assignment for you. I could fax this story to you within three weeks of receiving your go-ahead.

I can obtain from the newspapers, at no cost, file photos of the principal editors and publishers, and camera-ready shots of typical front pages of both papers. I can arrange for a photographer colleague to shoot action photos to your specifications for $25 per photo published.

I will telephone you in a week to answer any questions you might have.

Sincerely,

- As in our first paragraph, outline immediately and concisely the central thrust of your story idea—a "hot competitive fight" in this instance.
- Quickly address the question of whether your story fits into the magazine's pattern of coverage. The editor alone will ultimately answer that question, but get your thoughts on record. We do that in the second paragraph: "This story fits nicely into your pattern of coverage for newspaper professionals and journalism educators...."
- Note also in the second paragraph how we outline the story's wider appeal: "... instructive to editors and publishers of all newspapers, regardless of where they are published." Anticipate the questions likely to arise in the editor's mind, then answer them in a manner that will sell your idea.
- Mention, as in our third paragraph, why the story is unique and whether you are offering it exclusively. Some writers offer ideas to several editors simul-

taneously, then take the first or best offer. However, editors don't like to be played off against each other so, in general, a beginner is advised to develop the intimacy of an exclusive offer. It can lead to an ongoing relationship that will help you sell the editor on future ideas.

- Display, as in our fourth paragraph, your ability and willingness to write to requested style and length. But, importantly, specify what you have in mind ("700–800 words, structured around. . . ."). And emphasize, once more, why the story is important (one paper already cut its ad rates, a development of significance for any publisher among *Editor & Publisher*'s readers).

- Attach your résumé and, as in our fifth paragraph, use your cover letter to draw attention to your single most important characteristic. In this case, it's that you regularly contribute to a campus magazine (and thus are an established writer) and are ready to handle the assignment.

- Mention, as in our fifth paragraph, when you can submit the story. Consider carefully the time you'll need to "file" or deliver your story, then tack on a week to be safe. The editor may schedule your story based on your promise, and you'll destroy your chances of any ongoing relationship if you don't meet your self-imposed deadline.

- Offering to arrange photos or other illustrations improves your chances of a sale. Your story may be secondary in the overall scheme of *E&P*'s coverage plan, and Consoli probably would pass it rather than go to great effort and cost to arrange illustration independently. Also, illustration will help your story get better play (or position) in the magazine, which will improve its impact in your clip file.

- As in our last paragraph, retain initiative for a follow-up. Editors get busy. They put letters and story ideas aside. Sometimes you can speed the process with a gentle prod by telephone. Don't write, "I eagerly await your response."

- Finally, note our sample letter doesn't mention your costs or fee expectations. Try to maneuver the editor into making an offer. If it's higher than you expect, grab it! If it's too low, say so and negotiate. With experience and a publishing track record, you'll have a stronger negotiating position. Right now, you might have to take a low offer and regard getting published in a leading magazine as compensation. Incidentally, note for future reference: Big-league editors often pay a commission fee to retain the services of an accomplished free-lance writer. That helps the writer cover costs of travel and research. Some editors also pay a "kill fee" for stories they commission but don't use. Until you build a reputation for excellence you'll probably have to submit finished stories "on spec"—on speculation that they'll be accepted.

Some writers, particularly those whose byline editors recognize, prefer to submit story ideas in concise memos. Let's look at that form.

Writing Idea Memos

However you submit a story idea, the fundamentals we discussed earlier must be laid before your target editor. In memo form, a story idea could be presented along the lines of Figure 9–2.

If you have a good handle on this story—that is, if you've figured out how you'll write it—you may want to open your story memo as shown in Figure 9–3.

Whether you offer your story in person or by letter or memo, keep three points in mind.

First, explain immediately and concisely your story's central thrust and its relevance to the target magazine's audience. Practice your in-person presentation or edit your letter ruthlessly to eliminate verbiage that forces the recipient editor to work to understand your meaning.

FIGURE 9–2 An Idea Memo

Story Offering

January 19, 1993
116 S. Basil Avenue
Hometown, Ill. 61701
(309) 542-9874

To: Editor John Consoli, *E&P*
From: Beginner Writer
Subject: Exclusive story on head-on competitive fight between two Hometown University campus newspapers.

- Well-financed newcomer, *The Daily Bulldog,* is challenging 100-year-old college daily, *The Barker.*
- Battle for readers and advertisers is forcing *Barker* to give ground, reducing ad rates. In an industry where few head-on fights occur, this battle shows editors and publishers everywhere that no newspaper has a safe, secure hold on its market franchise.
- I am a magazine student at Hometown University (résumé attached) and have direct access to principal editorial and management executives involved in the fight, plus advertisers, readers and, for analysis and interpretation, journalism and business school professors.
- I can deliver the story, accompanied by illustrations and photos taken to your specifications, within three weeks of your go-ahead. . . .

Second, don't get cute. Don't write, "Subject: Story idea that will knock your socks off. . . ." or, "Mr. Editor, I've got a story that can really improve your magazine. . . ." In the first instance, editors seek performers, not boasters; in the second, you've told the editor the magazine needs improvement—a direct challenge of how it's edited by current management.

Third, with every story offering, present a résumé that *sells you.*

Writing a Résumé That Sells

Selling your work requires selling yourself, and that, in turn, requires fashioning a résumé very carefully. As you write yours keep two points in mind.

FIGURE 9–3 Another Story Memo

To: Editor John Consoli, *E&P*
From: Beginner Writer
Subject: Exclusive story on unique newspaper war

Envisioned lead:

HOMETOWN, IL—A newspaper war, rare anywhere in the industry these days, has erupted on the campus of Hometown University. It proves not even well-established newspapers are safe from damaging competitive attacks.

Details:

Well-financed newcomer . . .

First, your résumé must highlight—briefly and honestly—the experience and personal traits that will build an editor's trust in you.

Second, it must be shaped for fast reading. After a few seconds, if your résumé hasn't caught an editor's eye it may end up in the wastepaper basket.

The résumé example in Figure 9–4 raises a few issues.

First, be certain everything in your résumé is accurate. Don't exaggerate, even mildly, what you've accomplished. Sadly, editors have learned they must check out résumés, and the slightest sniff of dishonesty will finish you.

Second, if you have professional experience, as does "Beginner Writer," emphasize it. But if you've had to wash dishes 40 hours weekly to pay your bills and thus haven't had time to work on campus publications, mention that and emphasize, instead, your academic preparation. In Figure 9–4, that would mean substituting "Education" for "Professional Experience."

Third, enclose full-page clips to show editors how your stories were played and what they competed against. Ask a trusted advisor to help select your best clips. Your own judgment needs confirmation.

Fourth, include names, titles, addresses and telephone numbers of at least three references who can comment on your reporting and writing professionalism. That doesn't include your pastor (editors know pastors feel compelled to say something nice about everyone) or your father (listed by one of our students as, obviously, a sure thing!). Ask references in advance: "I'd like to list you on my résumé. Could you give me a good reference?" That puts the person on record as promising a favorable reference.

Now, let's assume your résumé/story idea package scored with an editor and you're ready to formalize an agreement to write the article. What's next?

Guard Your Ownership Rights

Under the law, you own what you write unless you relinquish your property rights. Beware that you don't relinquish those rights unknowingly—or without adequate compensation.

You may feel as a beginner writer that getting published is so important that you don't want to risk offending an editor by squabbling over property rights. But keep in mind that magazine articles sometimes become the basis for profitable movies or books, and that some articles are sold as reprints. Such secondary usage can have substantial economic value. Because of that, you need a written agreement with the magazine on what rights you are selling.

Try for agreement to sell only "first North American serial rights." This gives the magazine a one-time right to publish your story in North America, and reserves to you the opportunity to sell it to foreign magazines or share in proceeds from secondary use. This agreement also retains your right to expand your article into a book or screenplay.

Under some circumstances, you might want to sell one-time publication rights that are more restricted. For example, you could sell geographically limited rights— giving a city magazine rights to your article in just that city or region. Another limitation on sale could be topical, providing an aviation magazine first-time exclusive rights among aviation magazines.

You can expect difficulty obtaining written agreement from campus publications or small off-campus magazines, which often are mildly disorganized and tend to overlook such niceties. In that case, write your own letter of agreement. Figure 9–5 is a form recommended by the American Society of Journalists and Authors Inc. (ASJA).

Obviously, the letter suggested in Figure 9–5 is written to fully protect your rights. As a beginner you might not have the leverage to get all the protection you want. If not, *negotiate.*

FIGURE 9–4 A Sample Résumé

Beginner Writer
116 S. Basil Avenue
Hometown, Ill. 61701
(309) 542-9874

Professional Experience

Assistant managing editor, September 1992–present, *Viewpoint,* a quarterly magazine of 9,000 circulation published by Journalism Department for Hometown University faculty/students. Am responsible for all staff writer assignments and copy editing.

Staff writer, Viewpoint, September 1991–September 1992; wrote one major feature for each of four issues during that year; also wrote front-of-book "Around Town" column reviewing student bars, restaurants, entertainment.

Editorial internship, Hometown City, June 1991–September 1991; paid internship with this monthly city magazine of 11,000 circulation; edited letters-to-editor and did editorial research for staff writers handling cover stories in three issues.

Part-time reporter, Hometown Daily News, September 1990–June 1991; wrote weekend prep sports for this daily of 19,000 circulation.

Publishing Record (clips attached)

- Profiled university president during budget controversy; *Viewpoint* (cover story), November 1991.
- Surveyed university policy, student reaction on switch to semester system; *Viewpoint* (cover story), January 1993.
- Question-and-answer with university athletic director on football team grade scandal; *Viewpoint,* November 1991.
- Free-lanced "tail-gate party scene" for *Chicago Tribune* entertainment section, October 1991.
- Free-lanced "pressures on prep athletes," *Hometown Daily News* Sunday sports section, September 1992.

Education

Expect A.B.J. from Hometown University, June 1993.
Major: Magazines. Courses included Introduction to Professional Newswriting, Public Affairs Reporting, Introduction to Magazine Writing, Contemporary American Magazines, Advanced Feature Writing.
Minor: Business.

References

Mr. John Lother	Mrs. Betty White	Prof. Milton Lawser
Managing Editor	Asst. Managing Editor (sports)	*Viewpoint* Faculty Advisor
Hometown City	*Hometown Daily News*	Box 118
239 Wilson Blvd.	1876 Third St.	Department of Journalism
Hometown, Ill. 61701	Hometown, Ill. 61701	Hometown University
(309) 543-6789	(309) 543-0980	Hometown, Ill. 61701

FIGURE 9–5 A Sample Publishing Rights Agreement (*Reprinted with permission from The ASJA Handbook © 1992 by The American Society of Journalists and Authors*)

Date
Your address

Editor's name and title
Publication
Address

Dear [Editor's name]:
This will confirm our agreement that I will research and write an article of approximately [number] words on the subject of [brief description], in accord with our discussion of [date].

The deadline for delivery of this article to you is [date].

It is understood that my fee for this article shall be [$ amount], with one-third payable in advance and the remainder on acceptance. [ASJA recommends that if the publication refuses to pay an advance you may want to substitute this wording: "If this assignment does not work out, a sum of one-third the agreed-upon fee shall be paid me."] I will be responsible for up to two revisions.

[Name of publication] shall be entitled to first North American publication rights in the article. [ASJA recommends that if your discussion included sale of other rights, this clause should specify a basic fee for first North American rights, additional fees and express rights each covers, and total amount.]

It is further understood that you shall reimburse me for routine expenses incurred in the researching and writing of the article, including long-distance telephone calls, and that extraordinary expenses, should any be anticipated, will be discussed with you before they are incurred. [ASJA recommends any other conditions agreed upon, such as inclusion of travel expenses or a maximum dollar amount for which you will be compensated, should also be specified.]

It is also agreed that you will submit proofs of the article for my examination, sufficiently in advance of publication to permit correction of errors.

This letter is intended to cover the main points of our agreement. Should any disagreement arise on these or other matters, we agree to rely upon the guidelines set forth in the Code of Ethics and Fair Practices of the American Society of Journalists and Authors. Should any controversy persist, such controversy shall be submitted to arbitration before the American Arbitration Association in accordance with its rules, and judgment confirming the arbitrator's award may be entered in any court of competent jurisdiction.

Please confirm our mutual understanding by signing the copy of this agreement and returning it to me.

Sincerely,
[Signature]
Your name [printed]

Publication
by _____
(name and title)

Date _____

Two things to watch closely:

First, in the fourth paragraph, if the editor demands rights beyond "first North American rights," see if you can obtain additional payment. Whatever the outcome, make sure the fourth paragraph explicitly outlines which rights you are selling. Ensure it specifies the basic fee for first North American rights and each additional fee for other rights.

Second, you may have to agree to pay all or most of your own expenses. So, determine in advance, as precisely as possible, what total costs you will incur in doing the story. Ensure the fifth paragraph explicitly states which costs you will pick up and which the magazine will cover.

Many magazines have standard letters of agreement, of course, and you'll be expected to sign one for free-lance assignments. A key provision in most agreements comes out of this language in the Copyright Act:

> Works Made for Hire: In the case of a work made for hire, employer or other person for whom the work was prepared is considered the author for purposes of this title and unless the parties have expressly agreed otherwise in a written instrument signed by them, owns all the rights comprised in the copyright.

Note "Works Made for Hire." If that language or "All Rights Transferred" appear in a letter agreement, the magazine or publishing company will own the copyright. Figure 9–6 is a letter agreement used by Crain Communications, publisher of *Advertising Age, Automotive News* and other excellent trade magazines, to commission free-lance articles. As you read, note the special emphasis we've added to material in the first, second and third grafs.[2]

Note in Figure 9–6 that first-graf language (in italics) gives Crain Communications exclusive ownership of articles that its magazines commission from free-lancers.

In the second graf, free-lancers agree ("you represent and warrant") that articles they sell are original, don't include any libelous or unlawful matter, haven't been published previously and aren't being submitted to another party. This is legally binding language, so don't sign such an agreement unless you are absolutely certain you can meet all conditions.

In the third graf, Crain reserves the right to edit articles it buys. Writers agree to rewrite, if necessary, without additional payment.

Of all conditions in such agreements, the "work-made-for-hire" language causes most problems between writers and magazines. That's because it gives magazines full ownership of free-lancers' work. The controversy led the American Society of Journalists and Authors to issue a position statement on authors' rights (note Box 9–2).

In negotiating an agreement with a magazine, you should take care to protect your rights in other areas. First, note the ASJA's "Code of Ethics and Fair Practices" in Box 9–3.

You'll note in Box 9–3 that ASJA's code really is a set of guidelines you can follow in protecting your author's rights, and not a journalistic code of ethics (which we'll discuss in Chapter 15). These are among key rights ASJA—and we—recommend you guard carefully:

- Retain the right (paragraph 1) to maintain the sense or intent of your article, which can become distorted in the editing process. You'll have to submit to often rigorous editing, of course—but you do have the right to ensure that your article's basic thrust isn't rewritten without your consent (paragraph 9 in Box 9–3).
- Your story idea is *yours,* even if an editor rejects your offer to write it (paragraph 3).
- You have the right to be compensated if, during an assignment, your editor removes you from the story (paragraph 7). (Of course, you have responsibilities to your editor, too. For example, you should make every effort to keep

FIGURE 9–6 Rights Agreement Used by Crain Communications (*Reprinted with permission of Crain Communications Inc.*)

Dear _____:

As we have previously discussed, and in consideration of the payment of _____ , and other good and valuable consideration, you have agreed to prepare an article *specifically ordered or commissioned for use* as a contribution to the periodical _____ and *you expressly agree that the article will be a work for hire* of Crain Communications Inc ("Crain"). The commissioned article will relate to _____ , and may include photographs and other related works such as graphs and charts, (the "Article"). Since *it is intended that all rights to the Article, including all copyrights, shall belong to Crain,* you agree to sign any documents, including assignment documents, or copyright registration applications and related materials, that may be deemed necessary or appropriate by Crain to reflect Crain's ownership of all rights to the Article.

With the exception of any portions of the Article for which you have obtained all rights, including all copyrights, from the owners of such portions, *you represent and warrant that the entire Article will be your own original work of authorship. You further represent and warrant: that you own all rights to the Article, including copyrights, that production, publication or any other use of the Article by Crain will not infringe the rights, including the personal or proprietary rights, of any other party; and that the Article will be factually accurate and will not contain any libelous or otherwise unlawful subject matter. You also represent and warrant that the Article has not been published previously, nor has it been submitted to another party for publication.*

Crain reserves the right to make any editorial changes to the Article that it considers necessary or appropriate to conform to Crain's requirements, and *you agree to rewrite the Article to conform to Crain's requirements without any additional compensation.*

If you agree to the above terms, please sign and date the enclosed copy of this agreement and return it to me. Also, if there is any other person who made or will make a contribution to this Article, including supplying photographs or other materials, please have them sign and date the agreement as well.

In the event that you prepared the Article or any portion thereof in connection with your employment by someone other than Crain, please have an authorized representative of your employer sign and date the agreement.

Very truly yours,

Crain Communications Inc.

By: _____
Its: _____

Agreed:

_____
Name

_____
Date

| BOX 9-2 | ASJA Position on Work for Hire |

In an effort to protect the rights of authors who sell articles, the American Society of Journalists and Authors, Inc., has issued the following position statement on "Work Made for Hire":

It has long been the established practice for responsible periodicals, in commissioning articles by free-lance writers, to purchase only one-time publication rights—commonly known as "first North American serial rights"—to such articles, the author retaining all other rights exclusively and all revenues received from the subsequent sale of other rights reverting to the author.

This practice is affirmed by the Code of Ethics and Fair Practices of the American Society of Journalists and Authors (ASJA), the national organization of independent nonfiction writers. The philosophy underlying this tradition has been further affirmed by the Copyright Law of 1976, which took effect in January of 1978 and states explicitly that copyright is vested in the author of a work and commences at the moment of creation of that work. "Copyright" is, literally, the "right to copy"—i.e., to publish in any form; that right is the author's, transferable only by written agreement and only to the degree, and under the terms, specified by such agreement.

It has come to the attention of the ASJA that certain periodical publishers have recently sought to circumvent the clear intent of the law by requiring independent writers, as a condition of article assignment, to sign so-called "all rights transferred" or "work made for hire" agreements. "All rights transferred" signifies that the author, the recognized copyright owner, transfers that ownership—and the right to all future revenues that may accrue therefrom—to the publisher. A "work made for hire" agreement specifically relegates the independent writer, so far as the article under consideration is concerned, to the status of an employee and creates a mythical—but nonetheless presumably legally binding—relationship in which the author agrees to function as a hired hand, while the publisher assumes the mantle of "creator" of the work, with all the rights of ownership vested in the creator under the law.

Both types of agreement clearly presume that the work being produced has an inherent value beyond one-time publication. Both the law and the ASJA Code of Ethics recognize that presumption, and it is the intent of both documents that the transfer of any rights beyond one-time publication take place only as the result of negotiation that assigns monetary value to each such specific right a publisher seeks to acquire. Both types of agreement described above deny the author's basic role as owner and creator and seek to wrest from the writer, even before the work has been produced, all future interest in revenues that may derive from that work.

This effort, subverting the intent of the law and contrary to ethical publishing trade practices, is condemned by the American Society of Journalists and Authors. The demand for blanket assignment of all future right and interest in an article or other creative work simply will not be met by responsible independent writers. Publishers who persist in issuing such inequitable agreements in connection with commissioned works will find that they have done so at the certain risk of losing a healthy flow of superior professional material. The result, for those periodicals, is likely to be a sharp and inevitable decline in editorial quality—an erosion and debasement of the standards on which periodicals must rely in order to attract readers and maintain their own reputations.

(*Reprinted with permission from* The ASJA Handbook © *1992 by The American Society of Journalists and Authors*)

---

your editor advised of your progress, particularly if you're running behind schedule and might not make your deadline.)

- You should insist on a byline for your article (paragraph 10). It's particularly important to have bylines when you're getting started as a free-lance writer and trying to become known in the industry.

- Try to negotiate a kill fee, which compensates you if an editor accepts your idea and orders an assignment, then cancels it through no fault of yours (paragraph 13). ASJA reports that kill fees average about 30 percent of the total agreed-upon fee.

- You have a right to prompt payment of your fee and any agreed-upon expenses within 30 days of submission of your article (paragraph 14). *Never* agree to payment only when your article is published. That may take months.

- You have the right to use an agent who contacts editors and attempts to sell your work (paragraph 20). A generally accepted fee is 10 or 15 percent of what you are paid. It's best, however, to make your own contacts, get to know editors personally and learn how to negotiate for yourself. Anyway, agents deal mostly in books and films and seldom are interested in beginner magazine writers, most of whom must scrape for years to make a living!

ASJA Code of Ethics and Fair Practices

BOX 9–3

Preamble

Over the years, an unwritten code governing editor-writer relationships has arisen. The American Society of Journalists and Authors has compiled the major principles and practices of that code that are generally recognized as fair and equitable.

The ASJA has also established a Committee on Editor-Writer Relations to investigate and mediate disagreements brought before it, either by members or by editors. In its activity this committee shall rely on the following guidelines.

1. **Truthfulness, Accuracy, Editing.** The writer shall at all times perform professionally and to the best of his or her ability, assuming primary responsibility for truth and accuracy. No writer shall deliberately write into an article a dishonest, distorted, or inaccurate statement.

    Editors may correct or delete copy for purposes of style, grammar, conciseness or arrangement, but may not change the intent or sense without the writer's permission.

2. **Sources.** A writer shall be prepared to support all statements made in his or her manuscripts, if requested. It is understood, however, that the publisher shall respect any and all promises of confidentiality made by the writer in obtaining information.

    (In 1991, the U.S. Supreme Court ruled that a source whose name had been revealed contrary to a promise made by a journalist was entitled to sue, even though the agreement was not a written contract.)

3. **Ideas and Proposals.** An idea shall be defined not as a subject alone but as a subject combined with an approach.

    A proposal of an idea ("query") by a professional writer shall receive a personal response within three weeks. If such a communication is in writing, it is properly viewed and treated as business correspondence, with no return postage or other materials required for reply.

    A writer shall be considered to have a proprietary right to an idea suggested to an editor.

    (A beginning writer should enclose a self-addressed, stamped envelope, to be used for the magazine's reply, along with an article proposal. *All* writers should enclose such envelopes when submitting *unsolicited* manuscripts; no magazine can be expected to assume the cost of returning material it has not assigned or invited. If the material is stored on a computer disk, the writer may wish to advise the magazine that an unwanted manuscript need not be returned.)

4. **Acceptance of an Assignment.** A request from an editor that the writer proceed with an idea, however worded and whether oral or written, shall be considered an assignment. (The word "assignment" here is understood to mean a definite order for an article.) It shall be the obligation of the writer to proceed as rapidly as possible toward the completion of an assignment, to meet a deadline mutually agreed upon, and not to agree to unreasonable deadlines.

5. **Conflict of Interest.** The writer shall reveal to the editor, before acceptance of an assignment, any actual or potential conflict of interest, including but not limited to any financial interest in any product, firm, or commercial venture relating to the subject of the article.

6. **Report on Assignment.** If in the course of research or during the writing of the article, the writer concludes that the assignment will not result in a satisfactory article, he or she shall be obliged to so inform the editor.

7. **Withdrawal.** Should a disagreement arise between the editor and writer as to the merit or handling of an assignment, the editor may remove the writer on payment of mutually satisfactory compensation for the effort already expended, or the writer may withdraw without compensation and, if the idea for the assignment originated with the writer, may take the idea elsewhere without penalty.

8. **Agreements.** The practice of written confirmation of all agreements between editors and writers is strongly recommended, and such confirmation may originate with the editor, the writer, or an agent. Such a memorandum of confirmation should list all aspects of the assignment including subject, approach, length, special instructions, payments, deadline, and guarantee (if any). Failing prompt contradictory response to such a memorandum, both parties are entitled to assume that the terms set forth therein are binding.

    All terms and conditions should be agreed upon at the time of assignment, with no changes permitted except by written agreement signed by both parties.

9. **Rewriting.** No writer's work shall be rewritten without his or her advance consent. If an editor requests a writer to rewrite a manuscript, the writer shall be obliged to do so but shall alternatively be entitled to withdraw the manuscript and offer it elsewhere.

10. **Bylines.** Lacking any stipulation to the contrary, a byline is the author's unquestioned right. All advertisements of the article shall also carry the author's name. If an author's byline is omitted from the published article, no matter what the cause or reason, the pub-

BOX 9–3 *continued*

lisher shall be liable to compensate the author financially for the omission.

11. **Updating.** If delay in publication necessitates extensive updating of an article, such updating shall be done by the author, to whom additional compensation shall be paid.

12. **Reversion of Rights.** A writer is not paid by money alone. Part of the writer's compensation is the intangible value of timely publication. Consequently, reasonable and good-faith efforts should be made to schedule an article within six months and publish it within twelve months. In the event that circumstances prevent such timely publication, the writer should be informed within twelve months as to the publication's continued interest in the article and plans to publish it. If publication is unlikely, the manuscript and all rights therein should revert to the author without penalty or cost to the author.

13. **Payment for Assignments.** An assignment presumes an obligation upon the publisher to pay for the writer's work upon satisfactory completion of the assignment, according to the agreed terms. Should a manuscript that has been accepted, orally or in writing, by a publisher or any representative or employee of the publisher, later be deemed unacceptable, the publisher shall nevertheless be obliged to pay the writer in full according to the agreed terms.

If an editor withdraws or terminates an assignment, due to no fault of the writer, after work has begun but prior to completion of a manuscript, the writer is entitled to compensation for work already put in; such compensation shall be negotiated between editor and author and shall be commensurate with the amount of work already completed. If a completed assignment is not acceptable, due to no fault of the writer, the writer is nevertheless entitled to payment; such payment, in common practice, has varied from half the agreed-upon price to the full amount of that price.

14. **Time of Payments.** The writer is entitled to full payment for an accepted article within 30 days of delivery. No article payment, or any portion thereof, should ever be subject to publication or to scheduling for publication. (Writers are strongly urged to reject agreements that specify payment at any time later than this.)

15. **Expenses.** Unless otherwise stipulated by the editor at the time of an assignment, a writer shall assume that normal, out-of-pocket expenses will be reimbursed by the publisher. Any extraordinary expenses anticipated by the writer shall be discussed with the editor prior to incurring them.

16. **Insurance.** A magazine that gives a writer an assignment involving any extraordinary hazard shall insure the writer against death or disability during the course of travel or the hazard, or, failing that, shall honor the cost of such temporary insurance as an expense account item.

17. **Loss of Personal Belongings.** If, as a result of circumstances or events directly connected with a perilous assignment and due to no fault of the writer, a writer suffers loss of personal belongings or professional equipment or incurs bodily injury, the publisher shall compensate the writer in full.

18. **Copyright, Additional Rights.** It shall be understood, unless otherwise stipulated in writing, that sale of an article manuscript entitles the purchaser to first North American serial rights only, and that all other rights are retained by the author. Under no circumstances shall an independent writer be required to sign a so-called "all rights transferred" or "work made for hire" agreement as a condition of assignment, of payment, or of publication.

19. **Reprints.** All revenues from reprints shall revert to the author exclusively, and it is incumbent upon a publication to refer all requests for reprints to the author. The author has a right to charge for such reprints and must request that the original publication be credited.

20. **Agents.** An agent may not represent editors or publishers. In the absence of any agreement to the contrary, a writer shall not be obliged to pay an agent a fee on work negotiated, accomplished and paid for without the assistance of the agent. An agent should not charge a client a separate fee covering "legal" review of a contract for a book or other project.

21. **TV and Radio Promotion.** The writer is entitled to be paid for personal participation in TV or radio programs promoting periodicals in which the writer's work appears.

22. **Indemnity.** No writer should be obliged to indemnify any magazine or book publisher against any claim, actions, or proceedings arising from an article or book, except where there are valid claims of plagiarism or copyright violation.

23. **Proofs.** The editor shall submit edited proofs of the author's work to the author for approval, sufficiently in advance of publication that any errors may be brought to the editor's attention. If for any reason a publication is unable to so deliver or transmit proofs to the author, the author is entitled to review the proofs in the publication's office. (In the past, magazines have sometimes pleaded time constraints, with turnaround within hours, to explain failure to submit proofs. With the advent of the fax machine, a publication's inability to transmit proofs to the author, or to some facility in the author's vicinity, would be extremely rare.)

(Reprinted with permission from *The ASJA Handbook* © 1992 by The American Society of Journalists and Authors)

Managing Your Money

If you're serious about selling your writing (and we hope you are), you should establish precise money-management techniques.

First, unless you're careful, what you spend to research and write an article can get completely out of hand, outrunning by far what any editor will pay you. Over time that's a formula for financial disaster.

Second, what you earn will be subject to federal and, probably, state income taxes. Remember this: It's not what you earn *before* taxes that counts; it's what you keep *after* taxes that matters.

So, if your free-lance career takes off, *get expert advice from an accountant or tax advisor.* Following are some additional tips from your non-accountant co-authors.

Before contacting an editor with a story idea, calculate carefully all out-of-pocket expenses you'll likely incur. In your mind, "walk" through the research, interviews and travel you'll have to do for the article. Pay particular attention to transportation, hotel and food costs. They're the big ones. But don't overlook seemingly insignificant costs—long-distance telephone calls, entertaining (lunch for a source?), books or other materials you might have to buy. These "small" costs can amount to big numbers.

Total all envisioned expenses for your story. Add 10 percent for "contingencies," expenses that, inevitably, you've overlooked. Then add 10 percent more. Now, you have a cost estimate as a basis for fee negotiation with the editor. Right? Wrong! We haven't discussed inserting in that estimate a reasonable charge for your time.

Obviously, if your primary goal is simply to get published and get your free-lance career under way, you might want to negotiate a fee that covers only your out-of-pocket expenses. But don't do that too often. Your time is valuable and limited, and you should be paid for it.

Editors frequently suggest changes in your story idea or request research, interviews or travel you didn't anticipate. Beware: You must quickly estimate any additional costs involved. You may have to renegotiate your fee. Keep separate expense files for each story. You frequently should review which types of stories and magazines are paying off and which are costing you money.

You can establish yourself as a "business" for tax purposes when you free-lance. Some expenses are deductible and will reduce the taxes you must pay. If your free-lance income becomes substantial, your accountant might advise setting up a Keogh plan (a self-employment retirement program) or establishing another tax status to reduce income taxes. Sometimes, accountants can find ways to deduct major, hidden expenses, such as a portion of your housing costs (if you have an office at home) or the cost of magazines, newspapers and books (if used in research or professional advancement.

If you do become a "business," you'll have to file additional tax forms with your federal return, including Schedule C, Profit or Loss from Business, Schedule E, Supplemental Income and Loss, Form 2106, Employee Business Expenses and Form 8829, Expenses for Business Use of Your Home.

Meanwhile, when you conduct research, routinely obtain receipts for every expense. At day's end, note on each receipt the precise details of each expenditure, then enter all costs in an expense file. Don't stuff receipts in a drawer for sorting out six months later. By then, you will have forgotten why you took someone to lunch in Minneapolis, and a receipt from a taxi driver in Dubuque will be unintelligible.

Come tax time, you'll need precise figures on every deductible dollar spent on a story. And, as much as three years after you've filed your tax return, the Internal Revenue Service may audit your return and demand a receipt to prove you took that taxi ride in Dubuque.

NOW, ABOUT YOUR CAREER . . .

If you are interested in a magazine career, you should start the job-hunting process long before graduation. We recommend you take these steps:

First, seriously reflect on your strengths and weaknesses as a writer. What type of writing do you (and your instructors) think best suits you? Are you a strong feature writer? Or are you best at timely, topical writing that's closer to the news—the type of writing favored by trade publications?

Second, of all magazines you've studied, in this and other courses, which appeal to you the most? We've discussed newsweeklies, trades, general interest consumer magazines and others. Given your druthers, which type would you like to work for?

Third, *write for publication*. We cannot emphasize this enough. Write for newspapers and magazines, on campus and off. If you do, you'll answer many questions about yourself and your ability as a writer, in addition to building experience and a clip file.

Fourth, contact magazine writers and editors who visit campus to lecture or meet with classes. How do you arrange a meeting? By walking up, sticking out your hand and saying, "Hello." Telephone off-campus editors and tell them you're a student of magazine writing and would like to drop in and introduce yourself. Many professionals welcome contact with students. Push yourself forward. Develop the professionalism that comes from talking with professionals.

Fifth, when you've decided what type of magazine career to seek, strive for an internship or summer job. Offer to do anything, even the magazine equivalent of hewing wood and hauling water. You need hands-on experience in a magazine environment to make you attractive to potential employers after graduation.

Sixth, immediately write a résumé and hand it out to anyone remotely connected with magazine work. It's called networking, and it means alerting a network of friends and contacts that you're a hard-working, enthusiastic person anxious for an opportunity in the magazine industry.

Writing a Job-Hunting Résumé

The résumé you use in job hunting should differ somewhat from one used in submitting story ideas. Figure 9–7 follows an approach we favor.

You should note a few points about Figure 9–7.

First, by inserting "long-term objective," you provide some sense of your career objective, the sweep of your imagination. That aids a hiring editor in figuring out how you might fit into a magazine's organization.

Second, however, hasten to add, in "short-term objective," that you know you're a beginner, that you have much to learn and that you are willing to do the grunt work that involves.

Third, in listing professional experience, include *any* writing or editing experience. It's all valuable in preparing you for a magazine job.

Fourth, expand your "education" category to include any courses in your major or minor that back up your contention that you're prepared to help an editor get out a magazine. Obviously, in this sample résumé, listing minor courses in business backs up the long-term objective of eventually writing for a national business magazine.

Fifth, in "other," list anything that makes you stand out from the crowd—backpacking, scuba diving, reading Civil War history. As best possible, show the totality of your personality and experience.

FIGURE 9–7 A Job-Hunting Résumé

Beginner Writer

Permanent Address   *Campus Address*
c/o Mr. and Mrs. John Writer   116 S. Basil Ave.
2398 Wilson Blvd.   Hometown, Ill. 61701
San Diego, Calif. 92101   (309) 542-9874
(619) 765-9870

Long-term objective:	Staff writer, national business magazine, covering personal finance and investment.
Short-term objective:	Entry-level editorial position that will involve me quickly in magazine writing and editing.
Professional experience:	*Assistant managing editor,* September 1992–present, *Viewpoint,* a quarterly magazine of 9,000 circulation published by Journalism Department of Hometown University for students/faculty. Write cover stories on various subjects; assign staff writers and edit copy.
	Staff writer, Hometown City, June 1991–September 1991; paid internship with this monthly city magazine of 11,000 circulation. Edited letters-to-editor and did editorial research for staff writers.
	Part-time reporter, Hometown Daily News, September 1990–June 1991, wrote prep sports for this daily of 19,000 circulation.
Education:	Expect A.B.J. from Hometown University, June 1993. Major: Magazines. Courses included Introduction to Professional Newswriting, Public Affairs Reporting, Introduction to Magazine Writing, Contemporary American Magazines, Advanced Feature Writing. Minor: Business. Courses included Accounting (two courses), Computer Science (two), Macroeconomics, Economic Development of the United States, Money and Banking, Financial Management, Commodity Markets.
Other:	Experienced in IBM and Macintosh word processing systems. Dean's Honor List, four semesters. Member, Magazine Club and Society of Professional Journalists. Have backpacked extensively throughout Europe. Hobbies are scuba diving and reading Civil War history.
References:	(As in Figure 9–4)

Writing Sharp Cover Letters

Never simply stuff your résumés in envelopes and scatter them helter-skelter across the landscape. Target potential employers with the same precision you use in selecting magazines for your story ideas.

Ideally, the process of self-examination we described earlier in this chapter will help you locate magazines whose editors likely will be interested in a person with your background. Approach them with a cover letter carefully crafted along the lines shown in Figure 9–8.

The sample shown in Figure 9–8 shows several techniques you can use in a cover letter.

First, your initial paragraph states explicitly what you seek and when you will be available. Don't make the recipient editor guess what you're after.

Second, your second paragraph shows you know *Southeastern Business,* and its type of coverage, and that you've not simply plucked the magazine's name out of a hat. Note also how this paragraph logically ties in your long-term career objective with *Southeastern*'s concentration on personal finance. This paragraph demonstrates that you are a *thoughtful* job applicant.

Third, the letter highlights the single-most important strength of your attached résumé—your substantial experience plus course work in career-related subjects. And, note the pledge to be a "productive member" of the staff from the first day. Editors don't wonder how to further your education or broaden your background. Rather, their question is: "Can this person help me get my magazine out every week?"

Fourth, in your last paragraph, you retain initiative for the follow-up. *Pursue.* Show determination and tenacity.

FIGURE 9–8 Sample Résumé Cover Letter

February 1, 1993
116 S. Basil Avenue
Hometown, Ill. 61701
(309) 542-9874

Ms. Betty White, Editor
Southeastern Business
1165 Wilste Street
Atlanta, Ga. 30302

Dear Ms. White:

I want to apply for an entry-level editorial position with *Southeastern Business* after my graduation from Hometown University on June 6.

I am a long-term reader of *Southeastern Business* and find your concentration on personal finance and investing most appealing. Your current series on home buying hints is superb. My long-term goal is to specialize in this type of magazine writing.

As you will note from the enclosed résumé, I have substantial hands-on experience in magazine writing and editing and have taken many writing and business courses. I believe this combination of classroom and "real world" preparation will make me a productive member of your staff from the first day.

I will telephone your office in a week's time to see if it would be convenient for me to call on you for an interview.

Sincerely,

Winning in a Job Interview

For some beginners, a job interview is torture. It need not be, if you prepare properly.

Recognize first that practice makes perfect, in interviews as in everything else. Seize every opportunity during your college years to interview for internships and jobs, even if you don't want them. After a few interviews your anxiety will disappear, and by the time you interview for a job you really want, you'll be a pro.

Recognize, also, that to succeed in an interview you must do more than simply answer questions. You must make a statement about yourself and *sell yourself.* So, prepare a strategy well before the interview opens. That involves several steps:

- Think through the four or five characteristics that make you unique and desirable as an employee. Write them in a paragraph each. These attributes could be your on-campus experience in magazine writing, your course work, your determination to succeed. Practice sliding them into a conversation, but if the opportunity doesn't present itself, conclude the interview by saying, "There are a couple more things I want to say about myself. . . ."
- Seize the initiative with questions about the magazine, career paths within it and so forth. Take notes. That gives you a chance to break eye contact, which some beginners find difficult to handle, but it also demonstrates you have developed methodical, professional techniques in interviewing and note-taking.
- Have in your notes the minimum salary you *need* and what you *want*— expressed in dollars per week, month and year. That's so you won't lunge unthinkingly at $13,000 annually, which perhaps sounds like a lot of money to an impoverished undergraduate but which isn't. (It works out to only $250 weekly.) But, try to get the interviewer to put the salary on the table, on the theory, again, that if it's more than you expected, you can grab it; if it's less, you can negotiate.
- Dress neatly in appropriate professional attire—jacket and tie for men, the equivalent for women. But don't feel you must mortgage your future to buy hugely expensive clothing.
- Be alert, even a bit aggressive, but avoid any hint of boasting. Your résumé will show your strengths; your job in the interview is to demonstrate you have good skills and can handle yourself in a conversation.

Finally, remember that no matter how "smooth" you are in interviews, it's your substantive preparation—in hands-on writing experience and the classroom—that will sell you.

So, let's continue that preparation by turning, in the next chapter, to another aspect of magazine writing.

SUMMARY

You advance from the ranks of amateur to professional writer by getting your stories published and *getting paid for them.* Devise a strategy *now* for getting into print.

Target a local magazine whose audience you know and write on a local subject you understand, using a story structure you can reasonably master. Don't expect to score at *Esquire,* for a fee of, say, $10,000, with your first story.

When submitting articles, learn all you can about your target magazine—its content, audience and, importantly, the stories it has published recently. Submitting an idea that duplicates a story published a couple of months ago stamps you as an amateur.

Editors you approach will wonder: Does your story fit into their coverage pattern? How is your story unique? Why should they trust you to deliver an accurate, professional reporting and writing job?

Try for a personal appointment so you can answer those questions. If that's not possible, write a query letter or story idea memo that concisely outlines the core of your story, describes how the story fits the magazine's needs, and whether you are offering the story exclusively. Also describe the structure you envisage (personality profile, or whatever), how long the story will be and when you can deliver it.

In writing your résumé, remember that busy editors will give it just seconds. So, use lean, clean language to emphasize your experience in any form of written communication, especially any hands-on work in magazines. List any course work that supports your contention that you are, if not yet a professional, at least a semi-pro.

In preparing for job interviews, practice makes perfect. Take all interviews you can, even if they involve a job you don't want. Handling yourself in a real interview is the best way to master techniques that will win when you finally interview for the job you really want. When that one comes along, go in with a strategy to present, tersely but effectively, the four or five attributes that make you a promising hire.

RECOMMENDED READING

For beginners intent on a serious free-lance career, this is *must* (not merely recommended) reading: *The ASJA Handbook,* 2d ed. (New York: American Society of Journalists and Authors Inc., 1501 Broadway, Suite 302, New York, N.Y. 10036, telephone (212) 997-0947, FAX (212) 768-7414).

NOTES

1. Conversations with Consoli were in November 1991 and April 1992.
2. Special thanks to Editor Fred Danzig of *Advertising Age* for permission to reprint the contract.

Part Three

Writing for specialized magazines

Although prestigious general-interest consumer magazines have the largest circulations, smaller specialized magazines are a writer's biggest—and most rapidly expanding—market.

For every *TV Guide* or *Life,* with their millions of readers, there are *dozens* of specialized magazines catering to audiences with narrowly defined reading interests. And many new specialized publications are launched each year in search of ever more narrowly targeted slices of the reader market.

We turn, in Part III, to the special reporting and writing skills you need to get published in specialized magazines. Note we emphasize *reporting*. When writing for specialized magazines, you are serving an audience that very likely has a high degree of expertise in your subject. Caution: Your readers will spot immediately any weakness in your reporting or any technical errors in your writing. And, they will expect you to advance their knowledge in the subject. That means you must truly understand your topic and be able to find and interview authoritative sources.

We start with business writing in Chapter Ten, "Writing for Your Readers' Pocketbooks." This is one of the most rapidly expanding types of magazine and newspaper writing.

In Chapter Eleven, "Writing Sports," we pass along hints on a type of writing that is both great fun and demanding. Fans expect a high degree of expertise from sports writers.

Chapter Twelve, "Writing for Technical Magazines," addresses the challenge of writing for engineers, scientists, technocrats of all kinds. This fascinating sector is open to non-engineer writers if they take strong reporting skills to the job.

In Chapter Thirteen, "Writing for Entertainment Magazines," we pass along hints on how to get started immediately in a serious career of writing about fun. Magazines on campus and off offer you a market right now.

Chapter 10

Writing for your readers' pocketbooks

Are you interested in money—how to make it, how to save it? Join the crowd. It's a hot topic these days, on campus and off. Everybody is interested in how to make money and how to spend it wisely on tuition, books, cars, rent, vacations and so on.

For more evidence of how popular money is as a magazine topic, check (once more!) your favorite magazine sales rack. Note the number of magazines that cover making and spending money. The obvious titles—*Money, Forbes, Fortune*—are just the beginning. *Time* covers money stories, as do *Lear's, New York, Atlantic, Modern Maturity, Travel & Leisure* . . . virtually all consumer magazines carry regular coverage of "pocketbook" issues.

There also are thousands of trade and specialty magazines that focus narrowly on specific industries and how money is made and spent in them: *Marketing Insights, Beverage Journal, Crain's Cleveland Business, International Fiber Journal, Food Product Design* and many—very many—more.

Such panoramic coverage of business, industry and finance shows that magazine editors understand the reading public's great interest in money. Editors devote major space to stories about money. They also pay premium rates for writers who can sift through the complexities of business news, extract elements important to readers and present them in clear, concise terms.

In this chapter we'll discuss ways you can develop expert skill in this type of magazine writing. We'll also show how you can get a head start on a career in writing about business. Finally, we'll discuss how business news is defined, where it can be found and how it can be written with strength and clarity.

"PITCH" TO YOUR AUDIENCE

As in all magazine writing, your first step in writing about money must be to understand your audience. You must know who reads money stories—and why. Broadly, two characteristics mark this audience.

First, the audience is growing rapidly. More than ever, Americans realize their personal lives—their own pocketbooks—are affected every day by even seemingly remote developments in business and finance. Readers want to understand those developments, to learn how they and their families are affected by world, national and state economic and business trends. From you, the writer, they expect *translation* of those trends into terms they understand.[1] They expect even the most distant, most esoteric development to be reduced into clear, simple language that explains how their lives will be affected.

Second, many magazine readers are financial heavy hitters. As a group they are upscale demographically and, thus, represent a fairly sophisticated level of understanding of money matters. That will challenge you, in turn, to be sophisticated in your reporting, insightful in your writing and, above all, precise and accurate. Note, for example, the following financial profile in Table 10–1, published by the Magazine Publishers Association. This compares financial activity by adult magazine readers to activity by TV viewers—and compares both against a U.S. average of 100.

You can draw two major conclusions from Table 10–1 on how to approach business writing.

First, you should define business writing very broadly. Many magazine readers are affected by virtually any significant development in the general economy, business, industry or finance. As a writer, you'll have an eager audience for stories on interest levels offered for regular checking accounts or individual retirement accounts. Note also that Table 10–1 shows evidence that stories concerning the stock market or other investments are of prime concern to magazine readers. In defining business news, then, work backward from your readers' pocketbooks. If an event might affect wallets or purses, you have a story worth writing.

Second, Table 10–1 makes clear that many readers already are aware of investment devices used to make (and, of course, lose) money. *However,* many readers do

TABLE 10–1 Financial Profile Index, Magazine Readers Versus TV Viewers

Financial Activity	Magazine Readers	TV Viewers
Regular checking account	116	86
Individual retirement account	121	82
Investment property	132	72
Tax-sheltered annuities	141	68
Brokerage account	120	77
U.S. Savings Bonds	127	75
Common stock	123	79
$100,000-plus homeowners insurance	126	75
American Express Gold credit card	133	64

Note: U.S. average = 100.
Source: The Magazine Handbook, 1990–1991, p. 42.

not have investments or tax-sheltered annuities. Some don't know a stock from a bond. And, therein lies a major challenge you'll face in writing this specialty: You must accurately gauge your readers' level of understanding and "pitch" your writing with great precision. But how?

Here's a simple three-step process that can help you.

First, if the magazine deals exclusively with money stories or some narrow aspect of business, finance or commerce, you almost always can assume that many of your readers are fairly knowledgeable. *Beverage Journal* obviously isn't read by casual readers outside the beverage industry, for example. You'll not find *Food Product Design* lying around your dentist's office. Those specialty magazines are edited for targeted readers who earn their living in the beverage and food industries. You'll succeed in writing for such readers only if you add to their already somewhat advanced understanding of a subject. Don't write for experienced brewers that hops are an ingredient of beer (brewers have known that for centuries). Your brewer-readers might be captured and held, however, with a story on, say, a scientific breakthrough in use of hops substitutes in beer making.

If a magazine's editorial content leads you to assume that its readers are experts, you can double-check your assumptions by studying the magazine's advertising. If ads, like editorial content, speak the language of specialists, you know you must write for expert readers. That is, if ads offer goods and services to brewers, not people who drink the stuff, you can assume readers have a fairly sophisticated understanding of how beer is made.

The second step in calculating how to "pitch" your writing: If you are writing money stories for a magazine that covers business or finance as only a relatively minor ingredient in a general mix of many other subjects, you can pitch your writing at a lower level of understanding. For example, *Lear's* targets mature women with editorial content on family, personal health, good looks, travel as well as business in general and personal finance in particular. For *Lear's* general audience you must refine your writing pitch with great precision—aiming at women who are, say, 50 or so and interested not so much in broad economic trends as in how developments in business, commerce and finance affect them personally. Of course, personal finance in itself is a broad subject, so you must carefully refine your approach further. Don't write, for example, as you might for 19-year-old college women, about how to get a credit card or how to read an apartment lease. *Lear's* readers are far beyond that. Rather, write for those 50-year-old women on, say, how to find a trustworthy investment counselor if suddenly widowed, or how to start a small business after the children have left home.

A third step in analyzing the level of reader understanding is, of course, to read carefully the structure and language of money stories previously published in the magazine you target. Editors base their careers on correctly gauging their readers' interests and capabilities and consistently offering appropriate copy. Read what is published and you'll note over time that definite patterns emerge in (a) types of stories published, (b) general writing structures, (c) subtleties in such things as financial terms used and whether they are translated for understanding.

For example, consistent reading of *Money* reveals a strong emphasis on personal finance (how to buy a house, how to invest savings). *Forbes* publishes, year after year, strong profiles of business executives and companies. And *Forbes,* which boasts millionaires among its readers, uses language quite different from language appropriate for a general audience of, say, *Lear's* readers. Writing for *Forbes* about bonds, for example, you could refer simply to "tax-exempts." For *Lear's* readers, you must explain how those bonds are exempt from certain taxes.

Another translation example: It's a good bet that *Forbes* subscribers know what "short-sellers" do for a living. Martin Mayer didn't make that bet when writing for a more general audience attracted to "The Business World," a special supplement published by *New York Times Magazine.* Note his lead on a story about short selling:

> Short selling was, until recently, an activity conducted mostly behind closed doors by consenting professionals who talked about why the stocks they had sold were terrible investments that everyone ought to sell. Short-sellers borrow the stock they sell; they make money when its price drops and they can replace what they borrowed with shares they can buy at a lower price.
>
> Theirs has always been a detested occupation because it's not considered nice to wish bad luck to other people. When a company's stock plummets, it usually means that employees and suppliers and customers as well as stockholders will take a beating.... (*Martin Mayer, "The Business World,"* New York Times Magazine, *9 June 1991, 6*)

In sum, no matter how authoritative your reporting or how expert your writing, you'll fail if you don't ascertain precisely your audience's level of understanding and pitch your story accordingly. Look at it this way: Would you stick with us in this book if, for example, we discussed how to write Dick and Jane stories or how to describe Spot running? We clearly would be on the wrong wavelength for college readers. In writing economic, business and financial news, make certain you are on your readers' wavelength.

Be Accurate

Accuracy must be your primary goal in writing about money, for two obvious reasons.

First, money ranks high on the list of things really important to your readers. If you cause them, through inaccurate writing, to waste their money they'll not forgive you! Editors won't either. Being inaccurate on, say, yards gained in Saturday's football game is one thing; it's something else to present erroneous information that leads your readers into disastrous investments. Money news—like news on health, family, safety and other intensely personal subjects—requires extra-careful handling because readers make important decisions on what you write.

Second, because money topics tend to attract knowledgeable audiences, even the slightest error in your writing will be obvious to some of your readers. For them, accuracy means not only being correct in a broad structural sense but also presenting a great deal of precise detail. They don't want to hear that the Consumer Price Index rose "a couple of points" but, rather, that it rose exactly "2.1 percent."

Handling numbers with accuracy is mandatory in business writing. That's so obvious we won't dwell on the need for precision reporting—and rigorous double-checking the moment you suspect something is wrong with your numbers.

But there is more to *accurately communicating* numbers and their meaning than merely ensuring you heard the correct figures in a speech or press conference and got them down, as spoken, on paper. A couple of hints:

First, when your story involves numbers, make sure the individual components add up. For example, if your lead mentions three million are unemployed in three states, make sure the state-by-state listings total three million. (Then add them again to be doubly certain). If you mention four reasons for a company's bankruptcy, make certain your story clearly explains all four.

Second, to communicate the *meaning* of figures accurately, express them several ways—both in dollars and percentages, for example—and characterize their importance. Note how *Business Week* reporters did that:

> It's no surprise that, over the last 10 years, state and local taxes have increased far faster than federal levies. In 1990, state and local governments collected more than $500 billion in taxes. That's more than 9% of the nation's gross national product—and it's nearly 10% higher than the level a decade ago and more than double the share of GNP in 1970. By contrast, the federal take has hovered at 19% of GNP for the past four years and is still well below its peak of more than 20% in 1981.... (*Howard Gleckman in Washington, with Ronald Grover in Los Angeles, Joseph Weber in Philadelphia and Keith H. Hammonds in Boston, "Pity the Poor Taxpayer,"* Business Week, *2 Sept. 1991, 32*)

Frankly, accurately understanding how much $500 billion actually is will be beyond many readers. But when that number is characterized as in *Business Week,* its meaning becomes clearer.

Here's another example: Suppose we want to describe how an Avon lady in China makes $1,500 a month. Can you fully grasp the significance of that? No? Never mind, a *Forbes* writer puts it in perspective for you:

> Liang Yungjuan, 40, is a pediatrician in the city of Guangzhou (Canton), capital of free-wheeling Guangdong Province in the People's Republic of China. What does a Chinese pediatrician earn? About $120 a month. But Dr. Liang earned more than ten times that much last month—though not from practicing medicine. As a part-time Avon Lady, she netted $1,500, her share from the proceeds of selling $5,000 of makeup and skin care products.... (*Andrew Tanzer, "Ding-Dong, Capitalism Calling,"* Forbes, *14 Oct. 1991, 61*)

Another reason to be on guard over accuracy when writing money news: Disreputable people can make a great deal of money by influencing you to handle business stories certain ways. Money moves on news; into whose pockets it moves and how quickly often depend on how the news is written. For example, recall the previous illustration about short-sellers. They trade in stocks by betting prices will fall. You can see how they would gain by quietly selling a stock short, then influencing you to write a story that, when published, would drive down the stock's price.

Readers of stories on business and finance count on you for more than getting names and addresses right, for more than getting the facts straight in a press conference. Readers also count on you to objectively and dispassionately sort through often conflicting reports and get the accurate picture despite any efforts to unduly influence your writing.[2]

But, you may wonder, how can a college student grasp fundamentals of writing such complex subjects? How can a beginning writer develop background essential to translating for readers stories about short selling and other business world esoterica?

You start by developing disciplined reporting skills. Now.

Develop Authoritative Sources

Nothing gets a beginning writer off to a faster start in business news than learning how to develop and use authoritative sources.

It's important to remember that you're not required personally to be an instant expert in economics, business or finance if you want to write on those topics. However, you *are* required to find sources who are experts, then develop their confidence in you as a painstaking, professional writer who will treat their information with great care. Once accepted as a reliable professional, you'll be able to unlock business world information that will make your writing sparkle with authority and precision.

The best sources are people acknowledged as leaders in their fields, including chief executive officers of corporations, government officials, university scholars and others with in-depth expertise in a specialty area. The best sources are positioned properly to know what is happening and how it affects your readers. These sources are near the origin of power, in business, government and politics. They are situated to see (and explain to you) important developments. It's an old rule for reporters: Move upstream to the headwaters of money and power, in private business or government, and you'll find sources you need.

A few additional pointers:

Economic, business and financial news is extremely complicated at times, and even the most expert magazine writers must check sources and recheck them, in a circular, never-ending process. It takes hard work to ensure your reporting is up-to-date, accurate, balanced and authoritative. You don't have to independently assess developments and predict for your readers how they can best manage their business lives. You must, however, present the views of truly authoritative sources so your readers can make their own informed judgments on how to order their lives.

It's often difficult to develop authoritative sources in the corporate world. Believe it: An almost traditional view among business executives is that reporters cannot be trusted to make the required effort to understand business complexities or to pass along to their readers an accurate, balanced viewpoint. Indeed, many business executives regard writers as anti-business. You'll have to work harder and longer to develop sources in the business world than you would in sports. But in business, economic and financial writing, the effort to develop sources is worth it. "Working" expert sources can yield news tips and background information that give your copy an authoritative ring for editors and readers alike.

Once you develop sources and start to build personal background in business news, your challenge is to present information in a style that communicates effectively. Let's look at some ideas on that.

Basic Writing Hints

The best business writing is, above all, accurate and clear. But close behind in your writing priorities must be creating an attractive style and easy narrative flow to capture the great drama of many business stories, the clash of powerful business personalities, the fascinating swirl of economic developments that affect the lives of every American.

Lesson: You can create impact in this specialty writing if you write with the excitement and verve that the very best sports writers give to their craft or leading Washington correspondents to theirs. Business isn't dull; your writing about it cannot be dull, either.

Note how *Lear's* Contributing Editor Patricia O'Toole uses a catchy lead to ease her readers into a complex story on a struggle over control of Time Inc.:

> Not so very long ago, debt was a four-letter word. All but a fortunate few had to resort to mortgages and the odd loan, of course, but persons of character were expected to regret it. As for boasting about one's borrowings—well, that was unthinkable.
>
> Things have changed, and there is no more striking display of the sleight of hand that has turned debt from vice to virtue than this year's struggle for control of Time Inc. It started peaceably—and cheaply—enough. At the beginning of March, Time and Warner Communications Inc., an entertainment conglomerate, announced that they would merge in a deal that was virtually debt free; they would simply swap shares of stock. Both companies hailed the deal as the marriage of the decade. . . .

Deeper in her story, O'Toole maintains her writing momentum with a light touch on a serious problem that arose during merger talks: Some *Time* employees feared Warner accountants (the "abacus boys") would cut spending on news coverage. Here's how she explained that:

> . . . journalists at *Time* Inc. magazine feared for their editorial independence. Would *People* stories about Warner stars like Spielberg and Streisand have to be valentines? Would the lights go out at far-flung *Time* bureaus when the abacus boys at Warner found out that readers always skip those earnest but mind-numbing pieces from Burkina Faso and Djibouti? (*Patricia O'Toole, "Silk Purse Chronicles,"* Lear's, *Oct. 1989, 29*)

Writing hint: With nimble lead writing and skillful play on words you can draw even casual readers of a consumer magazine into a story that without deft writing would bore many. Read again how O'Toole's lead did that. Note also that once she "hooked" her readers, O'Toole didn't lapse into dull, routine writing. She maintained her writing pace to draw readers deeply into the story.

Next, free-lance writer David DeVoss dresses up a serious, dollars-and-cents business story with a nicely crafted lead. Note also how quickly, in the second paragraph, De Voss draws readers into his central thrust—the growth of a famous department store chain.

> If shopping is the great American reward for hard work and virtuous living, then entering a Nordstrom is, for many people, a little like going to heaven. Nordstrom is a phenomenally successful specialty department store chain based in Seattle, founded 88 years ago as a family shoe store. Later it became a retail-apparel chain, which, for the most part, it remains. In the 1980's—a decade during which a bewildering variety of retail markets went soft and companies as entrenched as Gimbels, Goldwater's, and J. L. Hudson were restructured or collapsed—Nordstrom grew beyond retail-industry analysts' most optimistic expectations.
>
> Ten years ago Nordstrom was strictly a regional retailer whose 26 Pacific Northwest stores earned respectable combined annual revenues of about $293 million. Today the company—still family controlled—has 49 branch stores scattered across 5 western states and suburban Virginia, with revenues in excess of $2.3 billion a year—an almost 800 percent increase. (By way of contrast, Lord & Taylor and Neiman Marcus, both successful, have doubled annual income since 1980.) In the next few years Nordstrom plans to extend throughout the Midwest and the Northeast corridor, launching 15 more stores by 1993. The newest, called Pentagon City, is due to open September 29 in Arlington, Virginia. . . . (*David DeVoss, "The Rise and Rise of Nordstrom,"* Lear's, *Oct. 1989, 35*)

In the last example, "annual revenues" and other dollar details so important in a business story can get a bit heavy for a general audience of readers of a consumer magazine such as *Lear's*. So, in the third paragraph (which we don't have room to reproduce in full), DeVoss maintains reader interest with this informative gem about a Nordstrom store with "something for everyone":

> Its Champagne Exchange offers 103 brands of bubbly, beluga at $50 an ounce, and 16 varieties of chilled vodka. . . .

"Wow," readers think, "that's fascinating . . . lead on." And DeVoss does:

> Women's rooms are universally decked out with leatherette changing tables, free disposable diapers, and wipes for the kids. (third paragraph)
> In a hideaway penthouse there is even a spa where drop-in customers can enjoy herbal footbaths or mint-scented algae facial scrubs while listening to seamless New Wave music tinkling in the background. (fourth paragraph)
> Women's shoe departments at the branch stores stock up to 70,000 different *styles* of shoe, all in sizes 4 to 12. (sixth paragraph)

You get the picture: With writer David DeVoss leading the way, readers leap ahead, searching for more fascinating tidbits. Before they know it, they have read a thorough story about retail marketing and have absorbed an understanding of how a top-of-the-line department store is managed.

Incidentally, look again at the second paragraph in the DeVoss story above. Note how neatly he inserts Nordstrom's growth record ("Ten years ago," "today"), compares it with growth by other chains (Lord & Taylor, Neiman Marcus), then pitches the story ahead ("In the next few years Nordstrom plans . . ."). Whatever your business story and however you write it, that kind of comparative data is mandatory.

Now, note how *not* to write a business story. This writer gets comparative data into the lead, but merely dumps them in, making no effort to entice you into reading.

> At 13,632, final attendance figures for the National Spa and Pool Institute's (NSPI) 34th Annual Convention/Expo in Anaheim, Calif., were significantly lower than the more than 17,000 people who turned out for 1989's event in Orlando. A sluggish economy and cutbacks in travel expenses may have played a role in the lower attendance figures, according to Molly Finney, director of conventions and expositions for the NSPI. "Instead of bringing 10 people as they've done for previous shows, they may have brought five or even three this year," Finney explained. . . . (*"Show Wrap-Up,"* Swimming Pool/Spa Age, *Jan. 1991, 28*)

The only readers who will work their way through the preceding example are those who desperately want to learn about a swimming pool convention. Don't make your readers work that hard. They have too many reading options, too many demands on their time, and they'll switch to something else rather than fight their way through verbosity.

Remember that in business writing, you often ask readers to absorb much complex material and many numbers. You can help them by pacing yourself carefully, by limiting the bursts of information you fire at them. The next example is from a writer who ignored that advice. Read the following paragraph once (only once) and write down its central meaning.

> Football television contracts in the 1991–92 season will cost the networks about $1 billion in rights fees, including about $900 million for the National Football League and $100 million for various college football and World League of American Football deals, but tight fourth-quarter budgets among advertisers are likely to hinder the networks' efforts to recoup the costs. (*"First Down and $1 Billion in 4th Quarter,"* Broadcasting, *12 Aug. 1991, 38*)

Were you able to absorb, in a single reading, the meaning of this paragraph? No? We couldn't either, and that's because the writer jammed five separate thoughts into one sentence ($1 billion, $900 million, $100 million, tight fourth-quarter budgets, networks' efforts).

Your challenge, then, is to juggle twin responsibilities: making your writing readable (and, whenever possible, enjoyable) while simultaneously inserting operative, fact-filled information desired by hard-core business readers. You can do it.

Here's how a writer for *Forbes,* a hard-core business publication if there ever was one, crafts a lead to entice you gently into a story about root beer marketing wars:

> Anyone who lives near bayou country has probably known about Barq's root beer for years. Barq's has been a local institution since 1898, when Edward Barq gave up on his dream of planting champagne vineyards in Louisiana and started brewing root beer in backyard tubs. In southern Mississippi, Barq's once held 30% of the soft drink market—ahead of even Pepsi—despite the fact that Barq's ran virtually no advertising.
> These days, though, Barq's reach goes far beyond the bayou. . . .

Make no mistake: This story isn't designed for simple reading pleasure. Its mission is to inform marketing executives and investors of competitive shifts in root beer marketing and possible investment opportunities. So, the *Forbes* writer puts aside cute writing about bayou country and gets operative information into her story. Note how clearly she does that, presenting comparative percentages in readable form:

> Thanks to a smart expansion plan and an unconventional advertising approach, Barq's new owners have pushed Barq's from its Deep South stronghold into over 70% of the country—and they're still moving. In fact, Barq's has become the second-ranked root beer in the country, with 8% of the $1.8 billion root beer market. In the past five years Barq's 37% annual growth rate has propelled it past Pepsi's Mug (6.6%), Monarch Co.'s Dad's (4.8%) and Cadbury Schweppes' Hires (4.8%). Barq's still has a way to go to catch number one A&W with 30% of the market, but there's no doubt what the goal is: Barq's recently had T-shirts printed that read, "A&Who?" . . . (*Claire Poole, "Beyond the Bayou,"* Forbes, *24 June 1991, 94*)

Sometimes, such factual details are best set off from the body of your story, in an accompanying chart, graph or box. Editors normally decide how material is to be presented, but writers increasingly are expected to suggest page designs and typographical devices that best present the total information package and highlight essential elements. *Working Woman* took the "package" approach in a major story on career opportunities for women. Writers briefly described different careers (physical therapist and international accountant, for example) and set off additional facts. After describing careers in international accounting, *Working Woman* set off this data:

Education: An undergraduate liberal-arts degree in accounting is required. A master's degree in taxation, accounting, business, or law and proficiency in a foreign language are highly desirable.

Salary: Entry level brings $25,000 to $32,000, while midcareer accountants earn $35,000 to $55,000. At the top, $250,000 to $300,000 is possible. (*Pam Carroll, "The Growth Careers,"* Working Woman, *July 1991, 58*)

You often achieve two major results by handling data as did *Working Woman.*

First, you improve readability, sometimes dramatically, by removing dense masses of detail from the body of your story. Jumbled masses of facts and figures, frequently difficult to absorb, can bog down the narrative flow of your writing.

Second, you improve information accessibility for your readers. It's easier to understand dollar figures by glancing at a chart or graph, for example, than it is to try to pluck them one by one from a running narrative and comprehend them. In its story, *Working Woman* presented education and salary information for each career possibility, all in the standardized format. At a glance, readers can pick out the essentials.

U.S. News & World Report, which bills much of its content as "news you can use," employed a combination of body copy and other devices to lead readers carefully through a complicated story on health costs. First, *U.S. News* used this lead:

Senior citizens are about to get some relief from a large headache—deciphering medigap insurance. The often confusing coverage, bought by 65 percent of Americans over age 65 to fill in Medicare's gappy coverage of hospital and doctors' bills, has been the target of complaints and fraud investigation since the mid-1970's. Many seniors have been pressured to buy several or even dozens of policies when one would have been enough. Limited reforms didn't vanquish the abuses. Now, following Congress's mandate for a sweeping overhaul, the National Association of Insurance Commissioners has devised 10 standard policies that will soon replace the 250 or so variations on the market. The group has also added major benefits and set new rules by which the policies must be sold. . . .

Note how easily you can make your way through the last lead. One careful reading and you can comprehend its central thrust. But, obviously, readers with health care problems need meatier stuff—facts and figures for their decision making. *U.S. News* set off those facts.

First, a separate story listed what medicare policies will and will not cover. (For example, which hospital costs policies will cover: "For first 60 days, 100 percent after deductible of $628". . . .)

Second, separate boxes enticed readers with detail that, while fascinating, would seriously impair the readability of the main story. An example:

A MOUNTAIN OF BILLS
A serious illness burdens you with $24,850 in expenses.

■ Hospital: $16,500 (21 days)
■ Doctors: $4,500
■ Nursing Home: $2,800 (28 days at $100 per day)
■ Home Care: $1,050 (14 days at $75 per day)

WHO PAYS?
(*"Plugging the Medigap,"* U.S. News & World Report, *1 July 1991, 60*)

In business writing, your basic mission is to communicate operative information to readers. To do that, you sometimes must use many writing, packaging and design devices.

Important: Stay fresh in this process. Reach for new ways of presenting information in palatable form. But don't reach so far that you grab a tired old cliche, as did a writer for *Modern Maturity:*

The good news is that the majority of older Americans still live in their homes. The bad news is that. . . .

We don't know about you, but we've heard enough "good news, bad news" stories to last two lifetimes. So, undoubtedly, have your readers. Don't try to be too cute in your writing; sometimes you're best off just letting a story tell itself.

Let's look at how you can "tell" your business story better by carefully selecting the writing structure most appropriate for the type of information you are delivering to readers.

MASTER FUNDAMENTAL STORY STRUCTURES

In structuring business stories you are limited only by your imagination. Even casual reading of business magazines reveals a wide variety of story forms and narrative frameworks. Editors increasingly are casting aside old-fashioned rules of writing and seeking writing approaches that are unique and innovative. If a writing approach works, use it.

Of all structural possibilities, three are most important for beginning business writers: The straight or hard-news approach; the how-to structure and the profile. Let's look at all three.

The Straight or Hard-News Structure

Let's say you awaken some night and see your neighbor's house is on fire. How would you communicate the news? How about running across the lawn and shouting: "The good news is that I've called the fire department . . . The bad news is that your house is on fire."

That scenario is ridiculous, of course. It's equally ridiculous in business news to try to be so cute in your writing that you delay for very long delivering hard, operative facts or disguise crucial information your readers need—now—for making important decisions. Your writing defeats your primary mission of communicating effectively if, in an undisciplined effort to be readable, you disguise news behind thick layers of verbiage.

Obviously, however, there are problems in writing a hard-news approach for magazines. Other media, particularly newspapers and TV, can reach your readers more quickly with news than can magazines. So, the straight writing structure works best in weekly magazines that can stay closer to business developments than can monthly or quarterly magazines. Still, even for weeklies the "straight" approach works only if you meet at least one of three conditions.

First, you'll clearly succeed with a straight hard-news structure if you have a story exclusively. But it's difficult for a magazine to be exclusive in general business news. Much breaks from government or corporate sources who routinely make it available to daily newspapers and TV. However, in writing for specialty magazines you can focus on a narrow segment of business and often break stories that general-interest media simply don't cover. When you do, write to take your readers straight into the news. And for that, nothing beats recalling the writer's mantra you studied in basic newswriting: who, what, where, when, why and how.

Second, the hard-news structure for a magazine story often works splendidly if daily newspapers and TV break a story, but just skim the surface of its news. For example, general-circulation newspapers revealed Hearst Corp. and Dow Jones & Co. might jointly publish a magazine. But many newspapers, with an entire world to cover for readers of enormously varying interests, published only a few paragraphs. That permitted the weekly *Advertising Age,* though it didn't break the story, to put a straight lead on its story:

NEW YORK—More than eight months after the concept was revealed, Hearst Corp. and Dow Jones & Co. are gearing up to test a new personal finance magazine.

The media companies last week signed a partnership agreement that covers next March's test of *Smart Money* and—if the test is a success—its launch.

The magazine will be subtitled *The Wall Street Journal of Personal Business.*

Jack Heistand, publisher of magazine development at Hearst, will serve as managing director, overseeing a board made up equally of executives from both companies. Board members include John Mack Carter, director of magazine development at Hearst, and Norman Pearlstine, executive editor of *The Wall Street Journal.*

The joint venture combines Hearst's experience with testing, launching and publishing magazines and Dow Jones' editorial resources and expertise with business and personal finance issues. Steve Swartz, 28, a former front-page editor of the *Journal,* will serve as editor. . . . (*Scott Donaton, "Hearst, Dow Jones Title Test Set,"* Advertising Age, *19 Aug. 1991, 4*)

The straight lead in this story works because it gives *Ad Age* readers operative details not available from newspapers or TV. (Incidentally, the lead would work in a daily newspaper if it concluded; ". . . personal finance magazine, *it was learned to-day.*") Insertion of a today time element isn't possible in a weekly magazine, of course, so the writer subordinates his time element ("last week") to the second paragraph and then neatly pitches the story ahead ("next March").

Next, *Business Week* fashions a straight news lead for an event already covered on almost a minute-by-minute basis by daily newspapers and TV, the attempted coup against Soviet leader Mikhail Gorbachev in 1991. This lead works because it focuses on a narrow element of the story important to *Business Week*'s specialized audience—joint ventures in the Soviet Union—that newspapers and TV didn't cover well.

As the tanks rolled into Moscow on Aug. 19, John Mitchell dispatched a message to his colleagues at Imperial Chemical Industries PLC: All visits to the Soviet Union were canceled. Families of employees there were ordered to leave the country. As chairman of ICI East Europe, he also called a halt to several joint ventures that he had been negotiating with the Soviets.

But 48 hours later, Mitchell did an about-face. As the tanks retreated and reform-minded politicians appeared to regain control, Mitchell overruled his earlier messages and prepared to resume joint-venture talks. "After one step backward, it's two steps forward to a free market," he says. . . . (*Richard A. Melcher in London, with Mark Ivey in Houston, Jonathan B. Levine in Paris, David Greising in Chicago and Joyce Barnathan in New York, "For Investors, 'After One Step Backward, It's Two Steps Forward',"* Business Week, *2 Sept. 1991, 28*)

A third way to succeed in magazine writing with a straight lead is to use the traditional Five W's and How but to surround them in analytical detail normally not found in daily business writing. For example, note below how *New York,* a weekly, handled a breaking news story about an advertising agency, Scali, McCabe, Sloves. This story was strongly covered in daily newspapers and TV before *New York* could get it:

If Scali, McCabe, Sloves had proposed only the controversial sonogram spot—in which a fetus floats to New Age music while a voice-over asks, "Is something inside telling you to buy a Volvo?," the crash could have been avoided. But it didn't, and the massive tires that crushed Volvo's competitors and dented the reputation of the "car you can believe in" have proved to be, if not fatal to Scali, at least a nightmarish interlude.

On November 13, one week after Volvo ran corrective newspaper ads apologizing for its "Bear Foot" spot, and after several days of tense conferences, Scali resigned the $40-million account, its biggest and oldest. Under pressure from Texas Attorney General Jim Mattox, who called Volvo's ad "a hoax and a sham," Volvo admitted that the commercial shot in Texas—in which a monster truck with huge tires runs over various cars but only Volvo withstands the pounding—was based on a car-crushing exhibition that had taken place in Vermont. If only the ad had noted that this was a dramatization. . . . (*Bernice Kanner, "Crunched,"* New York, *10 Dec. 1990, 22*)

The Economist, a London-based weekly, sticks close to major news developments and attracts a large and influential audience throughout the world, including the United States, because of its interpretative writing. *The Economist*'s reputation for analysis is so strong, in fact, that it often proceeds as if competitive media don't exist. *The Economist* lead here, you'll note, mentions an 11-day-old time element—September 17—in a magazine dated September 28.

> WASHINGTON, "A debate that wasn't supposed to happen is now going on in Washington." With those words Les Aspin, the Democratic chairman of the House Armed Services Committee, opened a speech to the Air Force Association on September 17th—and broke a taboo. He said that if changes in the Soviet Union permanently reduce the reach of its armed forces and diminish the power of its military-industrial complex, substantial further reductions in America's own defence budget will have to follow.
>
> That was exactly what a senior person like Mr. Aspin was not meant to say. For between the autumn of 1990 and the spring of this year, Congress and the administration took a series of decisions both on the federal budget generally and on an orderly rundown (by about 22% in the years from 1990 to 1996) of the defence budget. Outside the left wing of the Democratic Party and the right wing of the Republican Party, everybody hoped that the agreements would stick. They will not. . . . (*"The Pentagon Goes on the Defensive,"* The Economist, *28 Sept. 1991, 25*)

In sum, the hard-news approach to business writing works best if you carry an event forward, revealing something your readers don't know, or if you surround a complex development in understandable analysis. Think back to our fire scenario: If you're the first to run across the lawn to your neighbor's burning house, stress the real news: the house is on fire. If you are the second good Samaritan to arrive, bring "new news"—that you've called the fire department and it will arrive soon (a look-ahead angle!) or that you saw the fire start in the kitchen (helpful analysis).

The "How-To" Structure

This structure works well for alerting readers, step-by-step, about how they can solve a money or business problem. Recall from Chapter Six that it looks like Figure 10–1.

Following is an example of how free-lancer Joseph A. Harb used that structure for a *Modern Maturity* story on how to buy a car (the magazine titled it, "Never Pay Sticker Price Again!"). First, an anecdotal lead:

> When (Fred Smith) of Springfield, Virginia, accompanied his daughter to the new-car dealership for her first auto purchase, they had three aims in mind: The total cost would not exceed $9,000, the monthly payments would not exceed $150, and the sales agreement would not be signed that day. At least those were their resolves before they encountered the Human Buzz Saw, a.k.a. the new-car salesman.
>
> Four hours later, the (Smiths) walked out the door with signed papers for a new car. "I think I got a good deal," Linda says today. "But I wish I hadn't bought so quickly. I really didn't know what was happening."
>
> What was? . . .

Quickly, a summary of the problem:

> Most cars carry built-in profit margins of 10 to 20 percent. Profits on dealer-added options can be 100 to 1,000 percent or more. As a result, the less wary buyer can pay several thousand dollars more for a car than he or she has to.

Now, a step-by-step examination of "ploys" used by car sellers—and how buyers can handle them:

> Following are 10 ploys you'll probably encounter next time you go to buy a new car. How the (Smiths) handled them is worth noting.

FIGURE 10–1 The "How-to" Article Structure.

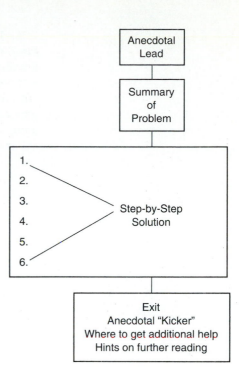

1.   I know just what you want. As they greet you, car sellers begin smoking out your greatest concern—price range, trade-in, extras, monthly payments, etc.—and focusing on that concern to convince you to buy. ("I know you're paying $2,500 more than you planned. But with a five-year loan and a large down, your monthly payments are what you wanted, right?") . . .

Defense.   The (Smiths) couldn't be sweet-talked. They did what they came to do and ignored the rest.

2.   What will it take for you to buy? Don't fall for this one, which is followed by: "If I can do that for you, will you buy a car today?" If you do, you'll identify what's most crucial to you and make you feel like you've made a verbal commitment to buy. Instead, don't commit yourself.

Defense.   Unfortunately, this ploy worked on the (Smiths) in the matter of Linda's monthly payment. To escape it, remember you're the one holding the money. Tell the salesman you're ready to buy (if you really are), but only if you're given (1) the car you want, (2) the features you want, (3) the price you want, and (4) the terms you want. And don't be swayed from your position. . . .

Then, after carefully discussing each selling ploy, writer Harb exits with this kicker:

Postscript: Linda (Smith) bought her new car for $8,834, more than $3,000 less than the original asking price but roughly equal to the manufacturer's suggested list price—which left the dealer with a healthy profit and Linda with a car she wanted and could afford (although she and her dad still think she could have done better). (*Joseph A. Harb, "Never Pay Sticker Price Again!" Modern Maturity, Aug.–Sept. 1987, 66*)

Note several things about Harb's writing skill.

First, the story flows easily, almost in conversational tempo, yet is packed with dollars-and-cents detail and firm advice on how to buy a car. It is "news you can use" in highly palatable form. Gently weave facts into your narrative.

Second, the story progresses in a logical, chronological manner that's simple to follow. Walking through a car purchase with the Smiths makes it easy for readers to understand the buying process.

Third, no concept or term in the entire story (including the portions we don't have room to reproduce) goes unexplained or untranslated. You don't need an advanced degree in accounting to understand this story.

A strength of the how-to structure in business writing is that it can be used for any audience, whatever its level of expertise—not only for simplistic explanations for general audiences of such things as car buying. For example, *Medical Economics,* with an upscale, well-educated audience of physicians and surgeons, takes this approach to the complexities of insurance:

> When was the last time you thought about business insurance? We figured as much. But go ahead and let your policies gather dust in the filing cabinet. There's probably nothing to worry about. Unless, of course, you overlooked something when you first bought your insurance. Or you've added or cut staff since you last reviewed your policy. Or taken on a partner. Or bought equipment. Or rented out office space.
>
> Maybe a quick check is in order, after all. Here's what to look for.... (*"Bring Your Coverage Into the '90s,"* Medical Economics, *29 Oct. 1990, 68*)

Note two factors about this story.

First, this is trade journal writing done with engaging informality and rhythm that make for easy reading. Don't think that business writing for the trades has to be stodgy or colorless. Liven things up a bit!

Second, note the use of "we" (*Medical Economics*) and "you" (the physician-reader). This is an effective device for bringing readers into a story and personalizing its impact. Note how we, your authors, have tried to do that for you, our readers, throughout this book.

The Profile: A Winning Structure

Would you like to steal some time from your busy day and read about oil wildcatters? No? Think it's a subject of interest only to other wildcatters?

Wrong.

Look at this:

> Mayer Billy (Duke) Rudman, 81, recalls that when he won an oratory contest at age 15, his father accused him of cozying up to the judges. "He was always telling me I was no good," says Rudman. "I've been trying to forgive him for 40 years since he died, and I can't seem to do it."
>
> Maybe he hasn't forgiven, but Dallasite Duke Rudman has done a pretty good job of proving his father wrong by becoming one of the country's most successful wildcat oil drillers. Known as "Duke" for his flamboyant wardrobe, he likes to flaunt a red satin tuxedo, a green velvet jumpsuit and an Edwardian overcoat and owns 50 pairs of cowboy boots and upwards of 250 hats. He can afford these vanities: Rudman is worth an estimated $220 million.

Ready now to read more about oil wildcatters?

That's what personality profiles can do for you in business writing: They can brighten your topic, bring your writing alive and pull readers deeply into your story.

As discussed in Chapter Six, the profile is a strong story structure in many subject areas. We're discussing it again here because in business news you must redouble your efforts to place lively, palatable writing before your readers. You'll lose them if you don't. The profile is perfect for holding them because it enables you to highlight the most interesting aspect of business—people.

Bit of advice: In writing profiles in business news don't get so wrapped up in the personality that you overlook the underlying responsibility of any business writer: You must address the dollars-and-cents factor, the lessons readers can draw for their own business or investment purposes. There must be a factual, instructional foundation beneath a business profile.

The preceding introduction is from a *Forbes* profile that, after catching your interest (a "red satin tuxedo"?), moves smoothly into how this wildcatter operates.

For example, the *Forbes* writer neatly slides from the wildcatter's flamboyant dress habits to how he will gamble against 100-to-1 odds in making investments. Then:

> But if he's a gambler, Rudman is a disciplined gambler. He rarely takes more than 25% of any particular well. "He won't allow himself to fall in love with a deal," says John Aubrey, president of Houston-based oil prospector Tepco Inc. He makes his picks in tandem with his geologist of 32 years, James Trimble. Together they evaluate some 1,100 drilling prospects a year, from which they pick the 40 or 50 they think show the best risk/reward profiles.
>
> They choose well. Rudman's gambles succeed more than 1 time in 4—a high score for risky wells where the usual success ratio is 1 in 15. With no debt, low costs and his high success ratio, Rudman can make good money even at today's low oil and gas prices.
>
> Rudman tends to work with partners—notably Tepco and Paramount Petroleum—that have proved themselves as oil finders. He has no trouble coming up with his share of the financing. Thanks to some almost uncannily smart timing, he is highly liquid.

At this point, the *Forbes* writer must decide how to end the story. Let it trail off with a few more facts and figures? That would be criminal, when the writer has such a colorful personality to work with. The *Forbes* writer wisely goes back to the human element in fashioning a superb kicker to conclude the article:

> For an elderly man worth nearly a quarter of a billion dollars, Rudman has few extravagances beyond his wardrobe, a chauffeured Lincoln limousine and the three months he spends abroad each year.
>
> With his wife of 56 years, Josephine, Rudman still lives in that house (they've owned for years). He keeps a strict regimen of calisthenics, aerobic exercise and mac-robiotic diet; Rudman is still vigorous. His mother died two years ago at age 101. "I'm going to live to 120," he vows with a wink, "and get shot by a jealous husband." One place he'll never find himself is in bankruptcy court. (*Toni Mack, "My Father Said I Was Stupid,"* Forbes, *2 Sept. 1991, 98*)

Note next how a *Forbes* writer superbly ties an intriguing glimpse of a personality to an underlying investment message of interest to business readers. We'll reproduce only the first two grafs to illustrate the profile's rhythm—personality to instructional tidbit and back to personality:

> Charles Albers, 50, is a methodical man. He runs 4 miles three times a week—always on Saturday, Sunday and one weekday—and he double-ties his shoelaces. He also manages the $275 million Guardian Park Avenue Fund with the assistance of a mechanical stock-scoring system. "It's practical," he says.
>
> Albers began experimenting with stock-scoring systems while working as an analyst for the *Value Line Investment Survey* in New York City.... (*Suzanne L. Oliver, "Momentum and Value,"* Forbes, *2 Sept. 1991, 190*)

That's how to use the profile to make business writing come alive!

Now, we've discussed selecting, reporting and writing business news stories. How can *you* get started in this writing specialty? Let's turn to that.

START IN BUSINESS NEWS. NOW!

Are you searching, as you read this chapter, for the secret that will unlock the mystery of business newswriting?

If so, you can stop. We hope we demonstrated there is no mystery, no secret. Business news is just another writing specialty (although we think it's a particularly fascinating specialty), and you must apply to it the same news values you apply to any form of magazine writing—the same determination to write accurately and dispassionately, with balance and enthusiasm.

Broadly, there are two types of business news stories that even a beginner can start writing immediately.

Localize National Stories

In business news, even the most distant or seemingly esoteric development can unleash a cause-and-effect reaction that in time will strike the pocket of nearly everyone you know. War in the Middle East, bank failures in faraway cities, car production in Detroit—all can have impact on your friends, your campus.

Just think:

- War in the oil fields can generate price increases in the gasoline you and your friends buy. When the first cannon booms, interview university economists on the likely impact on local gas prices. Talk to regional executives of gas companies, distributors, gas station owners, student drivers—the list is endless. The story: A local view, from local experts, of the local impact of that faraway event. It's the stuff of cover stories in local city or regional magazines of local newspapers.

- Distant bank failures can have almost immediate impact on local bank regulation and operation. University experts in the business school or economics department can interpret those distant signals for you. Local bank executives can give you their reaction. The story: likely changes in interest rates students will have to pay on education loans, or how the cost of financing a car will increase. That, too, is cover story stuff.

- Car production in Detroit is a basic indicator of the health of the general U.S. economy. Substantial production increases spur economic growth; decreases depress it. Again, experts on your own campus can interpret the likely impact—and, importantly, can help you trace the cause-and-effect chain to your university and town. Will a local tire manufacturer hire or fire? Will graduating seniors pay more or less for new cars?

In just that manner, by thinking deeply about distant economic developments and consulting local experts, you can develop meaningful and strongly localized business news stories.

These story ideas will occur to you almost instinctively if you develop the habit of reading national newspapers (*The New York Times, The Wall Street Journal, USA Today*) and thinking, each time you read a story, "What is the local angle on this?"[3] National, regional and state business magazines are sources of story ideas, as are television news programs and cable TV's business news shows.

Important economic indicators are issued regularly from Washington and reported urgently in national media. They can trigger meaningful story ideas. For example:

- *Gross Domestic Product* (GDP)—The Department of Commerce issues the GDP, a measure in dollars and percentages of the total goods and services produced *in* the nation. (The older Gross National Product also covers production by Americans *outside* the United States.) If it's up, do local merchants, bankers or chamber of commerce executives say local business is up? Down? It's a story either way.

- *Consumer Price Index* (CPI)—The CPI is a monthly measurement by the Bureau of Labor Statistics of the movement of "market basket" prices—the cost of clothing, food, housing, fuel and so forth. Again, what's the impact on local consumer prices—particularly for goods (potato chips, beer!) that students purchase?

■ *Unemployment rate*—It's reported monthly by the Labor Department, and a fine story for you is what it all means for student internships, part-time jobs, jobs after graduation. Interview your campus placement director, employers or officials of local state employment offices.

Well, you get our point: Even a beginner in business news can spot a distant economic development, interview local authoritative sources and get into print with meaningful and important—if basic—stories of interest to student or local readers. There's another way to get started in business newswriting.

Write Student Money Stories

Want to know which business news stories will get published in a campus magazine? Check your fellow students' pocketbooks (figuratively, of course).

You'll find many students concerned with "pocketbook issues," such as how to get a student loan, how to guard against traps in apartment leases, how to get a job, how to make more money and spend less. And, if you factor into the definition of business news your *own* money concerns, you'll find story ideas surface quickly.

For example, let's examine beginner stories that flow from, say, apartment leases. You can interview university housing officials, local realtors and building managers on apartment availability and rental levels. This could be a what-to-expect story for apartment seekers. Or you could ask law school professors or other authoritative sources to explain how to avoid legal problems over leases—explaining how renters are responsible for damage to apartments, for example, or the limitations on the number of people who can share an apartment.

You have a winning story for any campus magazine or newspaper if you take readers, step by step, through how to qualify for student loans and complete the application process. Examine loans, and interest levels and conditions available from off-campus lending institutions.

When you venture into business writing, experiment with all of the story structures we've discussed. Following is an example of how an anecdotal lead is used by free-lance writer Robert McGarvey to pull you into a story he sold to *USAir Magazine:*

> The job interview was proceeding evenly until Sid Wing asked the candidate about that one curious item on his résumé—the two doctorate degrees he claimed. That's when the applicant exploded: "We nearly came to blows," remembers Wing, president and CEO of Chatsworth, California-based Datametrics Corporation. "He threatened me that he had not one, but two black belts in judo." Did this job-hunter bag a job with Wing's high-tech firm? When asked, Wing only chuckles.
>
> Maybe that pugnacious job-seeker is worse than most when it comes to surviving the interview, but not by much, says Bob McCarthy, an outplacement consultant in Century City, California: "Most job candidates have terrible interviewing skills. Put them in an interview, and odds are high they'll succeed only in shooting themselves in the foot. . . .

Now, you just know that many of your fellow students are deeply interested in how to handle themselves properly in a job interview. So this anecdotal lead is perfect for introducing them to "The ABCs of Interviewing," the title *USAir Magazine* put on the story.

Picture yourself interviewing your university's placement officer, or the personnel chief of a local corporation, and getting that type of anecdote. What substantive information do your readers want? McGarvey bet his readers want lots of how-to detail. Here is some he included in his story:

> For starters, remember this "don't": Never agree to a prescreening telephone interview. To cut expenses, many employers lately are conducting preinterviews—telephone chats. But as Richard Irish, recruiter and author of *Go Hire Yourself an Employer,*

explains, "Your job is to capture a face-to-face interview. Nobody is going to hire you—sight unseen—on the phone." Since this interview can only lead to elimination from the race, beg off talking by pleading a hectic schedule and ask for a face-to-face meeting.

But getting an interview is just the beginning. According to consultant Judith Schuster, the prime error made by job hunters is going into the interview unprepared. "Do that," she explains, "and the employer worries you'll be the kind of person who shows up to work unprepared—and who wants to hire that kind of employee?"

As you write this type of how-to business story for a student audience try to answer questions *you* would like to ask an expert on interviewing. It's likely your fellow students want to ask the same things.

Then, weave in lots of helpful detail, right down to how to dress. Writer McGarvey did:

> Another interviewing basic is your attire. "Dress inappropriately," says John Molloy, author of *Dress for Success,* "and you will not get the job." Research backs up his claim. When asked if their companies turn down people who show up at job interviews inappropriately dressed, a staggering 93 percent of a cross section of executives responded "yes." Granted, a particular corporate culture may dictate a different attire, but barring evidence to the contrary, Molloy tells men to get clothing on their side by wearing a good solid blue suit, a white shirt, and a conservative, nondescript tie. For women, the rules are less concrete, but a good policy is to stick with a conservatively cut suit or a dress in subdued colors and fabrics. Both sexes also ought to avoid wearing flashy jewelry (if in doubt, take it off), and never use an interview to make a fashion statement. If you follow this advice, is the job yours? Not necessarily, but at least your look won't rule you out at the starting gate. . . . (*Robert McGarvey, "The ABCs of Interviewing,"* USAir Magazine, *Aug. 1991, 14*)

Can you have impact on people's lives through business writing? With the last type of story, yes!

SUMMARY

Magazines offer an expanding market for business writing because the lives of so many readers are touched by even seemingly remote and esoteric developments in business, economics and finance.

Define business writing broadly, including any issue that affects readers' pocketbooks. Study your target magazine's content for clues about the level of reader understanding. It's imperative to pitch your business writing to your readers' level of expertise.

Most importantly, your business writing must be accurate. Translating terms and concepts into language your readers can understand is another important goal.

Communicating numbers accurately is a challenge that goes far beyond simply reporting correctly the figures you get in an interview or press conference. You must characterize and place in a proper context all crucial numbers in your story. Expressing concepts in numbers *and* percentages aids reader comprehension.

Nothing gets a beginner off to a faster start in business writing than developing authoritative sources. You're not expected to become an instant expert in business news. You *are* expected to find expert sources and report their views to your readers.

Although accuracy comes first in business writing, a close second is creating colorful, engaging copy that will pull in readers and maintain their reading momentum throughout your story. Weaving interesting, anecdotal material in with hard dollars-and-cents information will do that.

Magazine editors decide how your material will be presented. But writers increasingly are expected to suggest ways to improve reader comprehension through graphics and layout. For example, you can suggest that statistical material be broken out of your main story and presented in an accompanying box or graph. That also can improve your story's readability.

Fundamental story structures important for beginning business writers include straight structures for delivering hard news, the how-to stories and profiles.

To get started in writing business news, look for ways to localize, for a campus or city magazine, a distant economic development (the likely effect on local gas prices of a war in the Middle East, for example). Also, write "pocketbook issues" stories of interest to your fellow students (say, how to conduct a job interview).

RECOMMENDED READING

Next to minoring in business, the best preparation for *writing* about money is *reading* about it.

Through selective, regular and *disciplined* reading, you can learn how professional writers and editors define business, economic and financial news, then report and write it. Our favorite source for learning about the world of money—and the favorite of many writers and editors—is *The Wall Street Journal*. Other sources include *Business Week* (for regular weekly and panoramic coverage), *Forbes* (for short, punchy and beautifully written profiles of companies and people who run them), *Money* (for down-to-earth writing of personal finance stories.)

The *Journal,* in the words of Joseph Nocera, *Esquire* contributing editor, in many ways "resembles a great magazine more than a newspaper." For beginning writers, the *Journal* provides strong guidance in two areas: Its editors consistently show superior judgment in what's news in the world of business, and many of the writing techniques displayed in the *Journal* are fully applicable to magazine writing. Read the *Journal* for guidance on what to cover, how to translate its meaning and how to write it with strength and flair.

Other reading hints:

- The *Journal's* "Education Edition" is an annual, 12-page special edition that explains in lay language how to read the *Journal* itself and, importantly, how to understand stock market price lists, earnings reports, commodity news and other basic business, financial and economic stories. The special edition can be obtained from the *Journal* at Dow Jones Educational Bureau, P.O. Box 300, Princeton, N.J. 08543-0300.
- Also see Richard Saul Wurman, Alan Siegel and Kenneth Morris, *The Wall Street Journal: Guide to Understanding Money and Markets* (New York: Access Press, 1989).
- For learning how to analyze a company's financial position, see "How to Read a Financial Report," published by the brokerage firm Merrill Lynch, Pierce, Fenner & Smith, and available at its headquarters, P.O. Box 30441, New Brunswick, N.J., 08989-0441, or Merrill Lynch local offices.
- Start reading specialty magazines that cover subjects you might want to make your own specialty. Read *Advertising Age* if you want to write about the business of advertising; read *presstime* if covering the newspaper industry interests you. Whatever writing specialty appeals to you, there are periodicals that cover it.

NOTES

1. For beginning writers, note a section on business writing and a glossary in *The Associated Press Stylebook and Libel Manual.* Dow Jones & Co. publishes an excellent glossary.
2. The ethics of business writing are discussed in Conrad Fink, *Media Ethics: In the Newsroom and Beyond* (New York: McGraw-Hill, 1988). Also see codes of ethics published by American Society of Newspaper Editors and Associated Press Managing Editors.
3. Major metropolitan newspapers are excellent sources of story ideas for city or regional magazines. We particularly like business coverage in the *Seattle Times, Los Angeles Times,* the *Milwaukee Journal, Chicago Tribune, Philadelphia Inquirer, Washington Post, Charlotte Observer, Miami Herald* and *Dallas News.*

Chapter 11

Writing sports

Sports offers writers a huge market: Hundreds of magazines are dedicated exclusively to sports, of course, but virtually all magazines, whatever their overall editorial strategies, occasionally feature stories dealing with some aspects of sports or the business of sports.

For those of you with sports expertise, however esoteric, somewhere there is a magazine for you. Niche publications cover not only principal spectator sports, such as football, baseball and basketball, but also narrowly defined special interest areas. Note *Car Craft,* for example, or *Guns & Ammo*, *Backpacker*, *Running* or *Fur-Fish-Game*.

But, what if you don't have expertise in sports? What if you don't know a linebacker from a left fielder? Well, sports still offers you opportunities to get published—if you can report thoroughly and accurately and write in clean, straightforward style. For example, picture yourself handling the following stories. Despite their wide diversity, all are sports or sports-related stories:

- *Vogue,* a fashion magazine, publishes a story on snowboarding, a cross between surfboarding and skiing, *and,* of course, features what every well-dressed woman should wear for the sport.[1]

- *Insight,* a current affairs magazine published in Washington, devotes major play to the *politics* of sports in South Africa.[2]
- *Modern Maturity* provides its audience of older Americans with hints on how to play tennis when "you no longer have quite the up-and-at-'em physical ability you once had. . . ."[3]
- *Sky,* an in-flight magazine you find in your airliner seat pocket, features an article for non-expert TV watchers on the new World League of American Football.[4]
- *Backpacker,* a bible for those who hike and climb for sport, accords major space to an article on where to buy, of all things, the best pocketknife—and how to care for it once it's yours.[5]

You get the point: The subject list of sports-related stories is lengthy, and every magazine, whatever its principal editorial thrust, is a potential target for you.

Your challenge in exploiting these publishing opportunities is to understand thoroughly your target magazine, its audience and editorial strategy, then select an appropriate sports subject and writing angle.

In Chapter Eleven, we'll discuss how you can fashion a winning strategy for sports writing. We'll look at magazines that publish sports stories and discuss writing skills that can help you get in them. We'll discuss in detail many of the techniques used by writers successful in sports subjects.

YOUR FIRST DECISION: WRITE FOR INSIDERS OR OUTSIDERS?

Broadly, your first decision in sports writing is whether to write as an insider for other insiders (fans) or for non-expert outsiders—readers who don't follow sports regularly.

If you want to write for insiders, be prepared to spend as much time and energy learning your craft as does a writer specializing in foreign policy or the intricacies of high finance.

Fans *do* know the difference between a linebacker and a left fielder. Indeed, they likely know how many sacks the linebacker had last season, what the left fielder batted in the minors and whether he tends to lose high ones in the sun. Now, if *you* don't understand the nuances in that preceding sentence, you've got a lot of learning ahead before you try for the prestige national magazines that narrowly focus on finer points of sports for expert readers—*Sports Illustrated, Golf Digest, Inside Sports, Sports Afield* and so forth.

But don't be discouraged even if you're not an expert in sports. You can get into sports writing by using sound reporting techniques, seeking out authoritative sources and interviewing experts, then writing with precision to make sure you're on exactly the right wavelength for your intended audience.

Let's assume you're relatively new to both magazine writing and sports. We'll look first at writing for outsiders, readers who don't follow sports daily but who can be attracted to the subject if the right story is written the right way.

How to Write for Sports Outsiders

Although many magazine readers probably consider themselves sports "outsiders" who aren't interested in sports, all of us are touched by sports in one way or another. Note:

- Americans spend $180 billion annually on sports and athletic events—more than they spend on rent, twice what they spend on religion and more than half what the United States spends on defense.[6]

- U.S. companies spend more than $23 billion annually to sponsor golf tournaments, football bowl games and other sporting events. This sports marketing—designed solely to thrust the name of the corporate sponsor before the public—is expected to more than double by the mid-1990s.[7]
- And, of course, it's difficult to find any newspaper or TV news program that doesn't cover sports.

So, whatever the demographics or psychographics of your target magazine's readers, it's likely you can find among them an interest in, if not a need for, a sports story. Locating it is largely a matter of thinking deeply about the magazine's principal editorial thrust and how you can appeal, first, to the editors who fashion it and, second, to the readers who pay for it every week or month.

We'll run through the process a couple of times to illustrate our point.

Let's start with *The Atlantic,* one of America's most distinguished "thought-leader" magazines. *The Atlantic* appeals to reader intellect on serious topics. Check the table of contents: One issue carries stories on current events in the Far East, hyperactive children and what psychiatrists say about them, environmentally damaging farming, and "The Novel as Status Symbol,"[8] Another features articles on how the United States can cope with victory after the Persian Gulf War (and quotes Thucydides' writings on the Athenian defeat of the Persians in the fifth century B.C.), the tensions between courts and legislatures, the outlook for a reunified Germany.[9]

Heavy stuff! Certainly makes *The Atlantic* an unlikely candidate for a story on something as unintellectual as sports, right? But, wait... what commonality runs through *Atlantic* articles? It's their high-brow tone, their appeal to thinking readers. Is there a peg for a sports story in that?

Sam Toperoff found one. He did a piece on Princeton, pride of the Ivy League. Its basketball coach, Pete Carril, puts together winning teams from *student* athletes who can meet the university's rigorous academic admissions standards, go to class, pass their courses and get an education. In selecting this subject, Toperoff plays counterpoint—using a writing angle that flows against the usual story about academic scandals in collegiate basketball, which employs scores of semiprofessional players, some of whom leave school unable to read the scorecard that lists their own names.

Isn't that a great sports angle for a "thought-leader" magazine? *The Atlantic's* editors thought so. They put this headline on the story: "Playing The Cerebral Game: Princeton's Carril Is A Thinking Man's Basketball Coach."

As you must anytime you write sports for a non-expert audience, writer Toperoff structures his story on two realities.

First, he does not assume his readers have detailed background in basketball.

Second, he chooses his language carefully. He doesn't offer a steady diet of one-syllable words used by some sports writers to catch the grunts and groans of the locker room.

Note, for example, the tone of Toperoff's lead:

> When knowledgeable college-basketball fans discuss the game's excellent coaches, they mostly mention men who direct teams that are almost always among the highest ranked nationally.... To connoisseurs and among coaches themselves, however, Pete Carril, about to start his twenty-third season at Princeton, is renowned for getting remarkable results from players whose natural abilities are usually significantly below those of players at schools well known for basketball....

"Connoisseurs"? In a *sports* story? Yes, and there is more:

> But adversaries continue to underestimate (Carril's) team, and the tenacious intelligence of Princeton's players keeps the Tigers very competitive against teams with more skillful athletes....
>
> Princeton is an automatic underdog when it plays any major basketball school, because its stringent recruiting rules limit it to players of high academic achievement.

Academic excellence doesn't preclude basketball excellence, of course, but the pool of players who can maintain both is minuscule. . . .

Nowhere in his article does writer Toperoff lapse into the dialect spoken by truly dedicated basketball fans. There is no "full-court press" or "fast-break offense" or other basketball esoterica. Instead, Toperoff describes Princeton's offensive strategy in terms basketball fans would find incredibly elementary—but that are just right for *The Atlantic*'s non-expert readers:

> Players must move the ball and themselves continually; they must remain constantly alert to opportunities; they must be masters of deception. (*Sam Toperoff, "Playing The Cerebral Game,"* The Atlantic, *Nov. 1989, 115*)

That's how to get a sports story into a "thought-leader" magazine that also writes about Thucydides and the art of war in the fifth century B.C.

Okay, let's imagine this time we want to get into *Life,* a general-circulation monthly, with a sports story on, say, racing greyhounds. Impossible? Not for Jack McClintock. This is his lead:

> One day in 1988, while looking for the lavatory in her veterinarian's office, Helen Banks opened the wrong door and found 12 dead greyhounds stacked like sandbags in a corner. Though she had been working at the Naples-Fort Meyers dog track for two years, it had never occurred to her to wonder what happened to greyhounds when they got too old to race. She was horrified. . . .

This story is about something little known outside the tight circle of greyhound racing enthusiasts: Greyhounds that don't win are killed. For their non-expert readers, *Life* editors highlighted that with the headline, "Run Or Die."

Writer McClintock built his story around Helen Banks who, after finding those 12 dead dogs, began a campaign of adopting loser Greyhounds, and Prize, a loser saved by adoption. Throughout, McClintock strums the theme: beautiful dogs, harsh treatment, win or die. An example:

> People who use animals to make money often seem to think of the money first and the animals second. Greyhounds, seen by their owners as business investments, are expected to produce or die. Although Prize seems never to have been deliberately mistreated, her life has not been a walk in the park. From the age of 18 months she was confined, day and night, to a three-foot-by-three-foot wire-mesh crate stored, along with 50 other crates containing 50 other greyhounds, in a cement-block kennel behind the tote board. Like a piece of factory equipment, Prize was efficiently serviced. Every day she was fed horse meat, vegetables, brown sugar and vitamins. Four times a day she was muzzled, taken outside for a pit stop and then brought back to her crate, where she waited, gazing at the world through the wire mesh, waiting to run her twice-a-week, 30-second race, after which she would be hastily hosed down and returned to her crate. . . . (*Jack McClintock, "Run Or Die,"* Life, *June 1991, 63*)

How many *Life* readers are deeply committed fans of Greyhound racing? One in 1,000? One in 10,000? We don't know. But we'll make a bet: A very high percentage of *Life* readers—even sports outsiders—likely were deeply moved by writer McClintock's sports story.

The *Life* and *Atlantic* articles both are classic "outsiders-looking-in" stories. Both reach into sports and pull out an angle of great interest to non-fan readers of general-circulation magazines. Nevertheless, both stories are consistent with the general editorial strategies of the magazines—"thinking" basketball for readers of a "thought-leader" magazine; dramatic, heart-touching copy on beautiful dogs for a magazine filled with human interest copy.

But how about this challenge: Can you get into a general-interest magazine with a sports story that is *in*consistent with the magazine's overall editorial strategy? With proper planning and precision writing you can, because editors often like to play counterpoint themselves, running stories with angles contrary to their usual offerings.

Joy Williams exploits that tendency in a story for *Esquire,* a magazine with mostly male readers and, at times, more than a little macho swagger in its copy. Her story, "The Killing Game," is a direct attack on the love some have for hunting. Her lead:

> Death and suffering are a big part of hunting. A big part. Not that you'd ever know it by hearing hunters talk. They tend to downplay the killing part. To kill is to put to death, extinguish, nullify, cancel, destroy. But from the hunter's point of view, it's just a tiny part of the experience. "The kill is the least important part of the hunt" . . . they say . . . For the animal, of course, the killing part is of considerably more importance. . . .

Then, Williams takes the macho spirit and slam-dunks it:

> For hunters, hunting is fun. Recreation is play. Hunting is recreation. Hunters kill for play, for entertainment. They kill for the thrill of it, to make an animal "theirs". . . . (*Joy Williams, "The Killing Game,"* Esquire, *Oct. 1990, 113*)

Here's a challenge: Sell the editors of *Forbes,* a magazine that celebrates money, on a sports story. Peter Newcomb does it with this lead.:

> The young celebrity at last appeared, a fashionable 45 minutes late. A barrage of flashbulbs and a sea of microphones. Movie star? Madonna? Nope. Just a normally attractive 17-year-old who happens to be a whiz of a tennis player.
> Having already won two of the three Grand Slam tennis tournaments held so far this year, Monica Seles, the youngest woman player ever to hold the number-one ranking, should easily earn over $1.5 million in 1991. That's just on the court. Off the court? Four times that amount. . . . (*Peter Newcomb, "Madonna Is The Model,"* Forbes, *19 Aug. 1991, 80*)

Yes, of course, the *Forbes* story above is about the *money* in sports. Writer Newcomb appeals to his business-executive readers (*Forbes* claims one in three is a millionaire) by detailing the huge sums to be made in sports (heavyweight Evander Holyfield led at press time with $60.5 million earned). Why don't *you* write about the money in local sports for a city or regional magazine?

We can draw some lessons from our look at writing for sports outsiders.

First, for the writer, sports involves more than a sports angle, more than the "inside dope" on the pure technicalities of sports understood only by sports technicians. Sports also has drama, anger, pathos, good guys, bad guys—the list of writing angles is virtually unlimited. And, if properly researched and reported, such angles can carry you into writing sports stories that are considered not only meaningful by non-fan readers but *imperative.*

Second, you must thoroughly understand the editorial strategy of your target magazine as well as the psychographics and demographics of its readers. You must get on those readers' wavelength, emphasizing angles you know will interest them, then *translating* the story into terms they understand.

Third, whatever your personal background in sports, you can report and write such angles for local magazines. Don't overlook any published on campus or in nearby cities. You *can* start in sports writing with copy for non-fans who read, say, city or regional magazines or general-interest student publications.

Of course, much sports writing is done with an insider's view for insiders—expert writers writing for reader-fans with a high degree of expertise themselves. If you want to write in that league, you face a wholly different challenge. Let's look at it.

How to Write for Sports Insiders

Try this lead on readers of *The Atlantic* or a similar magazine:

> Let's look at the worst case. Joe Montana goes down in the first game. What happens to the 49ers then? Say they go 2–6 in games they trail after halftime instead of last year's 6–2. That makes them 10–6 instead of 14–2. That's still good enough to win the NFC West.

It could get worse than that, of course. Without Montana, the defense could play with less confidence.... (*"NFC West,"* Sport, *Sept. 1991, 26*)

How about offering the following to editors of *Vogue* for their fashion-oriented readers?

The flood of opposing pass rushers eventually tore the rotator cuff of quarterback Don Majkowski, the cornerstone of the franchise. He's optimistic about playing in September, but when Jim McMahon recovered ahead of schedule from a similar injury in 1987, he wasn't ready until October. The Packers signed ex-Bear Mike Tomczak to stand in for him, which makes sense unless it means they've given up on Anthony Dilweg after 193 NFL passes and.... (*"NFC Central,"* Sport, *Sept. 1991, 30*)

These two examples are from *Sport,* a national magazine written by sports experts for expert readers. And, unless they also happen to be sports fans, readers of *The Atlantic* or *Vogue* would labor over deciphering the jargon—"Joe Montana goes down..." and "tore the rotator cuff...." (That means Montana, San Francisco 49er quarterback, is hurt and out for the season; the rotator cuff is in the shoulder, and injuring it impairs a quarterback's passing ability.)

There, in the paragraph above, is the distinction between writing sports for outsiders and insiders: Outsiders who read *The Atlantic* or similar magazines need an explanation of sports jargon, much as you would explain "prime rate" or "Dow Jones Industrial Average" when writing about finance for non-experts. But for sports experts, such as *Sport* readers, inserting such basic explanations is a sign of amateurism. It slows the readers' pace, tells them what they already know, talks down to them.

The strong expertise needed in writing any type of sports for expert readers requires you to develop personal background in sports and excellent reporting abilities to stay ahead of your readers.

When writing for insiders, whatever the sports news specialty, successful writers possess several characteristics.

First, they define sports writing very broadly. News isn't limited to action on the field or court. It includes player salaries, contract haggling, personal lives of athletes, drugs and crime—all the off-field developments that so often make sports a topic of everyday conversation.

Second, their writing is deeply analytical. As in so many areas of magazine writing, sports writers confront the reality that TV and newspapers get to their readers first. Magazine writers must assume readers saw it on TV or read about it in their daily newspaper—and now want the story moved ahead. That means you must get deeply beneath the "what" of the story—which team won, which lost—and into the "real what," the "why" and "how."

Third, successful sports writers develop conversational styles of writing. This is not stocks and bonds we're writing about here. It's whether the Pirates need stronger pitching; whether Joe Louis really could take Mike Tyson. Successful writers develop the ability to write with accuracy and discipline about such things, yet intimately and warmly, as if chatting over a beer or two.

Fourth, successful writers find—and prize—the human element in sports. Good sports writing is not about home runs, it's about people who hit them. It's not about records in the 100-yard dash, it's about people who train for years, people who sweat and hurt and strive to set those records.

Let's look at how professional writers use such techniques in covering organized spectator sports.

WRITING MAINSTREAM SPECTATOR SPORTS

For many people, August 1991 isn't remembered as the month of an attempted coup against Mikhail S. Gorbachev's government in Moscow. Rather, it's when coach Ray

Handley chose Jeff Hostetler over Phil Simms as starting quarterback of the New York Giants.

Now, you may not like hearing that in sports circles the debate over Hostetler versus Simms was as hot as any, in other circles, over the future of the Soviet Union. But for many, it was. Ira Berkow, a leading sports columnist for *The New York Times,* referred to the "genuine passion" that erupted, and opened his next-day column this way:

> "Did you hear the news?"
> "What news?"
> "Who's back in?"
> "Yeah. Unbelievable."
> "Who would have thought it."
> "Yep. Gorby's the man."
> "What Gorby? I'm talking about Hostetler!"
>
> In some areas, the events the other day concerning the Giants football team were taking precedence over the coup news in Moscow. One man's world is another man's neighborhood.
>
> As soon as the decision was made that not Phil Simms but Jeff Hostetler would be the man hunkered behind the center for the Giants, there was a great reaction. For one thing, the switchboard at the Giants' office was lit up by callers complaining about it. . . .
> (*Ira Berkow, "That Quarterback Bombshell,"* The New York Times, *23 Aug. 1991, 11*)

If you write mainline sports—football, basketball, baseball and a few others— you're deep into something that for many magazine readers is serious business, indeed. Many writers, sports writers among them, sometimes make sneering noises over writing about games and people who play them. Red Smith, one of the greatest (he won a Pulitzer Prize for sports essays), once said he worked in the "toy department." But are Kremlinologists more serious about what's happening in Moscow than football fans are about the National Football League?

So, lesson one: Aim for big-league sports writing only if you're serious not only about writing but, also, the sports you cover.

Lesson two: You won't get far if you take to sports writing the unquestioning, myth-making boosterism—the worshipful, unwavering support of the hometown team—that marked much sports writing in the past. Puffery still haunts much sports writing, of course, even as it has disappeared from writing on other subjects, such as politics. James Taub, a New York free-lancer, explains: "Few political correspondents are likely to have grown up lionizing their local congressman, but practically every red-blooded male has dreamed of the broken-field scamper and the slam dunk, sportswriters almost certainly more than most. Thus the adulatory prose, the open partisanship. . . ."[10] But hero worship is for amateurs these days.

So, what *does* mark professional writing on mainline sports? Let's look.

Professionals Get Inside the Story

Free-lancer Taub, referring to the "malignant side effect" of television sports coverage, poses the challenge: "Now that the ardent fan can see practically every inning or every free throw of the home team's schedule, the Olympian rendition of the events of the day that the sportswriter once offered has become obsolete. The fan says: I *know* that; give me the inside scoop. . . ."[11]

Look at it this way: With TV coverage of sports so complete, who won is old news by the time tomorrow morning's newspaper is delivered. It's ancient history by the time your magazine arrives, next week or next month. To compete, then, you must go inside the story, searching for angles that carry the story forward *and* meet the true fan's near-insatiable desire to know what really is happening.

Note, for example, how a *Sport* writer takes fans not only into the Chicago Bears' training camp but into what Bears coaches actually are talking about among themselves:

> The Bears' offensive coaches work the word "balance" into their conversations more often than accountants. It's a code word for passing. The Bears gained only 51 percent of their yards on pass plays last year. As they learned in January, they can win the division that way, but they can't beat many playoff teams.... (*"Who Else But The Bears in The Black-And-Blue?"* Sport, *Sept. 1991, 30*)

Editors of *Sports Illustrated,* the largest-circulation sports magazine, know their readers watched Otis Nixon come alive as a batter for the Atlanta Braves. So, they strive to explain the inside story of why and how he is hitting so well:

> Nixon attributes his improved average to hitting guru Harry (the Hat) Walker and to Hal McRae, the Royals manager who was Nixon's batting coach in Montreal. "Stay back, stay compact, keep your stroke short, be selective, be patient," says Nixon, rattling off his plate routine. He attributes his speed to a five-minute pregame stretching regimen and to genes passed on from his mother, Gracie.... (*Hank Hersch, "End of The Slide,"* Sports Illustrated, *19 Aug. 1991, 24*)

Note the thrust of the last two examples. In the Bears story, the writer addresses overall team strategy. It's war out there in professional football, and your readers are armchair generals. The inside scoop on "balance" gives reader-fans something to think about in comparing the Bears to other teams.

In his story on Otis Nixon, *Sports Illustrated*'s Hank Hersch takes his readers inside the fundamental drama of sports—the very personal effort of a single athlete to improve performance. Writer Hersch even works in Nixon's bloodline!

The inside story can be written on many levels: league against league, team against team, player against other players but, importantly, also players against their own personal best.

Professionals Write "Look-Ahead" Angles

To write for true sports fans, you must understand two realities.

First, every game or contest is merely preparation for the next one. For fans, it's important that their team or star wins. To win *and* get positioned properly for the next contest is even more important to them. So, remember to not only write deeply analytical copy on how and why the win (or loss) occurred, but also to interpret how the win (or loss) likely will affect the outcome of the next contest.

Second, for really serious fans, the season for their favorite sport never ends; it just shifts into a new phase. Whatever the month, for example, reader-fans are interested in articles on academic performance (and, thus, eligibility) of your school's football players. The signing of new basketball players, even for a playing season six months away, is a hot topic for fans. So, there is no "off-season" for writers; writing angles are numerous—*if* you write with a look-ahead angle that carries reader-fans ahead to when their favorite team next takes the field or court.

It's not difficult to insert the look-ahead angle into writing for those season-preview magazines that, months before play begins, overflow magazine sales racks. You simply aim at giving reader-fans highly detailed information they use to "scope out" action during the coming season. In September, for example, *Sport* publishes a "Pro Football Preview" so reader-fans can predict gridiron action all the way to the season finale, the Super Bowl. Articles predict for fans where each team will finish in the final standings and answer "why" and "how" questions by addressing these points:

First, each team's central offensive and defensive strengths (and weaknesses) are compared to those of other teams.

Second, individual stars are examined along with their health and playing ability and how they can (or cannot) assist the team in the season ahead.

Third, particularly important games or competitive challenges in the forthcoming season are discussed. *Sport* calls this "Hot Date": The single most-important game each team must play and win.

Fourth, coaching, draft picks, contract negotiations, player holdouts and other off-field events likely to affect on-field performance are scrutinized.

The preceding elements are required, obviously, in look-ahead stories for any sport.

Within individual stories, it's important to move seamlessly from what happened to what's next.

For example, Pat Putnam writes for *Sports Illustrated* a detailed story on how unbeaten heavyweight Riddick Bowe knocks out Bruce Seldon. It is a left hook, Putnam explains; Seldon foolishly is expecting a right hand. We see Seldon facedown on the canvas, trying to rise. Then, Putnam moves us ahead:

> "Cancel Christmas," said Bowe, staring down at Seldon.
> After 26 bouts in 29 months, a remarkable pace, Bowe has decided to turn his guns, for the moment, in another direction. . . .

At this point, writer Putnam explains Bowe is going to work for awhile with anti-drug activists in Little Rock, Ark. Then, the transition to the look-ahead angle that fight fans want:

> While Bowe wages that war, his manager, Rock Newman, will continue negotiations with Larry Holmes, the former heavyweight champion who came out of retirement in April. The 41-year-old Holmes is scheduled to fight Eddie Gonzales, a slick but light-punching cruiserweight, in Tampa on Tuesday night. Holmes also has a bout set for later this month in Honolulu.
> "We're getting closer on the money," says Newman. "Before tonight a lot of people said they wanted to fight us, but we couldn't get any names on a contract. They say Bowe is afraid of them, but they are always saying it while they are running away. After tonight, I don't know. I just hope Holmes answers his telephone tomorrow." *(Pat Putnam, "Short Work,"* Sports Illustrated, *19 Aug. 1991, 57)*

Professionals Focus on People

In perhaps no other type of writing is the human element as important to your writing style and eventual success as it is in sports.

Diplomatic correspondents worry over the clash of nations.

Political writers focus often on party ideologies, political action committees, voter blocs.

Business writers deal frequently with inanimate objects such as stocks, bonds and commodities (although they sometimes give them human characteristics: "The market decided to move up today.")

For sports writers, it always comes back to the *heavyweights* and their left hooks, the *batters* and their averages, the *quarterbacks* and their rotator cuffs. Scoff, if you will, at personalized sports writing as "hero worship." Call it "star fixation," if you wish. But ignore it, and you will fail in sports writing. Does that overstate the importance of the human element? Team owners don't think so: They pay multimillion-dollar salaries to individual stars because they draw fans (who also read magazines). Coaches don't think so, either: They often construct their entire on-field strategies around one or two key players.

The obsession of sports writers with individual athletes isn't new, of course. Check magazines of a few generations ago and you'll be able to read thousands of words about Babe Ruth, Jack Dempsey, Joe Louis and other stars. But you won't be able to read *all* about them. You'll see in the files a writing style that sanitized the sports world with one-dimensional portraits—hokum and ritualistic adoration that, bottom line, often is a lie. Generally absent is detailed coverage of the drinking, gambling and womanizing that so often marred sports then, as today. That's where responsible, conscientious magazine writers today differ so dramatically from their predecessors: Their focus on the human element transports readers far from idolatry and into the off-field personal (and sometimes dark and disreputable) lives of sports stars.

By striving for such balanced, well-rounded writing, you do more than present readers with an honest picture. You open for yourself wonderful writing opportunities to do personality profiles and to probe deeply into what, on field and off, makes for athletic greatness.

Note here how Mike Lupica spurns cliches and hero worship as he writes about Adrian Dantley, a relatively unknown but high-scoring basketball player for the Dallas Mavericks. Dantley, who has roamed from team to team, drives Lupica around the neighborhood where his gypsy-like career started.

> He puts the Mercedes back in gear. The car moves as easily as A.D. once had in his life as a basketball gypsy. At Georgia and Irving, he points to Bruce-Monroe Elementary School, where he first played on a real court. The car keeps going. Dantley points out all the boyhood landmarks, this 7-11 and that McDonald's, a grocery store called Miles Long, where you could get five cookies for a penny. In between, there is always another hoop or another playground. "I've played long enough to become a dinosaur," he says now, his voice weary with the long road from Irving Street to Dallas. Gypsies like to keep traveling; last year, A.D. wanted to settle for a while in Detroit. . . . (*Mike Lupica, "Have Gunner, Will Travel,"* Esquire, *Feb. 1990, 43*)

Is that *sports* writing? Yes, and good writing, too.

Next, free-lancer Larry Platt does a people story, warts and all, on Jerome Brown, all-pro defensive lineman for the Philadelphia Eagles. Not ignored are reports that Brown lost more than $30,000 in card games and flew girlfriends to Eagles road games. Platt spends much time with Brown and lets *him* respond, in his own words:

> "The media blew that all out of proportion," he says. "Man, losing $30,000? It never got over $3,000, but that's owed to a bunch of guys. And hardly anyone pays anyway. My agent and my accountant would kick my butt if I lost that much. . . ." (*Larry Platt, "Jerome Brown,"* Sport, *Sept. 1991, 21*)

Babe Ruth had girlfriends. He also ate and drank himself sick on occasion. But you'll find not much was written on that at the time. Note, incidentally, the fascinating insight writer Platt conveys by letting Brown talk: Today's pro football player isn't complete without an agent and attorney! That's the way to write with well-rounded focus on the people of sports.

Professionals Write the Hell out of Sports

Rejoice. In sports, you are expected—nay, *required*—to let your writer's juices flow. For pure writer's fun, nothing beats sports. That's because editors today, as always, give what Red Smith called the "toy department" latitude that they deny writers of more "serious" topics.

Inevitably, that means you will see a great deal of *over*writing in sports, much stretching and grasping for a new, more amusing, more colorful twist of words. That, in turn, means more bad writing and real clunkers in sports, page-for-page, than in other types of magazine writing.

But the good sports writers are really good! If you want to make it in their league, you'd better be good, too.

Let's join Mike Lupica again, this time watching Canadian hockey star Wayne Gretzky practice with the Los Angeles Kings:

> Gretzky had come across center ice in his long gray sweat shirt, moving like a swan, and had gotten ready to shoot the puck at the goalie. But then, in an instant, the shooting motion was gone, his stick was dropping in front of the puck, Gretzky was making a blind pass behind him, and the man skating on right wing had put the puck into the net. I waited for someone to cheer, the man fixing the boards, or the man behind the skate-rental counter, or the blond girl waiting for the ice so she could become the next Katarina Witt. But it was just Gretzky being Gretzky, on an 80-degree Friday morning in his new city.
>
> It was like finding Baryshnikov in an Arthur Murray studio. . . . (*Mike Lupica, "Hockey's Only Hope,"* Esquire, *Feb. 1989, 55*)

There, in the second paragraph, is a point we want to emphasize: Truly strong writers in sports are well-read, expansive and knowledgeable men and women. They tuck into their writing not only the nuances of winning hockey but also a grace and fluidity of style that can come only from reading about and experiencing things more widely than sports—such as dance—and knowing not only jocks but the likes of Baryshnikov, as well. You cannot prepare for big-league sports writing only by learning what down-and-out patterns are. Mike Lupica, Red Smith and the other sports-writing greats before you earned the right to be called *essayists* in the fullest sense.

Listen as John Edgar Wideman takes flight on basketball:

> When it's played the way it's spozed to be played, basketball happens in the air, the pure air; flying, floating, elevated above the floor, levitating the way oppressed peoples of this earth imagine themselves in their dreams, as I do in my lifelong fantasies of escape and power, finally, at last, once and for all, free. For glimpses of this ideal future game we should thank, among others, Elgin Baylor, Connie Hawkins, David Thompson. . . . (*John Edgar Wideman, "Michael Jordan Leaps the Great Divide,"* Esquire, *Nov. 1990, 139*)

Now, we'll quickly agree with what you're probably thinking: Swans, Baryshnikov and levitation will wear thin on sports fans who, after all, seek not so much poetry as, rather, information and insights they can lay on fellow fans at the corner pub. But for even your most literal readers you can draw deeply from your reservoir of creativity and make their search a readable, enjoyable experience.

Gary Cartwright, for example, describes manager Lou Duva importing sparring partners to help Evander Holyfield train to defend his heavyweight title against George Foreman:

> To get his man ready for the fight, Duva imported a series of Foreman look-alikes as sparring partners. They arrived at camp like logs at a sawmill, each a never-was posturing as a has-been, most strong enough to give the champ a taste of the mugging and mauling he could expect one month later in Atlantic City. With a ghetto blaster at ringside playing what sounded like rock music from Hell, Holyfield went progressively longer each day. . . . (*Gary Cartwright, "The Real Deal V,"* Texas Monthly, *June 1991, 116*)

And, isn't this a *fun* way to read about a Notre Dame football star who signed to play Canadian football:

> When Raghib Ismail, better known in leading social circles as "Rocket," ran his memorable postseason fly pattern—zipping past those golden Notre Dame memories, scurrying by all those startled National Football League representatives, and spiking the ball in downtown Toronto—football fans across America couldn't hide their disappointment. You mean we won't have Rocket's afterburners lighting up our TV screens on Sundays the way he used to on Saturdays? You mean no more blurring kick returns? No more flashy sprints from scrimmage with the game on the line?
>
> Hey, no sweat, say his admirers from the good old U.S. of A. He'll be back soon enough. He won't like playing on those weird-sized fields, in front of those hockey-crazed Canadian fans. They go bananas over pucks in the net, not All-Americans in the endzone.

They prefer 40-foot slapshots to 60-yard runbacks. I mean, get serious. They don't even get ESPN up there, do they? (*Steve Bisheff, "Run For The Border," Inside Sports, Sept. 1991, 52*)

When turning you loose in sports to *write,* many editors grant you special dispensation to drop any pretense of objectivity and to insert your personal views. It's a dispensation not given all writers in other departments. Seldom, for example, do you see diplomatic correspondents freed to write that the secretary of state "can't negotiate his way out of a wet paper bag." But note the latitude these writers have:

- A *Sport* writer on quarterback Steve Walsh of the New Orleans Saints: "... Walsh had bad enough stats last year to make a skunk hold its nose, and he can't throw a football through a windowpane."[12]
- A writer says fans pay millions to see an aging, slow Sugar Ray Leonard fight: "In return, the public gets to see Ray Leonard throwing punches as if underwater ..."[13]
- A *Sports Illustrated* writer reports a Jacksonville University basketball player quits, citing the coach's disciplinarian methods, and enlists in the Air Force. The piece is titled: "Mild Blue Yonder."[14]

Have fun in sports writing! This isn't the Fate of the Free Western World you're dealing with.

WRITING PARTICIPANT SPORTS

Leisure-time and personal fitness sports are growing explosively in America, and so is the number of magazines for people who participate in them. For the writer, a huge market is building.

Two areas of participant sports offer a beginning writer greatest opportunity: "white shoe" sports, such as golf, tennis, running; and "black boot" sports, such as hunting, fishing and camping. Many specialty magazines are published for each sport, and general-circulation magazines open their pages to stories about them.

Broadly, you can get started writing about participant sports with two types of stories: the "how-it-is-done" story, for which there is never-ending demand, and the "armchair adventure" story. Let's look at both.

The "How-It-Is-Done" Story

For a great many Americans, improving their tennis serve or perfecting their golf putting is very important stuff. Helping them—along with others who want to run, swim or walk better—gives you many chances to get published.

Obviously, you'll not be able to write from personal experience how it is done in every sport. So, it's important that you use the reporting techniques we discussed earlier in this book and find authoritative sources whose hints you can relay to readers.

Note we say *authoritative* sources. The first strength of how-it-is-done writing must be a high degree of technical expertise. Though amateurs, many of your readers are devoted to their sport. They read about it, watch it on TV, study it—and you'll have to advance their understanding of it to succeed.

The second most important strength is focusing on a limited aspect of a sport and writing about it in specifics, not generalities. That is, don't attempt to write about "golf." For readers of golf specialty magazines, golf is a many-splendored thing and they're way ahead of you in understanding its general nature. They want what *Golf*

Digest gives them when staff writer Cliff Schrock collaborates with a teaching professional, Todd Anderson, to write how to "build a strong swing." Notice the instructional specifics (each tied to an accompanying photo that illustrates the point):

> First, stand in a relaxed position, with your arms by your side and the club in your hand (Photo 1).
>
> Second, raise the club in front of you until it is horizontal, then place your right hand on the grip (2).
>
> Third, lower the club and bend from your hips, until the clubhead is a foot above the ground (3).
>
> And fourth, lower the clubhead to the ground by relaxing your arms, wrists and legs and let the weight of the club bring it to the ground. You should feel "springy" (4)....(*Todd Anderson with Cliff Schrock, "How To Get Set Up,"* Golf Digest, *Sept. 1991, 98*)

Note the obvious expertise in a *Runner's World* article by a writer who consulted an expert on the proper way to run:

> To analyze and improve your running style, you must assess the major moving parts of the body as they relate to running as fast and as smoothly as possible. You will no doubt find that your form is already good in certain areas. Others will need attention. Let's begin at the bottom and move upward and outward.
>
> **The feet: Run Straight.** When you run in a straight line, your successive foot placements should be parallel to each other (or very nearly so). This will reduce the rotation or twisting of the ankles and knees and will help to prevent shortening of your stride due to turning out of the foot. Because the hip, knee, and ankle joints all must bear the severe stresses and impact of running, you should always try to concentrate on preventing any twisting or sideways motion and keep feet and legs moving directly forward.... (*Peter Coe and David Martin, Ph.D., "Fix Your Form,"* Runner's World, *Sept. 1991, 38*)

Note how Coe and Martin personalize their writing: "When *you* run in a straight line, *your* successive ..." The how-it-is-done story is best told in intimate, one-to-one conversational tones.

Incidentally, the large market offered a writer by participant sports is illustrated by the single issue of *Runner's World* just mentioned. It carries many articles of the type that can be written by authors who lack personal expertise in running—if they know how to find and interview knowledgeable sources who do have it. Subjects include what runners should eat, "the country's best races with a historical theme," features on outstanding runners and so forth. Free-lancer Jim Harmon writes about Shelby Coffey III, editor of *The Los Angeles Times.* The article focuses on how running helps Coffey handle the stress of executive life. Note that the reporting and writing in the following excerpt could be used by you in submitting a similar article to almost any type of *general-interest* magazine, as well as a runner's specialty publication:

> Coffey rises every morning by 5:30 to read the paper and usually takes off on his 40- to 50-minute run by 6:30. "It's a clarified period of the day," he says.
>
> "Running has a soothing, calming effect on him," says his wife, Mary Lee, an emergency-room doctor at the Huntington Hospital. "When he doesn't run, he gets a little frazzled, a little crabby. He's sort of living proof of endorphin and encephalin theory."
>
> Coffey himself obviously recognizes how running keeps him in balance. "One of the interesting things about this job is you never know whether the next phone call's going to be routine or an all-systems-go problem," Coffey says. "Running helps give me a little more equanimity with which to greet the unexpected".... (*Jim Harmon, "Meet The Press,"* Runner's World, *Sept. 1991, 35*)

One way to personalize a how-it-is-done article is to cast it as "how I did it." Curry Kirkpatrick, senior writer for *Sports Illustrated,* did that in an article on President Bush's sometimes frenetic involvement in sports. Kirkpatrick played doubles in tennis with Bush:

> . . . when I drifted back, set up perfectly, swung and . . . missed the ball completely, it was the single most embarrassing moment in the history of my life. The worst part was, I couldn't blame my whiff on the blazing sun, the soft ocean breezes, the Laykold hard-court surface or, especially, the footsteps behind me, which belonged to my partner, who also happens to be the leader of the free world. "Shake it off. Tough shot. Let's go," said George Herbert Walker Bush. . . . (*Curry Kirkpatrick, "Playing in The Bush League,"* Sports Illustrated, *19 Aug. 1991, 32*)

The self-effacing vignette beautifully hooks readers into the five-page article that follows on Bush's sports activities.

Hodding Carter IV, an All-American swimmer in college and now an *Esquire* staff writer, uses the same plunge-right-in technique in an article on Mark Spitz, a 1972 Olympics gold medalist trying a comeback in swimming:

> He pushed off the wall first, plowing through the water like a mako shark, and with one stroke resumed his race against the past seventeen years. I waited five seconds and swam after him, a determined blowfish. . . . (*Hodding Carter IV, "Comeback,"* Esquire, *May 1990, 140*)

It's important to note that you need not be an All-American in college to use the how-I-did-it writing approach. Even if you are a rank amateur, you can write an entertaining article on how you flubbed your way through a tennis match, a golf lesson or a training session in the pool. To get published, however, you'll need to work into your article an informative dimension by quoting an expert on hints helpful to readers.

Let's turn now to a type of sports where personal adventure and involvement are major writing themes.

The "Armchair Adventure" Outdoor Sports Story

We know a business executive who dresses specially in corduroy trousers and plaid shirt to read his outdoor sports magazines. He sits in his basement, where he can smell gun oil and look at fishing rods while he reads.

What's that executive looking for in his magazines? Adventure! And immediate transportation to adventure is what editors provide, along with how-to-do-it hints, in *New York Sportsman, Sports Afield, Outdoor Life, Gray's Sporting Journal* and the great many other specialty magazines that cover hunting, fishing and other outdoor sports.

Note how one writer transports *Sports Afield* readers into a confrontation with a bull moose. His lead:

> The stillness that hung over southwest Alaska's Mulchatna wilderness was short-lived. A bull moose had moved into a small clearing and was boasting about the harem of two cows he had collected.
> Waauuuggh! Waauuugghh! The bull chipped away at the alpine quiet with more throaty grunts. Then he shattered the tranquility of the forest with a series of raspy, guttural bellows, bellows that issued a challenge to any and all takers in the area.
> High above the autumn-dyed boreal forest, we heard the challenge and accepted it. . . .

A couple points about this lead: First, it "sets up" the armchair adventurer in a direct, one-on-one challenge with the moose. Second, the author "writes the hell" out of the story. Note the colorful scene-setting detail. Can't you *see* the forest and *hear* the moose? Lesson: Writing outdoor sports, like writing mainline spectator sports, works best if you involve your readers personally and spin a tale in vivid and dramatic you-are-there detail.

Of course, there *must* be an instructional dimension in outdoor sports writing, as in writing about participant sports. Readers of the moose story get this expert advice:

> When you're hunting Alaska moose, the best cartridge is one you can shoot quickly and accurately. My favorite is a 338 Winchester Magnum because it has consistently put moose down for me fast, especially when using a 250-grain Nosler Partition bullet. . . .
>
> Many hunters might argue that smaller calibers—including the 7mm Remington Magnum—are adequate for moose. Unless you're a sharpshooter who has taken moose in the past, avoid the smaller centerfires. Unless it's a neck or spine shot, moose don't drop as quickly when the standard chest shots are taken with the smaller calibers. I saw one moose hit five times with a 7mm, all in the boiler room, and that 61-inch bull ran 50 yards before dropping. . . . (*Christopher Batin, "Adventures With Alaska Moose,"* Sports Afield, *Sept. 1991, 63*)

Confrontation with nature—humans against the angry elements—is another theme in successful outdoor writing. *All* trout fishermen will stop for this one:

> I love trout, but I would not want to die for one. I came close once. Even now I'm not sure exactly how close, but close enough. . . .
>
> My first step never touched bottom. The current hit me low, like a blindside block at the knees, knocked me off my feet and carried me quickly downriver into deep water. Before I had gone a hundred feet, before fear had even registered, I hit a sweeper, a dead softwood stretched like a loving arm into the river. I embraced the tree with all four extremities like a possum, then slowly, carefully pulled myself on top. My lower half was still submerged, my legs locked around the tree, but for the moment I was safe. I started tossing gear onto the bank, less than twenty feet away. First the rod, then net, vest, hat, glasses. Then I shinnied, crawled, clambered to shore. I pulled off and drained my boots and stretched out in the sun. For the first time in a week, I didn't feel like fishing. . . . (*J. H. Hall, "Swimming The Selway,"* Gray's Sporting Journal, *Summer 1990, 29*)

Note (if you're not claustrophobic) how this writer takes you out of the armchair and into "caving," the sport of exploring caves:

> I'm not happy. The cave passage is only 20 inches high, three of which is cold, muddy water that I'm lying in. . . . (*Thomas Engle, "Caving in New York State,"* The Conservationist/NYSDEC, *March-April 1991, 34*)

But, what if you want to write about outdoor sports without shooting a moose, risking your life in a raging trout stream or getting caught in a cave deep underground? Then you use reporter skills, as you would in covering any sport, and add a free-swinging writing style. Rick Bass does that for *Esquire*:

> It's a sometimes wonderful and peculiarly Texan affliction to search for and label things as being the Best this or that, and I was amused to find myself having fallen prey to it—like a doodlebug falling into an ant lion's trap is what it felt like . . .

And with that, Bass is off and running on a delightful story about visiting a bird-dog trainer, Jarrett Thompson, renowned for producing the best quail hunters. Bass doesn't know quail, doesn't know dogs. But he *does* know how to find—then report and write in engaging detail—an outdoor sports story. Note his writing grace:

> The long, narrow road through the woods leading to Thompson's farm is canopied, like some tunnel of love. Sunlight comes down in dapples through the big pines, and through heavy hardwoods, the oaks and hickories. . . .
>
> Each breed seems to have its own little camp on the farm, and after a long drive down the dusty road, I begin to pass their kennels—dogs leaping, when they see me, in acrobatic twists, entire kennels of all setters, and then, a little farther down the road, also rising and jumping in the sun, all pointers, and then the friendly hound-looking Vizslas, and so on; and finally, at the end, Thompson himself. He's friendly, too, and, shaking hands with him, I wonder, what must the dogs think of him? He's a sturdy man, smiling,

with wheelbarrows full of control, all around him, inside him, I can tell that, or want to believe it, just meeting him.... (*Rick Bass, "A Dog in The Hand,"* Esquire, *Oct. 1989, 150*)

Like writer Bass, many successful outdoor writers don't shoot nature or struggle against it. They *love* it, and attract readers who want to trek along, to top the next rise in the trail and see distant horizons. Note how a writer for *Backpacker,* in an article on animal speed and grace, takes a delightful side trail:

There is little doubt that speed is of survival value to animals like the pronghorn. But it is hard to believe that animals don't move just for the enjoyment of speed, at least once in a while. Once I sat on a hillside during a Lake Superior gale and watched a trio of crows. They would plough into the wind, rowing with their wings, until it seemed the strength of the storm would snap the bones in their wings like dry sticks. Just at the instant it seemed they could not possibly survive, they would bank into the wind and be blown at incredible speeds back out across the sky. For as long as I could sit still in the storm, the birds returned again and again, like children swinging on a rope out over a mud puddle, pushing it just to the edge of disaster and all in the name of fun.... (*Jeff Rennicke, "The Athletics of Survival," Backpacker,* Aug. 1991, 18)

Got a little poetry in your writer's soul? If so, dig into it for successful outdoor writing!

SUMMARY

Sports offers writers a huge market. Hundreds of specialty magazines are dedicated exclusively to sports writing, and general-interest magazines welcome sports stories—if they're strongly reported and written with the proper angle.

Decide first whether to write for sports insiders—fans with a high degree of expertise—or for outsiders, those non-fans who need technical terms translated. For either audience, you can write from your personal experience in sports or as a reporter who interviews authoritative sources.

If you plan carefully, you can place a sports story with virtually any magazine. *The Atlantic,* a "thought-leader" magazine, carried a story on a Princeton University coach whose student-athletes play "The Cerebral Game" and win in basketball. *Forbes,* a business magazine, carried an article on the money of sports.

Writing for sports insiders requires you to assume a higher degree of understanding among your readers and to write with precision and expertise that *doesn't talk down to them.*

Define sports writing broadly, including personal lives of athletes, contract haggling, drug use and other topics in off-field sports activity. Strong writers are deeply analytical, carrying readers beyond the who-won approach of daily journalism. They write in conversational style and focus strongly on the human element in sports.

If you want to write mainstream spectator sports such as football, basketball or baseball, you must develop your own expertise in sports as strongly as, say, diplomatic writers do in their specialty. You must get inside the story for exclusive details and write with a look-ahead angle that takes reader-fans to the next contest, the next season. And you must "write the hell" out of sports. Good sports writers are essayists of the highest order.

In writing participant sports you can concentrate on "white shoe" sports (golf, tennis, running) or "black boot" sports (hunting, fishing, camping).

One superb structure for outdoor writing is the how-it-is-done story, for readers who want to learn how to improve their tennis or golf game or how to run or walk more effectively. Write from personal experience or take your strong reporting skills into interviews with authoritative sources for a story that's solidly based in their expertise.

Another effective structure is the armchair adventure outdoor sports story. It transports readers to distant adventure, meeting one-on-one an Alaskan moose or struggling against the elements of nature. Dig deep for poetry in your writer's soul when writing this type of story. Let your readers walk with you over the next rise in the trail.

RECOMMENDED READING

If you're interested in a career of writing sports for magazines, we recommended three steps.

First, read again what you've learned about basic writing techniques in this book and elsewhere. Sports writing is, above all, *writing*. And, as in all forms of magazine work, great sports writing careers are built on great writing.

Second, read widely and voraciously to develop your own personal writing style. Read newspapers (all three New York City dailies are strong in sports. So are the *Chicago Tribune, Los Angeles Times, Seattle Times, Dallas Morning News* and others). Watch especially the great sports columnists: Jim Murray of the *Los Angeles Times,* Ira Berkow of *The New York Times* and Frederick C. Klein of *The Wall Street Journal.* Much of their writing skill is transferable to magazine writing.

Third, read widely to learn something about many sports but, importantly, to also learn a great deal about a few. Read to develop a specialty in sports, an expertise that will permit you to write for sports insiders as well as outsiders.

NOTES

1. Pamela Kaufman, "Fitness," *Vogue,* Jan. 1991, 90.
2. John Holmes, "The Lure of Sports and the End of Apartheid." *Insight,* 24 June 1991, 26.
3. Peter Schwed, "Tennis Tactics," *Modern Maturity,* Aug.-Sept. 1991, 38.
4. Walter Roessing, "Football Goes Global," *Sky,* May 1991, 20.
5. Dave Getchell, "Looking for That Edge," *Backpacker,* Aug. 1991, 54.
6. From an Associated Press study quoted in Darrell Christian, "Lots More Than Fun and Games," *AP Log,* 19 Aug. 1991, 1.
7. *Ibid.* Also see Mike Greehan, "Sports Marketing vs. Mass Marketing," *The SRDS Report,* March 1991, 1.
8. *The Atlantic,* Nov. 1989.
9. *The Atlantic,* May 1990.
10. James Taub, "Please Don't Mash the Sportswriter," *Washington Journalism Review,* July/ Aug. 1991, 35.
11. *Ibid.*
12. "NFC West," *Sport,* Sept. 1991, 26.
13. Mike Lupica, "Here's to the Wieners!" *Esquire,* Sept. 1990, 83.
14. "Mild Blue Yonder," *Sports Illustrated,* 19 Aug. 1991, 14.

Chapter 12

Writing
for technical
magazines

Beneath the surface of everyday news, hidden from those who read only consumer magazines and newspapers or watch TV, flows a torrent of information crucial to an important and expanding audience.

This information "river" reports on industries and companies, their technologies and the goods and services they produce. The writing is aimed at helping readers produce better goods and services more efficiently and profitably and, thus, advance their careers.

We turn, in Chapter Twelve, to how you can find career advancement in writing this type of copy for the thousands of "technical magazines" that target incredibly narrow markets.

We put "technical magazines" in quotes because the term no longer adequately describes the style of magazine writing we'll discuss in this chapter: exciting, creatively fulfilling and multidimensional writing that goes far beyond technical nuts and bolts reporting.

The market for such writing is expanding. Every year, more technical magazines are launched, bearing titles such as *Food Processing* ("The Magazine of the Food Industry"), *Advance* ("For Medical Laboratory Professionals"), *Commuter Air* ("The International Magazine for Regional, Commuter, and Short Haul Airlines"), *World*

Wastes ("The Independent Voice of the Waste Management Industry"), *Modern Paint and Coatings* and *Shopping Center World.*

We'll also look at exciting opportunities available in health and environment writing and corporate writing.

TECHNICAL WRITING: ITS MODERN MISSION

Not long ago, technical writing could have been described as copy unimaginatively ground out by technician-writers for technician-readers willing to plow dutifully through writing about as exciting as a calculus textbook and *labor* to extract needed information.

No longer. Technical writing today must follow all the guidelines of good writing we've discussed elsewhere in this book and simultaneously be enticing *and* meet the highest standards of accuracy, authoritativeness and reliability.

Richard M. O'Connor, editor-in-chief and publisher of *Successful Meetings,* explains why he and other editors demand alluring, engaging writing of even the most esoterically technical subjects:

> "Trade publications, like all publications, compete for a reader's time. Today's readers simply do not have the time to go through all the periodicals that come across their desks or arrive at their homes. If you want your book to be noticed, to grab a reader's attention and sustain that reader's loyalty, it must look and read as good as a top consumer book. Anything less is unacceptable." (*Richard M. O'Connor, "Why Trades Get No Respect,"* Folio, *Aug. 1991, 79*)

You face special challenges in technical writing.

First, your readers often know more about your subject than you do. That obviously requires you to immerse yourself in the subject through disciplined reading or formal education. Most importantly, you must develop skillful, aggressive reporting techniques that will lead you to authoritative sources whose input can advance your readers' knowledge. It's worth emphasizing: You don't need to be the world's leading expert in a subject; you *do* need to be a highly professional reporter who can find sources who *are* experts.

Second, in technical writing you must meet the challenge of writing accurately for readers who make important decisions on what you report. We're talking about profit-and-loss decisions and, perhaps, life-and-death decisions. *The New York Times* recognizes that in reporting that Dr. Jerome P. Kassirer is "one of the world's most powerful doctors" because he is editor of *The New England Journal of Medicine. Journal* editors have enormous power, *The Times* says, "because of their role as stewards of medical knowledge."[1]

With the challenges of technical writing, however, come rewards. One is a ready market for your writing—if you turn out professional copy. Another is the satisfaction of writing important copy for sometimes incredibly loyal audiences. For example, readers of *Aviation Week & Space Technology* reward that technical magazine's writers with an 81 percent subscription renewal rate—far higher than many general-interest consumer magazines or newspapers can boast.[2]

Yet another reward in technical writing is the demand today for widening varieties of writing styles and structures. Whatever your personal interests and writing style, there likely is a niche for you somewhere in technical writing.

For example, *Aviation Week* employs specialist writers in military, national and congressional affairs; space, transportation, aviation and space engineering, the aerospace business and other subjects related to the magazine's central thrust. Those writers have varied backgrounds: One-third are pilots, one-third engineers and one-third began as general assignment newspaper reporters. The success of ex-newspaper reporters in covering aviation and space illustrates how basic reporting and writing techniques can succeed in any form of technical writing if you immerse yourself in a subject and cultivate knowledgeable, authoritative sources.

Another example of magazines that publish writers of widely varying backgrounds and styles: *Fire Chief,* a slick, prosperous technical journal for readers who fight fires for a living or who sell services and products to those who do. *Fire Chief*'s editor, Don Michard, says his writers cover "the economic, technological, legal and sociological trends that are likely to affect the fire service...."[3]

We see developing, then, three broad areas of reporting and writing that will offer you career opportunities in technical magazines:

- writing about the *business* of an industry,
- covering its *technology* and
- writing about its *operations.*

Let's look at each.

Writing About the Business of Industry

Of all forms of technical writing, covering the business of an industry is most general in nature and, thus, often the best starting point for inexperienced writers.

The mission is to provide readers a broad overview of developments in their industry that are important to their own careers. For the writer, the best approach is the survey or summary story that taps authoritative sources throughout the industry and then presents a *wrap-up* of informed opinion. The primary mission is to give readers meaningful context for their own professional lives.

For example, let's say you are writing for *Midwest Real Estate News,* a monthly primarily for developers, brokers and others in real estate in 10 states. Many of your readers are highly expert in real estate financial and legal complexities—and you're not. How can you write for such an audience? You can do as Jerry DeMuth did in producing an article that led the magazine: Pick a subject (availability of financing) that even a non-expert knows is certain to interest readers in all 10 states, then interview sources intimately knowledgeable about it.

Then, write a survey or summary lead that wraps up what your sources say and back it up with well-chosen quotes:

> Financing is available, even during today's credit crunch, but it's harder to get, and developers and owners have to give up more to get it.
> "There's money around; people want to loan money," says Fred Smith, president of Smith Realty Partners, Burr Ridge, Wis. "All their questions can be a pain, but they want to make sure it's quality real estate, sponsored by experienced people, that has every chance of surviving an economic shift. If so, it's going to get funded, but it'll probably take more cash and a little more time...." (*Jerry DeMuth, "Funding Still Around, But Only at A Higher Price,"* Midwest Real Estate News, *Oct. 1990, 1*)

In the several thousand words of this story, writer DeMuth presents views obtained in telephone interviews with real estate experts scattered throughout the magazine's 10-state circulation area, insuring a true overview for readers. The story is structured almost entirely of direct quotes and paraphrases of what the experts say. DeMuth isn't required to insert—or, indeed, possess—extraordinary personal expertise. The techniques required for this type of story are reporting accurately and honestly, then writing in direct, clear, concise language—precisely the techniques we've discussed for other forms of magazine writing.

Often, writing about the business of an industry in fact is newswriting, only with a radically different sense of timing.

For example, for a daily newspaper's business or food section you write immediately about a surprisingly high orange crop estimate from Florida, if the development likely will have impact on prices your readers pay at the supermarket. If you are writing for a weekly newsmagazine, you have a little more time, but the crop estimate still is the news. What if you're writing for a monthly and you cannot get into print until long after the estimate is issued?

Well, for Winston Smith of the monthly *Frozen Food Age* ("The Industry Magazine of Marketing and Distribution"), the industry's *reaction* to the estimate becomes the news peg:

> Frozen concentrated orange juice marketers, reacting to last month's surprisingly high Florida crop estimate, slashed prices sharply in October, positioning themselves for a strong promotional effort during their peak winter selling season.
>
> Specials as low as 69 cents on 12-ounce product were already popping up in scattered markets around the country at month's end.
>
> Private label packers dropped their card prices on 24/12 FCOJ $4.70 a case to $19.15 October 15, a cutback of nearly 20 per cent. This figure was 27 per cent below the record-high quotations that had prevailed before the industry's August price decline.
>
> The latest reduction came on the heels of a 50-cent drop in Brazil's export price to $1.35 per pound solids—two cents under last December's level prior to the Christmas weekend freeze that devastated Florida groves.
>
> Among advertised brands, Minute Maid 24/12 product fell $3.36 a case to $28.40 October 29. Particularly aggressive was Tropicana, which knocked $4.80 off its card to $25.20 and, according to trade sources, retained a $4.02 promotional allowance that put its bottom-line figure within $2 of the private label price.... (*Winston Smith, "Prices Plummet As FCOJ Reflects Big Florida Crop,"* Frozen Food Age, *Nov. 1990, 1*)

Let's examine the last story.

First paragraph: Gives industry readers a business overview that pitches the story ahead of the crop estimate and into marketers' reaction. This overcomes the monthly magazine's inherent inability to deal immediately with spot-breaking news.

Second paragraph: Presents specifics ("69 cents on 12-ounce product") that back up the lead's reaction angle. General summary leads often work well in technical magazines, but you must move quickly into operative details your readers need so they can make their own business decisions.

Third paragraph: More specifics, this time on futures trading ("FCOJ"), in which marketers estimate how prices in months ahead will react to current developments. Note the reference to a previous record-high quotation puts this story's news in a broad context.

Fourth and fifth paragraphs: The story's overview is broadened (Brazil's export price, prices of advertised brands) to give readers even more specifics for laying down their own marketing and pricing decisions.

What other characteristics mark the orange juice story above?

Well, it is accessible and structured so readers can easily absorb principal details. But it lacks any attempt at fancy writing. The writer doesn't stretch for color or human interest angles.

The orange juice story's fundamental appeal is based not on a beguiling or, certainly, particularly cute lead but, rather, on (a) an assumption that *Frozen Food Age* subscribers read the magazine to begin with because they have professional interest in its content and (b) that they'll read any article that gives them operative business information in clear, concise and easily understandable language.

Those are the keys to effectively writing about the business of an industry.

Of course, you should never ignore an opportunity to get real people into your technical writing. *Journal,* published for dairy-farm families, gets people (and cows) into a wrap-up story on spending by dairy associations to promote and advertise their products:

> Most dairy farmers can tell you the exact lineage of every cow in the barn, the age and model of all of their tractors, and perhaps some good history surrounding every acre

of farmland within a 20-mile radius. However, if you ask one of them how much money is deducted from their milk check for milk promotion purposes every month, where it goes, and how it is spent—almost every dairy farmer draws a blank.

To start with, every dairy farmer in the country has $.15 per hundredweight (cwt.) deducted from their milk check which goes toward milk promotion thanks to the 1983 Dairy and Tobacco Adjustment Act.... (*"New England Milk Promotion Dollars—Where Do They Go? How Are They Spent?"* Journal, *April 1989, 6*)

In the preceding story, the anecdotal intro sets up readers by leading them gently into a technically complex story. But note how quickly (in the second paragraph) it gets into dollars-and-cents specifics.

Now, an example of how *not* to write an overview. This is from a magazine for medical laboratory professionals:

"Allies in health education" is one way to describe the relationship that has been fostered of late between educators at Thomas Jefferson University's College of Allied Health Sciences, Philadelphia, PA, and educators and administrators of medical educational facilities in China....

We venture to say not even participants in the exchange program described here can easily get through that lead paragraph! Why? Because it fails the test of clarity and conciseness that must be applied to all writing, not only technical writing.

A dividend in covering the business of industries: You often can draw attractive assignments. *Aviation Week* writers roam the world for aerospace stories crucial to readers in U.S. and foreign aviation industries; *TV Technology* writers cover Washington stories important to TV executives and technicians; *Food Engineering* writers cover global marketplaces.

Exciting news beats aren't exclusive to war correspondents.

Writing About Technology

Your first requirement in writing highly technical copy is accuracy. The second requirement is accuracy. So is the third. Accuracy, accuracy, accuracy. Nothing—not writing flair, not story structure, nothing—is as important as accuracy in this type of writing.

Further, technical writing requires you to produce copy that's accurate in all its parts as well as its totality. A travel story about New Delhi for a general-consumer magazine can succeed, even if you get the address wrong for a temple, as long as your overall thrust correctly concludes there is adventure and color in visiting the capital of India.

Not so in technical writing. Correctly concluding that water is a combination of hydrogen and oxygen will fail if, internally in your story, you incorrectly state the mix is three (not two) parts of hydrogen to one of oxygen.

Accuracy is so important in technical writing because (a) your readers are mostly experts who'll read your story as they would study a mathematical equation and will quickly spot any inaccuracies, (b) important technological decisions may be made on information you report and (c) technical magazines base their reputations (and, thus, their business success) on delivering accurate, meaningful, helpful information, not articles written for reader amusement or leisure-time titillation.

Recall from Chapter Two that a high percentage of trade magazine subscribers read technical articles in their workplaces (not homes) on Mondays and Tuesdays (not leisurely weekends)—an obvious signal they seek career-oriented information that will help on the job throughout the week.

Note the following, written by *Broadcast Engineering*'s technical editor, Rick Lehtinen, clearly is designed to provide operative news of broadcasting technology:

Broadcasting was once a glamorous industry. There was plenty of money to spend on elaborate production tools. Having "the latest and greatest" meant more than saving a few dollars here and there. However, changing times have reshaped the economics of broadcasting. Broadcasters now want to be "lean and tough." They want to use fewer tools, and use the ones available to their utmost capacity.

Broadcast equipment manufacturers, by necessity, have followed a similar path. Today's equipment is cleaner, simpler, and more reliable than that offered a few years ago. If it isn't, stations won't buy it.

Consider the automated spot playback machine. It was once a sprawling walrus of a device, built of thick steel plate with gadgets of every kind, from pneumatics to optics, inside of it. To make it run required enormous amounts of electricity, plus vacuum, compressed air and a lot of engineering attention.

In comparison, today's automatic library systems are tame. Modern analog systems not only do more than their predecessors, they do it better and they cost less. Today's digital versions also do more, and they cost about the same as their forerunners, considering inflation . . .

Examine the last story.

First, writer Lehtinen clearly demonstrates in his lead a grasp of broadcasting history and, importantly, the *economics* of the industry and its technology. The first paragraph exudes the writer's personal authority.

Second, the article immediately strikes a theme crucial to technicians in broadcasting (or any industry): how to do the job better but more cheaply. The best technical writing uses nuts-and-bolts details to show readers how they can implement improvements.

Having lured readers with the promise of helpful, operative information, writer Lehtinen delivers:

Simplicity is one of the attractions of the new systems. It is only logical that they don't fail as often because there is less to break.

Consider the case of two simple structures built out of steel conduit with flattened ends. Although the rectangle uses more steel and should be stronger, it can deform and disable the system. Unnecessary complexity has added a failure mode. The triangle is not only a simpler system than the rectangle, it is also stronger. The triangle can only fail if one of the conduits fails. It can be the same with equipment. . . . (*Rick Lehtinen, "A Case For Refinement,"* Broadcast Engineering, *Oct. 1990, 10*)

Throughout the preceding article (a full page in *Broadcast Engineering*), the writer translates technical developments into dollars-and-cents terms (reporting, for example, that "One broadcast manufacturer replaced $80 worth of metal with $2.50 worth of plastic and improved its panel in the process.").

Guide *your* readers to improved job performance at lower cost and you'll have a loyal audience.

Another comment on Lehtinen's story: Despite his obvious personal expertise, he adds this:

Acknowledgment: The author wishes to thank Tom Meyers, vice president of engineering, Dynair, San Diego.

By citing an authoritative source, the author anticipates a question asked by magazine readers—especially expert readers—when presented with important information: "Who says?"

Before they accept your technical information as accurate and, certainly, before they adapt your ideas to their own technology, readers of technical journals want to assess for themselves how authoritative and reliable your sources are. Writer Lehtinen strengthens his story with such prominent sourcing.

In writing for *Communicator,* published by the Radio-Television News Association, Kim Standish quotes *four* executives of firms that design news sets for TV stations. Then, she quickly delivers operative technical detail her readers can use:

More stations today are updating their look by giving their old set a facelift—new carpeting, a fresh coat of paint, and perhaps a change in background.

For news executives thinking of making a change, here are some design trends today:

- The Desk: One new look has an oval table which allows talent to sit closer together.
- The Background: Designers are using a modeled background to make the anchors appear to "pop off the screen."
- The Colors: Shades of blue and gray are "in," with accents of earth tones, scarlet and green.
- The technology: This generation of sets is being designed with robotics in mind. . . . (*Kim Standish, "Local News Sets For The 1990s,"* Communicator, *Sept. 1990, 22*)

Some technical writers have great fun on the job—flying the latest jet fighters, for example, or driving new autos—and then writing of their adventures (in precise technical detail, of course) for stay-at-home readers.

It doesn't measure up to flying a jet, but one effective way to describe technical detail is to walk your readers through a manufacturing technique or process. Greg Erickson, managing editor of *Packaging* (a "magazine for decision-makers"), does that to illustrate how a new machine works.

More or less, a stretch bundler works like a down-sized spiral stretch-film pallet wrapper lying on its side.

Using one generally involves these steps: The product or product group to be wrapped is placed on a conveyor and moved into the machine. The wrapping process is switched on and off, and the machine-held film is cut loose. The product is then either moved down the conveyor a bit for another band of film or passes on through. . . . (*Greg Erickson, "Stretch Bundling Stretches Profits,"* Packaging, *Feb. 1991, 41*)

The last example illustrates a reality of writing about technology: For a general audience of, say, consumer magazine readers, the information you report is "far out" or unintelligible. To understand how a "stretch bundler" works you first must know the operation of "a down-sized spiral stretch-film pallet wrapper lying on its side."

Here's a lead in *Dairymen News* that will frighten off all but dairy farmers:

Pseudomonas aeruginosa is an infrequent cause of mastitis that typically occurs sporadically in dairy herds. Herd outbreaks, however, in which a high proportion of cows are affected also occur. . . . (*"Water Supply May Harbor Pseudomonas,"* Dairymen News, *April 1989, 8*)

And, check out this lead from a cover story in *Prepared Foods* ("The Magazine For Packaged Foods"):

Personal computers already labor alongside human operators at every work station on the biscuit line at The Pillsbury Co.'s largest bakery products plant in New Albany, Ind. At present, those microcomputers monitor only the results of line automation. Actual control is performed by programmable controllers installed or embedded in the dry ingredients mix room, the dough line, packaging equipment and the inventory handling system. . . . (*Paul Bush, "Pillsbury's Predictable Quality,"* Prepared Foods, *Jan. 1991, 43*)

If you write technical articles, forget dreams of huge mass audiences, coast to coast, clamoring for your byline.

However, you will write stories that are extremely important to a relatively small core of readers. And they will make important decisions, sometimes spending millions of dollars, in part because of information you deliver, not your colorful writing. Paul Bush does that with the preceding story on Pillsbury.

There also is the reward of building byline reputation—personal recognition—among specialist readers. Develop a record of accurate, reliable writing and you can achieve the intimacy with your readers that Mike Ballai has with his readers of *Photomethods* ("For the Compleat Visual Communicator"):

You already know I love quartz lighting, but you probably don't know how much I *really* care. Sure I have my impetuous moments with flash, but quartz' abiding illumination is so reassuring. With flash you never know if the moment is right or you worry about completely open communication; flash just seems to flirt. But quartz lights are truly passionate "creatures" that are sometimes too hot to handle once they're turned on. . . . (*Mike Ballai, "More Romantic Quartzship,"* Photomethods, *Aug. 1991, 9*)

Now, we've studied two broad areas of technical writing: the business of industry and technology. Let's look at a third, operations.

Writing About Industry Operations

If you understand trends in an industry and grasp its technology, you can write effectively about operational methods within that industry.

This involves accumulating and analyzing a great deal of information, then writing articles that top executives and virtually everyone down the managerial ladder can use to help improve a company's overall operational efficiency.

Mind you, we're not suggesting you immediately launch forth with articles that tell the chairman of General Motors how to operate its assembly lines or lecture banks on how to attract customers.

We *are* suggesting you can achieve career success writing about industry operations if you build substantial expertise in your subject *and* develop authoritative sources who can help you fit technical bits and pieces together in an overall mosaic of importance to operations managers.

Obviously, this type of writing carries enormous responsibility because how you select and present information can be perceived as telling your readers how to run their own businesses. Nevertheless, there are ways to edge cautiously into writing about operations by using careful reporting and writing techniques.

For example, writing in *Airline Executive,* Douglas W. Nelms opens with a four-paragraph survey intro explaining that airline demand for pilots is exceeding the number trained by military or civilian flight schools. His writing is solidly based on *reporting* from the Future Aviation Professionals of America, which provides statistics to back up his summary lead.

In his fourth paragraph, Nelms moves to the point of his article: an explanation for airline executives on what their airlines can do about the shortage of pilots. Note the writer's transition into where to find pilots:

So—where do they come from?

Three major airlines have now taken it upon themselves to train pilots literally from the ground up, using established college and university programs for Ab Initio ("from the beginning") airline training. . . .

Later, writer Nelms provides specific guidance for operations chiefs of airlines confronted by shortages:

Northwest Aerospace Training Corporation (NATCO), the training arm of Northwest Airlines, has affiliated itself with the University of North Dakota's (UND) Center for Aerospace Studies (CAS). While CAS has had an aeronautical program for several years, the new NATCO/CAS will be a separate entity with a curriculum that is specifically airline oriented.

Under UND's standard aeronautical curriculum, a student can earn a four-year college degree while gaining the necessary ratings that can eventually lead to a job with the airlines. However, the standard program is not geared specifically in the airline direction. The student begins flight training at the beginning of his or her freshman year, and generally will graduate with commercial, multi-engine and instructor ratings. . . . (*Douglas W. Nelms, "Training Pilots From Zero Time to Left Seat,"* Airline Executive, *March 1988, 28*)

Two points about the story above: (a) It could be written by any accomplished reporter able to find authoritative sources in the airline industry and (b) though of little interest to a general audience, the story is important news for airline operations managers eager to start their own pilot training programs.

Here is the intro of an *Aviation Week* article very important to airline operations chiefs:

> Pan American World Airways succumbed finally to a defect intolerable to the world of commerce. It would not or could not adapt to changing times.
>
> A series of final blows brought to an end an airline conceived 64 years ago as the "Chosen Instrument" of the U.S. government in international aviation. As a private company representing America abroad, it rose to preeminence even before the Allied victory 45 years ago in World War 2. But its inability to adjust to political change, a new era in aviation and deregulation caused its slow fall to oblivion.
>
> By the 1970s Pan Am became a relic of a pioneer age, seeking to preserve its unique relationship with the government that was impossible in an era of mass transportation and competitive carriers. Some say the government hindered Pan Am from reforming more than it helped.
>
> Nevertheless, burdened with debt throughout the modern era, hampered by bad management and poor direction, union problems and hard luck, Pan Am in the 1980s slipped into an unrecoverable tailspin. . . .

The preceding story, a cover piece, was reported by six *Aviation Week* staffers, then written by two of them. Many technical journals use team reporting to weave varied expertise into a story.

Now, you'll note that professional reporters who don't really know much about airline operations could produce the first four paragraphs of the Pan Am story. They could check aviation history sources and, for the fourth paragraph, consult airline executives on Pan Am's debt and management problems.

But airline operations managers cannot be content with such generalities. They need specific guidance on how to run *their* companies—and that's what the *Aviation Week* article provides. An example:

> Earlier, in 1965, Pan Am arranged a $100-million revolving credit agreement with 36 U.S. commercial banks, enabling it to borrow and repay as its needs dictated. By year's end, its capital structure consisted of $200 million in senior debt; $80.4 million in convertible debentures, a common type of bond issued by large, well-established corporations; and $70 million in capitalized aircraft leases.
>
> Debt-to-equity, a fundamental measure of a business' financial health, was at a dangerously high level: 1.3 to 1. Between 1965 and 1969, Pan Am was required to lay out $1.08 billion in capital. The expenditures averaged $270 million annually to pay for the 747s. By 1969, long-term debt more than doubled to $400.7 million and debt-to-equity climbed to 1.75 to 1. Pan Am incurred its first operating losses in 1969 and 1970 of $26 million and $16 million, respectively. Long-term debt in 1970 topped $1 billion. . . .
> (*James Ott and Anthony L. Velocci, Jr., "Inability to Adapt in New Era of Aviation Doomed Pan Am,"* Aviation Week & Space Technology, *Dec. 16/23, 1991, 28*)

All to say that you need considerable expertise to report in big-league technical journals if your subject is industry operations.

Note the expertise evident in this intro that Erica Shames, a New York free-lance writer, did for *Videography,* a monthly for video producers:

> How do facility owners divine what equipment they will need in the coming year to remain competitive, and how do they calculate how much they can afford to spend on it? These are sticky questions for which there are no strict guidelines or mathematical formulas that yield solid answers. The more straightforward theories such as a three-to-five-year depreciation-accounting guideline are not as reliable as they once were, thanks to the fast-paced forward movement of new technology.
>
> The continuing emergence of equipment with new capabilities virtually obsoletes existing hardware years before it is depreciated and even longer before it wears out. Consequently, the factors guiding people in their equipment purchases are often as individualistic as the people who manage the facilities in which the equipment is used.

> Discussions with a variety of facilities, ranging from rental houses to duplicating facilities and postproduction studios, reveal some of the thinking that goes into these decisions. . . . (*Erica Shames, "Calculating the Incalculable,"* Videography, *Sept. 1989, 42*)

In the last example, did you note how writer Shames laid her reporter's credentials before her readers? (It's in the second paragraph: "Discussions with a variety of facilities . . . reveal some of the thinking. . . .") *That* is the way to combine reporting and writing skills for technical journals.

GETTING STARTED IN TECHNICAL WRITING

Every college or off-campus local community offers you many chances to get started in technical writing.

Story ideas? They're all around you. You'll find them at your college (a business), which is involved in an industry (education). Both have their own technologies (and technocrats). Faculty and staff are operations managers who need accurate, reliable information on their specialties, written in clear, concise language.

Off campus, your local community, regardless of its size, and local companies, no matter what their business, originate and use technical information.

For starters, we'll explore four areas where technical writers are needed: in the university community, and in health, environment and consumer news.

Technical Writing on Campus

Officials once started to count the magazines, newsletters and other periodicals issued by the University of Georgia. They halted after the count reached 300, so nobody really knows just how large the university's publishing business is.

This *is* known: A great many university publications carry technical copy and, further, the university's 13 separate colleges—agriculture, veterinary medicine, forest resources and so forth—use technical writing to communicate with audiences on and off campus.

In sum, campus publishing is a happy hunting ground for technical writers eager to sell their talents. And, whatever your personal interests or hobbies, you probably can find a campus publication that needs your background, as well as your writing talents.

Broadly, such technical writing has two missions.

First, it *translates* technical news that breaks on campus for *non-technical readers*. This, of course, requires writers who can understand the language of the colleges of consumer sciences or pharmacy, then communicate effectively in non-technical language for non-expert readers.

Second, it communicates technical information in the technical language of, say, medicine or pharmacy, to expert readers.

For example, following is a story from *Research News,* a magazine published by Georgia's vice president for research. The story obviously is written in "lay" language for non-technician readers, as well as researchers in all disciplines.

> It's like Mom always told you: Be careful when talking about religion, politics or sex. Perhaps the same advice applies to research into similar subjects.
>
> Any research, from mail-out surveys to studies on emotionally-charged issues like illegal drug use, sexual habits, or the treatment of criminals, can be a political "hot potato," or worse, a ticking time bomb. Citizens displeased with or skeptical about published results may ask to see researchers' data. As employees of a state-funded institution subject to Georgia's Open Records Law, University researchers may have to comply when data has been publicly released, published, copyrighted or patented.

Because all research information is not protected under the law, investigators need to be aware of the controversies their research may spawn.

"Under the law, any citizen can request data concerning published research and then reinterpret it to come up with their own conclusions," said University Vice President for Legal Affairs, Bryndis Roberts. According to Roberts, the reinterpretation of data is not prevented by the state statute.... (*"Protecting Research Under Georgia's Open Records Law,"* Research News, *Jan. 1992, 1*)

Note the catchy lead for the last story. Don't overlook the need to be readable in technical writing. Don't try to jam facts down your readers' throats; *entice* readers into your copy. Note also, in the last paragraph, the reporter at work. This writer (a) understands the issue (research law) and (b) knows how to find an authoritative source (Roberts) to interview. The result: a technical story researched with general-assignment reporting skills and written for technicians and non-technicians alike.

Here's an example of technical writing, from the same university magazine, that requires special knowledge to write and understand.

Researchers working with nucleic acid and protein separation and purification in small quantities may use the College of Veterinary Medicine's new Applied Biosystems high performance electrophoresis chromatography system (HPEC 230A). For more information, contact Dr. (Fred Smith), 542-5000. (*"Electrophoresis Chromatography System Available,"* Research News, *Jan. 1992, 1*)

What if you're a student in a non-technical department—journalism, say—and really feel more comfortable writing about something you understand (like journalism education)? How about doing a story for your department's newsletter on the equipment students use in studying television or the new computers in your newspaper editing lab?

Or, if you're looking for experience as a technical writer, start with your university's news bureau or director of information and the director of publications in a department or college whose research subject matches your personal interests.

Writing Health News

Everyone, it seems, is concerned about being too fat or too thin, whether they get enough exercise and whether their blood pressure is okay.

Sensing those concerns, virtually all magazines carry health articles. Virtually *all?*

Well, even *Corporate Video Decisions,* a technical journal aimed at readers in charge of corporate video departments, carried a health article on how to handle executive stress. *Industry Week* ("The Industry Management Magazine") informed its executive readers of how Adolph Coors Co., the brewer, instituted wellness programs for employees.[4] *The Los Angeles Times* regularly publishes a special section, *The Good Health Magazine.* Consumer magazines are filled with stuff about everything from hair loss to corns.

Specialty magazines dealing exclusively with health have enormous circulations: *Weight Watchers* (in June 1991) had 1,006,396 circulation; *American Health,* 812,672; *Self,* 1,140,635; *Prevention,* a whopping 3,109,562.[5]

You get the picture: Health news is *big* news, and like other subjects covered in this chapter, is written for expert or non-expert audiences alike.

In searching for stories that likely will interest non-expert readers, use the same news definitions you apply to any type of magazine writing: If a subject has impact on your readers' health, is timely and can be written in interesting, non-technical language, you likely have a winner—particularly if you deal with types of ailments, availability of cures or help and quality and cost of help. Then write it with imagination.

Note how Thomas H. Maugh II handles a piece on strokes. First, a human-interest intro:

> The old man sits alone in his wheelchair, watching his beloved Kansas City Royals struggle through another televised spring training game, or simply staring out the window at the squirrels emerging from their winter doldrums.
>
> At 77 years of age, he is an enigma. His right side is paralyzed and virtually useless. His speech is limited to yeses and noes that often don't seem to make sense. But his eyes burn with pride that reflects the intelligence that was once there—and may still be. . . .

Now, writer Maugh introduces a personal note—with telling effect:

> My father had a stroke on July 17, 1985. At 5:30 in the morning, he arose, exhaled sharply and collapsed to the floor. In the briefest of seconds, a black wall descended across his mind, muting his communication with the outside world, severing control of the right side of his body, and irrevocably changing the lives of his family.
>
> His—our—experience is not uncommon. Every year, about a half-million Americans have a stroke and nearly 149,000 die from it, making stroke the third leading cause of death behind heart disease and cancer. . . .

With readers firmly "hooked," writer Maugh turns to technical details written in language lay readers can understand:

> . . . strokes are caused by the rupture of a weak spot, called an aneurysm, on a blood vessel in the brain. When the aneurysm ruptures, blood flow is interrupted. If the blood vessel is on the surface of the brain (subarachnoid hemorrhaging), the blood leaks into the fluid surrounding the brain. If the vessel is within the brain (cerebral hemorrhaging), the blood accumulates within the brain. In addition to injury caused by loss of circulation, the pooled blood can damage brain cells by putting pressure on them.
>
> Aside from the use of aspirin to prevent clot formation, the most common approach to preventing strokes is a surgical procedure called carotid endarterectomy, in which the fat deposits that clog the carotid arteries in the neck are surgically cleaned out so that clots are less likely to form. . . . (*Thomas H. Maugh II, "The Silent Scourge,"* The Los Angeles Times' The Good Health Magazine, *29 April 1990, 31*)

Note how the writer assumes his readers have *no* specialized knowledge and explains each technical term.

Next, a writer for *Medical Laboratory Observer* assumes in her lead that readers, clinical technicians all, understand her subject—operation of testing labs. She then writes to their level of understanding:

> In satellite buildings, in corners of the emergency room and surgical suite, at the bedside, and elsewhere, a wide variety of testing is being done that was formerly restricted to the main laboratory. Many institutions that have not yet spread their labs' wings in this way are considering doing so in the near future.
>
> In fact, more than half of the respondents to MLO's recent national survey of supervisory laboratorians expect such testing to increase at their institutions in the next three to five years. While some laboratorians embrace the concept heartily, others are less enthusiastic—even wary. . . . (*Marcia Ringel Barman, "Alternative-Site Testing: Mixed Feelings About The Inevitable,"* Medical Laboratory Observer, *Dec. 1990, 22*)

We suggest you try your hand in health writing with stories aimed at lay (not expert) readers. For example, how about reporting, then translating into lay terms, these stories for readers of a campus magazine (or, if your college doesn't have one, a newspaper):

- Alcoholism—its prevalence among students; how to spot it if you think you or your friends are drinking too much.
- Eating disorders—what is (and isn't) a healthy diet; bulimia (insatiable hunger) and anorexia (rejection of food); signals of disorders.
- Stress—what are its danger signs; what causes it; what experts say are ways of handling it.

For all three story ideas, authoritative sources include the student health center, local hospitals and physicians (interview several), and university counselors. Include in each story complete information on where to get help—including names, addresses, telephone numbers of counseling services on and off campus. Also provide details on cost of care.

Writing Environmental News

Environmental news is *big* news—one of the biggest stories in decades. You can write this specialty for two broad audiences:

- general reader audiences, who increasingly are concerned with the safety of what they eat, drink and breathe and preservation of the world around them.
- officials of companies, industries and communities who know they must manage in environmentally sound ways.

John R. Cady, president of the National Food Processors Association, outlines the scope of media coverage in an article for his association's magazine, *Process*:

> For an industry so driven by consumer demand, it is a confusing time for the food business when it comes down to answering these questions: "What do consumers really want?" "What direction on products and environmental issues should our company take?"
> Much of the attendant hand-wringing has been due to the current fixation on questions about pesticides as they relate to the safety of food and the sustainability of Spaceship Earth. And, no wonder, because "the environment" and things "green" are everywhere we turn, particularly in the news media.
> According to a scan of top daily newspapers, wire services, and business and trade publications conducted by Mead Data Central, during a five-year period (1984–88), the print media generated 80,980 news stories addressing environmental issues.... By comparison, fewer than 40,000 articles were written about AIDS, and roughly 16,000 stories reported on the growing use of crack. The top environmental issue was the dangerous effect of pesticides, which accounted for 29 percent of the environmental stories, a full 10 percentage points above next-ranking toxic waste.... (*John R. Cady, "The Great Pesticide Debate,"* Process, *Dec. 1990, 3*)

Trade journals published for many industries allocate considerable space to environmental news and thus are markets for technical writers. Additionally, some magazines deal exclusively with environmental issues for industry readers.

For example, *World Wastes,* published 13 times annually, has 35,000 circulation among managers of landfills and waste disposal companies. Talk about narrow focus! Note this writing style directed at industry readers:

> In Camden County, Conn., the concept of recycling is enjoying a burst of popularity unseen since the early 1970s. About one-fourth of all refuse in the county is recycled, and the Camden recycling plant processes more than 50 tons of bottles and cans a day. Countywide, resident participation in the voluntary recycling program is running at more than 60 percent.
> The reason behind the push for recycling in Camden County is not the monetary return residents or the county will see for returning glass or newspapers to recycling centers; the real saving is of the county's dwindling landfill space.
> The state's Department of Environmental Protection (DEP) has estimated that Connecticut's landfill capacity will be exhausted by 1990. It is hoped that by combining recycling with refuse incineration at waste-to-energy facilities, the state's landfill life can be extended an additional 50 years.... (*Susan Darcey, "Landfill Crisis Report,"* World Wastes, *May 1987, 22*)

Obviously, writer Darcey's intent is to provide managers nationwide with information they can use in operating their own companies.

For writers just starting in environmental news, a much larger market awaits in general-consumer magazines. This is a huge market. *Greenpeace* has over 1.5 million in circulation; *Sierra,* over 500,000. Both are published by clubs. Smaller, independent magazines include *Countryside* (300,000 circulation), *Garbage* (100,000), *Buzzworm* (86,000).[6]

Your best beginning strategy, however, is to pick a local environment story you can report firsthand for a local magazine you can contact personally. Some story ideas:

- On-campus waste—how much tonnage is produced; is any toxic; which departments/colleges produce it; how is it handled and disposed of? Sources include physical plant officials, department/college deans, Environmental Protection Agency.
- Dorms/residences and their safety—are all free of asbestos; do any have "sick" air (a safety hazard in some air-conditioned buildings); what can individual students do to ensure the safest possible living environment? Same sources as the first idea.
- Localizing distant stories—don't overlook the many story possibilities in interviews with faculty and staff officials on environment and public safety. Comments by faculty experts can add local relevance to stories on, say, toxic waste or landfill problems that develop far from campus.

Writing Consumer News

Do you have hobbies or compelling personal interests—a love of cars, cooking, photography, home repairs?

If so, you're nicely positioned as a beginning writer in consumer news. Like health and environmental news, consumerism is an expanding area for technical writers with personal interest or expertise in specialized topics.

The market for consumer articles is huge. From *Consumer Reports,* the giant of consumer reporting, to the smallest local magazine, editors search for articles dealing with their readers' cars, kitchens and homes.

The key to effective consumer reporting is writing from the viewpoint of the consumers (your readers), who are seeking technical details and analysis to help them live better, more comfortable lives with products and services that are reliable and priced right.

For example, *Consumer Reports* has an international reputation for explaining in basic, lay language the technical strengths and weaknesses of products and, bottom line, what's a good buy and what isn't. Many readers consult *Consumer Reports* before any significant purchase is made.

For beginning writers, the best route into consumer writing is through in-depth interviews with experts whose authoritative guidance you can pass to readers. Unless you're *really* an expert in a subject, stick to reporting rather than interpretive writing. Story ideas litter the campus:

- Personal computers—expert views on strengths/weaknesses of models suitable for students; availability and cost; software capabilities.
- Textbooks—do some comparative shopping in your college bookstore and off-campus shops. Where are the best values for your student readers?
- Personal credit—how can students obtain credit cards? Can bouncing a check in a local bar harm a student's application for credit later in life? Ask bankers, credit bureau officials, business school professors.
- Vacations—where to go for a weekend or on spring break, how much it costs and what to do when you get there. Compare air fares and hotel rates.

Now, About Corporate Writing . . .

Corporate writing arguably is a public relations function and not a proper subject in a discussion of magazine writing.

Unquestionably, corporate writing is designed to further the image and profit goals of corporations and so, yes, it is a PR function. *However,* if you work for the right corporation, association or university, you can do ethical, straight writing on behalf of a product, service, idea, personality or cause in which you strongly believe.

This type of writing has two broad goals:

- to explain a corporation's mission and viewpoint to an *external* audience, such as customers, a local community or the public at large and
- *internally* to communicate management information, instructions and views to employees.

PR and advertising departments normally generate such communication, and they need highly professional writers who can handle technical subjects.

For example, all publicly owned companies (those whose shares trade on stock exchanges) are required by law to publish detailed information about their management and operations. This includes detailed financial information and news about a company's competitive position, its production techniques and sales methods.

Publications that in every sense are magazines often are the vehicles for getting this information out.

For example, annual reports issued by publicly owned companies often are beautifully crafted magazines filled with strong writing and graphics. Ask your central library or business school to see annual reports issued by Times Mirror Co. or New York Times Co. Both are major publishers of magazines. (Say! There's an idea: Could your background in journalism and magazine writing prepare you for a corporate writing job with a media company?)

Shareholder information of many kinds is generated by major corporations through newsletters, periodicals, speeches and audiovisuals, and all require strong writing.

Company magazines, for both external and internal audiences, are a huge market for writers. Gannett Co., one of the nation's largest media companies, publishes a monthly, *Gannetteer,* that discusses operations in Gannett newspapers, television stations and outdoor advertising companies. The magazine is highly regarded by communications professionals throughout the nation.

Employee newsletters are a major function for corporate writers. Gannett, for example, issues *Health/Works* ("Gannett Guide to Good Health") for employees. Its writers must possess strong writing skills, obviously, and a knack for translating technical details of health care for a lay audience.

Corporate writing? Check it out.

SUMMARY

Beneath the surface of everyday news floats a torrent of information on industries and companies, their technologies and the goods and services they produce.

This river of information is carried, in part, by technical magazines whose mission is helping readers produce better goods and services more efficiently and profitably and, thus, advance their careers.

The modern mission of technical writing requires writers to follow all the guidelines of good magazine writing, be enticing and meet the highest standards of accuracy.

Writing about the business of industry involves giving readers a broad overview of developments that likely are important to their own careers. An example is a summary story that wraps up, say, availability of financing for readers who are developers and investors in real estate.

Writing about technology requires extra care to be accurate, because readers most likely are experts in the subject you're covering, and because they may make important decisions—involving profit and loss or even life and death—based on what you write.

Writing about industry *operations* involves accumulating a great deal of information for executives and others on the managerial ladder who are striving to improve a company's overall operational efficiency. This type of writing requires writers who understand how an industry works and who can write effectively about its technology and operations.

Get started in technical writing by covering campus stories from your college's various departments (i.e., agriculture, veterinary medicine, forest resources). Many use technical writing to communicate with audiences on and off campus.

Writing health news takes you into concerns shared by your student colleagues (and, perhaps, yourself): alcoholism, eating disorders, and so forth.

A huge market exists for stories on environmental concerns. Write for two audiences: general readers concerned with the safety of what they eat, drink and breathe, and for officials of companies, industries and cities (and universities) who know they must manage in environmentally sound ways.

Consumer news can be attractive for writers with hobbies or compelling personal interests—a love of cars, cooking, photography, for example. Write from the consumers' viewpoint on how they can live better, more comfortable lives with the products and services they purchase.

Corporate magazines and newsletters employ writers, too. Check 'em out.

RECOMMENDED READING

To prepare for a career in technical writing, your best bet for additional helpful reading is in trade and technical journals and selected newspapers that cover your chosen specialty.

For example, if general science writing is your goal, *never* miss science writing in *The New York Times* (particularly its special science section on Tuesdays). Science writing there, in *The Wall Street Journal* and in *Time* and *Newsweek* often illustrates perfectly how professional writers can absorb and analyze highly technical information, then place it carefully before general readers in terms they understand.

If you want to write technical articles for an expert audience, select (with your instructor's help) the best trade journals in your chosen field and read them religiously. For example, if you want to write about, say, advertising, read *Advertising Age*. You'll learn a great deal about both advertising and technical writing.

For other hints on specialty writing, see Conrad C. Fink, *Introduction to Professional Newswriting* (White Plains, N.Y.: Longman, 1992) and chapters on public relations in Conrad C. Fink, *Inside the Media* (White Plains, N.Y.: Longman, 1990.)

NOTES

1. Lawrence E. Altman, M.D., "Editor of Journal Envisions New Directions and Lighter Tone," *The New York Times,* national edition, 5 Feb. 1991, B7.
2. "Pilots at the Controls of *Aviation Week,*" *McGraw-Hill World,* 22 Aug. 1991, 2.
3. Don Michard, "Forecasting the Future," *Fire Chief,* Jan. 1991, 30.
4. In order, these stories are Ron Marans, "Stressed Out," *Corporate Video Decisions,* June 1989, 16, and Shari Caudron, "Wellness Works," *Industry Week,* 4 Feb. 1991, 22.
5. Diane Loupe, "A Healthy Dose of Competition," *The Atlanta Constitution,* 15 Oct. 1991, B4, quoting Audit Bureau of Circulations.
6. Rodney Ho, "Environmental Magazines Defy Slump," *The Wall Street Journal,* 10 Sept. 1991, B1.

Chapter 13

Writing
for entertainment
magazines

Can you build a *serious* magazine career in writing about *fun*?

Yes. Big time.

Note the huge number of magazines devoted exclusively to entertainment. Flip through "serious" magazines and note the many stories about films, music, dance, television—and the just-plain-fun stories—positioned among all those deep-think pieces on politics, economics and other "meaningful" subjects.

Clearly, entertainment is big news in America. Readers love it. And advertisers love to be in any magazine, alongside any story, that readers love. So, editors of nearly all types of magazines are receptive to well-written copy on some aspect of entertainment.

Some magazines devoted purely to entertainment are virtual American institutions. *Rolling Stone*, *TV Guide* and *People* are among titles that pop to mind.

New entertainment magazines are launched every year, often aimed at incredibly narrow market segments. For example, *Strings,* published by amateur cellist David Lusterman, has a 9,000 circulation among players, teachers and makers of stringed instruments. Lusterman's *The Piano Quarterly* has an 8,000 circulation.[1]

Many entertainment magazines are hugely popular with both readers and advertisers. For example, *TV Guide,* with its balanced content of TV listings and commentary on television, had 15.8 million circulation in 1990. Each copy sold was read, on average, by 2.5 readers. The magazine thus claimed an astounding 39.5 million readers. For advertisers, those readers were highly attractive: The average reader was 37.2 years old, had household income of about $32,000 and leafed through each copy of *TV Guide* 4.7 times (thus being exposed repeatedly to ads) before tossing it out.[2]

In this chapter, we'll look at various types of entertainment writing (it's a multidimensional field) and pass along some hints on writing style. We'll also discuss some ways you can get started, on campus or off, in this specialty writing.

YOUR FIRST DECISION: WRITE FOR INSIDERS OR CONSUMERS?

Two general approaches are open for beginners in entertainment writing. Your choice should depend primarily on your own expertise in the subject you want to cover.

First, you can write for readers who are consumers (not producers) of entertainment and who read about it for fun. Many of these readers are knowledgeable about entertainment and entertainers, but their level of expectation often can be met, even by beginning writers, through diligent, careful reporting.

Second, you can write for entertainment insiders, readers who create entertainment or those who are intimately familiar with the entertainment industry's financial and other complexities. Many of these readers are as expert in their fields as are scientists who read *Scientific American* or Wall Street investors who read *Forbes*. For entertainment insiders you'll need to possess—and communicate clearly through your writing—a high level of expertise.

Let's look at how you can get started in these two broad categories.

WRITING FOR ENTERTAINMENT CONSUMERS

So, you've always been fascinated with movies or rock music or dance or the bar scene, and now you want to write for people who share your interests.

Where to start?

Short answer: Virtually wherever—and however—you want to start.

In perhaps no other sector of magazine writing are so many options open for beginners. We can't think of a general-interest or consumer magazine that doesn't publish entertainment copy. Trade or specialty magazines are good markets, too.

As for story topics, let your imagination run. Consumers of entertainment—the fans—are interested in an enormously wide array of subjects: from Elizabeth Taylor's latest diet (or husband) to the string quartet visiting your campus to next month's movie schedule at your university theater.

We hasten to point out that for beginners there is danger in writing entertainment copy: Many inexperienced writers believe that from Day One they must approach entertainment writing as critics or commentators, and the more viciously critical, the better. Beware. Nothing falls flatter than inexperienced writers seized by an attack mentality and lashing out wildly at every art form in sight. In getting started in entertainment writing (as in any magazine writing specialty) you should ease into the task. Start with reporting the basics and convey them in simple, clear, straightforward language. With solid experience in reporting entertainment news you can move on to more sophisticated commentary if you write in a lively, informed, reasonable way.

When writing entertainment copy (and most other forms of magazine articles), focus on people. Even casual study of magazines reveals editors are serving readers who are more interested in film stars than films, musicians than music, dancers than dance. And the more "inside" information you deliver, the better. Deborah Paul, co-publisher and editor of *Indianapolis Monthly,* puts it this way: "Readers are a little like cat burglars—they like to sit and look in the windows of other people's homes."

Also, you must develop a writing style that builds special intimacy with your readers. Don't try the type of journalism you might practice if writing about, say, Yugoslavia's civil war for a "thought leader" such as *The Atlantic*: "Here, read this; you need to know this." Many people read entertainment copy for, obviously, entertainment. Don't force-feed those who seek diversion, relaxation, titillation. And for even those more serious readers who are deeply interested in an art form (opera buffs and dance fans can be near-fanatics), you must develop a writing style that glides, not charges, ahead; a style built around vignettes, insights, subtleties. The Five W's and How must be in your copy, all right. Just don't jam them all into your first paragraph.

Many story structures are available to you. Let's look at how professional writers handle some of the most important ones.

The Personality Profile

Because the entertainment industry revolves around personalities, the profile is one of the most important story structures you have for writing about it.

Broadly, you can use the profile most effectively for two purposes: (a) To "chat" with your readers about a well-known personality without getting too serious about communicating some underlying, compellingly important message or (b) to use the personality merely as a vehicle for pulling your readers into a wider subject.

First, an example of a shoes-off, gentle and non-challenging chat with readers still on their Sunday morning cup of coffee:

> "When it comes to the sophisticated world of TV," says Willard Scott, the weatherman for the *Today* show, "I'm a mutation. If you put me on an audition tape, everything is wrong—except for the fact that I have a nice voice." He breaks into his familiar gaptoothed smile. "Look at me," he adds. "I'm 57, overweight, baldheaded and corny. Not exactly your leading man, and yet I'm on top of the heap."
>
> Indeed, Scott has shown amazing staying power in a business known to be fickle. Though his antics on the air haven't pleased all viewers, and critics have come down hard on him, for 11 years Scott has been a decided hit with TV viewers. What accounts for his popularity?
>
> To be sure, Scott is no ordinary weatherman. What he gives his viewers is a combination of folksy chatter, corny humor and, of course, the weather. Scott acknowledges that he's a performer, not a meteorologist. "Anybody can read the weather," he says. "You have to have a gimmick. You need an act to set you apart from the other weather guys in town."
>
> His clownish act is something that comes naturally to the 275-pound, 6-foot-3 Scott—whether it be with the funny hats he wears, the flower in his lapel or the toupee that comes on and off. But he asserts, "I'm a buffoon with substance. . . ." (*Marvin Scott, "Why They Love This Guy,"* Parade, *8 Sept. 1991, 4*)

Above, note the folksy tone: "gaptoothed smile," "corny humor," "clownish act. . . ." The author is saying, Hey, readers! This guy Willard is just like a lot of us—a good ole' boy, balding, overweight, a real down-home guy. Nothing in the entire story (*Parade* gave it two full pages) takes readers beyond that. The story is a quick, warm, friendly Sunday morning read—and nothing more.

Now, let's look at a story that appears, at first glance, to be a typical personality profile on Woody Allen:

> Woody Allen has always insisted on complete creative control over the movies he makes. They're his babies. He writes them; he directs them.

As long as he kept them under a certain limited budget, Orion Pictures, which has financed and distributed all his movies since 1982, let him do what he wanted. Sure, they like to joke in Hollywood, no one outside New York ever went to his movies, Orion wouldn't even bother to book them in the Corn Belt, but Woody's core New York audience, together with a few cultish fans in half a dozen other cities, kept his pictures in the black.

Most of the time.

Not that profit was ever the object, anyway.

But now, with Orion close to bankruptcy, Allen has been talking to other studios. Every studio head would love to do a deal with the Woodster. He's America's one true auteur filmmaker. He's prestige. He's class. But few studio heads seem to be as willing as Arthur Krim, Woody's old friend and a founder of Orion, to grant him unlimited freedom.

Earlier this month, Allen signed a deal to make one movie with TriStar Pictures. The details have remained secret, but everyone is intrigued.... (*John Taylor, "Woody Wonderland,"* New York, *30 Sept. 1991, 35*)

Well, you might say, there's nothing in that story about Allen's age, weight or teeth, so it cannot be a personality profile. But it *is*. The story is a narrowly focused and insightful profile of a single dimension of Allen's personality—his business skill.

The Woody Allen piece differs from the Willard Scott article in another way: The Willard Scott story is all about Willard Scott; however, in the Woody Allen article, author Taylor uses the filmmaker's personality as a vehicle for discussing an underlying topic taken very seriously in film circles: how much control artists should have over creative content and marketing of their own work.

There is middle ground between those two extremes: The profile that neatly balances physically descriptive and biographical data against what an entertainment figure says about art, performing or subjects of public interest. Writer Leonora Langley took such a balanced approach to actress Holly Hunter, concentrating on her activist support of abortion rights but also sprinkling her story with profile material such as this:

Whether at an abortion rights rally or on screen or in an interview, Holly Hunter doesn't mince words. A petite 5'2", with straight shoulder-length hair and elfin features, Hunter, 33, is not a woman of rounded and polished phrases, but she is by no means taciturn. In fact, once she starts talking, she barely pauses for breath.... (*Leonora Langley, "Hunter's Game,"* Elle, *March 1991, 120*)

Obviously, a key to writing effective personality profiles is presenting just the right balance: information on how a star walks, talks, looks but also details on what the star says, the quality of performance, impact on audiences and so forth. Each story requires its own balance. How to find that balance? Try and try again. With experience you'll find the right formula.

The personality profile clearly is a wondrously flexible story structure you can bend to many uses. It works so well because it's built around people, and people are what people most like to read about.

But magazine readers have other interests in entertainment, too. Let's look at ways to write to those other interests.

The Survey Story or Updater

In entertainment, as in virtually all sectors of our society, important changes are under way. New art forms are emerging, new personalities and trends becoming important. And for entertainment buffs, nothing is more crucial than being on the cutting edge of those changes. You can succeed if you bring first word of change or deliver true insight into the meaning of change.

A structure perfect for this is the survey story. Use this to pull together bits and pieces to reveal trends, to sweep across a subject and update your readers on what is happening.

Note how a writer looks at American filmmaking, finds a trend—increasing success by black directors—and eases you into the subject with a superbly crafted opening vignette:

> John Singleton pulls his slightly battered silver Peugeot into the empty two-car garage of his new house in Baldwin Hills, a prosperous black neighborhood of contemporary homes sitting high above Los Angeles. The house itself, with impressive views from each oversize window, is mostly unfurnished, testament to a recent windfall and a lack of time to spend it. Singleton, whose first feature film, "Boyz N the Hood," opened nationally on Friday, lives alone, except for an albino cat who floats down the stairs to greet him.
>
> "That's White Boy," Singleton says, stooping to rub the cat behind his translucent ears.
>
> The metaphor is irresistible at the moment, John Singleton, a 23-year-old black man, has the notoriously insular and mostly white Hollywood establishment purring. . . .

Note two points about this illustration.

First, the story has a current time element ("Friday," in the first paragraph). The survey or "updater" story is most effective if your subject matter is current.

Second, the first three paragraphs don't really survey anything. They focus on one man and give only a whiff of something larger to come ("... notoriously insular and mostly white Hollywood establishment purring . . ."). So, if this story is to present a wider view of filmmaking and truly reveal a trend, the writer must quickly broaden the approach. This is done in the sixth paragraph:

> "The Singleton thing," as it's referred to in current Hollywood parlance, is the latest bold-relief example of Hollywood's sudden open-door policy toward black filmmakers, particularly those telling black stories. Several studios—among them Warner Brothers, Columbia, Goldwyn, New Line and Island World (which is releasing "Juice," the first feature by Ernest Dickerson, Spike Lee's longtime friend and cinematographer)—have black films in the pipeline. By year's end 19 will have been released, more than in all of the previous decade. The frenzy for black product that allowed Singleton, who has no previous professional credits, to direct his own film has become so great that black film properties may be to the 90's what the car phone was to the 80's: every studio executive has to have one. . . . (*Karen Grigsby Bates, "They've Gotta Have Us,"* New York Times Magazine, *14 July 1991, 15*)

Next, a writer opens a survey story by creating a vision in your mind ("Saturday night in Manhattan . . . cabs . . . trendy supper club . . ."), then updates you ("jazz is bouncing back") and quickly (second paragraph) tells you *why* jazz is bouncing back.

> On a Saturday night in Manhattan, cabs pull up in front of a trendy supper club and unload slicked-up men and women for a night of fun and frolic. Only they're not going to disco, rock 'n' roll, or hip-hop. Tonight, a warm buzz of conversation blends into the sonorous highs and lows of jazz ascending in mighty clouds of joy. Once relegated to the dustbin of history, jazz is bouncing back, not just among old-timers or audiophiles in love with their new CD players, but with a whole new audience that's just beginning to recognize the difference between Miles Davis and Duke Ellington.
>
> What happened? Not too long ago, jazz was a moribund anachronism indulged in by purists who stayed home wearing out the grooves of record collections that ended around 1967, the year John Coltrane died. Ten—or even five—years ago, talk of a jazz revival was met with the skepticism normally reserved for those who went on about the forthcoming fall of Communism. (Yeah, right.) But thanks to a confluence of events—social, political, and economic—we find ourselves looking backwards into the future. Welcome to the post-Cold War, recession-proof jazz age, where an esoteric cultlike music with an image problem, only barely heard on hard-to-tune frequencies, radically

out-of-place in the age of ubiquitous sampling, becomes the next big thing.... (*David Hershkovits, "Jazzmatazz,"* Elle, *March 1991, 128*)

Incidentally, did you catch, in the second paragraph, the tongue-in-cheek reference to the "fall of communism" and the slangy "(Yeah, right.)"? That's the writer's effort (successful, we think) to get chummy with you, to build that intimacy we mentioned earlier. It's just the two of you, two music fans—writer and reader alone.

The survey story can work beautifully for magazines that offer readers a little armchair adventure—an opportunity to vicariously "see," through the written word, paintings they otherwise would never see, to "hear" music they otherwise never would hear. *Town & Country* does that in this survey story:

> We keep hearing about the cultural reawakening in Spain, and the explosion of talent in the arts. Barcelona and Seville are building contemporary art museums while, in Madrid, institutions like the Reina Sofia museum, the Caixa de Pension bank and the Palacio de Velazquez are hosting world-class contemporary art exhibitions. ARCO, the annual contemporary art fair in Madrid, has become a must not only for the Spanish but for critics and gallery owners the world over. And dealers—from New York's Leo Castelli, Blum-Helman and Brooke Alexander to various outposts in England, Germany, Japan and France—have taken a serious interest in showing—and selling—work by Spanish artists.
>
> There seem to be two distinct trends in Spanish art today.... (*Deborah Gimelson, "An Art For The 90s,"* Town & Country, *April 1990, 209*)

The Nostalgia Story

Remember Dr. Seuss? "Cat in the Hat"? How about, "How the Grinch Stole Christmas"?

If you're like millions of Americans you remember Dr. Seuss—author Theodore Geisel—and the stories he wrote. You may even remember the day you learned he died, in 1991. Nostalgia swept American campuses that day as young Americans raised on Dr. Seuss stories mourned his passing. His death was one of those occurrences that, if even for a short time, unites millions of people in nostalgia. For older Americans, the same thing happens with mention of the Japanese attack on Pearl Harbor, the assassination of President John Kennedy, the slaying of the Beatles' John Lennon.

Those nostalgic moments are threads of universal understanding you can use to weave tales that will transport your readers back to better times and fond memories. (See Figure 13–1.)

Magazines are wide open for nostalgia stories of virtually all types. (Some magazines, such as *Victoria,* specialize in it.) Using a little imagination, you can exploit that market with unusual stories. Take, for example, the wonderful old TV series, "Star Trek." You're an atypical American if you haven't seen at least an episode or two. Indeed, Americans now in their 30s and 40s remember "Star Trek" as part of growing up. Writer Walter Roessing recognized that. He also recognized that Delta Airlines (like all airlines) courts travelers in their 30s and 40s. He wrote a nostalgic piece on "Star Trek" for *Sky* magazine, which you'll find in the seat pockets of Delta airliners. Roessing's lead:

> Its array of flashing consoles, an alien-world look, and the padded chair of Starfleet Captain Jean-Luc Picard make the bridge of the starship Enterprise the most beguiling set on the Paramount Pictures lot in Hollywood. Some of its mesmerized visitors have included ex-President Ronald Reagan, General Colin Powell, and a delegation of Tibetan monks.
>
> "Everyone wants to sit in the captain's chair," says Michael Dorn, who portrays Lieutenant Worf on the hit television series, *Star Trek: The Next Generation.* "Our show is so captivating that, even when we're not shooting, the visitors tiptoe around our set and speak in whispers."

FIGURE 13–1 News events often give writers marvelous "pegs" for nostalgic stories. The *Campus Observer,* serving the University of Georgia campus, used stories, editorials and this drawing by cartoonist Mike Moreu to touch thousands of hearts when Dr. Seuss (author Theodore Geisel) died. (*Used with permission*)

Indeed, the fascination with Star Trek—boldly taken to worlds where no TV series has ventured before—has continued for 25 years.

With his readers now thinking back fondly to their early years of watching TV, writer Roessing faces a decision: Should he stick with nostalgia and simply milk the "old days" for all they're worth? Or, should he pitch the story ahead into new territory with facts likely to interest business travelers in their 30s and 40s? Roessing decides to use nostalgia only as a peg for his story and later build into his narrative substantive, dollars-and-cents reporting:

> Star Trek, the imaginative creation of Gene Roddenberry, has been evolving all that time through two television series, an animated children's show, and five major motion pictures. It's estimated that these productions, plus an extensive line of merchandising, have rewarded Paramount with more than $1 billion in revenues.
>
> That's not bad for a show whose most notable acting line to date has been, "Beam me up, Scotty."
>
> Paramount has such a profitable and popular commodity on its hands that—as part of Star Trek's 25th anniversary year—it will unveil a sixth major motion picture in December.... (*Walter Roessing, "Hey, Scotty! We're 25!" Sky, Sept. 1991, 30*)

Pegs for nostalgia pieces are unlimited. Here's how Kenneth Shouler, a sports writer, elbows into Delta's *Sky* with a piece on, of all things, old-time baseball songs.

> It was ten seasons ago, during the strike-interrupted summer of 1981, that baseball was saved by a song.
>
> Feeling the sadness of the strike like any baseball zealot, Terry Cashman wrote the lyrical "Willie, Mickey, and the Duke," offering a consolation prize for lost fans forced to listen to radio replays and watch minor-league games for two months. At its nostalgic best, the song sprightly highlights some episodes of 1950s baseball....

Following these two paragraphs, writer Shouler reproduced lyrics of the song, which mentions the nicknames of baseball players of that era. He then pulls his readers into participating in his story:

For fun, try naming the players whose nicknames are used. Not only is Cashman, baseball's balladist par excellence, hankering for the innocent times of baggy-pants baseball, but he also started something. As Yogi himself might have said when Cashman came out with his 1981 ballad, "It was déjà vu all over again."

You see, some 500 diamond songs had already extolled the game, beginning with the tune "Slide Billy Slide" which came along in the 1890s. That early rhapsody praised the exploits of a Hall of Fame speedster, Slidin' Billy Hamilton. Since then, baseball has been romanticized in song—and literature for that matter—more frequently than any other sport, anywhere. The breadth of music and writing suggests that no sport captures the rhythms of a season the way baseball punctuates the languorous, untroubled times of summer. . . . (*Kenneth Shouler, "Diamond Songs," Sky, Oct. 1991, 12*)

Why is the nostalgia structure so effective? Note in the baseball song story: ". . . the innocent times of baggy-pants baseball . . ." and ". . . the languorous, untroubled times of summer . . ." *That's* what the nostalgia piece does—takes readers back to the summers of their youth, to joys and sadness, even back to times that perhaps never were but should have been!

WRITING ENTERTAINMENT SPECIALTIES

Magazine editors regard "entertainment" as a multifaceted subject. They divide it into narrow segments, grouping stories under headings of "Movies," "Eating Out," "Music" and so forth.

You'll improve enormously your chances of getting published if you pick one or two such specialties and concentrate on learning the reporting and writing skills needed to cover them.

Let's look at some of those specialties.

Writing Restaurant and Bar Reviews

For millions of Americans, eating and drinking out are primary forms of entertainment. Magazines, like newspapers, devote major resources to covering them.

In this specialty, two factors should drive your writing style.

First, your readers want *operative information* for deciding where to seek entertainment. That includes addresses, telephone numbers (for making reservations), prices, tipping practices and so forth.

Second, *your writing style should match your subject*: Let your language swing and sway when reporting on the club scene; in writing about, say, a restaurant, get quickly to what readers seek—prices, dining room ambiance, menu and so forth.

Note below how Gael Greene (dubbed by *New York* "The Insatiable Critic") lets 'er rip when reviewing a bar in New York City, Le Bar Bat:

An anthropologist, a chiropterist, and a psychoanalyst—preferably high on Jungle Fuzz (Kahlua, coconut, and cream)—could do justice to the determined herd at **Le Bar Bat.** A lineup of young Studs Lonigans hangs off the balcony rail assessing the merchandise. Early, it's suits and briefcases for guys and dolls, unanimous. Young melting-pot faces, beautiful faces with do-it-yourself hair crinkles, so young and unfinished they don't know how to walk in high heels yet. Scatterings of dirty old men eyes crazed, practically drooling. Suddenly, a clotted clump of what could be family at a wedding in Cleveland. Tourist bus? Then husky guys in cut-rate suits. Policemen from Boston. . . . (*Gael Greene, "Best Bats," New York, 30 Sept. 1991, 58*)

Writer Greene obviously had great fun writing the story above (deeper in the story Greene describes the bar as "wildly funky, a soaring stage-set saloon or bordello in a Far Eastern country at war, Vietnam perhaps" . . .) But throughout

Greene weaves in dollars-and-cents information: a drink called the "Volcanic Bat Bite" is priced at $24, for example, "and the food scores mostly between not bad and pretty good."

Reviewing restaurants for *Esquire,* writer John Mariani devotes less wordage to scene-setting. Instead, he gets directly to what gourmets want to know:

C H E C K E R S

The Checkers Hotel

535 South Grand Avenue

213-624-0000

Despite the economic roll downtown L.A. is enjoying, few notable restaurants have opened in a section of the city that pretty much clears out after office hours. Not since Rex opened in 1983 has a restaurant as good as this one opened in this neighborhood. . . . The dining room itself is delicately bright and cheerful. . . . You might begin with a pea soup that is nothing more—and nothing less—than the essence of fresh flavors, then move on to fried zucchini blossoms in a smoked tomato sauce and the kind of soul-satisfying pork chops with mustard greens and baked beans or grilled duck with peppered mayonnaise and buckwheat salad you thought you could never find at a restaurant like this. The desserts by Dana Farkas are pure American delights: strawberry shortcake, homemade ice creams, and tapioca pudding that will bring you complete bliss. (*John Mariani, "Cheers!"* Esquire, *Nov. 1989, 187*)

In both of these reviews, note the writers are critics but in a rather subdued sense; mostly, they are reporters. Both make subjective judgments (the Checkers' dining room is "delicately bright," for example), but their principal goal is to report for readers on where and what to eat and drink.

Writing TV and Movie Reviews

Magazines (and newspapers) of consequence treat TV and movie entertainment as serious news, of course, and solid careers are carved out by many reviewers who become experts in that writing specialty.

In fact, editors regard TV and movie writing as so important that it deserves a book (or books) by itself. We don't have space for that, so we can pass along only a few hints that may help you get started.

First, any review, to be effective, must outline dispassionately the plot line and reveal enough about overall content to give your readers a firm idea of whether the film or TV show would appeal to them. (That does *not* include, of course, revealing the twists and turns of a plot or, say, the outcome of a murder mystery.)

Movie fans get deeply into plots, a fact exploited by Robert Seidenberg in the following example. Note how he plunges directly into the plot, with "Meet the Flaxes"—saying, in effect, Let me introduce you, movie fans, to the principal characters of the film, "Mermaids."

Meet the Flaxes, America's most atypical typical family. Mrs. Flax (Cher), the libertarian mother of two in "Mermaids," prides herself on her hors d'oeuvres. "Mrs. Flax's main cookbook," complains Charlotte, her 15-year-old, "is Fun Finger Foods. Anything more, she says, is too big a commitment." Which just about sums up her modus operandi. Self-centered and promiscuous, Mrs. Flax avoids intimacy; every time one of her many affairs turns too hot and heavy, she packs up and moves to a new spot randomly picked by a blind poke at the pages of a road atlas.

Charlotte (Winona Ryder) rebels. . . . (*Robert Seidenberg, "Mermaids,"* American Film, *Dec. 1990, 48*)

A second thing to remember when getting started in reviewing is that both movies and TV programming are, of course, *art forms,* and you'll need to display some knowledge to achieve credibility with readers. It's not enough to praise what *you* like and fume against what *you* don't like. Your subjective views must be cast against a backdrop of objective fact—firm grasp of moviemaking history, for example, or understanding of filmmaking technique. That is, your central role in reviewing, as in so many types of magazine writing, should be to report.

Note, for example, the unmistakable authority in this TV review by *New York*'s John Leonard:

> The Commish (Saturdays; 10 to 11 p.m.; ABC) is the latest from Stephen J. Cannell, the bearded executive producer/auteur who has more lives on network television than Dracula or Nixon . . . he's been rethinking masculinity. Why not a police commissioner with feelings? A sort of Frank Furillo, only cuddly—so long as we understand that deep down, Tony Scali is a fist of repressed menace. Hurt any member of his clan, and he'll hurt you back.
>
> As Scali, Michael Chiklis will remind you of Bob Hoskins, the private eye in "Who Framed Roger Rabbit". . . . The Commish works, not only because Chiklis is genuinely appealing but also because Cannell is so playful. He's been around since "The Rockford Files." He has given us "The A-Team," "Wise Guy," and "21 Jump Street," among many others. If this doesn't fly, he'll try something else. Television is his paint box and his Legos and his Erector Set. If he ever looks over his shoulder, I imagine it's merely to shrug. He enjoys himself. . . . (*John Leonard, "Feelings, Whoa, Oh, Oh, Feelings," New York, 30 Sept. 1991, 62*)

Certainly, once you've developed experience and a reputation as a movie critic—as David Denby has—editors will let you cut loose with strong opinions. Note:

> Of all the many kinds of bully, a life-affirming bully is perhaps the worst. I mean the kind of man who takes you by the lapel and screams, "Live, you moron!" Terry Gilliam, the American ex-Python who has made some of the most spectacular messes in the history of movies ("Time Bandits," "Brazil," "The Adventures of Baron Munchausen"), has become that sort of shouter. "The Fisher King" is a huge fable of moral decrepitude and regeneration, set in Gilliam's cracked, visionary New York—a medieval-modernistic nightmare city—and along with a few things that are touching and funny, the movie offers such fervent stupidities as Robin Williams lying naked in Central Park and mooning the moon. It's the oldest of "daring" cliches: The mad and foolish are closer to God than the rest of us are. . . . (*David Denby, "Mork and Terry," New York, 30 Sept. 1991, 60*)

For starters, try your hand at reviewing movies and TV programming from the *student viewpoint* for campus magazines. Give yourself the advantage of writing for an audience whose movie interests you understand!

Writing Theater, Dance and Music Reviews

Warning: When you write about theater, dance and music, you're moving into a writing specialty that requires an extremely high level of expertise.

People who seek out drama or dance reviews or who read deeply about music aren't the casual, non-expert types you'll often find sampling your articles on, say, movies, TV sitcoms or the local bar scene. Many theater, dance and music buffs are deadly serious in their love of the arts, and the slightest technical error in your writing will bring howls of protest.

So, if arts criticism is your long-term career goal, start now gaining the requisite background: an arts degree, perhaps, or at least a minor in music, the theater or whichever art form you pick as a specialty.

Start now in arts writing as a reporter. Don't feel you must begin with criticism, shouting from the mountaintop *your* opinions or reactions to a performance or performer. Start by writing about, say, dance companies on your campus, about local dance directors and dancers. Report *their* views on dance and opinions on the future of local dance. Many leading writers build expertise carefully, starting with stories of limited scope, then gradually expanding into true commentary and criticism as their experience broadens.

Actually, much so-called "critical" arts writing featured in major magazines is mostly expert reporting of trends and developments. Note here, for example, how a leading dance critic, Tobi Tobias, opens an article, as all good reporters must, by updating readers on recent developments:

> After a three-year stint with his company at Brussel's Theatre de la Monnaie, Mark Morris is home again in the States. His group isn't slated to perform in New York yet under its own aegis, but the choreographer and his dancers have hardly been idle. Recently, at the Brooklyn Academy of Music, they formed the dance component of John Adams's new opera, The Death of Klinghoffer, directed by Peter Sellars with a libretto by Alice Goodman. The same team of four gave us the 1987 "Nixon in China". . . .

This writing flows from good reporting. Limit yourself to stories of narrow scope and, using basic reporting skills, you can edge into arts writing. However, read more deeply into Tobi Tobias' story and you'll see why a high degree of expertise is required to succeed in big-league arts writing. Note the following paragraph from the same story:

> What the choreographer has come up with is logical and adequate, nothing more. He complements the music in setting the choral showpieces as dance-choir passages and assigning dance alter egos (sort of guardian angels) to the solo singers. Morris's group work, like that of Adams's score, is formal and imposing. It is dominated by simple, clear gestures—frequently literal "signed" equivalents of words in the sung text—with lots of space and time around them to heighten their effect. The singers perform similar movements, which may explain why the dancers aren't allowed the more complex and subtle elaborations on this basic vocabulary that you wish they'd make. . . . (*Tobi Tobias, "Mostly Morris," New York, 30 Sept. 1991, 68*)

In this last example, writer Tobias obviously is using a language spoken primarily (if not only) by dance fans. Amateur writers need not apply!

Kay Larson, art critic for *New York,* takes a reporter's approach to a new show of Pop art:

> LONDON—What you might call the mom of all Pop shows opened here at the Royal Academy of Arts in a fever of promotion. A custom-painted bus offered free rides to the exhibition. The BBC did an entire Saturday evening's programming after the opening. A national radio station broadcast live bands from the courtyard; one of the musicians, asked what he remembered of Pop, grudgingly pointed out that it had all happened before he was born.
>
> Roughly 30 years old, Pop has sustained its presence into the nineties. For the aging gents who lived through it (and through the youth culture and the music scene that coincided with it), Pop hit the sixties with the force of the inevitable. Why it should be so is the topic of this huge exhibition—the biggest and most important Pop show of a generation, the one that will rewrite the textbooks. Brought in from cities as far-flung as Los Angeles and Milan, and dating from as early as 1950, the art is broadly revisionist. . . .
>
> According to the usual histories, Pop in the early sixties blasted away the tired debris of Abstract Expressionism in a clatter of Campbell's soup cans and comic-strip BLAM!s, horrifying the high-minded. That oversimplified picture is being amended by Norman Rosenthal, exhibitions coordinator of the Royal Academy, and Marco Livingstone, British art historian and Pop specialist. . . . (*Kay Larson, "Top of the Pop," New York, 30 Sept. 1991, 72*)

Note the story components: a *news* development (new show in London), a time element in history ("30 years old," in second paragraph) and the *what* of the event (third paragraph, Rosenthal is amending the "oversimplified picture" of Pop art). That's the stuff of good reporting—the sort *you* might do on the opening of an art exhibit on your campus.

Writing Travel Stories

Travel writing is an entertainment specialty that is an industry in itself. Scores of magazines offer travel articles exclusively, and virtually every other type of publication regularly covers the subject. Why? Because millions of affluent Americans love to travel and, it seems, those who don't travel want to read about it. Advertisers selling everything from exotic African tours to hiking boots flock to publications that can deliver such readers.

You can break into travel writing with a wide variety of subjects: methods and expense of travel, where to stay, what to see when you get there, how much it will cost. All are the stuff of travel writing.

Many writing approaches and story structures are available, too. Because we have limited space, we'll discuss only one. We call it the "come-along-with-me" structure, and we select it for discussion because you can use it to get started in travel writing.

The come-along-with-me story is just that—an invitation to readers to accompany you on a friendly, chatty tour. Here's an example:

> For more than two centuries, skilled fingers have fashioned beauty from strands of wool, streaks of paint, and mounds of clay in Winston-Salem, North Carolina.
>
> That handmade heritage is preserved today at the restored town of Old Salem, and contemporary craftsmen continue that Winston-Salem tradition, presenting their work in studios, galleries, and museums throughout the area.
>
> Along Trade Street, craftsmen work in small studios creating pottery, stained glass, jewelry, and fabric artwork. A few blocks away, a sunfilled gallery features contemporary works by members of the Piedmont Craftsmen, one of the South's largest and most respected craft guilds.
>
> Near Old Salem, the Museum of Early Southern Decorative Arts presents exhibits and programs on period furnishings from the 17th, 18th, and 19th centuries, while just north of downtown lies the Southeastern Center for Contemporary Art.
>
> The source of the city's arts and crafts tradition—Old Salem—is just a few blocks from Winston-Salem's bustling business district. Founded in the 1760's.... (*James T. Black, "Winston-Salem's Handmade Heritage,"* Southern Living, *Oct. 1991, 10*)

Deeper in the last story, writer Black walks his readers past houses "shaded by lemon-leaved trees" and lets them listen as a "horse-drawn carriage clops down the street" of reconstructed Old Salem. Sounds, aromas, shades of light, glimpses of history—all must be in the strong mood writing that is central to effective travel writing. *However,* good travel writing also is strong on operative, dollars-and-cents information that prospective travelers can use to plan vacations. Black and *Southern Living* present it in a sidebar this way:

> THE INNS AND OUTS
> OF WINSTON-SALEM
>
> For general information on the area, write the Winston-Salem Convention and Visitors Bureau, P.O. Box 1408, 500 West Fifth Street, Winston-Salem, North Carolina 27102; call 1-800-331-7018 or (919) 725-2361 in North Carolina.
>
> Old Salem is open daily 9:30 a.m. to 4:30 p.m. and Sunday 1:30 to 4:30 p.m. A fee of $10 for adults ($5 for children 3 through 14) gives visitors admission to seven museum buildings. For more information write ...

You are surrounded by travel/entertainment stories you can do. Just a few ideas:

- For your school's alumni magazine, how about a nostalgic tour around campus? Lead old grads by the hand, visiting buildings new and old. Point out new student hang-outs (and be sure to mention the old ones your readers will remember). Visit a classroom or two and let your readers "see" the new teaching technology and methods.

- For a campus magazine, take freshmen and new transfer students around the campus and through the town off campus. Lead them through watering holes and other sites of particular interest to students. Show them where the bookstore is, where to register for classes, where to buy football tickets.
- For a student magazine, do a come-along-with-me piece on weekend fun spots—a nearby beach resort or mountain area. How about a canoe trip on a nearby river? Where can your readers rent a canoe? How much will it cost? Where can they stop for lunch along the way?

In general, try for tightly focused stories. Write about the marketplace in a city, not about the city; describe Victorian homes in a town, not all homes.

How to get started in travel writing is no problem. *When* isn't either; it's *now*.

Though huge, the market for articles directed at *consumers* of entertainment is just part of what's open to you as a writer. Let's extend our discussion into a whole new dimension.

WRITING FOR ENTERTAINMENT INSIDERS

The *business* of fun in America is huge. People spend billions to create entertainment, people pay billions to enjoy it.

If you want to capture entertainment insiders, then you must take a businesslike approach to reporting and writing. Your copy must have the dollars-and-cents precision required these days in any form of effective business writing.

Don't panic. Even a beginner can write with such precision for an audience of experts. The key is methodically determining which types of stories are needed by the many specialty and trade magazines serving entertainment insiders and how those stories should be written.

How to Target Your Market

In Motion, published in Annapolis, Md., bills itself as a "film and video magazine." We'll use it as a case study on writing for a specialty magazine serving entertainment insiders.

Like virtually all magazines that accept advertising, *In Motion* provides advertisers a standard marketing kit filled with key information about readers, editorial content and ad rates. This kit is a gold mine of information for you as a writer.

Note in Figure 13–2 (p. 242), for example, how *In Motion* specifies who reads the magazine. Note particularly that 43 percent of the magazine's 15,000-plus readers are professionals in film and video production.

Your first clue: *In Motion* editors obviously will be receptive to story ideas dealing with equipment and techniques of compelling interest to those who produce video.

Now note, in Figure 13–3 (p. 243), the geographic distribution of *In Motion*'s readership: scattered nationwide but largest (29 percent) in the Mid-Atlantic states.

Second clue: You'll undoubtedly have the best chance with stories concerning video production in Mid-Atlantic (and Northeastern states) and less chance with copy aimed at Midwest or West Coast readers.

Turn now to Figure 13–4 (p. 244), *In Motion*'s "1992 Editorial Calendar." This outlines special coverage planned for each monthly issue. Note how individual issues often concentrate on video production developments in cities or states (Washington, D.C., in January, for example, and Miami in March). Now, analyze content themes: In March, *In Motion* plans an issue focusing on, among other things, "Shooting TV Sitcoms on 16mm."

FIGURE 13–2 Breakdown of an Entertainment-Magazine Audience (*For writers, media kits are filled with hints on how to structure and write stories. Note how* In Motion's *audience is broken down by readers' profession or job category. Reprinted with permission.*)

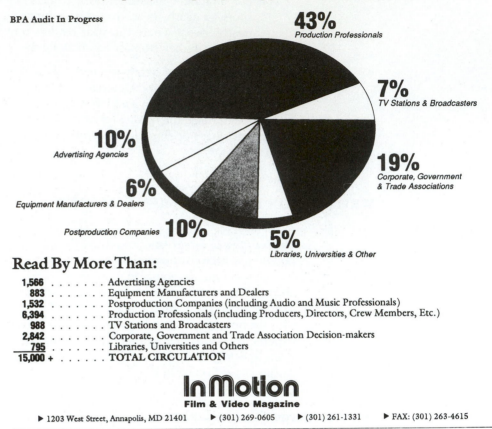

WHO ARE OUR READERS?

In Motion *magazine is read by people who count: decision makers. They influence every aspect of the rapidly growing film and video community.*

BPA Audit In Progress

43%
Production Professionals

7%
TV Stations & Broadcasters

19%
Corporate, Government & Trade Associations

10%
Advertising Agencies

6%
Equipment Manufacturers & Dealers

Postproduction Companies **10%**

5%
Libraries, Universities & Other

Read By More Than:

1,566	Advertising Agencies
883	Equipment Manufacturers and Dealers
1,532	Postproduction Companies (including Audio and Music Professionals)
6,394	Production Professionals (including Producers, Directors, Crew Members, Etc.)
988	TV Stations and Broadcasters
2,842	Corporate, Government and Trade Association Decision-makers
795	Libraries, Universities and Others
15,000 +	**TOTAL CIRCULATION**

In Motion
Film & Video Magazine

▶ 1203 West Street, Annapolis, MD 21401   ▶ (301) 269-0605   ▶ (301) 261-1331   ▶ FAX: (301) 263-4615

Third clue: If you contacted *In Motion* editors, say, six months ahead of that March issue and suggested a story on sitcom production in Miami—well, you get the point: You would be right on their wavelength with a story suggestion that could fit neatly into their editorial planning.

Incidentally, note in the lower right corner of Figure 13–4 (p. 244) the deadline schedule for *In Motion*. If you aim a story at the March issue your copy is due in by January 15, artwork by January 5. Weekly trades have much shorter deadlines, but many editors of other types of magazines must schedule copy months in advance.

In sum, If you analyze information available about a magazine, you can translate your desire to write about film or video into concrete story ideas aimed at entertainment insiders. What's next?

Strong Reporting Is Key

When they read, entertainment insiders want—above all—access to operative information. They want stories with professional insights that will help them advance their careers.

Clearly, strong, professional, analytical reporting is the key to success in writing for the many trade and specialty magazines serving entertainment insiders. Strive for facts more than figures of speech; dollars-and-cents precision rather than "color" writing.

FIGURE 13–3 Circulation Distribution for an Entertainment Magazine (*A discerning free-lance writer will recognize quickly from the area breakdown that* In Motion *magazine's editor will be receptive to a story submission affecting readers in Mid-Atlantic states. Seek such clues from target magazine media kits. Reprinted with permission.*)

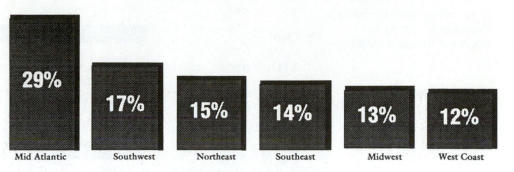

DISTRIBUTION BY MARKET

Over 15,000 subscribers in the film & video production trade!
Plus extra distribution to all major trade shows.

29%	17%	15%	14%	13%	12%
Mid Atlantic	Southwest	Northeast	Southeast	Midwest	West Coast

Breakdown By Area:

Mid Atlantic 29%
(DC, DE, MD, NJ, PA, VA, WV)

Northeast 15%
(CT, MA, ME, NH, NY, RI, VT)

Southeast 14%
(AL, GA, FL, NC, SC)

Midwest 12%
(IL, IN, MI, MN, OH, TN, WI)

West Coast 13%
(CA, HI, OR, WA)

Southwest 17%
(AZ, CO, LA, OK, TX)

BPA Audit In Progress

*Maximize your advertising with focused editorial on the
expanding multi-billion dollar Production Industry.*

InMotion
Film & Video Magazine

▶ 1203 West Street, Annapolis, MD 21401   ▶ (301) 269-0605   ▶ (301) 261-1331   ▶ FAX: (301) 263-4615

Of course, even the most fact-filled story will drive readers away if your writing is convoluted or fuzzy. So strive also for clear, engaging writing, even with the most technical material. Note here how a free-lance writer uses a catchy angle in her lead to pull you into an *In Motion* story that quickly gets down to hard-core detail:

> In treasure maps, X marks the spot. In mathematical formulas, X marks an unknown quantity. In the case of Panasonic's new ½-inch composite digital design (temporarily designated D-X) the "X" differentiates it from other digital formats. Perhaps the only mystery or unknown marketplace responds to the fledgling format.
>
> Immediately clear, however, is that Panasonic Broadcast Systems will garner more attention than usual at this year's NAB. Digital is one of the hottest topics around these days, and Panasonic will not only introduce a new digital format, but can demonstrate it through a range of products. Though some people are already calling the format "D-3", acknowledging previous arrivals D-1 and D-2, Panasonic executives note that only SMPTE can officially designate the format in that way. And though the company has asked SMPTE to designate a name for use by NAB time, for now at least, Panasonic prefers the desig-

FIGURE 13–4 Editorial Calendar for an Entertainment Magazine (*Magazines schedule editorial content months in advance. Free-lance writers can plan story submissions accordingly. Plan ahead. Editors do! Reprinted with permission.*)

1992 EDITORIAL CALENDAR

Our eleventh year calendar promises to be the best yet. Take a look at what's coming.

Our

11th Year

Of

Quality Editorial

For The

Film & Video

Production

& Postproduction

Industry.

JANUARY

- Spotlight On Washington, DC
- Duplication Facilities Survey
- Digital Step-By-Step
- Inter-Format Film Mixing
- On The Campaign Trail

FEBRUARY

- INFOCOMM
- Dallas Video Expo
- Texas Production Guide
- Music Libraries Survey
- CDI Versus DVI
- Motion Control Cinematography
- Business TV

MARCH

- Miami Production Guide
- Film Lab Survey
- Component Digital Suites
- Shooting TV Sitcoms On 16mm
- 10 Top Editing Boutiques

APRIL

- Annual NAB Issue
- Spotlight On New York
- Graphics Libraries Survey
- The All Digital Post House
- Shooting Features On S-8mm & 16mm
- Sports Edition
- 10 Top Paintbox Artists

MAY

- AICP Show
- IABC Show
- ITVA President's Meeting
- Spotlight On Atlanta
- Camera Support Systems
- DVE On $10 A Day
- Flatbed Roundup
- 10 Top Commercial Directors

JUNE

- Showbiz Expo (West)
- BPME/BDA Show
- Intelemart Show
- Soundstage Survey
- Teleconferencing
- Large Format Film: IMAX/Showscan
- Digital Audio For Film

JULY

- ITS Convention
- Video Expo: Chicago
- Directors' Directory
- Desktop Video Graphics
- 10 Top Cinematographers
- Redefining The Post Business

AUGUST

- Spotlight On Houston
- Stock Footage Libraries Survey
- Character Generators
- Nature Cinematography
- Medical Videos

SEPTEMBER

- Showbiz Expo (East)
- Video Expo: New York
- Spotlight On Philadelphia
- S-VHS Comes Of Age
- Super 16 Progress Report
- Interactive Makes The Grade: Education Revolution

OCTOBER

- SMPTE Show
- Spotlight On Nashville
- Equipment Rental Survey
- SMPTE Product Preview
- Matte Boxes

NOVEMBER

- Postproduction Facilities Survey
- Switcher Roundup
- Film-To-Tape Transfer
- Uncle Sam's $100 Million Marketplace
- 10 Top Editors

DECEMBER

- Video Expo: Miami
- Florida Production Guide
- Mobile Video Survey
- Converting To Digital
- Using Time Code
- 10 Top Producers

deadlines

TWO MONTHS ADVANCE
- **Editorial: the 15th**
- **Ads: the 25th**
- **Artwork: the 5th**

Example: For the January issue, editorial deadline is Nov. 15, ads Nov. 25, artwork Dec. 5.

In Motion

Film & Video Production Magazine

1203 West Street
Annapolis, Maryland 21401

410-269-0605
FAX: 410-263-4615

nation "½-inch composite digital" or, in a pinch, D-X. . . . (*Debra Kaufman, "X Marks the Format,"* In Motion, *April 1991, 41*)

The last story obviously is written for expert insiders. For non-experts it's almost unintelligible. Note writer Kaufman assumes her readers understand terms such as "composite digital design" and "this year's NAB" (which means, the National Association of Broadcasters' annual convention). Kaufman neatly writes to the higher level of understanding assumed to exist among production technicians who are *In Motion* readers.

Next, a writer for the same magazine casts her net more widely with a survey of how an editing system is used. She captures not only technicians but, also, *In Motion* readers involved in producing, directing and editing movies and TV commercials.

> Nonlinear editing has grown enormously in popularity since the mid-Eighties, when the first random-access editors were introduced by the Montage group, Droidworks (now LucasArts Editing Systems) and CMX. Editors of episodic TV shows and Movies of the Week have long been sold on the speed and cost-effectiveness of the nonlinear systems. Hey Vern, 21 Jumpstreet and the ABC Afterschool Specials are just a few of the programs that are edited on nonlinear systems.
>
> During the last year, nonlinear editing began to make serious inroads into the feature film and commercial editing markets. Sylvester Stallone's Rocky V was edited on the TouchVision system. Bernardo Bertolucci's The Sheltering Sky was edited on the CMX 6000. Nonlinear systems have been used to edit spots for McDonald's, L.A. Gear, Cadillac and Taco Bell, to name only a few.... (*Helen Shortal, "Walk on the Random Side,"* In Motion, *April 1991, 71*)

If by now you think despairingly that writing about CMX 6000 editing systems is beyond you—and that *In Motion* thus isn't a target magazine for you—take heart. Pick your topic carefully and you can get published in a technical journal by using the *general* news reporting and writing techniques you learned in basic newswriting. Note below how a writer does that with a story about the Persian Gulf War. He selects an angle likely to interest *In Motion*'s audience: not the war itself but, rather, advanced TV technology used to cover the war.

> As the war in the Persian Gulf moved through its second month, the coverage itself became the subject of increased interest. With this being the first war fought in the age of advanced technology, featuring such innovations as night vision and hi-tech phone lines, today's viewer experienced the horror of war with an immediacy no previous generation has felt.
>
> "During Vietnam, I remember when film would be flown back from overseas in a day and people would be impressed," marvels Peter Ford of NBC affiliate WAC-TV in Washington, DC. "Computers and satellites have really come to the forefront. The computers were remarkable; the message lines on the tops of the screens allowed access to anyone plugged in [to the system worldwide], so it was similar to a conference call. They were also valuable because of their memory."
>
> The improved technology, of course, has been evident on the battlefield as well as in the studio.... Dave Gardy, president of Gardy McGrath (GMG International) in Newington, VA, runs one of the few fullservice video facilities that has a security clearance. The firm was called upon by the Army to quickly produce a training video for Operation Desert Storm explaining the operation of a new component for tanks called a Mine Rake, developed late last fall. The apparatus, which can neutralize a land mine even after the elements cause shifts in the depth of the sand, was undoubtedly a factor in the early success of the ground war.... (*Mark Smith, "Bridging the Gulf,"* In Motion, *April 1991, 78*)

The last story illustrates perfectly that you can produce publishable stories on technical aspects of entertainment by interviewing experts and writing a story angled to the special interests of your target magazine's audience.

Magazines you might regard as being far off the entertainment track often are eager for stories that reveal inside details of the business aspects of the film or music industries.

Forbes, for example, explores for its broad audience of business readers the dollars-and-cents details of how greedy talent agents work in Hollywood. The story is a sure winner with this sprightly lead:

> The talent agent, his yacht capsized, is drowning at sea. Suddenly he is rescued and taken ashore by a man-eating shark. Professional courtesy, of course.... (*Kathryn Harris, "Feeding Frenzy,"* Forbes, *1 April 1991, 45*)

The *Economist,* frequently preoccupied with banking in Zurich or stock trading on Wall Street, focuses on a burst of economic success being enjoyed by black film directors:

> Police are at war with a gang of drug dealers; the dealers transform a huge Harlem apartment building into a crack factory that throws the city into a state of Boschian depravity. This is "New Jack City", a film that contains good-looking street-smart cops and villains, violence, sex and even a final triumph of good over evil. In its first weekend it took in $7m. Seats were so scarce that people killed each other to get them. Mortified, producers and director put out a statement insisting that their film, despite its brutality, showed "positive role models". The words are revealing; for this is a black film, not only with a mostly black cast but also with a black director, Mario Van Peebles.... (*"That Hollywood Shuffle,"* The Economist, *30 March 1991, 87*)

Advertising Age takes to its audience of ad agency and media executives the latest news about a new entertainment magazine:

> New York—Nineteen months after it stumbled out of the starting blocks, *Entertainment Weekly* is making strong circulation gains and winning acceptance from the ad community that once jeered it.
> Average paid circulation for the first half was 700,542, a 56% gain from the second half of 1990, said Michael Klingensmith, publisher of the Time Warner weekly.... (*Scott Donaton, "'EW' Is a Circulation Star,"* Advertising Age, *7 Oct. 1991, 63*)

You will note that what's needed to write any of the three stories above is (a) keen insight into the types of stories published by the three magazines, (b) strong reporting techniques to chase down dollars-and-cents details, then (c) flair and, especially, clarity in writing style.

SUMMARY

Entertainment is big news in America, and serious careers are built on writing about fun. Beginners should concentrate on reporting for consumers, not producers, of entertainment. Entertainment insiders, who create entertainment, demand precise reporting and writing, and you'll need a high degree of expertise to meet their expectations.

Beware the temptation to immediately write viciously critical reviews. Begin by reporting on the arts, then expand into commentary as your experience broadens.

Focus on people in arts writing and try for a style that builds intimacy with your readers. Remember, many people read about entertainment for entertainment, not for a force-fed lesson.

The personality profile enables you to chat with readers about a famous person or to use a well-known individual as the vehicle for pulling readers into a wider subject.

The survey story or updater enables you to pull bits and pieces together and bring your readers up to date on what's happening in the arts.

The nostalgia story can be pegged to an occurrence that unites readers, even if briefly, in nostalgia. The death of a famous person (Dr. Seuss) or an anniversary (the Japanese attack on Pearl Harbor) are examples.

Restaurants and bar reviews meet the needs of millions of Americans who regard eating and drinking out as primary entertainment. Deliver operative information—menus, costs, addresses—when writing this type of article.

TV and movie reviews should explain the plot line (but not give away the story). Build into your writing a knowledgeability that will create credibility with readers. Reporting objective facts about a performance can be more important than your subjective views. (Of course, your informed opinion is important *if* it's lively, fun and reasonable.)

Writing theater, dance and music reviews requires a high level of expertise because fans of those art forms can spot the slightest technical error in your writing. Get solid academic background in the art form you intend to cover.

In travel writing, use the come-along-with-me structure and take your readers by the hand on a friendly, chatty tour. Operative facts—travel routes, costs and so forth— are essential in travel writing.

Writing for entertainment insiders opens a huge market with trade and specialty magazines whose readers create movies, music and other art forms. Learn all you can about a magazine's target audience, then report and write fact-filled articles that entertainment professionals can use to advance their careers.

RECOMMENDED READING

If entertainment writing interests you, read on two levels: one to gain expertise in the art form you intend to cover, the other to study great contemporary stylists who cover it for magazines.

Opera News, Movies and *Dance* are examples of specialized arts magazines which, if you read them regularly, will help you build essential background.

The arts sections of leading metropolitan daily newspapers offer high-quality and continuing coverage of the arts. Our favorites are *The New York Times, Newsday, Chicago Tribune* and *Los Angeles Times*. For coverage of regional arts, see the *Boston Globe, Atlanta Constitution* and *Dallas Morning News*.

Forbes carries impressive coverage of the *business* of the arts, particularly filmmaking. Note *Business Week,* also. *The Wall Street Journal* carries outstanding business coverage of TV, Hollywood and entertainment in general.

NOTES

1. Liz Horton, "High Notes," *Folio,* Oct. 1991, 52.
2. *"TV Guide* Masters Narrow-Focus Publishing," *The SRDS Report,* Dec. 1990, 6.

Part Four

The legal and ethical context of magazine writing

Magazines, like all major communications media, operate within a societal context that greatly influences their behavior. Two important dimensions of that context are the law and ethics.

In Part IV, we turn to communications law and ethics because as a writer, you operate in that societal context, too.

Our goal is not definitive discussion of communications law or the history and practice of ethical behavior. Rather, we discuss here what a working writer must understand about legal traps awaiting the unwary and, then, our belief that a writer should fashion a personal code of ethics with all the care given to developing professional techniques of reporting and writing.

We begin, in Chapter Fourteen, with "You and the Law." We'll concentrate on the most dangerous aspect, libel, and on copyright law.

"Ethics and Social Responsibility" are the subject of Chapter Fifteen. We hope this discussion will help you begin formulating a personal approach to writing with a deep sense of integrity, responsibility and, simply, what is right.

Chapter 14

You and
the law

Y ou shouldn't touch a keyboard without considering possible legal ramifications of what you're writing. That's how bad the legal climate is these days for the media and people who write for them.

As a writer, you face many legal pitfalls, including, if you're not careful, loss of ownership over what you write. But libel suits are the big danger, of course.

Here is why we're devoting an entire chapter to "you and the law":

- If you or your magazine land in front of a jury in a libel case, you'll likely lose. The Libel Defense Resource Center reports news organizations lost 69 percent of libel trials in the period 1989–90.[1]
- If you lose, you can lose big. The average award against news organizations in the same period was $4.5 million.

The only good news is that about 90 percent of all libel actions are dropped, settled or dismissed before trial, and that only about one-quarter of libel awards against the media are upheld by appeals courts. But even this good news has a dark side: It can cost hundreds of thousands of dollars, sometimes millions, to defend against a libel suit, win or lose.[2]

Opinion research shows widespread public beliefs that the media are arrogant, self-centered and insensitive. Clearly, juries reflect those societal attitudes when they find so frequently against news organizations. Huge judgments against the media ($58 million in one case, $34 million in another) are evidence of that. So is an increase in punitive awards, which juries pass out to punish media defendants, rather than merely compensate plaintiffs for actual loss from being libeled.

Juries seem to be principally after "Big Media," the large publishing and broadcast institutions with deep pockets capable of paying huge sums. But writers often are included in libel actions, along with editors and other individuals involved, even peripherally, in transmitting material deemed libelous.

So, it's with considerable urgency that we recommend you master the basics of libel law. In the pages ahead, we'll provide hints on how to avoid traps in this and other aspects of communications law. One bit of advice right away: Neither of us is a lawyer, but we know how to get one on the telephone at the slightest hint of legal trouble. Quickly seeking expert advice on legal matters is a procedure you would do well to follow.

YOU AND THE FIRST AMENDMENT

Magazine writers have enormous freedom under the First Amendment to the U.S. Constitution: "Congress shall make no law respecting an establishment of religion, or prohibiting the free exercise thereof; or abridging the freedom of speech, or the press; or the right of the people peaceably to assemble, and to petition the Government for a redress of grievances."

However, your freedom as a writer is far from complete. In interpreting First Amendment cases, the U.S. Supreme Court has limited press freedom in publishing obscenities, for example, or jeopardizing a person's right to a fair trial.

For a writer, the most important limitation on the First Amendment is that it does not hold you free from civil actions by someone who sues you on grounds of defamation.

The Basics of Libel Law

Defamation is false communication that injures the reputation of persons or businesses by exposing them to ridicule, disgrace, hatred, dislike. By falsely harming reputations, defamation is held to lower people in the estimation of their community or deter others from associating with them.

Defamation has two forms: *Slander* is injury to reputation through the spoken word. *Libel,* our principal concern here, is injury to reputation through a tangible medium, such as writing, cartoons, pictures.

You should understand four important points about libel.

First, you're on potentially dangerous ground if your writing harms someone's professional reputation or causes financial loss. It's particularly dangerous to write that someone engaged in criminal behavior, is incompetent, inefficient, immoral, a fraud or otherwise engages in dishonorable conduct. Such accusations spark many libel suits.

Second, a libel must be published—but that doesn't mean only in a magazine for multitudes of readers. Even a private letter can constitute publication, if someone other than you and the target of your letter or memo sees the offending material. For example, don't write the editor of a local city magazine that you will offer an article on the drug scene, and "a focal point will be a gas station owner at Third and Broad. I've personally observed that he's a kingpin in local dope dealing." That written story idea (a) accuses a person without proof of criminal behavior and (b) constitutes publication when seen by the editor, a secretary or any other person.

Third, those who sue for libel must prove they were identified in the offending material. Warning: You're not protected simply by omitting a person's name. If identity can be inferred from what you write, you may be held to have identified a person as certainly as if you had included name, age and address. You certainly identify a person with a reference to a "gas station owner at Third and Broad." Another problem: If your identification is vague you might give a reasonable reader cause to identify more than one person. For example, if there are four gas station owners doing business at the corner of Third and Broad you raise the real possibility of *all* being identified by friends and business colleagues as drug dealers. That can mean four lawsuits, not just one.

Fourth, it's not only literal language that can be defamatory. The overall impression left by your writing, or its context, can defame, too. Even though you don't write explicitly that the gas station owner is a drug pusher, a jury might hold against you if it decides a reasonable person reading your account would reach an unfair, defamatory conclusion about the owner. Don't write coyly, "Police say drugs are being sold through small businesses on the north side, and they are very interested in what's happening these days at a certain gas station at Third and Broad."

Write Defensively!

Libel law is tricky stuff, and with multimillion dollar judgments against the media somewhat fashionable these days, you obviously must keep legal dangers firmly in mind each time you write. Your editors certainly do.

Unquestionably, a "chilling effect" sweeps through the publishing world with word of yet another huge judgment against the media or the enormous cost—$1 million or more, in some cases—of defending against a libel suit.

Some editors gut stories by eliminating potentially dangerous material. Some eliminate questionable stories altogether. How many stories, they ask, are worth $1 million in legal costs—or more in judgments if they lose a libel suit? One result is that some hard-hitting investigative stories never see print or, if they do, are shorn of essential detail.

We think you can write defensively to avoid legal problems and still fulfill your obligation to be probing, discerning and, yes, harshly critical when need arises.

Our first defensive recommendation springs from journalistic, not legal, considerations: Be fair, honest and balanced in your reporting and writing. In our experience, legal trouble erupts mostly over writing that is patently unfair, unbalanced and lacking in reportorial integrity. This scenario then often unfolds: Persons offended by what they perceive to be unfair treatment from a writer look for some form of redress. They get cold, arrogant treatment when they complain to writers and editors. A lawsuit follows. You often can head off trouble simply by doing what all writers should do: Be fair, responsible, balanced. In your reporting, give all parties opportunity to respond.

But, of course, you can meet your journalistic obligations to be fair and balanced and still draw legal fire. So, you should understand the legal defenses against libel charges.

Provable truth is an absolute defense against libel action. It means that you must be able to prove in court the truth of what you write, that you got your facts correct. Importantly, you also must be able to prove that allegations by someone you quote are substantially correct. It's not enough to prove you correctly quoted a neighbor as saying the gas station owner is a drug peddler. You must prove the neighbor's allegation is true.

Privilege is an important defense against libel charges. Qualified privilege flows from reporting public records and public and official proceedings. You're safe in accurately reporting from official police arrest records, or when a witness testifies in court or on the floor of the legislature that the gas station owner is a drug peddler, even if he isn't.

Privilege also sometimes extends protection on material you've reported from public records and public and official proceedings. For example, you have qualified privilege if you quote the police chief as saying in a press conference that the gas station owner was arrested on a charge of selling drugs. But you must be certain that you fairly and accurately report or summarize what the chief said. And, of course, you must write without malice. Don't "go after" the gas station owner because he cheated you on a car repair bill. Caution: State laws differ widely on who or what is "official." Although the chief of police may be an official source on drug busts in your city, the courthouse janitor undoubtedly isn't, even though he too is on the city payroll. State press associations are excellent sources for helpful background on such nuances of state libel laws. Most retain attorneys to answer questions.

Neutral reportage is a defense against libel charges in some states where courts have held that privilege sometimes exists for fair and balanced neutral reporting of charges by responsible individuals and organizations against public officials or figures. For example, if the Our Town Coalition of Gas Station Owners campaigns publicly to have the police chief fired for incompetency, you probably would not be required to prove the coalition's charge that he indeed is incompetent. The campaign is legitimate news about a public official. But you must demonstrate neutrality by being fair and balanced in your reporting, by giving the chief opportunity to respond and by not advocating the validity of the charges against him. Neutral reportage isn't an absolute defense, but it may give your attorney a stronger case.

In writing defensively, you must understand how actual malice is pivotal in many libel cases. This is the background:

In a 1964 landmark case, *New York Times Co. vs. Sullivan,* the U.S. Supreme Court ruled that public officials cannot recover damages for defamatory falsehoods in coverage of their official conduct unless they prove actual malice. That requires officials to prove those who published the article knew it was false or published it with "reckless disregard" of whether it was true or false. Of course, to defend yourself properly you should be able to prove in court that your reporting and writing were accurate, fair, principled, balanced. For example, you should be able to prove you consulted authoritative sources, checked your facts, then double-checked them. In other words, you should prove that you went through all the steps of doing a journalistically responsible, professional job.

In *Associated Press vs. Walker,* the Supreme Court in 1967 extended to *public figures* its ruling in *New York Times Co. vs. Sullivan.* The Court said that Edwin A. Walker, a retired U.S. Army general involved in integration riots at the University of Mississippi in 1962, "was a public man in whose public conduct society and the press had a legitimate and substantial interest." That places on public figures who sue for libel the burden of proving actual malice.

Important for a magazine writer: At the time of its *Walker* decision, the Court found that the *Saturday Evening Post* published with malice a story about Wallace Butts, a University of Georgia football coach. The Court said Butts was a public figure, but in its article about him, the *Post* ignored "elementary precautions" and engaged in "slipshod and sketchy investigatory techniques." The Court said AP's story about Walker was "hot news" but that the *Post's* article on Butts was not, and that the magazine published charges against Butts in "reckless disregard for the truth." The Court said editors recognized need for a thorough investigation before publication but didn't launch one.

The Butts case indicates the Court holds that writers doing long-term investigative stories, as contrasted with "hot news" stories, carry an extra burden of being careful and double-checking facts. Much of your magazine writing, of course, will not be in the "hot news" category.

Note again the need to be thoroughly professional in your reporting, in checking facts and taking all possible steps to prevent error. Also, make sure there is sound journalistic reason for what you write. AP was journalistically sound in reporting Gen. Walker's presence during the riots at Ole Miss. There was true news value in what happened, and the public had a legitimate right to know. There is danger in charging someone with criminal misconduct or with violating society's standards of ethics, privacy and behavior without sound journalistic reason.

Other Danger Areas

It's important to understand that the law is changing, evolving and always open to interpretation by juries and courts. Here are other areas where writers must be particularly alert:

Use of Quotes

In a 1991 ruling in *Masson vs. New Yorker Magazine, Inc.,* the Supreme Court seemed to open a new danger area for writers. The case involved a psychoanalyst who claimed a writer fabricated quotes after interviewing him and that those quotes defamed him.

The Court ruled the press is protected if a writer alters words actually spoken by a public official or figure—*unless* alteration "results in a material change in the meaning conveyed by the statement." Lyle Denniston, who covers the Court for the *Baltimore Sun,* warns that the decision means juries may be asked to act as editors and decide whether words published faithfully represent "meaning conveyed."[3]

Obviously, enormous difference can exist between what a person *says* and later claims to have *meant.* Your most important defensive measure is to put quote marks around only those words actually spoken in an interview. Use a tape recorder, if your story is particularly delicate, or use only verbatim quotes from your handwritten notes. If you want to clean up grammatical errors in what sources say, or protect them from looking foolish in an unguarded statement, take off the quote marks. Make it a rule: Everything between quote marks is precisely what was said.

Of course, most articles based on interviews can accommodate only a fraction of the quotes you get. You often have to paraphrase much that's said. Be careful to avoid giving juries an opportunity to decide those quotes and paraphrasing you select for use don't accurately reflect the interviewee's meaning.

Actually, principled journalists try hard to catch not only quotes but also meaning. Representing fairly and honestly what someone intends is the thing to do. But obviously this will be a potentially dangerous area of the law unless courts clarify the issue.

Fair Comment and Criticism

By its very nature, magazine writing, even for beginners, often involves commentary and criticism of the arts, books, theater, films, restaurants, hotels and so forth.

This type of writing can be as libelous as any, and often draws legal challenge. Restaurant owners sue because food critics pan their menus. Hotel owners sue because travel writers drive off business with tales of poor service and high prices.

However, you have an important defense: "fair comment and criticism."

Courts have held repeatedly that even the harshest criticism leaves authors, painters, musicians and other artists—including chefs—no legal recourse if critics are fair, write without malice and are accurate in their facts. "Fair comment and criticism" provides protection when you publish opinion and comment on services or products offered the public and write with honest purpose.

Note that in this sector of the law, doing the right thing journalistically—being fair and accurate, without malice—is once again the first step in writing defensively.

Note also the requirement that you write with honest purpose. That means examining the quality of food or service on behalf of your readers, not to seek revenge because you were served a lousy meal or couldn't get your laundry back from room service.

Incidentally, if you're getting started in writing for campus publications, two areas of criticism or commentary likely will draw threats (legal or otherwise) most quickly: reviewing arts performances by students, who are unused to being criticized in public; and reviewing off-campus bars and restaurants, whose owners can suffer real cash register loss if you criticize their drinks as too pricey or their music and entertainment as dull. It's when your review might cause financial loss that you should be particularly alert to meet the standards of "fair comment and criticism."

Privacy

Almost by definition, the best magazine writing focuses intently and in detail on people. Whatever your story structure—personality profile, survey, hard news—you'll spend much time writing about people, who they are, what they are, where they're from, what their past has been.

Be aware that two seemingly conflicting principles come into play under U.S. law: First, a person has the right to privacy, to be left alone. Second, however, courts have held that the right to privacy can be forfeited if a person is involved, even unwillingly, in a matter of legitimate public interest.

A key consideration in privacy law is whether what you are writing about a person is of "legitimate public interest." One standard to apply in deciding is whether there is current newsworthiness in a person or event and, if so, whether the right to privacy has been forfeited. Two examples:

First, you are doing a story on, say, sex offenders and you discover that a local minister, who runs a refuge for street children, has a history of being arrested on charges of child molestation, a subject of continuing public interest. You've got a good chance of proving there is newsworthiness in reporting the minister's past.

Second, you are doing a story on a local minister who is celebrating his 50th anniversary in the church and you discover that as a teenager he was convicted of drunk driving. Is there current newsworthiness in dredging up something that happened long ago to a person who subsequently lived 50 blameless years? Probably not.

Many privacy cases arise when people are involved unwillingly in events of "legitimate public interest," such as hotel fires, disasters or other circumstances that thrust them into the headlines. Courts generally have ruled that privacy rights are forfeited in such newsworthy events.

In general, you're on shaky legal ground if you intrude into the personal lives of private individuals or publish private facts about them. The sex life of a private person who hasn't sought the public spotlight or been thrust into a legitimate news event is off-limits.

You're on firmer ground in reporting on public officials or figures. Questions of ethics and good taste arise (some are discussed in the next chapter), but generally public officials and figures—sex lives and all—are open for comment.

Interestingly, intimate coverage of their private lives sometimes is challenged by film stars and others who spend years thrusting themselves into the public spotlight and creating public-figure status for themselves, then decide they want privacy. Although it would seem such persons truly are public figures and thus open for coverage, court rulings confuse the issue. For example, a woman who conducted press conferences and handed out public relations statements about herself was held to be a private person. So was a well-known attorney.

Be careful in deciding who is a private person and who isn't. Consult a lawyer if you're unsure.

Incidentally, if you decide you must push into someone's private life, be careful how you do it. Laws of trespass generally prohibit entry without permission into someone's private space, and those laws apply to magazine writers, like everyone else. Also, you may be liable for intrusion if you enter private space with secret use of wire taps, cameras, recorders or other electronic devices. Anyway, that's stuff for cops, not writers.

False Light

Even though not libelous, an article can hold an individual in "false light" if it creates a false image or impression of that person.

For example, you might not defame individuals by identifying them as avid members of anti-abortion groups. But if those persons are not militant, it might create false light that embarrasses them among friends and colleagues.

It's not only outright statements or explicit characterizations that can be held to create false light. Sometimes, lawsuits charge that omission of facts does so or that an article suggests or implies false light.

Generally, the First Amendment is a strong barrier to false light suits. Truth is the defense. If your article is true, it cannot hold a person in "false" light. It's worth repeating: Getting the facts correctly, then writing fairly and honestly, is your best across-the-board defense.

Guidelines for Non-Lawyers

We have a few other guidelines on how non-lawyer writers can protect themselves in legal matters.

First, treat *every* story you touch as big and significant. In our experience, many relatively insignificant stories create legal difficulty. That's because writers and editors tend to let down their guard on seemingly unimportant three-paragraph stories, reserving their energy and attention for the 3,000-word investigative takeouts.

You, your editor and probably the magazine's attorney will go over the investigative takeout repeatedly, searching for libelous material, while the small story gets dangerously sloppy handling. But you can libel someone in three grafs just as easily as in 3,000 words.

Second, level with your editors before publication if you think your story might be legally dangerous. Don't try to slip something by. Editors are paid to solve problems. Let them help solve yours—before an offended reader, with help from an attorney, points out problems in your writing.

Third, if you are contacted by an offended reader who threatens a lawsuit, listen only. Be courteous. Give the person a chance to talk—or rant and rave, if he or she prefers. Take details of the complaint. But never acknowledge that a libel or other legal problem crept into your writing. The law is complex, and what may appear to you to be libelous may in fact not be. And make it a rule: Never talk to complainants' lawyers. What you say could compound the problem.

Contact your editor immediately if a lawsuit is threatened. Don't try to "talk down" a complainant by promising a correction. You only dig yourself more deeply into trouble with something like, "Yeah, I guess you're right; I really screwed up that story, and I'll write another story for next week that will put things right." Any correction or acknowledgment of error must be made in consultation with the magazine's attorney.

If someone threatens you with a lawsuit, be completely forthcoming with your editor and attorney. It's only human nature to disguise the fact that you may have committed an error or written a libel. But your attorney needs *all* the facts to fashion a proper defense.

YOU AND COPYRIGHT LAW

There are strong reasons for all magazine writers to be familiar with the complexities of copyright law.

First, there are legal limitations on how you may quote from or otherwise use the writings of others.

Second, as discussed in Chapter Nine, you easily can lose ownership of what you write.

The Basics of Copyright Law

The U.S. Constitution (Article 1, Section 8) and a subsequent series of Copyright Acts make it clear: Writers have a legal right to own their original creative effort and, like photographers and other creative artists, can protect the right to profit from their creative expression.

A copyright thus is a property that its holder owns. Copyright automatically covers an article from the moment it is written. To gain full protection of property rights, a writer must take two steps:

1. Notice of copyright must be placed on the article. It can take this form: Copyright © (year of publication) by (author's name).
2. The article must be registered with Register of Copyrights, Copyright Office, Library of Congress, Washington, D.C., 20559. The article and a special form available from the Copyright Office must be submitted together.

Copyright lasts for the lifetime of the author plus 50 years (as property, it can be passed on to heirs). If owned by a magazine or employer of the author, copyright lasts 100 years from time of writing, 75 from time of publication.

Importantly, copyright covers the arrangement of words and sentences. For example, a written account of a news event can be copyrighted. However, copyright law does *not* cover news itself, facts, ideas or theories.

Two underlying philosophies are at play in copyright matters:

1. The law encourages creative effort by granting the right to profit from talent. The framers of the Constitution clearly had in mind encouraging writing and other creative efforts that place important issues before the public for discussion.
2. However, the law just as clearly inhibits public discussion to some extent because it limits how writers (and other creative artists) can quote from or use the work of others.

Let's look first at how the law applies to your use of work by others.

The Doctrine of "Fair Use"

Understand, first, that if you intend to use someone else's copyrighted work and ask permission, you can be charged a fee.

Other Issues to Watch

Although they don't constitute the danger of libel laws, other legal issues arise that writers should watch.

Shield Laws and Sources

Some states have moved toward permitting reporters to establish a confidential relationship with news sources that's akin to the confidentiality that clergy have with parishioners or physicians with patients. This right is embodied in "shield laws," which some state legislatures passed so reporters presumably can't be forced to reveal a source's identity, turn over notes or be compelled to testify in court or in administrative or legislative proceedings.

Our advice: Don't assume you're covered by a shield law without expert counsel from your attorney or state press association. In some cases, particularly if capital offenses are involved, courts rule that reporters' testimony is essential to the defense of an accused person. In New Jersey, which had a shield law, a reporter was jailed for refusing to turn over notes in a murder trial.

Reporters sometimes are subpoenaed in trials or administrative or legislative hearings. A subpoena is a court order to perform—to appear, testify, turn over notes or whatever. You can be jailed and heavily fined for refusing to perform as ordered. If ever subpoenaed, alert your editor immediately. Some magazines and newspapers take over the fight against subpoenas on principle.

Incidentally, don't lightly promise a source confidentiality and later publish the source's name. The Supreme Court has ruled that if your promise of confidentiality constituted a contract you can be sued for breach of promise.

Free Press/Fair Trial

An issue occasionally arising in spectacular trials is whether publicity deprives defendants of a fair trial. This can put the First Amendment in conflict with the Sixth Amendment, which guarantees public trial by impartial juries, and the Fourteenth Amendment, which guarantees everyone due process under the law.

If they fear coverage will prejudice juries, judges sometimes close courtrooms or issue gag orders that prohibit attorneys and witnesses from talking to reporters. The U.S. Supreme Court generally orders courtrooms opened and gag orders lifted. Less clear is whether *pretrial* proceedings can be closed by a judge. That's important, because many plea bargains are made behind closed doors, before trial begins.

Editors of some newspapers and magazines assign attorneys to fight gag orders or closed-door proceedings.

"Sunshine" Laws

Federal and, generally, state laws allow the media access to government meetings and records. They are laws that let the sun shine on the public's business.

On the federal level, the Freedom of Information Act is the umbrella law. For help, contact the FOI Service Center, 800 18th St., N.W., Suite 300, Washington, D.C., 20006. On the state level, press associations are well equipped to advise you of local access laws.

Misappropriation

This issue arises mostly in advertising, not news, criticism or commentary. It involves using a person's name, likeness or photo for commercial gain without consent. Don't provide material you've collected for a story to someone else who might use it for commercial purposes.

Photos

If you're asked to provide illustration for your article, be particularly careful about who is depicted and whether they relate directly to the story.

For example, let's say you are doing a story on street corner drug dealers and you take a few shots of a typical crowded intersection of the sort where narcotics are sold. An innocent passerby, briefcase in hand and on the way to work, ends up clearly recognizable in your cover photo for a story titled, "How Dope Peddlers Work Our Streets." See the problem? Suits for libel and false light invasion of privacy arise out of such scenarios.

Good rules: Never take a photo for one article, then use it for another. Use photos only of persons mentioned in your article.

Many magazines will provide you with consent forms that must be signed by anyone recognizable in your photographs.

Trademarks

Some trade names have carried enormous commercial value over many years for companies that spend millions to make them instantly recognizable. If those names are used generally and loosely they can slip into the public domain and lose their commercial value.

Therefore, you should use "soft drink" when that's what you mean—not "Coke" or "Pepsi," both of which are registered trademarks. And make it "photocopying machine," not "Xeroxing machine," and "bandage," not "Band-Aid."

If you don't ask permission, and if you use substantial portions of the work or diminish the property value of the owner's copyright, you can be sued for copyright infringement.

Two points are crucial.

First, the Copyright Act permits a writer to quote another without asking permission if limited amounts of material are used "for purposes such as criticism, comment, news reporting, teaching ... scholarship or research...."

Second, what constitutes "substantial" quotation or use of someone else's work hasn't been specified in the law or the many court cases involving copyright.

In considering individual claims of copyright infringement, courts apply four standards in the "fair use" doctrine:

1. Purpose of the use (whether for nonprofit educational use, for example, or whether a writer was trying to profit through unauthorized use of another's work).
2. Nature of the copyrighted work.
3. Amount quoted or used in proportion to the copyrighted work as a whole.
4. The effect quotation or use has on the potential market value of the copyrighted work.

If you're writing for profit (and we hope you are), and you quote substantially all of another written-for-profit article, thus destroying the writer's property value, you can have a big problem—unless you've obtained written permission.

The issue of destroying market value sometimes arises when magazines or newspapers obtain pre-publication copies of books and quote extensively from them. That is dangerous because it obviously can cause financial loss by taking the edge off book sales and give the copyright owner grounds to sue.

If, on the other hand, you quote just a paragraph or two from a lengthy history textbook to illustrate an angle in a news story, you might not have infringed on copyright.

In practice, editors develop their own rules of thumb on what is "safe" fair use. Some, for example, say quoting about 200 words from a lengthy book without permission is okay. Some say using only 75–100 words from a shorter article might be dangerous if it substantially "guts" the meaning and thrust of the article. Using without permission even a few words from a short poem or the lyrics of a song can be an infringement.

If you have any doubt, obtain written permission and give written credit to the original author (that's only good journalistic etiquette, anyway).

SUMMARY

The legal climate is so bad these days that you must always consider the legal ramifications of what you write.

Libel is the big danger. Juries frequently find against the media in libel cases and levy huge judgments—an average of $4.5 million in 1989–90.

The First Amendment gives writers enormous freedom, but it doesn't hold you free from civil action by someone who sues you on grounds of defamation.

Defamation is false communication that injures the reputation of persons or businesses by exposing them to ridicule, disgrace, hatred, dislike. Libel is written defamation.

Four important points: (a) You're on potentially dangerous ground if your writing harms professional reputations or causes financial loss; (b) a libel must be published—but a letter to one person can constitute publication; (c) those who sue for libel must prove they were identified, but that can be accomplished by inference;

(d) the overall impression left by your writing, not only your explicit language, can be defamatory.

Write *defensively* to avoid legal problems but still fulfill your writer's obligation to be probing and discerning.

Be fair, honest and accurate in your writing. Provable truth is an absolute defense against libel action. Privilege is another important defense. Qualified privilege comes from accurately reporting public records and public and official proceedings. Qualified privilege also can extend protection from fairly and accurately reporting or summarizing public records and public and official proceedings (a police chief's statement at a press conference, for example).

Neutral reportage is a defense, too. It can cover reporting charges by responsible individuals and organizations against public officials or figures, as long as you are fair and balanced, give the accused opportunity to respond and don't advocate the validity of charges.

Public officials and figures must prove actual malice to recover damages for defamatory falsehoods in coverage of their official or public conduct. That requires them to prove that those who published the article knew it was false or published it with reckless disregard of whether it was true or false.

Fair comment and criticism is a defense in libel actions stemming from reviews of arts, books, theater, films, restaurants and so forth.

In probing into the past of individuals, beware of using damaging material that doesn't have current newsworthiness. Individuals have a right to privacy.

Copyright law gives creative individuals legal right to control commercial use of their original creative effort.

The Doctrine of Fair Use permits quotation from copyrighted material under certain circumstances, but the law doesn't define precisely how many words may be used without permission.

RECOMMENDED READING

For superbly detailed coverage of issues relevant to writers, see Kent R. Middleton and Bill F. Chamberlin, *The Law of Public Communication,* 2 ed., Longman Publishing, White Plains, N.Y., 1991. Also see Ralph L. Holsinger, *Media Law,* Random House, New York, 1987.

For background on how to proceed under the Freedom of Information Act, see "How To Use The Federal FOI Act," published by the FOI Service Center, 800 18th St., N.W., Washington, D.C., 20006.

Excellent surveys on libel and privacy developments are published periodically by the Libel Defense Resource Center, 708 Third Ave., New York, N.Y., 10017.

NOTES

1. Alex S. Jones, "Libel Study Finds Juries Penalizing News Media," *The New York Times,* national edition, 26 Sept. 1991, A13. Also see, "Libel Awards Soaring in Suits Against Media," *Editor & Publisher,* 12 Oct. 1991, 16.
2. *Ibid.*
3. Lyle Denniston, "Masson Ruling Sets Up Jury As Editor," *WJR,* Sept. 1991, 61.

Chapter 15

You, ethics and honest writing

We have tried throughout this book to help you develop magazine writing skills and achieve your creative potential—to help you advance your writer's career and obtain reward for your artistic effort.

Now, we are going to reverse the equation and discuss, here in Chapter Fifteen, your ethical responsibilities as a writer—what you owe your readers and what you owe the society that confers on you the distinction of being a writer.

These are complex and controversial issues. Some writers, for example, say their sole responsibility is to write the story accurately, fairly and as they see it, and never mind this stuff about owing anybody anything.

And you may regard ethics as intensely personal, like discussing how you should run your private life or whether you should believe in a god.

We, however, can think of three good reasons to include "You, Ethics and Honest Writing" in this book.

First, we argue that you *do* take on special responsibilities when you assume the title of writer. You can enjoy many benefits in a writing career, including excitement, travel, creative fulfillment and (we hope) financial success. We also think there are responsibilities that flow down to you through centuries of humankind's search for what is right and good, for what is honest and truthful. Writers who turn their backs on all that betray a truly historic responsibility.

Second, as a staff or free-lance writer you must conform to your magazine's sense of ethics and social responsibility. It's not enough to meet professional standards for reporting and writing; you also must meet ethical standards shaped by editors who tussle daily with how to meet their journalistic obligations and do the right thing.

Third, society is ever more critical of what we in the media do and how we do it. Opinion polls prove our motives, our credibility, our *honesty* are questioned by readers, viewers and listeners as never before. An American Society of Newspaper Editors Poll in 1991 suggests American voters would not include freedom of the press if asked today to ratify the Bill of Rights.[1] If we writers and editors don't establish a sound, visible ethical context for our work, and convince the public we are striving to be responsible, the very concept of free expression may be in peril.

Let's turn, then, to ethical principles you might consider in fashioning your own writer's conscience, in deciding for yourself what is right and wrong. Libraries have been written on ethics, of course, since Aristotle and Plato argued the subject nearly 2,500 years ago. We'll not attempt definitive discussion of all that. Rather, we'll focus on a few issues we know to be most troublesome in magazine work today. We'll start by suggesting a process you can follow in thinking through an ethical dilemma the next time you confront one.

THE ETHICAL DECISION-MAKING PROCESS

If ethics were a science, someone long ago would have calculated for writers precisely what is right and wrong, good and bad. Well, ethics isn't a science, and we cannot give you a definitive list of a writer's ethical dos and don'ts.

We can however, point to a *decision-making process* that might help you find personal solutions to some of the troublesome ethical issues you'll inevitably encounter as a writer.

Broadly, four steps are involved:

1. assembling the facts
2. defining the issue
3. considering your alternatives
4. formulating your position

Assembling the Facts

It's important to have *all* relevant facts when confronting an ethical dilemma. Not having them invalidates the entire decision-making process.

Obviously, you'll need more than the simple factual framework you learn in basic newswriting—the Five W's and How. Look deeply into the complexities of each element of your dilemma.

For example, former U.S. Sen. Gary Hart ostensibly was the "who" when the *Miami Herald*, followed by magazines and other media, revealed in 1987 that he was having an extramarital relationship with a young woman in a Washington, D.C., hideaway.

But, there was a "real who" with deeper importance in that case: Gary Hart, leading candidate for the Democratic presidential nomination and a man who presumed to become leader of the United States. Editors decided that the real who distinguished this case from run-of-the-mill sex scandals.

The "what" ostensibly was infidelity by a man who, like many men, ignored marital vows to his wife. Editors decided, however, there was a more meaningful "real what"—that Hart's conduct in his personal life was an important indication of how he would conduct his official life as president.

You can see how editors revealed crucial ethical issues as they peeled back layers of facts in the Hart case. For example, in examining the "real who" and "real what," editors inevitably had to consider more than the superficial question of whether a man has the right to privacy in his personal life. They also had to consider the deeper issue of the public's right (or need) to know intimate details about that man who presumed to lead their nation.

In just that manner, by thinking deeply, you can assemble all the facts that will lead you to the second step in the decision-making process.

Defining the Issue

Assembling and truly understanding all the facts often lead to quick definition and comprehension of the ethical issue. Beware, however. Ethical issues often are more complex than they appear.

For example, snap analysis of superficial facts might limit the issue in the Gary Hart case to, simply, an individual's right to privacy versus the public's right to know. But there was more to it than that.

For starters, editors knew that publishing the story would not only kill Hart's campaign for the Democratic presidential nomination but likely would kill his political career as well. There was more: Publishing the story would inflict unspeakable agony on Hart's wife and family, adding the issue of whether wounding those innocents was a defensible price for serving the "people's right to know."

Then, another issue surfaced: ethics in reportorial technique. *Herald* reporters revealed they had shadowed the young woman involved and conducted an all-night stakeout around Hart's apartment. Tremendous criticism erupted, not only in the public but also among journalists, over what one *New York Times* editor described as reporters "hiding in the dark, listening for squeaking bedsprings."

Inevitably, editors' decision to publish the story expanded the ethical discussion to broader examination of whether the media in general sensationalize news simply for newsstand appeal—to sell more newspapers and magazines. Also discussed was whether the media apply unevenly whatever ethical standards they have. It was argued, for example, that the media of an earlier time didn't cover extramarital affairs of John F. Kennedy and other presidents. Why single out Gary Hart? Quickly, all media and their reportorial standards became additional issues.

In defining any ethical issue confronting you, be certain you examine it from many viewpoints. You may have more than one issue on your hands!

Considering Your Alternatives

Unfortunately, your alternatives in an ethical dilemma rarely are so simple as (a) writing a story or (b) walking away from it. That's because you are subject to many often-conflicting pressures as you consider what to do.

In the Gary Hart case, for example, writers and editors knew full well the wider impact their story would have. Yet, they felt obliged to publish it. Why? What in their training and experience influenced their decision? What influences will *you* be under when, inevitably, you face similarly tough calls? Let's look at some of those influences:

Ethical Precedents

Even for writers who haven't given them a thought since freshman philosophy, Socrates and his student, Plato, are alive and well in media ethics today. Their discussion nearly 2,500 years ago of "good" and "justice" began a process that down through the ages has yielded values and principles that are part of the societal framework in which you live and work today.

For example, Socrates taught that "good" can be identified and practiced. Plato suggested that good exists however society might conduct itself at the moment. Plato's student, Aristotle, placed on the individual the responsibility for making the right choice, doing the virtuous thing. You can see those concepts reflected today in attitudes of principled writers: Seek to do good through your writing, make the virtuous choice, do the right thing and take personal responsibility, even if that means running counter to critics around you.

Even though not codified as laws, ethical precedents come to bear on everyday decisions you make about how to act as a writer.

For example, not many writers chat about him over a beer, but John Milton (1608–74) influences journalists every day. He wrote, in *Areopagitica,* published in 1644, of an "open marketplace of ideas" in which all would be free to express themselves, creating a "self-righting process" that would yield truth. From this flows the conviction widespread among writers and editors today that if we give readers the full facts, they will determine truth.

Other names not discussed much these days around magazines but which, nevertheless, have direct bearing on what those magazines do: David Hume (1711–76) argued that "utility" or usefulness is a measure of ethical principle. That is, if an act helps humanity achieve happiness, it is utilitarian (justice serves the common good and thus is utilitarian). Immanuel Kant (1724–1804) wrote of the individual's *duty* to reason out what is good and act accordingly. John Stuart Mill (1806–73) interpreted utilitarianism as creating the greatest happiness or well-being for the greatest number of people. (Would *you* justify ringing the bell on Gary Hart—and wounding his family—on grounds that it served the wider interests of the American people?)

Religion

Religion brings to bear on your decision-making process an enormously wide range of values: The "Golden Rule," self-sacrifice, love of humankind, sensitivity to the welfare of others—all are inseparable from ethics discussions (even discussions among the nonreligious).

Question: Would truly Christian writers have such love for Mrs. Hart, and such sensitivity to her suffering, that they would feel compelled to walk away from the sex story? That's an example of how the ethical mainstream coming down through the centuries presents you with often conflicting influences.

Media Tradition and Values

By the late 1600s and early 1700s, the ruminations of ethicists and religious philosophers began shaping values applicable specifically to the press (which itself dates roughly to 1400, when Gutenberg popularized use of movable type).

An early concept was *libertarianism,* the idea of an independent, profit-making press freely disseminating news and opinion in a free society where the people could be trusted to make rational, truthful decisions. The press assumed responsibility for guarding against government infringement. These concepts are embodied in the First Amendment to the U.S. Constitution ("Congress shall make no law . . . abridging the freedom of speech, or of the press . . .").

Objectivity developed in the late 1800s as a guiding concept. It holds that journalists should present balanced and fair accounts of all sides of an issue, keep their personal views out of their writing and write as dispassionately as possible. Objectivity is a goal impossible to reach, perhaps, but is regarded by many writers as one to strive for. However, some writers feel equally strongly that objectivity is a concept better left to hard-news writers for newspapers, and that magazine writers *should* inject opinion, interpretation and passion into their work. Expressing a viewpoint in magazine writing is fashionable, but how to present and label it can raise ethical questions (more on this later).

By the early 1900s, many editors and publishers developed a sense of *social responsibility,* the concept of owing something to the society that engendered freedom of the press. This led to a sense of professionalism in the press and creation of journalistic societies that expressed journalistic ideals. The first written expression of major consequence was the "Canons of Journalism," adopted by the American Society of Newspaper Editors in 1923 (and supplanted by ASNE's "Statement of Principles" in 1975).

ASNE's "Principles" and ethical codes subsequently adopted by the Society of Professional Journalists and other journalistic societies give you only sweeping guidelines: serve the general welfare, scrutinize government at all levels, avoid impropriety and conflict of interest, write truthfully and accurately, be impartial and fair.

Importantly, no industry or society code provides for expulsion for code infractions. Because of that, some social commentators deny journalism the label of "profession" accorded to law, medicine and other endeavors that *do* require adherence to established standards as a condition of practice.

Often, media tradition and values are expressed in the judgment of peers—ethical stances taken by writers and editors of leading magazines and newspapers. Talking out an ethical dilemma with experienced colleagues frequently can clarify your alternatives on how to proceed.

Alvin P. Sanoff of *U.S. News & World Report* asked a colleague, one of the most famous journalists of our time, James Reston, whether the press should cover the private lives of politicians. Reston replied, in part: "As a general rule, I'm not at all sympathetic to those who say that we in the press are too nosy. I'm for being nosy. I don't even rule out the prospect that if a guy will cheat on his wife, he'll cheat on a lot of other things. I don't make any apology for feeling that there is a connection between character, keeping promises and telling the truth in private life and applying those principles to public life."[2]

Unquestionably, you—and your magazine—will be influenced strongly in ethical decision making by media traditions such as striving to be first with a story (the "scoop" mentality) or, if beaten, to not be far behind. Believe it: Editors who broke the Gary Hart story never forgot, as they considered the ethics of publishing, that they had a truly big story that would attract enormous reader interest (and sales), a story that would create long-lasting impact. (And they were correct; here we are, still talking about it!)

Another media tradition that can influence you is adversarialism, a concept that a writer's duty is to question, probe, criticize. This easily can degenerate into cynical thinking that a writer's duty is not so much to interview officials or cover institutions but, rather, to attack them.

So, ethical decision making is influenced by editorial traditions in defining news and establishing reporting and writing standards. There is more.

The Marketing Influence

Recall from Chapters One and Two how magazines, in pursuit of business objectives, define markets and fashion editorial content that will attract readers who then can be delivered to advertisers in those markets. This can lead to narrowly defining ethical conduct solely as what is deemed acceptable by those sought-after audiences—pandering to the marketplace, in other words.

Elaborately detailed reader research is behind marketing concepts that drive editorial strategies of many magazines. For example, note the predictable content of each issue of *Reader's Digest*: a little humor; at least one "human interest" story that makes you a little sad (but ends nicely); a little sex (often cloaked in instructional, sociological terms); an important medical or political story (beautifully crafted in basic, easy-to-understand terms), a "how-to" story and so forth. Such "formula" content, devised carefully in accord with research into reader wants, has lifted *Reader's Digest* circulation to the world's largest.

Only a few magazines exist without advertiser support: *Ms.* announced in 1990 that advertiser pressure on editorial content was enormous—and unacceptable. It pleaded with subscribers for support, received it and a year later announced higher-than-ever profit levels based solely on circulation revenue. Editor-in-Chief Robin Morgan expressed relief at being able to select and write stories without worrying about what advertisers might think.

Consumer Reports, with about 3.8 million circulation, carries no advertising. *Guideposts,* a religious publication with 4.1 circulation, and *Mad,* with 2 million, also rely solely on circulation revenue. Most magazines, however, carefully research which readers are desirable to advertisers, then research what types of editorial content will attract those desirable readers.

For a writer attempting to devise a personal sense of ethics, there is danger in listening too intently to the "echo" from such market-driven research. You may forget to apply independent ethical and editorial judgment to what and how you write. It's easy to concentrate so intently on what readers say they *want* that you forget what you, a trained journalist and writer, know they *need.*

Much magazine research has two goals: It asks readers, "Do you like our magazine?" And, if not, "How can we change our ways to make you like us more?" If such marketing impulses are your exclusive guide (or your editor's) to what is right or wrong, you've lost ethical control of your own keyboard.

Many magazines don't write formal codes of ethics. Editors simply explain "how we do things around here." Those with codes often structure them not to solve any ethical dilemma an individual writer might face but, rather, to protect the magazine's marketplace credibility, image and reputation.

Special-Interest Groups

As you consider your alternatives in ethical decision making, you'll find enormous pressure on magazines (and other media) from special-interest groups representing emotional causes of all kinds. Gay rights, abortion, gun control—you name it, there is a group vigorously propounding its special interest.

One goal of special-interest groups is "politically correct" reporting that handles sensitive issues gently or avoids them altogether. Howard Kurtz, media critic for *The Washington Post,* says the result is disastrous.

"There was a time," Kurtz writes, "when American journalism thrived on controversy, the very essence of the news business. But in an era when an ill-chosen phrase can spark a nationwide backlash, the profession seems infused with a new skittishness, a growing fear that some group or faction or minority might be offended. . . ."[3]

Kurtz sees wider problems in the "politically correct" pressures.

"The larger problem with such gale-force protests is that any attempt at rational discourse is swept away. Modern life, after all, is filled with unpleasant facts: Most prison inmates are black and Hispanic. Many poor women are having children that they are unable to care for adequately even with welfare assistance. The prevalence of AIDS is far greater in the homosexual community, particularly among gays who are promiscuous and do not take precautions . . . Yet to delve into these subjects is to risk charges of racism or sexism or homophobia. . . .''[3]

John Leo, *U.S. News & World Report* columnist, warns the move to smother controversial news "can shut down candid discussion with astonishing speed."[4]

Sometimes, economic clout—threat of reader or advertiser boycott—is used by special-interest groups. A financially weak magazine is extremely vulnerable to such pressure, and an editor's sensitivity to threat of attack surely will be translated into pressure (or guidance) on what and how you write.

Importantly, the most vociferous special-interest groups are *not* pressuring magazines or other media for particularly ethical writing or balanced and objective coverage. Rather, they are pushing for coverage skewed in their own interests. Keep that in mind when such influences bear on your ethical decision making.

Self-Interest

We would be less than candid (*much* less!) if we denied that self-interest (call it "careerism") is a major factor in ethical decision making by many writers.

Did writers and editors involved in the Gary Hart story stand to gain personally if it was published? You bet. Careers are built on developing exciting stories with such impact.

We've been there, and we can tell you that the day will come when you will have to strive mightily to keep self-interest and your own careerism out of your ethical decision-making process. After all, it's only human to balance what's right and wrong ethically against what's right and wrong for you personally. All we can say is, try your best to keep such personal considerations out of the equation. You need not stretch ethical limits to produce a big, exclusive story. It will come naturally, and you'll find that with careful handling you can produce copy that has strong impact, advances your career *and* is ethical.

In sum, principled decision making in ethics involves rigorous, systematic thinking. A structured approach devised by Dr. Ralph Potter of the Harvard Divinity School is favored by many ethicists.[5] In our discussion of ethics for magazine writers, Potter's compartmentalized approach, "The Potter Box," can be envisaged as involving the elements in Figure 15–1. Once you complete the process in Figure 15–1, you are ready for the final step in ethical decision making.

Formulating Your Position

Ideally, if you (a) methodically assemble the facts of an ethical dilemma, then (b) define the issue and (c) consider carefully your alternatives, you will (d) be able to formulate, with clarity and certainty, your ethical position.

FIGURE 15–1 An Approach to Ethical Decision Making

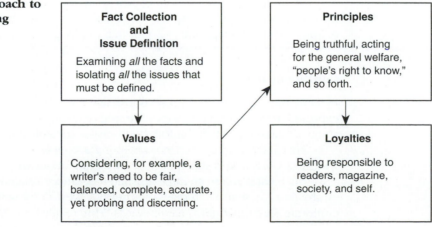

Unfortunately, thinking about ethics isn't like adding 2 + 2 to get 4, or mixing two parts of hydrogen to one part of oxygen to get water. Rarely does even the most painstaking examination of an ethical issue yield such clear-cut scientific results.

Reconcile yourself to two realities.

First, you'll come away from many ethical issues with a nagging feeling that you perhaps made the wrong call, that you decided on a course of action without fully understanding the facts or, particularly, the full impact of your decision. Perhaps years later it will occur to you: "My God, what I wrote was wrong!" Any professional (and honest) writer will acknowledge such misgivings.

Second, because ethics is so unscientific, so imprecise and often so personal, your thinking is wide open to doubt and, even, vigorous attack by others. That means what *you* decide is an ethical course can be considered grossly *un*ethical by others, including those who employ you or commission your writing. And that, in turn, means courage can be essential in formulating your ethical position. You can lose your staff writer's job in an ethical dispute or get a rejection slip instead of a free-lancer's check. In formulating an ethical position, you must decide how much you're willing to risk to stand by it.

COMPELLING ISSUES YOU'LL ENCOUNTER

Of the many ethical concerns writers face, two broad categories are most important for purposes of this book.

The ethics of reporting. This involves formulating ethical behavior and techniques you will follow in relationships with sources, for example. It means taking a stance on whether you'll accept gifts and favors from companies and institutions you write about or whether you'll maintain arm's-length independence.

The ethics of honest writing. This requires you to write not only accurately, fairly and with balance, but also to build structural integrity into each story and to create fundamental honesty in your relationships with readers.

Let's look at each category.

The Ethics of Reporting

For years, the ethical concerns of many editors focused primarily on the relationships of reporters, magazines, newspapers and broadcast media with the people and institutions they covered. From this arose guidelines widely accepted today on how individual reporters should conduct themselves.

In sum, principled editors expect writers to pursue truth aggressively and responsibly, without fear of special interests or favor to any. You can expect ethical editors of leading magazines to spell that out by prohibiting conflict of interest.

Conflict of Interest

In both their private and professional lives, writers for principled magazines are expected to demonstrate that they are free of entanglements that would destroy their ability to handle news and information dispassionately and evenhandedly.

That means, of course, not accepting a couple of free bottles of wine from a winery at Christmas if you specialize in writing about wine.

But what if you're an impoverished free-lancer struggling to get a career started on the East Coast and you get a big break: A West Coast winery offers to fly you in a corporate jet to its California vineyards. This might be a story for *Esquire,* but you cannot even reach it, let alone report it, if you don't accept the free ride. And, what's the harm? Can't you stay independent and dispassionate in your own mind?

Increasingly, leading magazine editors say you *cannot* avoid either the reality of conflict of interest in such a scenario or, importantly, cannot avoid creating a perception of conflict.

To avoid even a perception of conflict, which might impair their magazines' credibility, principled editors today insist their staff writers accept no such freebies. Further, many won't buy articles from free-lancers who do accept them.

However, Associate Editor Ed Avis of *The Quill,* the magazine of the Society of Professional Journalists, surveyed editors and found some still accepting free or subsidized travel for their writers and free-lancers. Those rejecting freebies mostly were profitable magazines with budgets large enough to afford turning down freebies.[6]

Travel & Leisure told Avis it pays for each of the more than 100 trips its staffers and free-lancers take annually. *Travel & Leisure* is owned by American Express, a highly profitable company. *Conde Nast Traveler* also has a policy against free travel, as does *New York Times Magazine.* Both are owned by large, profitable companies.

Obviously, you'll encounter situations in a magazine writing career that leave you no option but to accept free travel or special assistance. One of your co-authors accepted free travel in military aircraft while doing a series of aerospace stories in what used to be the Soviet Union. Your other co-author rode on U.S. helicopters in Vietnam. In both instances, official aircraft were the only means of getting to the story.

Many principled editors go far beyond a policy of no gifts or free travel. Some require writers to avoid financial investments in companies or industries they cover. Why? Well, let's say you owned stock in that California winery and what you write could cause the value of your stock to rise or fall. Could you really trust yourself to be dispassionate in writing about that company?

Leading magazines extend the prohibition against conflict of interest in personal investment to all sectors of writing: Real estate writers are expected to avoid land investments whose value could be influenced by what they write. Writers who specialize in autos, aircraft, commodities or the stock market itself are expected to avoid investment conflict of interest.

You may be tempted to do otherwise, because in a writing career you'll stumble across inside information that you *know* will move the share prices of a company, or the entire stock market, up or down when published. And who is to know if you trade for personal gain before publishing your story and letting the general investing public in on the secret? Well, using inside information for personal gain before it's published can be illegal and, for one, the U.S. Securities and Exchange Commission watches for (and helps jail) people who do. More to the point in our discussion: Such conduct is dishonest and unethical.

Some writers cannot resist the enormous temptations to compromise their writer's integrity.

The Wall Street Journal revealed in a major front-page investigative story that some writers for auto magazines were serving as paid consultants to companies they covered. Others were accepting lucrative speaking engagements, free use of cars, tickets for travel abroad and other freebies. One writer acknowledged making 20–25 speeches annually at a fee of $5,000 each paid by a company he covered.[7]

Increasingly, principled editors will require you not only to avoid such conflict of interest but to demonstrate that you do. That means editors sometimes will intrude into your private life.

For example, a principled editor of a city magazine will prohibit you from writing about education in your city if you serve on the school board or are an outspoken activist in educational issues. Don't expect to sell an editor a story on, say, the mayor's re-election campaign if you are employed part-time as a city hall speech writer. The principled editor of a campus magazine will reject your story offering on, say, your college's football team if you work part-time in the college's news bureau, a public relations office.

Sometimes, writers must handle stories that constitute apparent conflicts of interest. When that happens, reveal all to your readers. For example, in writing about media takeovers in Britain, *The Economist* was required to report on one of its owners. It revealed all this way:

> The Pearson publishing group, which owns the *Financial Times* (and, through it, 50% of *The Economist*), is the most likely buyer to have emerged so far.... (*"Who Is the Fairest of Them All?"* The Economist, *14 Dec. 1991, 62*)

In striving to avoid the reality or perception of conflict of interest, editors are demonstrating that their magazines are not beholden to any individual, group or special interest.

Identifying with Your Story

A danger in covering the same story over an extended period is that you can forget your primary mission is to serve your *readers,* not the industry you cover.

This is a hazard particularly for trade magazine writers who cover the same "beat" for years and can gradually slip—often unknowingly—from balanced, dispassionate writing into blatant (if unspoken) advocacy for the people and institutions they cover.

It's easy after years of reporting on, say, the U.S. military to come to believe in strong armed forces—and forget to regularly rethink the reporting basics and, for example, question such fundamental issues as whether changing world conditions mean more defense spending should be channeled into public health or highway construction. It's easy to report college football for years, basking in locker-room camaraderie and not periodically reexamining such basic questions as whether college football is too dominant on too many campuses.

In trade magazine journalism particularly, additional danger lies in two areas.

First, you can fear that your news sources, on whom you depend for your livelihood, will dry up if you are critical and don't "get on the team." Writers for advertising trade magazines, for example, may fear they wouldn't last long if they consistently attacked as social evils the advertising industry, the media and marketing companies.

Second, trade magazines depend, of course, on the industries they cover for their principal advertising and reader support. Advertising agencies or media companies won't advertise for long in magazines that consistently attack them.

There are strong reasons for magazines and writers to identify with the industries they cover. Unquestionably, however, trade magazines—and those who write for them—will fare better in the long run not by serving as uncritical mouthpieces of their industries but, rather, by publishing independent, balanced and, if necessary, critical coverage.

At issue is your fundamental credibility. A writer or magazine perceived to be "in the pocket" of a company or industry will have no credibility over time with readers or advertisers. Build a reputation for fair, honest writing and you will have credibility, even when being tough or critical.

Your Role as a Reporter

The technique of reporting is filled with ethical traps for the unwary.

The challenges begin immediately in two principal areas.

How you select stories. Writers can select from literally thousands of story options. The danger is in picking only those stories that will yield facts, information and viewpoints that agree with your personal thinking and your prejudices. For example, if you want to do a story on local education for a city magazine you can write on (a) the failures of local schools, (b) their successes or (c) a balanced, dispassionate account of *both* successes and failures. Now, if you're personally a critic—or admirer—of local schools, you'll need to guard against even subconsciously selecting a story that will prove you correct. Truly professional writers put aside personal feelings in selecting stories to write.

How you select sources. Ever notice how easy it is to talk with people who think as you do, who like the same things you do? In selecting sources to interview, you can find yourself unthinkingly heading for people with whose views you're comfortable. If you're a critic of local schools, you may find other critics just, well, make more sense than those who don't agree with you. You owe it to your readers to seek out sources on all sides of controversies.

A basic challenge in reporting, obviously, is to report without "making news." That is difficult, because your mere presence as a reporter sometimes changes the course of events. People act and talk differently when they know they're being watched. Next time you're viewing football on TV note how perfectly sane-looking people jump wildly, make insane faces and scream when the camera pans the crowd. Your presence, with notebook or tape recorder in hand, can have somewhat the same effect.

Another danger is that unless you're careful, you can turn an interview or press conference into theater by making statements, not asking questions; by attacking sources, not recording their views. Note in televised press conferences the adversarial, tendentious tone some reporters adopt. Watch others posture and strut their belief they know more about foreign policy or economic matters than the official being interviewed. Hard, direct questions often unlock news. Bulldog reporters can drag out facts that should be in the public view. But press conference theater can lead sources to freeze up.

In developing your reportorial technique, try to slide into your surroundings, quietly scooping up facts and catching quotes you need—*reporting your story, not making it.* If you make waves, you will distort the picture you're trying to record.

Some reporters go undercover and masquerade as police officers or physicians to secretly obtain "scoops." That may be storied technique in magazine history, but it generally is unwelcome today in editorial departments.

You'll find many editors require you to openly and fully identify yourself as a writer who interviews people on the record (establishing immediately that anything said can be published) and who gathers information for use with full attribution to the source by name.

Our experience compels us to advise you never to masquerade as anything other than a writer/journalist, except under most extraordinary circumstances. Identifying yourself as a cop or doctor to weasel into a story is, simply, dishonest (and illegal). It can destroy your reputation as a principled writer and seriously impair the image of your magazine.

Not all writers agree totally with such up-front openness, and, frankly, we can envisage situations in which being completely forthcoming may not be advisable.

For example, if you identify yourself as a travel writer for an important magazine, you'll get red-carpet treatment from any hotel, airline or tour company. And how can you report accurately for your readers if you are getting atypical treatment they never would receive?

And, of course, major stories sometimes are broken by writers who conceal their identities to obtain information. Other important stories get into print only because writers agree to go off the record to obtain information that sources don't want to be linked with publicly. *The Washington Post* still hasn't revealed the identity of its major source ("Deep Throat") for a series of articles that helped bring down President Nixon during the Watergate scandal in the 1970s. *New York Times* reporters (with other reporters quickly piling on) used what amounted to purloined documents (the

"Pentagon Papers"), handed over by a disgruntled former government employee, in a major investigative series on U.S. policy in the Vietnam war.

At the time, the *Post*'s and *Times*' reporting techniques were criticized by many. It generally is agreed today, however, that the nation's greater well-being was served by both papers ("utilitarianism"?).

In sum, the ethics of reporting are colored in many shades of grey, seldom unmistakably bold black and white. Sorting out your personal list of ethical dos and don'ts in reporting will be a major challenge in your magazine career.

The Ethics of Honest Writing

New (and numerous) ethical challenges arise the moment you touch your keyboard to start writing.

If you're attempting a balanced, dispassionate and fair story (not an opinion or interpretative piece), watch immediately for traps in several broad areas.

The timing and context of your story. Writing about failures in local schools two years before the school superintendent's contract expires has one meaning. That same story has quite another meaning if written two *weeks* before the board of education is to decide whether to extend the superintendent's contract. Unquestionably, timing and context can create wholly different meaning and impact for a story. We're not suggesting your first ethical duty is to make writing decisions based on likely impact; like many writers, we think your first duty is to write, as accurately and honestly as possible, stories that *should* be written. But any responsible writer must take the added step of considering timing, context and likely impact.

Story structure and fact selection. If you've done your job as a reporter, you have many more facts and quotes than you possibly can weave into your story. Your challenge now is to select facts and quotes that give readers an accurate, honest, balanced account. It's dishonest to write that local schools are plagued by violence, but omit what the superintendent told you in an interview: that the board of education repeatedly denied him funding for security patrols. It's dishonest, in writing an overview of local schools, to structure your story so powerfully on an anecdotal intro about a single schoolyard mugging that your opening vision of violence overpowers statistics showing the schools graduate an uncommonly high number of honors students and send many on to college. Where you place facts in your story structure also has ethical meaning: Devoting your first 2,000 words to school violence and only your last 200 to scholastic achievement distorts the story.

The language you use. Let's say you write, "Asked about skyrocketing school violence, the superintendent flushed angrily and rattled off statistics supporting his case."

Now, a writer's duty is to catch life's subtleties and nuances. In buying your magazine (and thus your story), readers pay you to go to see things they cannot see, to talk with people they'll never meet. They want those things and people described in colorful details they can see, feel, hear, smell.

But is violence truly "skyrocketing" or is that your assumption? Without supporting statistics, your language is a characterization that prejudices readers from the start. Did the superintendent flush—or blush with pleasure because he was waiting for you to ask for the facts? Was he really angry or just in a hurry? Were those statistics "rattled off" or is the superintendent a speed reader? And did he select statistics that supported his case (as you imply) or is that simply how the facts stacked up?

In sum, watch your language! Words aren't neutral instruments to be used loosely or interchangeably. They have very special meanings and, importantly, connotations. After you've decided what "flushed angrily" means to *you,* consider what it might mean to your *readers.*

As in story selection and reporting, thoroughly examine your *intent* when you start to write. If you simply don't like the school superintendent and, deep down, are out to bury him, you should (a) walk away from the story or (b) suggest to your editor that you write an opinion piece for clear labeling as interpretation.

Let's look at other concerns that arise in the writing process.

You, Truth, Fact and Opinion

If your goal as a writer is to reveal truth (about anything), you're in for a difficult career and, we venture to say, something less than complete success. Who, after all, knows what is true? Who knows where truth hides among the many shouting voices and numerous conflicting viewpoints that surround any controversial issue of our day?

Isn't it reasonable, however, to hope for success as a writer dedicated to revealing, interpreting, analyzing and balancing facts? Isn't there career fulfillment and satisfaction—*meaning*—in writing that dispassionately and fairly gives your readers the facts which they can use to find truth as they understand it? We think there is.

We're not suggesting you merely shovel facts at readers and, in effect, say, "Here, sort through all this and maybe you'll find truth." Rather, we're suggesting writing that is extremely cautious about promising truth and levels with readers and is honest with them. That means doing three things:

1. You should structure your story to present facts and quotes that give readers a balanced view. That in itself is difficult because it requires you to so thoroughly master your subject that you understand all sides of a controversy (remember how many issues cropped up in the Gary Hart case?). Then, you must weight, as objectively as possible, the importance of facts representing all sides by assigning them priorities in your story. Warning: Readers often find "truth" more readily in those facts you place first and most emphatically in your story and assign less importance to facts you position deep in your story.

2. You should explain honestly any holes in your story and why you don't have facts to fill them. For example, if school officials refuse to be interviewed on violence in schools, say so: "The president of the board of education refused comment on the report, and the superintendent of schools did not return five telephone calls to his office." That precise detail shows readers you know official views are important to the story and that you are attempting to present a balanced account—and explains why you cannot.

3. Anytime your writing moves beyond presentation of facts and into interpretation, analysis or opinion, you should inform your readers. This is necessary because magazine writing, by its nature, frequently requires opinion (passion, even) and analysis if you want to move your readers beyond what they find in the relatively straightforward newswriting of many newspapers or, certainly, television's superficial obsession with visual communication. Simple devices signal readers that opinion is coming their way: (a) You quote authoritative sources on their opinions, (b) you label your story "analysis" or "interpretation" or (c) you insert in your story the perpendicular pronoun: "Although the superintendent declined comment, I (or "this reporter" or "a writer") found school halls and playgrounds extremely violent."

You can fashion a fine career in advocacy writing. Just be sure to clearly label yourself as an advocate and your writing as opinion.

You, Your Sources and Your Readers

A writer often confronts seemingly conflicting ethical responsibilities to sources, essential to your trade, and readers, to whom you owe first allegiance.

First, you must honor (legally, sometimes, as well as ethically) any ground rules you accepted for your relationship. For example, if you agree to grant sources anonymity, you have an ethical responsibility to protect their identity. Writers have gone to jail rather than break their word on that. And, identifying sources can hurt them badly. *Newsweek* identified a prostitute with AIDS in a story on the disease, and police arrested her for attempted murder.[8]

Yet, it's implicit in your writer's relationship with readers that you will collect for them necessary facts and reliable views from authoritative sources. The best way to demonstrate you've fulfilled that obligation is to identify your sources by name, title and credentials. Readers have a right to judge for themselves the authenticity and reliability of information you are conveying.

A *New York Times* columnist, A. M. Rosenthal, noted that *Daedalus,* the magazine of the American Academy of Arts and Sciences, published an anonymous story, and commented: "For a newspaper or a magazine to use anonymous pieces is an invitation to mugging."[9] Rosenthal referred to a practice, common in politics, of sources using the media to launch "trial balloons"—controversial and anonymous statements—to judge public reaction. If reaction is adverse, such sources remain anonymous, of course. If favorable, they step forward.

You should take several steps in handling the ethical problems in source identification.

First, grant anonymity to sources only if there is absolutely no other way to pry out important information. Always suspect the motives of a source who demands to remain unidentified. Consult your editor before you agree.

Second, if you do grant anonymity, give your readers as much identification as possible so they can judge, even without the source's name, the reliability of your information. Quoting "a government source" is some help; quoting "a high-ranking official of the U.S. State Department" is better.

Third, if you must grant anonymity, tell your readers why. Here is how one writer protected a source in Zimbabwe, where critics of the government are dealt with harshly: "Reflecting the current political climate, the professor asked not to be identified." That single sentence helped readers understand why an anonymous source was quoted *and* actually strengthened the story's angle that democracy is threatened in the African nation.

You, Privacy and the "People's Need to Know"

One of a writer's toughest calls is judging whether individuals—perhaps innocent bystanders sideswiped by current events—should be spotlighted in a story and thus subjected unwillingly to the agony of public examination.

You'll recall from Chapter Fourteen that the law clearly recognizes the people's right to know intimate details about public officials and figures and, even, private individuals thrust unwillingly into events of compelling public interest.

But, what are the ethics of singling out individuals for scrutiny and revealing intimate—even sordid—details of their private lives? Do the people have a need as well as a right to know some of the ghastly things we write?

If you're unsure, you're not alone.

For example, controversy rages among writers over "outing" by gay publications—publicly identifying "closet" homosexuals who try to keep their sexual preferences private. *Outweek,* a gay magazine, and *Advocate,* a Los Angeles-based gay newspaper, both publish articles identifying closet gays. *Advocate* named a Pentagon official—and the argument began among writers on how to handle such revelations.

Advocate claimed there was news value in its story because the Pentagon discharges gays from the military. Columnist Jack Anderson said he made a "painful" decision to use the official's name although the official asked not to be identified. Anderson said, "A person's private life is his own business unless it affects the public interest. We made the decision that it had reached that point." Anderson asked why other writers publicize Gary Hart's heterosexual activities but won't publicly examine a man's homosexual life.[10]

Washington Journalism Review examined how writers handled the Pentagon story but didn't identify the official (although it almost certainly did pinpoint him for Washington insiders by specifying his title). That drew a charge of "censorship" against the magazine. An *Economist* writer, in a story on outing, identified a dead publisher outed while still alive but did not use names in discussing a living U.S. congressman and others publicly identified as homosexuals by gay publications.[11]

Similarly conflicting opinions exist over whether to identify rape victims. Many writers say no, that rape carries social stigma and that the victim should be spared the additional agony of being identified against her will. But some writers argue that's a double standard because media do identify alleged rapists (and accused child molesters) even while granting anonymity to accusers.

The potential harm you can do to individuals in stories on sexual preferences or rape is obvious. Sometimes, however, it's not so obvious in other types of stories.

For example, let's say you are writing that overview on school violence for a local city magazine and decide on an anecdotal intro. You single out one of scores of teachers unable to control violence in their classrooms. Or, let's say you focus a feature lead on one school principal among the city's many whose playgrounds are roamed by muggers. See the problem? By focusing public scrutiny on one individual—however gently or, even, unintentionally—you change their lives forever (you may even get the teacher or principal fired!).

Clearly, writers make decisions that can destroy lives. Certainly, the Pentagon official's life is changed forever. Who among us writers, mere mortals all, should make such god-like decisions that so dramatically affect the lives of others?

Whether we should or not, we do. When you face those calls, our advice is that you do as principled writers do and carefully consider a crucial question: People's right to know aside, is there need to reveal these details? For example, is the Pentagon official's ability to perform his duties compromised by his homosexuality and, therefore, does the public need to know?

You, Gore and Good Taste

We've discussed the need for vivid, graphic writing that makes readers *see, hear* and *smell* as if they're with you at the scene of the action.

But what if the sights, sounds and odors are so revoltingly gory that they make you ill? What if you encounter incredibly lewd language and behavior? How much of that belongs in your writing? It's not an easy call.

For example, your snap judgment might be that no writer needs to describe disemboweled or headless bodies. But, isn't that the stuff of war? And, if you're covering war, do you communicate to your readers a false picture if you omit such details?

Or, is it necessary to write, in covering AIDS, that homosexuals are at high risk because the disease can be transmitted through anal intercourse? Many writers omitted that detail when the disease entered public view in the early 1980s. Those writers denied their readers information essential for understanding AIDS and, in part, contributed to widespread panic among people who feared contagion from a handshake or the air around them. You cannot assume readers know.

For example, by 1991 there had been a decade of AIDS coverage in the media. Then basketball star Magic Johnson revealed he had the virus that carries the disease. The National AIDS Hot Line reported a flurry of telephone calls from thousands of people who—despite the years of news coverage—didn't know the differences between the virus (HIV) that carries the disease and AIDS itself. The second-most asked question: "What does heterosexual mean?"

Unquestionably, the American definition of good taste is changing. We remember when "Gone with the Wind" created quite a stir because Clark Gable uttered the word "damn" on screen. Today, live TV coverage of congressional hearings can include descriptions of oral sex. Writers can describe use of condoms in graphic detail.

Nevertheless, in matters of good taste, as in all questions of ethics, the individual writer has responsibility to avoid running with the herd and, instead, make sound personal judgments. We suggest you carefully consider two factors.

First, think of your audience. Detail and language appropriate for, say, *Esquire* or *Rolling Stone* readers may be unsuitable for readers of *Reader's Digest* or *Family Circle*. Good taste should be defined for *your* readers, not someone else's.

Second, is the questionable material *truly necessary* to communicate the point of your story? Or would its inclusion merely be for shock value? Sometimes extremely raw language is necessary. For example, *Broadcasting* used the "F" word (and others we will not repeat) in describing a documentary run by three TV stations. Why? Because the story was about Federal Communications Commission investigations into complaints of indecency at the stations. For *Broadcasting*'s audience of TV executives, the explicit language was not only appropriate but necessary.[12]

A FINAL—AND IMPORTANT—POINT

It's implicit in all we've said about professionalism and fairness, but we want to emphasize a final point about your writing: Stories or language that are sexist, racist or unnecessarily offensive to any sector of our society have no place in magazines today.

As a reporter and writer, thinker and agenda-setter, you're on the leading edge of change, with enormous power to influence how people think and act. Use that power wisely.

SUMMARY

Writers have ethical responsibilities to their readers and the society that confers on them the status of writer.

Four steps are involved in making ethical decisions: assembling the facts, defining the issue, considering your alternatives and formulating your position.

It's crucial to have *all* relevant facts when considering an ethical challenge. Dig beneath the surface to ensure you understand the true issue. Often, an ethical challenge really is several issues that need sorting out.

Numerous pressures bear on you in considering your alternatives: Ethical precedent—the history of ethical debate—is one. Socrates' search for "good" 2,500 years ago is relevant today. Religion also raises a wide range of values to consider, including the "Golden Rule," self-sacrifice and others.

Media traditions and values—libertarianism, objectivity, utilitarianism—have been debated for generations by ethicists and are important to your decision making today. So are social responsibility and a sense of professionalism, concepts that arose in the early 1900s.

One important factor in media ethics is the marketing influence, a tendency to measure what's ethically sound in terms of business strategies. Special-interest groups create enormous pressure, not for balanced, dispassionate writing but, rather, for writing skewed toward their interests.

In formulating an ethical position, expect to be unhappy—even years later—with your judgment. Seldom do you arrive at obvious, clearly correct judgments. Your ethical stand can be controversial, too, and might require courage to defend.

The ethics of reporting are enormously complex, involving conflict of interest and getting too close to your story and sources (and forgetting your mission is to serve your readers). You also must consider your technique as a reporter—how and why you select stories and sources. One common problem is reporters who make news (rather than report it) by being overly adversarial or feeling self-important.

The ethics of writing force you to think about the timing and context of your stories. When and how you write a story can dramatically change a reader's perception of its meaning. How you structure stories and the language you use can influence meaning, too.

Other ethical traps lie in whether to attempt to report "truth" or be content with reporting facts. Writing opinion is fine; just be certain to label it as advocacy writing.

An often agonizing challenge is deciding whether to invade a person's right to privacy on behalf of the public's "need to know." When is inflicting harm on an individual justified?

Although American standards of good taste are changing, individual writers must decide whether gory details or lewd language are appropriate for their readers and necessary for communicating the central meaning of their stories.

RECOMMENDED READING

The ethics of reporting and writing are explored more deeply in Conrad C. Fink, *Media Ethics in the Newsroom and Beyond* (New York: McGraw-Hill, 1988) and Conrad C. Fink, *Introduction to Professional Newswriting* (White Plains, N.Y.: Longman, 1992).

For writers, the best discussions of current ethical issues are published in *Washington Journalism Review, presstime, Broadcasting* and *Editor & Publisher.* For excellent surveys of reporter/writer opinion on ethics and in-depth analysis of compellingly important ethical questions, see the American Society of Newspaper Editors *Bulletin* and periodic reports issued by The Associated Press Managing Editors.

For a more historical look, see Robert C. Solomon, *Morality and the Good Life* (New York: McGraw-Hill, 1984) and Alasdair McIntyre, *A Short History of Ethics* (New York: Macmillan, 1966). Michael Emery and Edwin Emery trace the history of the American press in their *The Press and America*, 6th ed. (Englewood Cliffs, N.J.: Prentice-Hall, 1988).

NOTES

1. Poll results were published in "Free Expression and the American Public: A Survey Commemorating the 200th Anniversary of the First Amendment." It is available from ASNE Foundation, Box 17004, Washington, D.C. 20041.
2. Alvin P. Sanoff, "A Perspective on Power," *U.S. News & World Report,* 28 Oct. 1991, 81.
3. Howard Kurtz, "Our Politically Correct Press," *The Washington Post,* 20 Jan. 1991, B 1.
4. John Leo, "Smothering Controversial News," *U.S. News & World Report,* 23 Sept. 1991, 24.
5. Ralph Potter, "The Structure of Certain American Christian Responses to the Nuclear Dilemma, 1958–63," Harvard Ph.D. dissertation, 1965. The "Potter Box" is modified and superbly discussed in an excellent book: Clifford G. Christians, Kim B. Rotzoll and Mark Fackler, *Media Ethics: Cases & Moral Reasoning* (New York: Longman, 1991).
6. Ed Avis, "Have Subsidy, Will Travel," *The Quill,* March 1991, 20.
7. Joseph B. White, "Car Magazine Writers Sometimes Moonlight for Firms They Review," *The Wall Street Journal,* 15 March 1990, 1.
8. Katherine Bishop, "Prostitute in Jail After AIDS Report," *The New York Times,* 15 July 1990, 12.
9. A. M. Rosenthal, "On My Mind," *The New York Times,* 5 Jan. 1990, 23.
10. The Anderson quote is in David Astor, "Controversial Piece on Pentagon Official," *Editor & Publisher,* 17 Aug. 1991, 40. Also see Bill Monroe, "The Press Respected Privacy—Twice," *Washington Journalism Review,* Dec. 1991, 6, and "Hypocrisy Is News," letter to the editor of *Washington Journalism Review,* Jan./Feb. 1992, 10.
11. "Out and About," *The Economist,* 27 July 1991, 21.
12. "PBS Show Draws Indecency Complaints At FCC," *Broadcasting,* 29 July 1991, 70.

Part Five

You,
editors and
the production
process

To succeed as a magazine staff writer or free-lancer, you must do more than deliver strongly reported and well-written copy. You must understand and satisfy the technical needs of editors and others behind the scenes who put out your magazine.

You need not be an expert, of course, in every dimension of the editing, manufacturing and distribution process that puts magazines on newsstands and in subscribers' mailboxes. But you *do* need to understand how you and your writing must mesh with that process.

We won't attempt, in the single chapter of Part V, to describe the entire production process. That would require an entire book (perhaps several!). Rather, we will help you master some basic terms and techniques used in magazine production. Display a grasp of them, and you'll position yourself before editors as a true magazine professional.

Ahead is a brief overview of what's happening in the magazine industry's switch to a computerized future. Then, we'll provide hints on how to prepare and submit a manuscript, how to anticipate the mechanical needs of editors and, briefly, how the manufacturing and distribution process works.

Chapter 16

Overview:
The state of
our art

You've heard, of course, about how we used to produce magazines: grumpy editors in green eyeshades, wielding thick, black copy pencils, pastepots and scissors; the rattle of typewriters settling over the editorial department like a heavy dew; Linotype operators rekeyboarding everything in hot metal and, finally, the presses rolling.

We still can smell the pastepots and hear the typewriters; *you* can dismiss all that as a romantic carryover from an almost-forgotten past.

Enormous change is under way in magazine editing and production. Computers and associated technical innovations are transforming the magazine industry.

Editors (some still grumpy) now labor over electronic editing systems and some editorial departments are almost paperless. Pastepots and scissors are not in sight.

PRODUCTION REALITIES

Four realities are driving the change.

First, to remain competitive against other media in the battle for readers and advertisers, magazines must find ways of reducing their largest single cost—production. If costs get too high, subscription and advertising rates must rise, and readers and advertisers alike then may seek alternatives, including newspapers and TV.

Second, computerized editing and production systems can lower costs by reducing the number of people and amount of time needed to create magazines. People and time equal huge costs in the magazine business.

Third, computerized systems improve the entire editing and production results. Simply, we are able to put out better magazines than in pre-computer days. We are stronger and more timely, journalistically, as well as more cleanly edited, colorful and pleasing to the eye. And, computers help us marry copy, photos, graphs and other types of art in a total package that communicates more information more efficiently and quickly to our readers than did the relatively dull, unattractive magazines of yesteryear.

Fourth, computerized systems being installed in editorial departments today are relatively inexpensive. A nationwide survey by *Folio* of magazines of all sizes found the needed technology cost $140,000 on average. Using such low-cost technology to reduce expenses is a formula for profit.[1]

Don't fear you must wrestle with new technological mysteries as you learn to write. If you're a typical college undergraduate, you're already familiar with many of the computers and techniques used in magazine editorial departments. (It gets technically more complicated in the production departments, but mastering all that isn't crucial to writers.)

By a wide margin, Apple's Macintosh computers, used in many colleges, are most popular. *Folio* found that 60.7 percent of 84 magazines surveyed used Macs. Among smaller magazines, where you'll likely start, 70 percent used Macs; 43 percent of larger magazines did. The second most common system, reported by 26.2 percent of respondents, was a mix of Macs and personal computers.

Magazines that formerly relied on outside compositors are switching to in-house desktop publishing (DTP). The *Folio* survey found 86.9 percent of all editorial departments using DTP or electronic systems of some kind. DTP also was used by 82.1 percent for magazine design and by 76.2 percent for production. For many magazines, that pulled in-house the entire editing and much of the manufacturing process, short of the press. And half of those magazines that reported they weren't computerized said they would be in 12 months!

HINTS ON MANUSCRIPT PREPARATION

If you join a major magazine's staff you'll work only on computerized systems. Foreign correspondents and other writers use portable laptop computers to create copy while traveling, then send it via modem into their magazine's master computer. Editors massage the computerized files and the writer's own keystrokes eventually are used electronically to drive computerized typesetting equipment. In bygone days, the entire editorial file had to be rekeystroked by Linotype operators who set hot-metal type in a laborious, costly and time-consuming backshop process that followed editing.

If you submit free-lance copy to a magazine, you may be asked to "file" or deliver your copy electronically, on a diskette or by computer-to-computer hookup or fax. So, determine early in your conversation with any editor whether your PC is compatible with the magazine's system and how your manuscript should be coded.

However, some magazines, especially smaller ones open to beginning free-lancers, still take manuscripts on hard copy. They then manually re-key the manuscript into their electronic editing systems or use electronic optical scanners which "read" hard copy and digitize it—that is, convert copy to electronic form.

A writer's best friend: A copy editor, using modern electronic editing systems, can improve your writing by checking accuracy and rewriting for clarity.

Northern Light photo by Mark Fink

Even if you sell to larger, electronically edited magazines, you may work on hard copy in the back-and-forth process of editing and correcting proofs. So, a few hints on preparing hard-copy manuscripts:

Use 8½″ × 11″ bond paper. Do *not* use legal or odd-size sheets or onionskin paper, which most editors don't like to handle. Use a standard typeface—10-point pica or 12-point elite—that's easy to read. Avoid simulated script or other hard-to-read typefaces. If you write on a computer, use a letter-quality printer with a new ribbon, not a low-quality dot-matrix printer.

Double-space all copy and leave wide margins—at least 1½″—at the top, bottom and sides of each page. Good editors will have lots to say to you about your copy. Give them some room.

Each paragraph should be indented five spaces. Inserting subheads is the editor's responsibility (and prerogative), but you can signal your recommendations by including them in your manuscript like this:

Rock Fading on Campus

or

"New Wave" a New Hit

Most magazines have their own formats for manuscripts to ensure that copy, whether on paper or in an electronic file, is easily identifiable and simply to make certain it doesn't get lost among the millions of words that surge through editorial departments. If you faithfully follow the system used by your magazine, you'll come across as an "editor-friendly writer" whose copy is easy to "work." You need editors on your side, and anything you can do to ease their job will improve your relationship with them.

If you don't know the magazine's copy-handling system, you can follow logical procedures to help editors keep track of your story anyway. Start halfway down the first page (so the top half is available for the editor's handwritten instructions or for a headline.) Open with a "slugline" that clearly identifies you and your story:

(Your name)
(Date of submission)
College Music Trends (a brief "identifier" line that can be used as a computer file label.)

Editors normally accord bylines, but just to make sure, stick yours into that first page:

By Beginner Writer

Magazine styles vary, but to be certain you provide the essentials, start your story with a "dateline" (which, except for tradition, more properly would be called a "placeline"):

College Town, Ill.—College music trends. . . .

Don't divide words at the end of a line (which may be taken to signal hyphenation). Each page should be a self-contained unit, with no sentence or paragraph continuing on the next page. In industry parlance, that makes each page a complete "take." If more copy is to follow, type "more" at the bottom of the page.

Each succeeding page should be "slugged" at the top with something like this:

beginner writer/college music/add one
or
beginner writer/college music/p. 3

Your last page should conclude: "endit" or "-30-" or "###" or "-0-". (The storied "-30-" was used by telegraphers to signal end of a message in the old days. It's still widely used in this era of computers and communications satellites!)

If you file electronically from your PC to the magazine's master computer, the editors' queries and instructions likely will come back to you electronically. In large magazines, all editing will be done on computers. However, if you're filing hard copy, you and the editors can use time-honored, hand-written editing symbols (in black and dark blue ink, only) to change copy. Even new-age writers raised on computers should know these symbols, explained in Figure 16–1.

There! Now you'll be able to "read" the meaning of what editors write on your copy.

It's also important to be able to speak the "lingo" of your trade. Note the glossary in Box 16–1.

WHY EDITORS ACT THE WAY THEY DO

Throughout this book we've counseled you to take pride in your writing, to treasure your ability to communicate through the written word.

Now we must tell you that part of becoming a truly professional writer is learning when to accept—gracefully—heavy editing of your story or even a complete rewrite.

It's hard to believe when you see one of your masterpieces butchered, but strong editors who know their business can improve your copy dramatically and help you grow as a writer. Seek cooperative, not adversarial, relationships with editors. Ask their advice, and many will become your mentors and take great personal satisfaction in boosting your writing career.

Depending on the size and structure of your magazine, you may not deal directly with the editor-in-chief. On large magazines, this top editor normally is preoccupied with overall strategic direction of content, hiring and firing, budgeting and coordination with the publisher and representing the magazine to its external public. Your

FIGURE 16–1 Editing Symbols

¶ The rock band had great success,	indent
with one-night stands	run in
in small towns.	insert missing word
The band leader said once	transpose words
he thought this group would	separate words
Stick together forever.	lowercase; no cap
But he was wrong and he	insert dash
knew it⊙	insert period (also)
For two week ends	join together
he insisted, "We are blood	insert comma
brothers."	insert close quotes
In Benton, Illinois,	abbreviate
another band, the die-hards,	capitalize; uppercase
played for sixteen hours	use figure 16
straight. That was 4 hours	spell out four
longer than their record.	take out r
For them them, it was the	take out them
end. — stet	don't make correction
In Ill. the Die-Hards featured a	spell out Illinois
singer,	
Whoops.	spell as written (also use "Whoops (cq)")
Its not clear	insert apostrophe
awful but then the band	insert semicolon
Antirock fans	insert hyphen

Other Symbols

story continues	more
story ends	— 30 —
flush left	
flush right	
center	
set uppercase	
set lowercase	
set in italics	
set boldface	

BOX 16–1   Glossary of Publishing Terms

Agate   Technically, 5½-point type. But term is used loosely for any small type used for lists, boxed material and other non-text copy.

Art   Any photos, drawings or graphic elements on a page.

Author's alterations ("AAs")   Changes in proofs by author, not editors, compositors or printers.

Author's proof   Typeset copy of manuscript that author reads, corrects, approves.

Binding   Cutting, trimming, folding, stitching (or gluing) of magazine after printing.

Blueline (blue, blueprint)   A proof, done quickly in blue printing, of an article or a page.

Body type (type text)   Type size, usually 8- to 10-point, used for stories.

Book   What the pros call a magazine.

Box   Copy enclosed in borders, like this glossary.

Break-of-the-book   Decision, usually made in story conference, on allocation of space in a magazine.

Brownline   Fast proof, in brown printing, of article or page.

Budget (directory, schedule, digest)   List of stories for a single issue.

Bullet   Dots used typographically to separate material or set it off to catch reader attention. Dashes are used similarly.

Calendaring   Making paper specially smooth by rolling it during production. (Also, "coated paper.")

Caption (cutline)   Text explaining photos and other graphic material.

Close   Final deadline for sending all magazine copy to printer.

Cold type   Type produced through photocomposition, pastedown or desktop publishing techniques, not the generally now-outdated use of Linotypes and hot metal.

Collage (montage, composite)   Using several separate photos as one.

Color separation   Making press plates by converting a color transparency into its three primary colors and black.

Column inch   One inch deep in a single column.

Comprehensive   Hand-drawn layout (or "dummy") of page or cover.

Copy   Art or text to be printed.

Copyfitting   Editing, selecting type size to fit copy in allocated space.

Copyreading   Reading, correcting errors.

Cover stock   Special paper for covers.

Credit line   Information in caption identifying photographer or artist.

Crop   Editing and marking photos and other artwork to show how they should be reproduced.

Cutline   See "caption."

Cylinder press   Press that holds paper to a revolving cylinder, rolling it across an inked form to receive impressions.

Digital printing   Using ink-jet sprays or laser-etching, not plates, in a computer-controlled process that creates images.

Digitize   To convert hard copy into computerized (digital) form for use in electronic editing systems.

Dirty copy   Copy filled with errors; copy heavily marked up by copy editors.

Display type   Type larger than body (or text) type.

Dummy   Representation, often hand-drawn, of what page will look like.

Electrostatic printing   Using electrostatic charges to treat powder forms on paper and thus create images.

Engraving   Printing plate etched by acid.

Facsimile transmission (fax)   Transmitting text and graphic materials by scanning them and converting them into electromagnetic signals.

Flatbed press   Prints from a flat, not curved, type form, by pressing paper on type or engravings.

Folio   Page number; often includes magazine's name and date in a line at top or bottom of page.

Format   Magazine's size, style, shape, form.

Galley proof   Proof of typeset matter not yet made into pages/columns.

Gutter   Vertical white space between columns or pages; more commonly, inside margins of pages at binding.

Halftone   Reproduction from photograph or other graphic material. Tone gradations are produced by pattern of dots.

Hold (HFR)   Copy not to be published without release ("Hold for release").

Hot type ("hot metal")   Using molten metal to compose type mechanically.

Ink-jet printing   Using computer-driven ink jets, not plates, to create images on paper.

Jump   Continuation of a story on succeeding page.

Layout (dummy)   Representation, often hand-drawn, of how text, photos and other elements will appear on a page.

Letterpress   Prints by forcing paper on inked raised (relief) plates; has almost given way to modern cold type processes.

Makeup   Arrangement of text and other elements in page form.

Mark up   Providing instructions, in writing on copy or electronically, to compositors.

Mechanical   Photos, text and other elements made camera-ready in composition.

Montage   See "collage."

BOX 16–1

continued

Offset Lithographic printing process that transfers ink image from plate to rubber blanket to paper; offers higher quality than letterpress.

Page proof Text, photos and other elements in proof form.

Pagination Design and layout of pages on video display terminals.

Pasteup Positioning of all page elements for photographing in making printing plates.

Press proof One of first copies off printing press; provides opportunity for last-minute correction of major errors.

Process color Separation of colors in original color photographs for production of printing plates.

Proof Type, photos and other elements that are printed to permit correction of errors.

Refer (REE-fur) Text referring readers to another story, photo or accompanying graph.

Register Placing printing plates properly so they will reproduce sharp images without blur.

Reverse Reversing type from black on white to white on black.

Rotogravure Photomechanical printing process using an intaglio copper cylinder; often produces high-quality color reproduction.

Run Number of copies printed.

Saddle stitch Stapling (or stitching) a magazine through the middle fold of its pages.

Signature Number of pages printed on sheet of paper, which then is trimmed and folded.

Slug A few words identifying story and its author for editors.

Split page Magazine page containing both editorial and advertising material.

Spot color All color printing except process printing.

Stock Paper on which magazine is printed.

Take Portion of a story, such as one typed page.

Thermography Printing by powdering wet images on paper, then heating them to fuse powder and ink to create a raised image.

Typo Typographical error.

Velox Screened photographic print, usually more sharply defined than a photostat.

Webfed Presses that print on paper fed through from a roll, in contrast with flatbed presses that take single sheets.

Wrap Insert around a signature in a magazine.

Wrap type Type displayed (wrapped) around graphic material for special visual effect.

---

initial contact may be with an editor—variously titled executive editor or managing editor—who is in charge of day-to-day operations. You may also work with senior editors, department editors or other specialists. Ultimately, however, your copy will be "worked" by copy desk editors.

Copy editors don't get bylines or romantic assignments to far-off places on adventurous stories. In many editorial departments they have no say in overall content and don't attend "break-of-book" conferences, the strategy sessions where each issue's content is planned.

But copy editors are extremely important to any magazine and to all writers.

Copy editors have difficult tasks: They must dispassionately challenge facts and figures in your story and carefully check your spelling, grammar, sentence construction and whether your writing is consistent with the magazine's style. They must ensure your copy isn't libelous. They must improve your writing, eliminating gaseous verbosity and sharpening your imagery. They must trim your copy to fit allocated space. And, all of that must be done quickly, so that "copy flow"—the movement of copy through the editorial process—is maintained and deadlines are met.

In that process, copy editors are responsible to three constituencies: The magazine and its interests, of course, come first. But good editors also are surrogates for the readers, looking for holes in your story, questions or vague writing that might confuse them. Finally, copy editors serve you, the writer.

Copy-handling systems vary with the size and editorial missions of magazines, but copy editors normally work in several time frames. For example, *Aviation Week & Space Technology* works sometimes weeks in advance on cover stories while simultaneously pushing the current week's issue toward "close." That's the pre-dawn deadline on Fridays when *Aviation Week* sends to the printer the issue that bears a cover date of the following Monday.

How Deadlines Are Set

Deadlines are established by all magazines out of journalistic and marketing motives. Writers' copy must arrive on time so it can be processed through editing and production on time and be transmitted to the printer who, in turn, must roll the presses on time to meet circulation's deadlines for delivery to sales racks and mailboxes. For example, *Aviation Week* is a *news*magazine that readers regard as important for the career and industry information it contains. To help them on the job, it must be on their desks (in their offices generally, not their homes) at the opening of business on Mondays, the first day of the workweek. It's the editors' intent to provide information readers can use throughout the subsequent week. The entire copy-handling system, from writer deadlines to design and layout, is timed to permit this. (Some subscribers get special delivery on Saturdays. And single copies are sold only at selected sales racks.)

Aviation Week works with a minimum "editorial well" of 50 pages. That's the number of pages filled each week with news and information about the aerospace and defense industries. The number of pages over 50 open to editorial is determined by the amount of advertising sold. Sometimes the "well" is over 100 pages for special issues.

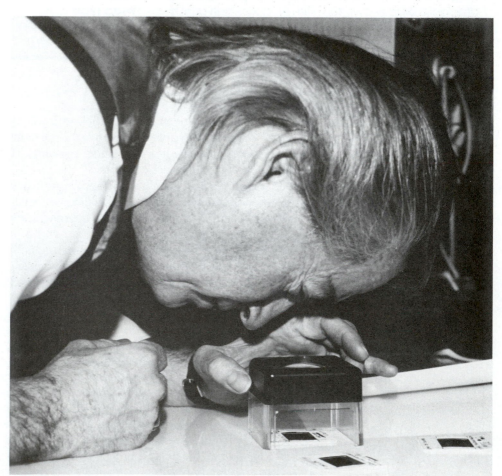

Aviation Week & Space Technology's art director uses a magnifying "loupe" and light table to examine a 35-millimeter transparency that will illustrate a story in the magazine.

Northern Light photo by Mark Fink

Copy for even 50 pages would overwhelm editors and choke the copy flow if all stories moved simultaneously through the system. So, the editing and the subsequent pre-press fact-checking, design/layout, artwork and pagination (page making) are divided into "early form" and "late form."

Editors select early-form copy each Thursday evening, 11 days prior to the Monday cover date that issue will bear. This involves assembling regular departmental features, special reports and other relatively timeless copy assigned to "back-of-the-book" positioning, under "standing heads"—that is, copy that will appear each week under the same sluglines or departmental headings, in back pages of the magazine. Early-form editing begins on Friday morning.

Simultaneously, work on late-form copy—late-breaking stories and new, timely information—proceeds apace so Friday's deadline can be met for next Monday's issue.

Each Wednesday, late in the day, and early on Thursdays the editors have a "bloodlet conference," so-called because they decide which stories must be "spiked" or "killed" and which must be trimmed drastically so truly important stories will fit into the magazine at the length they require. At many magazines this is a sometimes bruising process, with editors and writers competing to get their copy into print. The whole thing is akin to forcing 50 gallons of water into a 25-gallon barrel—quickly, under deadline pressure, and accurately, without spilling any. And this goes on day after day, week in and week out, with editors counting on writers to submit clean, accurate and well-written copy that meets deadlines.

Now do you understand why editors act the way they do?

THE POST-EDITING PROCESS

After copy editing, your story is a "digital database" or electronic file tucked into the editorial department's master computer under an identification number and adorned with all sorts of computerized instructions.

Electronic editing (done here with Adobe Photoshop software) permits enhancing a photo's color and quality. For ethical reasons, many editors forbid using the computer's ability to rearrange a photo's elements or change its content.

Northern Light photo by Mark Fink

The identification (or "file") number permits editors to find your story and call it up on their screens at any time. They can read your original manuscript, see what editing changes were made and trace who made them.

The copy editor's instructions order a headline (or perhaps deck lines, if additional headlines are desired).

Meanwhile, the magazine's art director is also at work on your story.

The art director and others who design and lay out the magazine must ensure each issue reflects the tone and character that publication strategists deem necessary to satisfy readers and advertisers. *Lear's* must look like *Lear's*; *Aviation Week* must look like *Aviation Week*—each week.

But design specialists have more in mind than mere packaging: They want the book to flow for readers, gently leading them in an orderly way between type and graphic elements, from page to page. Designers labor with type, photos, color and many typographical devices to focus reader attention on stories and features. Good designers strengthen copy and photos with layout, ensuring magazine content gets the best possible showcase.

In addition to selecting photos, drawings and other illustrations, the art director will order your story set in a certain typeface ("font") and designed to fit into a page layout. Photos, like your story, are converted into electronic form by most magazines for editing on screens.

At this point, you still have time to make changes or update your story, so don't think your writer's responsibility ends when your manuscript disappears into an electronic maw. One great benefit of new production systems is their ability to accept last-minute changes in copy.

Using an ARRAY overhead scanner, an editor captures a four-color image for electronic placement in a page layout. Such electronic wonders give editors, not outside technicians, last say on the magazine's appearance and lower production costs.

Northern Light photo by Mark Fink

A BiDCO output installation converts digitized magazine copy, pages and art into film for making printing press plates.

Northern Light photo by Mark Fink

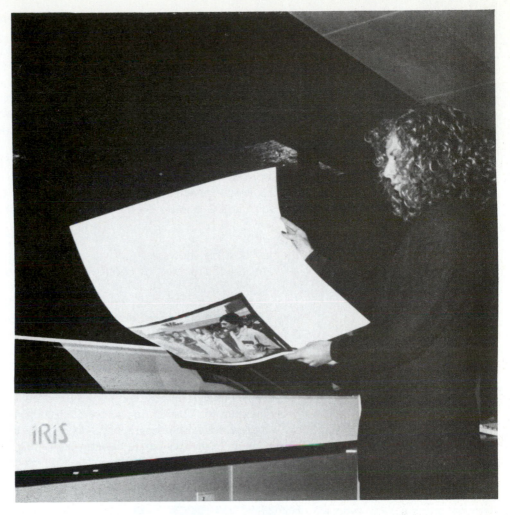

How Page Production Works

Next stop for your story and accompanying graphic elements is the page production department. Here, final copy, edited and coded to fit page layouts, is electronically melded into a page grid, template or skeleton, as many magazines term it. These grids command a final paging computer to insert copy, artwork and rules, those thin lines that define the page or separate columns of type.

During this process, today's electronic wonders of magazine publishing come into full play in two ways: First, they allow editors to control many processes formerly handled by non-editors who didn't always have a "feel" for the subtleties that go into publishing great magazines. Second, by bringing in-house many functions formerly contracted to outside firms, the electronic wonders lower magazine production costs.[2]

For example, *Fortune* reports enormous savings from establishing, in 1992, a 10-person in-house "imaging department" to produce the magazine. Film separations, a process for producing color that took outside engravers five days to supply, now take the in-house team less than two hours! Magazine quality improves, *Fortune* says, because production specialists are just down the hall from editors, not miles away, in an outside vendor's plant.[3]

For most magazines, the process moves to outside production houses when it's time to convert digitized copy, art and pages into film, which outside printers use to make plates for their presses. Enormous capital investment is needed for equipment required in this process, and it's usually affordable only by independent vendors who work for many magazines.

To hold magazine business, outside production houses must adhere to strict quality-control demands made by editors. This produces more magazines of outstanding technical quality than the industry ever did before.

With approval by magazine editors and the art director, film of page layouts is transmitted to the printing plant. For *Aviation Week,* that involves zapping the film images from New York offices up to a GStar 2 communication satellite hovering 23,000 miles above Baltimore, for relay to a printer in West Virginia!

As magazines come off the press, they go to the printer's bindery where they are glued or stapled into finished products. Then, it's to trucks, special delivery vans and the U.S. Postal Service, which will deliver your story (the one you started days, weeks or even months earlier) on the final leg to newsstands and subscriber mailboxes.

SUMMARY

To succeed as a professional writer you must understand and satisfy the technical needs of editors and others who put out magazines.

The magazine industry is shifting rapidly to computerized editing and production systems for these reasons: Magazines must reduce costs to stay competitive with other media; computerized systems reduce the number of people and amount of time (both costly) required to produce magazines; computers improve magazines journalistically and aesthetically; and the required editorial department systems are relatively inexpensive, costing on average $140,000, according to a *Folio* survey.

Typical college undergraduates already are familiar with equipment and techniques many magazines use in desktop publishing. Many systems are based on Macintosh equipment.

Throughout production, in-house or at an outside production house, strict quality controls yield dramatically improved technical quality in magazines. Here, a technician uses a controlled lighting booth to ensure color quality for the art director's final approval.

Northern Light photo by Mark Fink

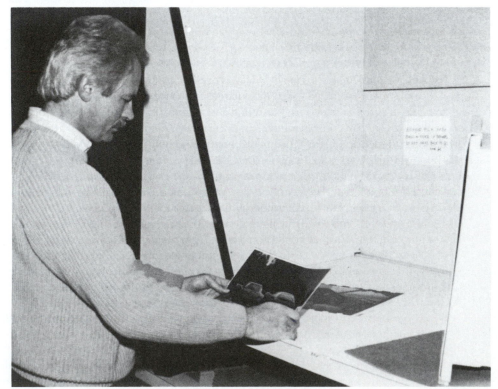

Whether you file your copy to a magazine electronically, by fax, computer-to-computer, on a diskette or on hard copy, you should prepare your manuscript in accord with the magazine's system or, at least, in a form editors will find easy to handle. Copy editors are crucial to your future; keep them happy by conforming to their methods and copy-handling systems.

You *must* meet your deadline for copy delivery so the copy flow—movement of copy through the editing system—can move on schedule. Only if all participants, starting with the writer, meet their deadlines will the production system permit presses to roll on time.

Because of new computerized techniques, the writer's responsibility for changing, correcting and updating copy continues almost up to press time. Don't think your responsibility ends when you deliver your raw manuscript.

RECOMMENDED READING

For those of you interested in magazine production, *Folio* regularly covers new techniques and systems for producing magazines.

For a broad look at magazine (and newspaper) production, see Russell N. Baird, Arthur T. Turnbull and Duncan McDonald, *The Graphics of Communication* (New York: Holt, Rinehart and Winston, 1987). On editing, see R. Thomas Berner, *The Process of Editing* (Boston: Allyn & Bacon, 1991).

NOTES

1. Jean Marie Angelo, "1992 Pre-press Trends," *Folio*, Sept. 1992, 57.
2. In its "Sourcebook 1992," *Folio* reported many magazines resorting to other cost-reduction measures to meet challenges of the 1991–92 recession. Magazines reduced the number of pages in issues, decreased the "text basis," or quality, of inside page and cover paper, and many decreased "trim"—the height and width of page size. See page 211.
3. Allan Demaree, "Editor's Desk," *Fortune,* 15 June 1992, 4.

Name Index

Subject Index

ISBN 0-02-337561-2

90000>

9 780023 375613